An Anthropology of Intellectual Exchange

WYSE Series in Social Anthropology

Editors:
James Laidlaw, William Wyse Professor of Social Anthropology, University of Cambridge, and Fellow of King's College, Cambridge
Joel Robbins, *Sigrid Rausing Professor of Social Anthropology, University of Cambridge, and Fellow of Trinity College, Cambridge*

Social Anthropology is a vibrant discipline of relevance to many areas – economics, politics, business, humanities, health and public policy. This series, published in association with the Cambridge William Wyse Chair in Social Anthropology, focuses on key interventions in Social Anthropology, based on innovative theory and research of relevance to contemporary social issues and debates. Former holders of the William Wyse Chair have included Meyer Fortes, Jack Goody, Ernest Gellner and Marilyn Strathern, all of whom have advanced the frontiers of the discipline. This series intends to develop and foster that tradition.

Recent volumes:

Volume 15
An Anthropology of Intellectual Exchange: Interactions, Transactions and Ethics in Asia and Beyond
Edited by Jacob Copeman, Nicholas J. Long, Lam Minh Chau, Joanna Cook and Magnus Marsden

Volume 14
Against Better Judgment: Akrasia in Anthropological Perspectives
Edited by Patrick McKearney and Nicholas H.A. Evans

Volume 13
New Perspectives on Moral Change: Anthropologists and Philosophers Engage with Transformations of Life Worlds
Edited by Cecilie Eriksen and Nora Hämäläinen

Volume 12
Where Is the Good in the World? Ethical Life between Social Theory and Philosophy
Edited by David Henig, Anna Strhan and Joel Robbins

Volume 11
Making Better Lives: Hope, Freedom and Home-Making among People Sleeping Rough in Paris
Johannes Lenhard

Volume 10
Selfishness and Selflessness: New Approaches to Understanding Morality
Edited by Linda L. Layne

Volume 9
Becoming Vaishnava in an Ideal Vedic City
John Fahy

Volume 8
It Happens Among People: Resonances and Extensions of the Work of Fredrik Barth
Edited by Keping Wu and Robert P. Weller

Volume 7
Indeterminacy: Waste, Value and the Imaginations
Edited by Catherine Alexander and Andrew Sanchez

For a full volume listing, please see the series page on our website: https://www.berghahnbooks.com/series/wyse

An Anthropology of Intellectual Exchange

Interactions, Transactions and Ethics in Asia and Beyond

Edited by

Jacob Copeman, Nicholas J. Long, Lam Minh Chau,

Joanna Cook and Magnus Marsden

berghahn
NEW YORK • OXFORD
www.berghahnbooks.com

First published in 2023 by
Berghahn Books
www.berghahnbooks.com

First paperback edition published in 2026

Library of Congress Cataloging-in-Publication Data
Names: Copeman, Jacob, editor. Long, Nicholas J., editor. | Chau, Lam Minh, editor. | Cook, Joanna, editor. | Marsden, Magnus, editor.
Title: An anthropology of intellectual exchange : interactions, transactions and ethics in Asia and beyond / edited by Jacob Copeman, Nicholas J. Long, Lam Minh Chau, Joanna Cook, and Magnus Marsden.
Description: New York : Berghahn Books, 2023. | Series: WYSE series in social anthropology; Volume 15 | Includes bibliographical references and index.
Identifiers: LCCN 2023007808 (print) | LCCN 2023007809 (ebook) | ISBN 9781805390701 (hardback) | ISBN 9781805390763 (open access ebook)
Subjects: LCSH: Learning and scholarship--South Asia. | Ethnology--South Asia.
Classification: LCC AZ776 .A67 2023 (print) | LCC AZ776 (ebook) | DDC 001.20954--dc23/eng/20230413
LC record available at https://lccn.loc.gov/2023007808
LC ebook record available at https://lccn.loc.gov/2023007809

British Library Cataloguing in Publication Data
A catalogue record for this book is available from the British Library

EU GPSR Authorized Representative
LOGOS EUROPE, 9 rue Nicolas Poussin, 17000, LA ROCHELLE, France
Email: Contact@logoseurope.eu

ISBN 978-1-80539-070-1 hardback
ISBN 978-1-80758-141-1 paperback
ISBN 978-1-80539-071-8 epub
ISBN 978-1-80539-076-3 web pdf

https://doi.org/10.3167/9781805390701

The electronic open access publication of *An Anthropology of Intellectual Exchange: Interactions, Transactions and Ethics in Asia and Beyond* has been made possible under a CC BY-NC-ND 4.0 licence through the generous financial support of the Consellería de Cultura, Educación e Universidade, Galicia, in collaboration with the Universidade de Santiago de Compostela.

Contents

Figures

Foreword

Sunil Amrith

In the late 2000s, I found myself in the town of Nagore, along the Tamil Nadu coast, in search of a saint I had first encountered in Southeast Asia. Stories of the saint, Shahul Hamid, recount his journey from the plains of North India to Mecca and back across the Indian Ocean, stopping in the Maldives and at Adam's Peak in Ceylon before settling in Nagore, where he died. When I visited, the shops that line the passageway leading to the main Nagore shrine sold small pieces of foil imprinted with the images of boats, which devotees offered at the shrine when they prayed for the safety of their voyages. My own path to the shrine had originated in my study of circulation of people, ideas and culture across the Bay of Bengal. Intrigued by the social and cultural world of the shrines to Shahul Hamid that still stood in Singapore and Penang, I was curious to see where they had originated. A trustee of the shrine told me that alongside the surviving Nagore shrines in Singapore and Penang, there were once shrines to the saint of Nagore dispersed in Burma, Ceylon, Indonesia and Vietnam.

Everything I needed to know, to understand what I was seeing in Nagore, I found in just a single paragraph of Susan Bayly's work (Bayly 2004). In her 2004 essay, 'Imagining "Greater India"', Bayly opened with the Nagore saint to remind her readers of the expansive moral and spiritual geographies that continue to shape people's lives in contemporary Asia. She argued that the Nagore saint and his cult were always situated 'in a wider world of *haj* pilgrimage, trade, and teaching, which his devotees still visualized ... as a living and expansive arena in which the saint continued to radiate his presence' (704). It took me about a decade of thinking and writing to fully incorporate that one profound insight.

I returned to the same essay, some years later, and found in it something completely different. By this time, I was working on a history of the South Asian monsoon – a history of monsoon science, and of how deeply concern with, even fear of, the monsoon had shaped postcolonial India. Returning to Bayly, I found a bracing and surprising intellectual history of the notion of 'monsoon Asia', a category that I found being used without self-consciousness in climate science. Bayly showed that Durkheimian anthropologists in colonial Indochina had embraced the notion of 'monsoon Asia' in their quest to understand what they saw as the vanished civilization of Champa. In the work of Paul Mus, above all, 'monsoon Asia' constituted a civilizational zone. He discerned an underlying core belief system, 'animism', that united the sweep of 'monsoon Asia', atop which Buddhism, Islam, Christianity sat lightly. As Bayly showed, the significance Mus attributed to climate drew on the French notion of *terroir*, climate and soil shaping individual and collective life. This is classic Bayly: seamlessly does she bridge intellectual and conceptual history with the history of lived experience, linking colonial meta-geographical categories that still shape how we see the world, with the paths of pilgrimage and migration that bridged the Indian Ocean.

Bayly's 2004 essay was written at a moment of transition in her intellectual trajectory. If Susan Bayly had published nothing beyond *Saints, Goddesses and Kings* (1989) and *Caste, Society and Politics in India* (1999) her place would already have been assured among the most insightful and generative scholars of modern India. Bayly's restless curiosity, however, led her to other shores. 'Imagining "Greater India"' was the first published hint of Bayly's growing engagement with the country that she would turn to study over the following two decades: Vietnam. Bayly's work on Vietnam drew upon her earlier experience in India; and in her focus on parallel and intersecting experiences, she was a true pioneer of what would come to be known as Inter-Asian scholarship.

This volume's focus on the anthropology of intellectual exchange is fitting acknowledgement of how central a theme that has been in Susan's work. Bayly, and the contributors to this volume, emphasize the importance of both individual and collective agency in shaping intellectual exchange. They insist that intellectual exchanges have an open-endedness and capacity to surprise, even in situations of unequal power and constraint. They conceive of intellectual exchange in a capacious way, going beyond the conventional focus on canonical texts or eminent thinkers ('intellectuals'). In the pages of this stimulating book, we glimpse the intellectual exchange embodied by the 'strikingly bold insistence' of Vietnamese architects that Soviet models of housing needed to adapt to local conditions, as in the chapter by Nguyen and Nguyen. We see the trans-regional scale of intellectual exchange, in Marsden's chapter, shaping profoundly local visions of how to live as a good Muslim in South and Central Asia. And we grasp the horror of what happens when intellectual exchange falters and fails, as in Christopher Goscha's moving account of French settlers clinging on to 'imperial time' in a Vietnam that had been transformed by war.

The roster of contributors to this book speaks volumes about Susan Bayly's influence not only as a scholar but also as a teacher and colleague. A generation of academics – now working in Europe, Asia and North America – owes a debt to Susan Bayly as a supervisor and mentor. I am privileged to count myself among them. Twenty years into my academic career, I have enough perspective to say that Susan has had a formative influence on all of the work I have done as a historian.

I encountered her not as a graduate student, but as a first-year undergraduate at Christ's College, Cambridge, where she was Fellow in History and Social

Anthropology. The first time I met her, at a formal dinner early in the term, I was ill at ease and still reeling from the culture shock of arriving at Cambridge from hyper-modern Singapore. Susan took me completely by surprise, and put me at ease, with a few words in Tamil. The following year, she taught me on the course that was still then called 'The West and the Third World'. I could not have imagined then that I would go on to become a professional historian of Asia.

What I learned from Susan in those weekly meetings in her college rooms has shaped everything I have done subsequently. As a graduate student I worked more closely with Susan's husband and intellectual partner, the late Sir Christopher Bayly; but for many years Susan's was – and perhaps still is – the voice in my ear demanding greater rigour, asking whether every dimension of a concept has been explored, whether all perspectives have been considered. Susan's depth of learning, the profusion of references that spilled forth from memory, the leaps and unexpected connections she would make in every conversation – these were then, and remain now, a profound inspiration.

It is fashionable to talk about boundary-crossing scholarship; Susan Bayly embodies it. Her oeuvre sits at the fruitful intersection between History and Social Anthropology – deeply archival yet richly ethnographic; conceptually sophisticated, yet never losing sight of the everyday. It has also crossed the borders of area studies – between the study of South and Southeast Asia – earlier and more boldly than many others. This volume is a tribute to her enormous influence on multiple fields. In keeping with the spirit of Susan Bayly's work, it is a volume that looks forward as much as back: it is pushing the frontiers of inquiry, towards a new history and anthropology of intellectual exchange.

Sunil Amrith is Renu and Anand Dhawan Professor of History at Yale University. He is a historian of South and Southeast Asia, and his work has covered environmental history and the history of public health. Amrith is the author of four books, most recently *Unruly Waters: How Rains, Rivers, Coasts, and Seas Have Shaped Asia's History* (Basic Books, 2018). He is a 2017 MacArthur Fellow and received the Infosys Prize in Humanities in 2016.

References

Bayly, Susan. 1989. *Saints, Goddesses and Kings: Muslims and Christians in South Indian Society, 1700–1900*. Cambridge: Cambridge University Press.

———. 1999. *Caste, Society and Politics in India from the Eighteenth Century to the Modern Age*. Cambridge: Cambridge University Press.

———. 2004. 'Imagining "Greater India": French and Indian Visions of Colonialism in the Indic Mode', *Modern Asian Studies* 38(3): 703–44.

Acknowledgements

The editors would like to acknowledge support from the Consellería de Cultura, Educación e Universidade, Galicia, in the context of its collaboration agreement with the Universidade de Santiago de Compostela (USC), which has enabled this volume to be made available open access. We would also like to thank Lindsay Graham for expert editorial assistance and Tom Bonnington, Charlotte Mosedale, Caroline Kuhtz, Marion Berghahn and the rest of the team at Berghahn Books for their support and assistance. We are grateful to all our contributors for their effort in producing such stimulating essays amidst the many challenges of the COVID-19 pandemic, to Sunil Amrith and James Laidlaw for kindly taking up our invitations to reflect on the chapters, and to Arkotong Longkumer and Filippo Osella for insights and support.

Above all we thank Susan Bayly for her guidance, inspiration and exceptionally generous intellectual gift-giving. This book – dedicated to Susan, a masterful practitioner of open-handed intellectual exchange as well as analyst of it – is our small counter-gift.

Introduction
An Anthropology of Intellectual Exchange

Nicholas J. Long, Jacob Copeman, Magnus Marsden, Lam Minh Chau and Joanna Cook

Intellectual exchange could be said to be the lifeblood of anthropology. Whenever we learn from and with our interlocutors in the field, discuss ideas with students or colleagues, teach, attend conferences or submit ideas to publishers and journals, we are engaging in forms of 'intellectual exchange'. You, now, reading this introduction, are participating in just such a process. Indeed, it would not be unreasonable to argue that intellectual exchange is not only the lifeblood of anthropology, but also of the very world that anthropologists inhabit. The buildings we live and work in, the economic systems in which we earn and spend our salaries, the healthcare systems that provide us with medical care and public health advice, the forms of statecraft that govern us: all of these have themselves been shaped in powerful ways by processes of intellectual exchange. The same is true for the worlds in which our interlocutors are embedded. Yet despite the apparent centrality of intellectual exchange for anthropologists and for anthropology, and burgeoning interest in intellectual exchange within adjacent scholarly fields, social anthropologists have yet to engage closely with the concept. In this volume we outline the promise of an analytic focus on 'intellectual exchange', as well as elaborating an ethnographically informed framework for its study across cultures and contexts. In short, we seek to develop an anthropology of intellectual exchange.

Our starting contention is that intellectual life – by which we mean the capacities to know, reason, understand and reach conclusions about various aspects of the world – is, to quote Fatsis (2016: 276), 'not the exclusive domain of a few, but a common attribute of the many'. It is thus as foundational to anthropological enquiry as other aspects of the human condition that have been highlighted in recent theoretical movements and 'turns', including our shared embodiment (Csordas 1994), our emplacement in a material world (Miller 2005) and our capacities to will and to feel affects and emotions (Gregg and Seigworth 2010; Murphy and Throop 2010). Moreover, while human intellectual life cannot be considered *reducible* to intellectual exchange (a proposition that would ignore the importance of such processes as inspiration, observation, deduction and so on), the very fact that people everywhere are socialized by others into culturally and historically specific intellectual traditions, as well as often being exposed to other traditions and perspectives over the course of their lifetimes, means that intellectual exchange is an integral dimension of both intellectual life and human existence.[1] By making this claim, we both build on and move beyond existing anthropological literature. A tremendous number of works have already addressed contexts and practices in which 'intellectual exchange' could be said to be taking place: from studies of schooling, training, scientific research and the workings of contemporary universities to ethnographic portraiture of childhood socialization and what Magnus Marsden (2005: 11, and this volume) terms 'the life of the mind' in everyday sociality. Yet despite this rich corpus of work, and a broader theoretical interest in the dynamics of cultural transmission (Bloch 2005; Ellen et al. 2013; Spiro 1997; Tindall 1976) – including an analysis of the different 'intellectual activities' demanded by different cultural settings (Cole and Scribner 1975) – the concept of 'intellectual exchange' remains curiously absent in most contemporary social anthropology.

By contrast, the term is used much more extensively in the fields of archaeology, education and, perhaps especially, history. In these disciplines, enquiries into 'intellectual exchange' have proven an important avenue for: firstly, highlighting the ways in which knowledge and understanding are created relationally; and secondly, tracing the specific relations that have had a formative influence upon particular bodies of thought, including subfields of anthropology (see, e.g., Magnarella 2003; Rivera 2000). Yet, valuable as such studies are, their focus is typically particularistic. Often it is the details of who said what to whom, and to what effect, that are attributed most significance in the authors' analysis. This comes at the expense not only of an interrogation of the term and its purported boundaries, but also of a full analysis of the factors that mediate the exchange and thereby determine its outcomes. Indeed, even one of the most prominent contemporary historians of intellectual exchange, Ian Merkel (2021), acknowledges that the concept remains 'undertheorized'. There are of course exceptions – trailblazing papers that analyse the dynamics of intellectual exchange in revealing ways, such as Nir Shafir's (2014) study of the ways in which the exigencies of 'the international congress' as a social form influence what kinds of intellectual dialogues can take place within such events, or Caoilfhionn Ní Bheacháin and Angus Mitchell's (2019) analysis of the role Victorian 'salon culture' played in facilitating intellectual exchanges between women whose diverse backgrounds would not otherwise give them any cause to meet. Such analytical insights, however, remain largely constrained to the case studies in hand. This volume builds upon these studies, as well as others available in the anthropological canon and our contributors' research findings, in order to develop a more systematic understanding of how intellectual exchange could be studied, and the factors that might influence its character and consequences.

While doing this, it is also our aim to celebrate, take inspiration from and build upon the insights of Professor Susan Bayly, a figure who has not only been a seminal influence within the intellectual lives of this volume's editors and contributors (whether as a mentor, colleague or friend), but who has also, throughout her career, made key contributions to the anthropological study of the ways in which knowledge and worldviews can be transformed through processes of (transcultural) encounter. Bayly trained as a historian in the Cambridge Faculty of History with the renowned historian of India Professor Eric Stokes as her supervisor. She became a Fellow of Christ's College, Cambridge in 1986, and joined the Cambridge Department of Social Anthropology in 2000, where we, the editors, all met her, and from where she retired in 2020.[2] Bayly's extensive publications, as we demonstrate in the next section, have addressed a wide variety of critical issues, including, but certainly not limited to, instances of intellectual exchange. Yet despite – or perhaps even because of – its diversity, Bayly's oeuvre proves a source of considerable inspiration for developing the methodological and analytical perspectives that we believe are necessary for understanding 'exchange' as an integral dimension of intellectual life.

Following an initial overview of Bayly's work, this introduction proceeds as follows. First, we outline why it is so important to pay attention to 'intellectual exchange', demonstrating the value of including the concept more fully within contemporary anthropological vocabulary. We show how the dynamism and acknowledgement of agency implicit in the 'exchange' framing serves as a valuable corrective to simplistic analytics of hegemonic domination, indoctrination and extraction, while simultaneously recognizing the power relations that constrain and enable such exchanges. It can also contribute to foregrounding hitherto unacknowledged voices within the academy and intellectual canon. Second, we address the question of where the boundaries of 'an anthropology of intellectual exchange' should be drawn. We argue that an analysis of intellectual exchange can be productively undertaken at a variety of scales, and suggest an approach in which intellectual life is recognized as being profoundly interconnected with other aspects of human experience, including our embodiment and our capacity to be affected. Third, we examine some of the factors that can shape the conduct of intellectual exchange. In particular, we argue that the framing of 'exchange' invites useful cross-pollination from parallel debates in linguistic and economic anthropology about the category of 'exchange' and the nature of its mediation. These debates, we suggest, can be used to set an initial agenda for a more systematic theorization of intellectual exchange across cultures and contexts. Finally, we ask why intellectual exchange is or is not undertaken, arguing that there is much to be gained from expanding the study of intellectual exchange beyond its practice in actuality to the way that it also exists as an object of desire, contemplation, or as a subjunctive possibility that may nevertheless prove consequential through the way it animates or eludes political and ethical subjectivities. A key point that emerges throughout is that intellectual exchange is intimately connected to ethical life – a domain which encompasses 'trying to do what [one] considers right or good, ... being evaluated according to what is right or good, or [being] in some debate about what constitutes the human good' (Lambek 2010: 1). Intellectual exchange may be seen as an ethical good in its own right, although it can also be considered a source of harm, especially when the institutional circumstances in which it takes place work to perpetuate unwanted social hierarchies, inequalities and exclusions (see Garnett 2006). It also has the capacity to challenge established ethical projects. It is a source of risk and uncertainty, that may be characterized by either anxiety or thrill. By exploring these issues, the chapters in this volume develop a theoretical toolkit with which readers can better understand issues associated with intellectual exchange, while simultaneously shedding ethnographic light on many of the transformations and complexities to which it has contributed in the part of the world to which Susan Bayly has dedicated her own life's work: the continent of Asia.

Bringing Intellectual Exchange into View: Susan Bayly's Work in Context

Susan Bayly's work has addressed some of the most complex and sensitive issues in the study of Asia, including syncretic forms of 'Indian religion', the historical context for the emergence of movements of so-called religious fundamentalism, the afterlife of socialism in Asian postcolonial societies, and, most recently, the experience of marketization in Vietnam, one of Asia's fastest growing economies. A consistent concern throughout her work has been the question of how particular cultural models and schemas become established and transformed on personal, community and (supra-)national scales: an issue that lies at the heart of research into intellectual exchange.

Bayly's initial work concerned the study of religious conversion in India. *Saints, Goddesses and Kings* (1989) broached the tremendously sensitive issues surrounding the nature of the historical interaction between Islam, Christianity and Hinduism in South India. At the time Bayly conducted this research, India's political landscape was being transformed by the growing political power of Hindutva movements and organizations seeking to establish the hegemony of Hinduism in India, which depicted the Abrahamic religions in general and Islam in particular as foreign to the Indian cultural environment. By analysing archival and interview-based materials through the analytical lens of anthropological debates relating to contested terms such as 'conversion' and 'religious syncretism', Bayly's study demonstrated that sharp distinctions between Muslims, Christians and Hindus were not an old but a recent feature of South India's cultural landscape. Just as crucially, Bayly demonstrated the active role of local actors in creating this interactive religious landscape, thereby challenging the notion that Islam and Christianity were not 'fully "Indian" religious systems' (1989: 454). *Saints, Goddesses and Kings* was a powerful and conceptually sophisticated study which demonstrated that Christianity and Islam were an integral part of religious life in South India rather than external penetrations. At the same time, by addressing the agency of Muslim, Christian and Hindu actors in processes of religious interaction, Bayly also brought attention to the dangers of treating 'Indian' religion as being inherently timeless and unchanging. This played a powerful role in enabling later scholarship to explore the historically diverse, layered and differentiated nature of Indian experiences of religious 'syncretism'. Bayly's sensitivity to complexity and nuance stands as an exemplar for the anthropological analysis of situations of encounter and co-existence, and such an approach is also fundamental to the way we envisage processes of intellectual exchange within this volume.

Bayly next turned her analytical focus to the study of caste in India in her celebrated *Caste, Society and Politics in India* (1999). The study of caste in Indian society was significantly polarized between scholars who depicted caste as an immutable core of Indian society, and others who sought to assert that clear-cut caste identities and roles emerged in the context of the British colonial state in India. As with *Saints, Goddesses and Kings*, in *Caste, Society and Politics in India* Bayly combined history and anthropology to provide a nuanced and varied depiction of caste's place in modern Indian society. The picture of caste society that Bayly presented in the book was grounded in the study of social and economic processes that had unfolded through early modern and modern Indian history. It also emphasized the role that Indians themselves played in re-inventing and refashioning caste as they integrated it with other aspects of their identities and of the changing environments in which they lived. Of critical and original importance too was the degree to which the book challenged caricatures that treated British scholar-officials' depictions of Indian society as one-dimensional manifestations of 'Orientalism', bringing attention to diverse understandings of caste among British officials in India and to the often unintended consequences of their policies on the shape taken by caste. Dealing as it does with the significance of caste to Indian society in the wake of the collapse of the Mughal Empire to the modern day, this book's scope was and remains unparalleled and it has had major and long-lasting ramifications for the ways in which caste in India is conceptualized by anthropologists and historians. The book's attention to the conscious ways in which Indian actors adjusted caste's role in Indian society in relationship to changing environments set it apart both from studies that depicted caste as the immutable core of Indian society and those that argued it to be the one-dimensional outcome of colonial classification and governance.

As the above summaries make clear, Bayly's first two monographs showed a commitment to highlighting both the active participation of Asian subjects in crafting their lived realities and the subtle nuances of the intellectual pursuits undertaken by colonial scholars and officials. Both of these commitments would feed through into the next phase of her work, which examined the nature and consequences of various forms of intellectual labour, including practices of intellectual exchange, in the context of the colonial enterprise. A series of articles and book chapters that she published in the 2000s (e.g. Bayly

2000, 2004) pointed to differences in the role played by anthropological scholarship in diverse expressions of European colonialism. Critically addressing debates about the degree to which nationalism in Asia was 'derivative' of colonial discourse, these works have also played an especially significant role in understanding supra-national forms of identity and political life. The articles not only compare different forms of imperial project (notably those of Britain and France) but also explore the active participation of actors who worked across and not simply within empires and cultural areas. Bayly demonstrates how the oft-made opposition between pre-modern expansive spatial imaginings that derive from historic world religious traditions such as Islam and those that are conceived of as forming a modern and 'unitary' imagination of the 'national-order-of-things' has had problematic implications for understanding the legacies of empire and colonialism. This opposition, Bayly shows, has led to an under-appreciation of the activities of actors – such as members of the 'Greater India Society' – who played a part in debates about cultural nationalist topics before and after independence from colonialism, but did not simply call for the creation of narrow and nationalist imaginaries. The 'Greater India Society', rather, was engaged in the forging of multiple and divergent visions of identity that were both translocal and supra-national. Inspired by historic connections between South and Southeast Asia, these visions were asserted in the language of scientific modernism, and forged through exchanges between nationalist intelligentsias, diaspora Indians and a consideration of 'Orientalist' scholarship. The original significance of Bayly's analysis lies in it bringing into sharper focus the ongoing vitality to the political cultures of postcolonial contexts of complex forms of identity and political imagination that are neither derivative of narrow cultural nationalism nor of world religious traditions. In this work too, then, Bayly challenges simplistic approaches to the nature of the role played by 'colonial knowledge' in the making of modern Asian contexts (see especially Bayly 2000, 2009a), while bringing attention to the agency of Asian actors – in this case intellectuals – in a domain (cultural nationalism) that was increasingly being treated as derivative of colonialism and Western ideas of the nation.

Bayly's third monograph, *Asian Voices in a Post-Colonial Age* (2007), builds on this interest in translocal forms of identity and affiliation that are self-consciously modern in nature and also forged in the context of colonialism. The book represents a significant step in Bayly's intellectual career, moving beyond the study of South Asia into Southeast Asia, drawing on long-term ethnographic fieldwork in Vietnam, as well as earlier anthropologically-informed archival research in India. Bayly makes a novel attempt to compare the experience of colonialism among Vietnamese and Indian nationalist intelligentsias. In so doing, she brings attention to Asian forms of modernity that are absent from studies based on mind-clamping comparisons between Asian and Western contexts. *Asian Voices*, then, prefigured the emergence of the critical field of 'inter-Asian' studies (on which, see, e.g., Chen 2010; Ho 2017; Yue 2017). It uses nuanced ethnographic data and oral history to demonstrate not only the importance of a language of socialism to the thinking and identities of Vietnamese and Indian nationalist intelligentsias, but also the role played by such actors in creating and sustaining an expansive 'global socialist ecumene'. As a result, and in a sophisticated and non-polemical way, the book questions the underlying arguments of social theorists such as Spivak (1985) and Chakrabarty (2000) who broadly treated nationalist intelligentsias either as the victims of colonial epistemic violence or as agency-less cogs in nationalist projects.

Susan Bayly's concern with understanding the agency of Asians in expansive social and economic processes has focused more recently on Vietnamese experiences of marketization and political transformation. One key theme associated with this work is what Long and Moore (2013) have dubbed 'the social life of achievement'. Drawing on ethnographic material regarding the experience of education in Vietnam, Bayly (2013, 2014) treats the ubiquitous measurement of achievement and urge to become 'creative' not as something imposed by the audit cultures or individualistic underpinnings of neoliberalism but rather as a contested moral site at which socialist ideas and marketization processes interact. At the same time, Bayly also connected her emphasis on the active participation of local people to the highly charged field of the study of propaganda. In a study of the ongoing significance of 'propaganda' to Vietnamese political culture, Bayly emphasizes that propaganda does not have a deadening effect on her interlocutors' moral and intellectual worlds. Instead, building on recent developments in visual anthropology and the anthropology of ethics and morality, Bayly attends to the ways in which her interlocutors differentiate between varying forms of visual propaganda on the basis of assessments they make of both its quality and the nature of the work invested by designers and producers (Bayly 2019, 2020). Highlighting that agentive moral life can be found in what are thought of as 'scopic contexts' (Jay 1993), Bayly contrasts the ways her interlocutors think of the moral agency of the 'individual who performs moral acts discerningly and reflectively' as qualitatively different from 'one who performs rightful action as a creature of mere habit or on command' (2019: 30) and argues this is evident in the way they value the display of taste and sensitivity in their interaction with propaganda.

***

From this necessarily broad overview of Bayly's works, we can distil two foundational principles which have also played a central role in much other contemporary scholarship on intellectual exchange. One of these is the importance of recognizing that transformations in intellectual traditions and cultural models do not occur automatically or unilaterally, but are the result of active participation and ethical judgement on the part of all parties involved. The other is the value of analysing social phenomena, including intellectual exchange, on a variety of historical and geographical scales.

Agentive Exchanges

Insisting on an approach that sees intellectual transformations as the outcome of agentive exchanges is important for several reasons. First, as noted above, it complicates work that represents populations that have been exposed to the ideas of powerful outsiders as either inevitably succumbing to those discourses' hegemonic force or, alternatively, showing a 'resilience' or defiant 'resistance' in the face of such ideas (see, e.g., Comaroff and Comaroff 1992; Scott 2009). Although such arguments are motivated by a commendable commitment to developing a critical analysis of power, they run the risk of reducing the populations they describe to their position within structural power relations. By contrast, framing (transcultural) encounters as moments of intellectual *exchange* affords a recognition of each person involved as a complex intellectual and ethical actor whose level of interest in the issues at hand and whose decisions over what to say, what to withhold, and how to respond to what is said cannot be presumed but must be understood in terms of both the specific cultural worlds they inhabit and the dynamics of the intellectual interactions in which they are engaged (see, e.g., Lewis 2004). In short, it is a way of thinking about social transformations that highlights the centrality of human agency and invites active consideration of the complex ways in which that agency is both experienced and deployed.

Attention to intellectual exchange not only highlights the agency of populations widely depicted as 'receiving' ideas and techniques from external sources, it also reveals the ways in which the generation of those ideas is itself a collaborative and often transcultural affair. Ian Merkel (2017, 2022), for example, shows how various celebrated French intellectuals, including Claude Lévi-Strauss, Roger Bastide and Ferdinand Braudel, have been 'remembered for their brilliance even when their work was indeed a much more collective production' (2017: 145). Merkel uses archival evidence to demonstrate that the time these thinkers spent living in Brazil and engaging with Brazilian intellectuals had a formative influence upon ideas and styles of analysis that would subsequently be considered quintessentially 'French'. Given that 'any study of Brazilian social sciences acknowledges the influence of French scholars' (2022: fourth cover), acknowledging that the reverse is true challenges the Eurocentricity of established scholarly canons (on which, see Burney 2012). Equally, however, a focus on intellectual exchange can challenge simplistic accusations of knowledge production as extractive or colonial. For Veronica Strang, critiques of anthropology as an 'externalised intellectual space of cross-cultural comparison' underplay the ways in which 'the knowledges acquired through ethnographic enquiry are mentally integrated and synthesised into the subsequent analysis and therefore emerge in the new understandings of the products of the research' (2006: 982–86). Strang emphasizes, by contrast, the ways in which anthropologists conducting fieldwork necessarily undertake a 'fluid and complex exchange of knowledges', for which they then serve as 'conduits', while highlighting how this process might be better acknowledged in scholarly publications by, for example, rethinking authorship criteria (2006: 990).[3]

As this discussion reveals, foregrounding exchange in accounts of intellectual life allows us to move past singularizing narratives and instead enable credit for intellectual accomplishments and transformations to be distributed in a manner that more precisely resembles the complex dynamics of inspiration and influence. Much is at stake in such a shift, since, as recent work in the anthropology of ethics has demonstrated, different ways of allocating responsibility can have far-reaching consequences for both subjectivity and sociality (see, e.g., Agrama 2012; Laidlaw 2014b; Long 2017). The move also serves as a valuable mitigation against the feelings of moral injury that can arise in contexts in which there is a failure to provide adequate recognition of the contribution of all partners (see Assmann 2013; Honneth 1995).

The present collection builds upon these traditions of writing about intellectual exchange, complicating simplistic narratives and highlighting the agency, ingenuity and ethical reasoning evident among the figures involved in the intellectual exchanges that we describe. For example, Nguyen and Nguyen's richly illustrated account of architectural developments in Hanoi (this volume) shows how the 'Soviet-style' apartment blocks that became ubiquitous in Hanoi from the late 1950s onwards should not be seen as mere recreations of architectural forms from North Korea and the USSR. While Vietnamese architects took inspiration and drew on guidance from architects in other socialist countries, they also made meaningful innovations in their own right, adapting designs to suit the tropical climate, Vietnamese cultural heritage and militarized context in which they were working. While such ingenuity is often overlooked, occluded by monikers such as 'Soviet-style', up-close ethnographic observation reveals sophisticated processes of agentive intellectual engagement with external hegemonic forces, in ways that cannot be classified as either passive, uncritical acceptance or outright resistance. Such dynamics are brought to the fore by thinking about architectural design as the outcome of intellectual exchange.

A coherent anthropology of intellectual exchange thus needs, at the very least, to entertain the possibility of conversation without domination, forms of dialogue 'in which we are not playing a game against each other but with each other' (Bohm 1996: 9), and acknowledge that ideas can be vital propellants of action, as much as power and economics. This is not the same thing as asserting the existence of free, equal, unconstrained intellectual exchange between sovereign subjects, communities or traditions. Rather, we argue that 'the power relations that constrain and enable, and weaken and empower' some parties to intellectual exchange in relation to others precisely give such free intellectual exchange as people are ever able to exercise both its shape and its scope (Laidlaw 2014a: 500). Bohm (1996: 8) recognizes something analogous in his framing of both 'freedom' and what he terms 'structure' as 'essential dimensions of any genuine dialogue'. If structure provides the backbone and freedom a spirit of exploration and discovery, it is the interplay between these dimensions 'that creates the dynamic tension and creative ambiguity that [can] make the dialogal process so exciting' (Freshwater 2007: 432). An anthropology of intellectual life must recognize the essential interplay of constraint and freedom as both the condition for and means of dialogue – an interplay that is foregrounded by using the concept of 'intellectual exchange' as an entry point to understanding how people have come to know, understand and think about the world in the particular ways that they do.

Scales of Analysis

As we have seen, the anthropological study of intellectual exchange can make vital contributions by attesting to the very existence of exchange processes within and between intellectual traditions, drawing attention to dynamics and participants that might otherwise be overlooked. Having recognized this, however, a question arises as to the *scale* at which instances of intellectual exchange are best analysed. One possibility is to examine them in their singularity, as components in the biographies of key figures, 'exemplars', or thinkers of particular interest to intellectual history. Another might be to treat them as representing 'intellectual exchange' within a certain time or space: under conditions of late empire, for instance, or within a particular regional or national tradition. Alternatively, one might seek to discern transcendent truths about intellectual exchange in general.

Such scalar dilemmas are not unique to an anthropology of intellectual exchange. As O'Connor (2020: 286) observes, the entire anthropological enterprise is 'fundamentally an exercise in scaling: to speak or write about anything we see, hear, or experience, we must first decide how to "scale" our approach' (see also Strathern 2004). Indeed, debates over whether anthropologists should devote their energies to identifying 'universal' principles and laws or instead focus on the particularity, even incommensurability, of individual cases date back to the origins of the discipline (O'Connor 2020) and continue to rage today (Miller et al. 2019). The challenge in determining how to proceed can be understood as twofold. Firstly, anthropologists must develop forms of writing which acknowledge that self-fashioning, self-cultivation and transformation experienced by people across the world, including via processes of intellectual exchange, never 'happens in isolation from scalar processes, but neither is it reducible to such processes' (O'Connor 2020: 293). Secondly, analysis must move beyond treating scale as a self-evident and objective quality of social ecology (cf. Berreman 1978), instead reflexively interrogating the scalar imagination of the anthropologist (Glück 2013; Carr and Lempert 2016; O'Connor 2020). Doing so not only ensures circumspection regarding the theoretical and personal commitments and assumptions underpinning particular strategies of scaling, it also promises openness to the alternative scales of analysis that may be suggested by one's research participants and ethnographic data.

Susan Bayly's work offers a compelling model for how the question of scale might be handled in the study of intellectual exchange. Bayly never loses sight of the immense personal significance that processes and moments of intellectual exchange can have for the individuals that she has worked with. Indeed, her scholarship is studded with vivid individual biographies, and a corresponding theoretical conviction that her interlocutors' 'tumultuous' and 'often very testing life experiences' are not just *products of*, but *central to* the Asian transformations with which her research has been concerned (Bayly 2007: 1, 7). Such a sensibility can also be seen in the contributions to this volume, which, read alongside each other, reveal the myriad ways in which intellectual exchange can transform, enrich, disrupt and damage individual lives. Yet Bayly's work does not merely 'contextualize' non-scalable individuality within abstracted analyses of processes occurring on greater historical and geographical scales. Rather, it sees those individual experiences as the very stuff of which social transformations are made, thereby disrupting simplistic meta-narratives and inviting more nuanced understandings of the changes afoot in Asia and the wider world. Bayly's early work on Catholicism in India (1989), for example, has been lauded as pioneering because, rather than simply asserting the arrival of Christian missionaries as an inaugural moment of transformation and rupture, it meticulously traces Catholicism's integration and transformation over the *longue durée* (Trento 2022: 8). Similarly, her more recent work on the mobile lives of Vietnamese and Indian intelligentsia families has pushed back against the 'amorphous, ahistorical and agentless conceptions of globalisation and diasporic connectivity' embedded in many analyses of 'late capitalism' and the scale of 'the global' (Bayly 2007: 223). Instead, by building on the work of Cooper (2005: 108) and attending to the specific 'units of affinity and mobilization' and 'collectivities that are capable of action' within her fieldwork, Bayly charts a portrait of a transnational socialist ecumene, all the while showing her readers why this may be a more useful scale than 'the global' for the analysis of socialist mobility and intellectual exchange.

Magnus Marsden's contribution to this volume makes a similar intervention, grounded in a personal account of how his own theoretical outlook has been shaped by his many intellectual exchanges with Susan Bayly, his former PhD supervisor. Marsden's concern is with how best to frame the many practices of debate, discussion and intellectual exchange that occur among Muslims living in an interconnected yet politically divided 'arena'. He notes how many currents in the anthropology of Islam, if not wholly particularistic, would encourage analyses rooted in methodological nationalism – as if the practices he observed, for example, in Chitral (a district of northern Pakistan) were somehow characteristic of *Pakistani* Islam. (Such methodological nationalism is widespread in many accounts of secular intellectual exchange as well.) Meanwhile, what was taken as exemplary of 'Islam' as a whole was often unduly reflective of the Arab Middle East. Marsden writes against these ways of approaching his material, instead advocating a practice of 'connective ethnography' which refuses to define Muslim thought as 'local', 'global' or related to a single knowledge ecumene, but instead shows how multiple ecumenes, geopolitical processes and temporal scales all mediate the character of intellectual exchange. The direction and nature of intellectual exchange in the arena which cuts across neighbouring regions of Pakistan, Afghanistan and Tajikistan was influenced by dense webs of historical connectivity to the wider Persianate world, including ties of kinship, trade and travel. The intellectual exchanges that Marsden observed during subsequent fieldwork in Afghanistan also reflected this history of Persianate connectivity, with additional influences including the cartographic projects and practical exigencies associated with various national and geopolitical processes, most notably those of the Cold War. Through his analysis, Marsden not only demonstrates the importance of conducting a wide-ranging and open-minded analysis of the many factors and scalings shaping practices of intellectual exchange; he also shows how detailed ethnography of intellectual exchange can contribute to a more nuanced understanding of self-transformation, world-bridging, and indeed world-making, revealing, for example, how 'the Islamic' is a field produced by human agency in time and space.

In her 2013 article 'Mapping Time, Living Space: The Moral Cartography of Renovation in Late-Socialist Vietnam', reprinted in this volume, Bayly further develops her concern with scales and scaling. Although 'the vision of a socialist ecumene in which Vietnam has played a role of heroic exemplification is still an active feature of collective and individual memory', contemporary Vietnamese inhabit 'a world of multiple chronologies and spatial orders', including those that celebrate it as a burgeoning 'middle income' market economy or label it a troubled 'country of memory' confronting the legacy of war. It is from the site of these frameworks' interpenetration that individual Vietnamese navigate the making and unmaking of the transnational socialist ecumene, something they do through practices of what Bayly terms 'moral cartography'. As in her previous work, Bayly uses the experiences and concerns of her interlocutors to move beyond the reductive framings through which they could otherwise be presented; to write of 'post-socialist Vietnam' would overlook the complicated ways in which 'a fully ethical life involves many different forms of geotemporal provision'. Such an analysis offers a timely reminder that we must not only pay close attention to the institutions, conventions and relations within which intellectual exchange occurs and by which it is mediated, but also be mindful that it is but a single component within often extremely complex and multifaceted projects of ethical life. Keeping both points in mind offers the promise of an anthropology that not only illuminates how the character of intellectual exchange may vary within and between cultural settings, but also unpacks its complex and variegated meanings.

Locating the Boundaries of 'Intellectual Exchange'

So far, our introduction has argued for the value of embracing the term 'intellectual exchange' as a way of highlighting the situated, agentive and ethical nature of the practices that inform the development of individuals' intellectual lives, as well as noting the value of analysing intellectual exchange on a variety of historical and geographical scales. Before thinking more systematically about how to theorize the mediation of intellectual exchange and its place within ethical life, some important questions arise regarding the definition and boundaries of the concept. While many of the examples we have discussed so far – from the activities of the Greater India Society to Annales School historians collaborating with Brazilian counterparts – seem to be straightforward examples of 'intellectual exchange', what is it that makes them so, and how can an anthropologist determine whether the processes they are observing in the field constitute 'intellectual exchange' or not?

As noted earlier, it is vital to acknowledge from the outset that all human beings, in all societies, are avowed of an intellectual life – capable of knowing, understanding and reaching conclusions about various aspects of the world – and thus embedded in processes of intellectual exchange. This point should not be controversial among anthropologists, whose fieldwork is frequently peppered with vibrant and thought-provoking discussions and debates (see, e.g., Bloch 2005; Marsden 2005). However, it stands at odds with a long academic tradition of foregrounding particular cultural elites – those who are understood as 'intellectuals' or 'intelligentsia' – in discussions of both intellectual exchange and the wider sociology of intellectual life (see, e.g., Fatsis 2016; Merkel 2021). Clearly, the question of whether subjects consider themselves to be 'intellectuals' or are seen as such by their interlocutors could have significant bearings on how any intellectual exchange unfolds. However, intellectual exchange itself must be recognized as ubiquitous, ordinary and partaken in by everyone.

What is it, then, that makes intellectual exchange 'intellectual'? Within secular Western thought, the 'intellect' has often been delineated as the sphere of knowledge, rational thought and logical reasoning, distinct from 'sensibilities' or 'the will' (e.g. Haven 1862). To some extent this distinction has value, and continues to inform our own framing of 'intellectual life' as concerned with the capacities to know, reason, understand and reach conclusions about various aspects of the world. For example, the question of how one has come to take an intellectual stance on the reality or otherwise of anthropogenic climate change is clearly a distinct empirical question to that of how one *feels* about the prospect of climate change, or about the narratives of climate change in public circulation. Either, or both, could be valid issues for anthropological investigation. The mistake has been to sometimes assume that just because these can be posed as two distinct empirical questions, the domains of 'sensibility' and 'intellect' are unrelated, as if intellectual life was purely cerebral and not profoundly connected to one's embodiment and emotional life (for further discussion of this fallacy, see Fatsis 2016: 278–79). As we discuss in the next section, one of the great contributions that anthropological (and specifically ethnographic) research can make to the interdisciplinary literature on intellectual exchange – hitherto strongly dominated by archival, textual research – is a close attention to its embodied, emplaced and affectively charged nature. These are dimensions of the process that will almost certainly shape the outcome of the exchange, but they do not make the exchange, or its outcome, any less 'intellectual' in nature. By defining 'intellectual exchange' as the dialogues, encounters and interactions through which particular ways of knowing, understanding and thinking about the world are forged, we hope to retain the clarity that is afforded from a focus on intellectual life, while nevertheless drawing deeply on the insights that can be afforded from attention to the full breadth of human experience.

Finally, it is important for any anthropological enquiry into intellectual life to recognize that the delineation of the sphere of 'knowledge' is not self-evident but geographically and historically contingent. It was eighteenth-century Enlightenment thinking, Shah-Kazemi (2002) emphasizes, that led the cosmos to be envisaged as 'empirical facts out there to be analysed and exploited to man's advantage', thereby creating an antinomy between 'science' and 'religion' which is not necessarily present in other cultural traditions (it has also been contested within Western faith communities: see, e.g., Anderson 1917). Similarly, Bayly's work in Vietnam (see especially 'Worlds United and Apart', this volume) offers rich portraiture of Vietnamese scholars and government administrators whose biographies reveal a 'confident traversing' of the realms of science and the supramundane. As Bayly acknowledges, these are knowledge realms that 'an outsider might think of as mutually antagonistic because they would seem to be based on radically conflicting views of human and cosmic nature'. Such difficulties are 'not insuperable'; her interlocutors would not 'regard the truths of science and the supramundane as incompatible or in rivalry as claims on the moral self'. And yet, as Alatas (2020) demonstrates with reference to Indonesian debates over the legitimacy of dreams as a source of historical knowledge, the boundaries of legitimate knowledge are not necessarily settled in any given cultural context, but can be matters of active discussion and contestation.

Given these complexities, it would be quite wrong for an anthropology of intellectual exchange to make bold proclamations as to what does or does not constitute legitimate 'understanding', 'reason', 'knowledge' or 'exercise of the intellect' – as opposed to, say, faith or fantasy. What it should do instead is determine how and why forms of knowing and thinking that *could* be considered 'intellectual' within the very expansive definition we have offered above come to have that status implicitly or explicitly affirmed, rejected or disputed through or within processes of dialogue and interaction. In other words, practices of 'intellectual exchange' can be understood as sites at which processes of cultural transmission intersect with the meaning-making and value attribution attendant on locally salient categories of 'the intellect' and its analogues.

In sum, an anthropology of intellectual exchange should encompass three key issues. Firstly, building on the broad definition of 'intellectual exchange' suggested by Carter and Spirling (2008: 375), it should document and analyse the full range of encounters, interactions or processes through which 'knowledge, ideas and techniques' (that is, propositional claims about the nature of the world and how it is possible to act in the world) are communicated, interrogated and/or defended, investigating why these occur in the ways, and with the consequences, that they do. Secondly, it must acknowledge that these are processes that often occur in everyday settings, sometimes fleetingly or unintentionally, even as they can also be undertaken self-consciously, both within and outside professionalized domains of intellectual practice, and investigate the extent to which such different contexts prove consequential for the trajectory and ramifications of the exchange. Finally, it must understand the cultural politics and narratives surrounding such exchanges, including the extent to which they are recognized as 'intellectual' by those participating in them, observing them and commenting upon them – including, perhaps, the anthropologist. It thereby becomes possible to bring the many insights afforded by anthropological methods and theory to our understanding of intellectual life without becoming complicit in reifying a domain of 'the intellectual' in ways that exclude or stigmatize alternative forms of thinking and knowing. Instead, the power dynamics inherent in delineating 'the intellectual' can remain in full view, with the ethnographic materials challenging readers to reflect more deeply on what they recognize as 'intellectual' or 'non-intellectual', and why.

With the value and scope of the term having been defined, we now consider what contributions – besides fine-grained ethnographic accounts – anthropological perspectives could make to existing literatures on intellectual exchange. In line with the insights proffered by contributors to this volume, we make two major arguments. Firstly, the enormous anthropological canon on 'exchange' offers potential axes for comparative study and theorization; secondly, recent turns in the anthropology of ethics allow us to think more deeply about the agencies and desires underpinning and shaping the intellectual exchange process.

Intellectual Exchange as Interaction and Transaction

The rubric of intellectual exchange invites us to see learning and knowledge as the outcome of 'exchanges' in two senses of the term. On the one hand, we can think of an exchange in its linguistic sense: as a conversation, debate or argument; in short, as an *interaction*. Yet we can also think of exchange in its economic sense, as a *transaction*. In both cases, anthropological scholarship offers a powerful analytic toolkit of concepts and perspectives that can be used to better understand how and why certain modalities of thought and practice take hold, transform and/or endure.

Exchange as Interaction

As Tindall (1976: 203) observed almost fifty years ago, any account of cultural transmission needs to attend carefully to 'the nature of the interactive encounters' within which knowledge is communicated. The study of intellectual exchange can thus be greatly enriched by many of the exciting perspectives that have arisen in recent years from anthropologists working at the interface of sociocultural and linguistic anthropology. This work departs from earlier 'cultural' forms of analysis, which saw anthropology's task as documenting and explicating *shared* systems of cultural meaning (e.g. Geertz 1973; Schneider 1984), instead taking its lead from the post-structuralist emphasis on multiplicity, incoherence and fragmentation (Stewart 1996) and from the processual accounts of how worlds come into being associated with actor-network theory (Callon 1984; Latour 1996). It emphasizes how social realities emerge through situated interactions and are thus influenced by both the rules, conventions and habits of interacting that prevail in any given time and place, and the vagaries of any particular interaction in its specificity (see, e.g., Berman 2020; Bielo 2019; Mathias 2020). This work is of considerable importance for an anthropology of intellectual exchange because it highlights not only that the spread of knowledge and understanding is far from automatic and uncomplicated, but also that, besides being subject to agentive reworking, intellectual exchange is mediated by topologies and traditions in ways of which participants themselves may not be fully aware.

Interactional perspectives on intellectual exchange are by no means new. A century ago, as Europe reeled from the impacts of the First World War, the philosophical anthropologist Bernhard Groethuysen turned his attention to how it might be possible to guard against what he considered the 'cultural derangement of hermetic ideologies that passed as normal' (Ermarth 1993: 679). Cultural dialogue and maieutic inquiry were seen as key to such a goal, reflected in his oversight of annual intellectual retreats that sought to bring scholars from across Europe into conversation with each other. But Groethuysen (1921) also highlighted the dangers attendant upon 'the declining use of what he called the "little words," "modest auxiliaries" and "crucial dubities" that foster comity and intellectual exchange rather than conceptual closure and ideological finality' (Ermarth 1993: 679–80). In other words, linguistic conventions such as the use of modifiers – 'perhaps', 'however', 'but' – were, for him, key to ensuring a mode of intellectual exchange that could foster open dialogue and combat the 'blinkering effects of mass ideologies' (Ermarth 1993: 685).

Interactions are not only influenced by linguistic choices. Structures of power – gendered, racial and institutional – may work to inhibit certain voices from either speaking or from being adequately heard (Allen 2021; Love et al. 2021), and can determine whether intellectual exchange occurs in a heterodox manner across different intellectual traditions, or within sealed disciplinary and theoretical silos (Garnett 2006). Broader cultural ideologies of 'how to interact' may have a similar effect.[4] Moreover, interactions never unfold in the abstract; as Csordas (1994) reminds us, the body is the existential ground of meaning-making and understanding. Close attention to embodiment and the ways in which felt experience is shaped by particular interactional topologies is thus essential for understanding how, why and to what effect intellectual exchange proceeds as it does (see, e.g., Long 2018). These concerns extend to the very material forms within which 'the intellectual' is made manifest. Such material culture is not confined to 'books, pamphlets, books and more books' (Nash 2019: 7). Physical means of exchanging knowledge range from paper and CDs to manifold scientific instruments and also one's hands (Sarbadhikary, this volume): knowledge 'travels in people's minds and in their bodies'; scientific communities likewise rely on memory and tacit knowledge (Robson 2019: 40). Conference presentations bring interlocutors together in the same room; social media, the internet and technologies such as Zoom lead them to meet in the realm of 'the virtual', their bodies positioned behind the screens of smartphones, tablets and computers, often many miles apart. But the various objectifications of knowledge that facilitate its exchange are not neutral: we must pay attention to 'the consequences of the particular materiality within which objectification … takes place' (Miller 2000: 21). Not merely reflecting their creators but social agents in their own right, their divergent material qualities – different levels of friction, adaptability and accessibility – enable the knowledge they convey differentially to find new partners and accomplices and join new conversations.

In sum, an anthropology of intellectual exchange needs to pay careful attention to how exchanges are mediated by linguistic and interactional conventions and dynamics, structures of power, and the materialities and affectivities of embodied practice. The chapters in this volume speak to this agenda in several ways. Jacob Copeman's chapter traces the motivations – and consequences – of Sikhs choosing to either renounce or embrace the characteristically Sikh family names of 'Singh' (for men) and 'Kaur' (for women). Such name exchanges can be generative of (as well as precipitated by) impassioned intellectual exchange, especially in cases where the Sikh in question is a public figure, whose actions may be widely debated by strangers on internet forums, comments boards and social media. When the hip-hop artist Taran Kaur Dhillon chose to adopt the stage name 'Hard Kaur', for example, many were outraged, arguing that her actions (her liberal consumption of alcohol, sexual frankness and dressing in revealing clothes) were out of step with the moral standards associated with the name 'Kaur'. Yet as some other commentators observed, there is an apparent double standard, with male artists able to use the word 'Singh' despite falling short of Sikh moral expectations, without experiencing anything like as much opprobrium as Taran Dhillon. Copeman's analysis reveals that the reasons for this double standard are complex – partly rooted in misogyny, partly reflecting the fact that 'Singh' is also used by some non-Sikh castes, and thus less profoundly associated with 'Sikhness' than its feminine counterpart. But it also shows that intellectual exchange, far from being the exclusive preserve of a cool and dispassionate faculty of 'reason', can be – and indeed often is – profoundly affectively charged, grounded not just in ideologies but also identifications (each with their own complex histories) that lead some participants in the exchange to consider certain intellectual positions as clear-cut and others as inadmissible. Of course, partaking in an intellectual exchange may do little more than shore up such outlooks, especially in cases where the medium of exchange leads them to find affirmation from within 'echo chambers' or to attract such hostile opposition that one holds one's ground and doubles down. However, there is also always the possibility that one's position will be reformulated by the exchange – when comments are moderated, or an insightful interjection (such as one questioning the possible misogyny underpinning one's attitude to the name Kaur) makes one think twice. Such open-endedness and riskiness, a point we return to at greater length in the final section of this introduction, is a crucial dimension of intellectual exchange, and one that is foregrounded especially usefully by thinking of it as an *interaction*.

Interactional conventions, structures of power, and materiality all play an important role in Caroline Humphrey's analysis of Mergen Güng Gombojab, a Mongolian hereditary noble and scholar born at the beginning of the twentieth century, who gave up his titles in pursuit of Soviet ideals and travelled widely within Mongolia, Russia and Europe before falling victim to Stalin's purges in 1940. Besides drawing our attention to forms and processes of intellectual exchange that have long been subject to silencing and erasure and showing how the contrasting intellectual currents to which he was exposed left a deep, and sometimes dissonant, impact upon Gombojab's subjectivity, Humphrey also highlights the importance of paying close attention to the governmental techniques that framed his travels through the international socialist ecumene. Intellectual exchange, for Gombojab, took place within the context of Soviet travel assignments (*komandirovka*). This meant that he was a bearer not just of personal but also institutional agency – embodying the goals and values of the sending organization but also endowed with a certain power to act, to proceed, and to expect respectful treatment at his destinations, and treated in specific ways by others as a result. Such a complex intertwining of personal mobility and institutional power even extended to the material presentation of the Soviet body, most notably through its clothing, which Humphrey argues should be understood as a form of equipment, demonstrating 'the social meaning and even the purpose of the person so dressed', even as it also affords scope for individuals to express their own personal takes on matters. Humphrey thus reveals the dangers attendant upon treating such analytic categories as 'transculturality', 'cultural mobility' or even 'intellectual exchange' as if they referred to self-evident or universal social realities, especially given the connotation of free circulation that such terms sometimes carry. Instead, careful attention needs to be paid to the governmental and interactional conventions that make certain forms of experience possible, for certain people, while precluding other outcomes. Her work thus signals the potential fruitfulness of a truly comparative anthropology of intellectual exchange, both within and beyond socialist settings.

Meanwhile, Sukanya Sarbadhikary's chapter takes up the theme of materiality and embodiment. In the spirit of a dialogue between Western and Indian philosophical-cum-anthropological traditions, Sarbadhikary draws on the philosophy informing the manufacture and playing of the *mridanga*, a sacred percussion instrument from West Bengal, to develop an innovative 'anthropology of hands' which foregrounds the primacy of the hands in all forms of exchange, both material and intellectual. When hand-crafting a *mridanga*, the body-self 'extends its own cosmic potential', externalizing the inner world of spiritual origin. When that same *mridanga* is played, having previously been exchanged via human hands in the market economy, sounds emanate from a union of hand and drum, penetrating the inner body of those who listen to it. The embodied, affective experience of listening to the drum and receiving its vibrations then serves as an existential grounds through which listeners reach and (re)affirm their own understanding of the ontological precepts underpinning Hindu cosmology. Equally, despite the tremendous salience of caste in this context, all bodies share the spiritual elements of clay-sound vibrations, and Sarbadhikary emphasizes how hands, by creating a seamless, intensely sensory exchange among the instrument-maker, player, listener and drum, allow intellectual exchange about essential equivalence among the drum sounders to be perpetually regenerated. As she notes, 'the intellectual discourse concerning the *mridanga* is exchanged among the participants as *both* sensory transmission *and* cognitive communication' (emphasis ours).

Through this analysis, not only is embodiment revealed as integral to the process of intellectual exchange, but the very straightforwardness of any distinction between 'material' and 'intellectual' exchange is called into question, since the transfer of *mridanga* for money is itself an essential component of the process by which core intellectual ideas, such as cosmological and ontological precepts, are circulated and sustained. This invites a broader consideration of how else anthropology's long history of thinking about exchange in the context of economic life might enrich our understanding of exchanges that we are prone to thinking of as primarily 'intellectual'.

Exchange as Transaction

Since knowledge itself is frequently a transactional good, numerous forms of intellectual exchange are already implicated in domains that are conventionally demarcated as 'economic'. For this reason, strict conceptual separation between economic and intellectual exchange is not usually tenable. Yet certain conceptual operations have to take place to make knowledge into a commodity due to its special property as a mode of 'immaterial labour' that is not physically manufactured in the same way as other goods. Jane Kenway et al. (2006: 55) explain how transforming knowledge into a commodity requires an understanding of its relation to the economy of scarcity: 'In terms of physically manufactured goods, if two people share the object, then each person's potential use of it is reduced. Rival goods are a precondition for the economic notion of "scarcity" as their depletion through consumption becomes the basis of a system of supply and demand that regulates a capitalist economy'. Knowledge, on the other hand, is a non-rival good because it does not diminish through consumption: its use by one does not preclude its use by another. If, then, knowledge – as 'a collectively shared, collectively produced, non-depletable (or non-rival) good' (Kenway et al. 2006: 56) – is to be exchanged for profit in the knowledge economy, it must be made 'artificially scarce by being turned into a privately-owned commodity' (Kundnani 1999: 52).

Making knowledge commercially exploitable thus requires its exclusion from free exchange – intellectual property rights (IPR) are an obvious example of this, with the knowledge owner gaining a monopoly on exploitation of the results of the research. We also meet here the 'black box' problem, known to anthropologists from the work of scholars such as Bruno Latour (1987) and recently discussed in reference to ancient knowledge networks by Eleanor Robson (2019). To claim ownership and hence restrict access to knowledge is to make invisible the manifold intellectual exchanges that contributed to its creation, a process of 'eras[ing] all traces of the process of production' (Robson 2019: 40) – what James Leach (2004) has called 'appropriative creativity'. In contexts where ownership of knowledge has been asserted, one person's generous, emancipatory, practice of intellectual exchange can be for another 'a form of copying or negative possession' (Reed 2011: 177), or even theft.

What these reflections reveal is that any anthropology of intellectual exchange ought to engage seriously with the anthropological literature on what Humphrey and Hugh-Jones (1992: 2) term 'types of exchange'. The core insight of this work was that 'exchange' can be broken down into different subtypes: barter, credit, formalized trade, gift exchange, monetized commodity exchange, theft and tribute, among others. Each has different 'rules' and moral valence, even as the boundaries between them were often blurred and contested, and individual transactions could sometimes be classified in multiple possible ways. Its value for an anthropology of intellectual exchange comes not only from the ethnographic specificity that is afforded by reflecting upon exactly what kind of exchange any given intellectual exchange might be for its constituent parties, but also from the leverage it offers anthropologists to *reclassify* instances of intellectual exchange, thereby resuscitating hitherto submerged dynamics.

Rather than always being a commodity exchange, for example, some instances of intellectual exchange might be better understood as gifting. In a note in her essay 'Worlds United and Apart' (this volume), Bayly explains how analyses of gift exchange influenced her understanding of Vietnamese intellectuals' participation in international exchanges of knowledge and modernizing expertise. As both givers and receivers of gifts of knowledge and skill, Vietnamese narratives do not neatly reflect the 'inequalities, power and patronage' (Mosse 2005: 20) that accounts of the gift in contexts of foreign development aid typically invoke. Rather, 'animated by feelings of selfless warmth', such exchanges were 'portrayed as something akin to the "empathetic dialogues" which Fennell (2002) sees as generated out of the giving of "illiquid", disinterested gifts between individual partners in exchange'. Bayly is here drawing on the work of Lee Anne Fennell (2002: 93), for whom a gift 'embodies and perpetuates empathetic dialogue between giver and recipient, facilitating and documenting each parties' imaginative participation in the life of the other'. Illiquid gift-giving, for Fennell, is not a form of market transaction but rather 'a specialized form of communication' that is empathetic in the sense that when selecting gift objects, parties imagine not what recipients would most like to possess but instead what they would most like to receive from this particular donor. While much can go wrong due to failures of imagination and gift selections inappropriate to the relationship, the forms of identification such dialogues can engender are unique: for instance, a donor's gift of jazz records might rest on their recognition of the 'higher order' preferences of a recipient who may know little about jazz but seeks to become the kind of person who does. Such a gift is insightful and empathetic since it successfully registers the hoped-for self-transformation of the recipient.

Meanwhile, and seeking to counter increased emphasis on the commercialization of research within the Australian Higher Education sector, Kenway et al. (2006) marshal the work of anthropological and other gift theorists (e.g. Gregory 1982; Carrier 1995; Frow 1997) to suggest parallels 'between the way the circulation of knowledge sustains an intellectual community, and the way the circulation of gifts maintains a gift community' (Kenway et al. 2006: 65). Arguing that knowledge is 'inalienable', they write of 'gifts of knowledge' and citation practices that acknowledge intellectual *debts* and give *credit* to intellectual influences. One need not agree with the normative thrust of Kenway et al.'s argument to recognize that its use of gift theory provides a stimulating perspective on intellectual exchanges and relations.

Economic anthropologists have long taken an interest in restricted modes of exchange, developing models that are likely to prove helpful in accounting for the intermittency or obstruction of certain instances of intellectual exchange. Jonathan Parry (1985) intimated something of this in an essay discussing how in classical Hindu theory only Brahman scholars are pure enough to be permitted to transmit Vedic knowledge. Pollution caused by death or birth can cause the process of transmission to be paused. Moreover, those belonging to certain 'unclean' castes are forbidden from hearing sacred texts: the ears of the Shudra 'are to be filled with mercury if he hears the Veda' (1985: 210); they are disbarred from being recipients of the Brahman's learning. Parry does not just compare the practice to the classical Indic form of gift-giving known as *dana* but argues that the Brahman's teaching actively partakes of – can only be understood in reference to – these gift logics. Brahman mortuary priests must not allow the gifts they receive at the time of cremation to accumulate. If they do, they become the rotting receptacles of sin, inauspiciousness and disease. In exactly the same way, the Brahman teacher who declines to transmit or exchange his knowledge will have to pay grave penalties in this life or the next.

The knowledge that they hold must circulate, but at the same time its circulation is highly restricted.

Parry contrasts the Brahmanical imperative to keep knowledge in circulation with Tantric traditions of secrecy and also regions of New Guinea where 'the most powerful knowledge is the most highly secret and where access to it is as narrowly restricted as possible' (1985: 208; see, e.g., Barth 1975). Other studies in economic anthropology likely to assist analysts of intellectual exchange include Eytan Bercovitch's work on 'hidden exchanges' in Inner New Guinea (1994), P.J. Hamilton-Grierson's on 'silent trade' (1903), Michael Walzer's on 'blocked exchanges' (1983) and in particular Paul and Laura Bohannan's work (1968) on 'spheres of exchange'. Indeed, exchanges, as anthropologists remind us, rarely if ever take place on an empty ground, but are always governed by rules and codes that are characteristic of social relations in a given time and place (Parry and Bloch 1989). Those rules and codes form *spheres of exchange*, understood as either a system of exchange in which objects are classified according to different spheres of values, and restrictions exist to prevent the exchange of objects in one sphere with those in another (Bohannan and Bohannan 1968), or a network of exchange regulated by specific norms regarding what can be circulated within the network (Pine 2002; Kwon 2007).

The notion of spheres of exchange guides the analysis in Lam Minh Chau's chapter in this volume. Chau examines the institutionalized discipline of anthropology practised by anthropologists employed in state research institutes and universities in northern Vietnam in the 1970s and 1980s pre-Renovation high-socialist period as a 'sphere of intellectual exchange'. Officially, only intellectual products of a certain kind could be circulated within this sphere: those that conformed to Soviet-style Marxist theories of social evolution. Non-Marxist, non-evolutionist theories and ideas were regarded as Western, reactionary and bourgeois, the circulation of which would contaminate the institutionalized discipline of anthropology as a means to facilitate social evolution among the country's ethnic minorities.

Anthropologists have not only paid attention to the ways spheres of exchange block, prevent and disrupt flows of ideas, knowledge and objects. They have also unveiled the many creative paths through which the supposedly rigid boundaries of exchange are overcome and worlds bridged (see Bayly, this volume). One way to transcend the boundaries is to engender the collapse of spheres of exchange altogether, notably by introducing a universal medium of exchange across all spheres (Kwon 2007). But boundaries can be transcended without leading to spheres' terminal destruction. Janet Carsten's work on 'cooking money' shows that Malaysian women who spent the money their husbands earned when working outside the home on the food they cooked and shared among family members converted money from a symbol of commercialized and individualized labour into embodiments of the spirits of collectivism, mutual sharing and non-calculation that could be safely exchanged within the home sphere as moral objects (1989: 132). Guided by Carsten's insights, Chau explores how a group of young Vietnamese state-employed anthropologists not only brought Western anthropological perspectives, particularly those associated with cultural relativism and structuralism, into the sphere of state anthropology as novel objects of intellectual exchange, but also, through their own distinctive interpretation of Western theories, 'cooked' those ideas into novel forms suitable to be circulated within the restricted sphere.

***

From contemporary interest in the mediating qualities of embodiment, materiality and linguistic and interactional conventions to the rich literature on forms and spheres of exchange, anthropology has an extensive repertoire of concepts and analytics that can be used to enhance interdisciplinary conversations on intellectual exchange, allowing us to understand it in nuanced and differentiated ways that go beyond, while nevertheless endorsing, the core observation that it is an agentive practice. We turn in the final section of the introduction to yet another way in which contemporary anthropological thought stands to both benefit from and offer valuable contributions to research on intellectual exchange. This line of analysis also builds upon the core recognition that intellectual exchange is an agentive practice. But if our discussion of 'exchange' analytics has been concerned with the minutiae of how such practice occurs, the next section considers its place and significance within the ethical lives of those undertaking it, and the others with whom they share their social worlds.

Intellectual Exchange and Ethical Life

Since cultural production is, as we have shown, underpinned by agentive – and yet contextually and materially mediated – processes of intellectual exchange, it is understandable that many scholars would be concerned with understanding what processes of intellectual exchange are taking place in any given context, in what ways, and to what effect. Such an enquiry may be driven by empiricist ethnographic modes of enquiry, but can also relate to more normative concerns. As seen in the previously cited example of Groethuysen's (1921) interest in fostering linguistic practices of intellectual exchange that guard against the dangers (for him) of hermetic ideologies, and as seen in many recent examinations of the shortcomings of established modes of academic practice (see, e.g., Brković 2022; Brodkin et al. 2011; Garnett 2006), those commenting on intellectual exchange are often keenly aware of divergences between the ways in which intellectual exchange is practised in actuality, and their ideals of intellectual exchange: how they would want it to be, or believe it *should* be. Intellectual exchange, then, is deeply bound up with ethical life: a site of possible moral flourishing, but also of possible compromise, complicity or moral failure. Equally, it is important not to take the occurrence of intellectual exchange for granted. Quite aside from the possibility of some people being excluded from intellectual interactions, ethnographic research has shown how even people with a vibrant intellectual life may actively withhold from, or simply be indifferent to, certain forms of intellectual conversation and enquiry (see, e.g., Last 1981; Long 2019). Conversely, the desire to participate in intellectual exchange cannot and should not be automatically credited to a transcendent cross-cultural domain of 'intellectual curiosity'. It must, instead, be located within an ethnographically contextualized understanding of the enquiring self, since this clarifies the impulses and modes of 'ethical reasoning' (Trnka et al. 2021: S59) that determine how intellectual exchange may be practised, and also sheds light on the affects and desires infusing the cultural politics that surround it.

Nicholas Long's contribution to this volume emphasizes the value of studying intellectual exchange not just as a practice but also as an ideal, developing this theoretical intervention with reference to ethnographic materials from Indonesia. Intellectual exchange, and specifically the prospect of high-achieving youngsters travelling abroad and then bringing knowledge back home – has a hallowed place in the national imaginary, since it is believed that such circuitry may rectify national problems of low human resource quality, educational deficiency and low international competitiveness. Studying overseas is thus a cherished aspiration for many Indonesians, and yet few are able to actually achieve it. While this in itself is a source of discontent, it also renders the endeavours of those who do partake in study overseas a matter of intense concern to their contemporaries back home. Such affective investment, Long argues, explains the shock and disbelief with which the Indonesian public responded to an incident in which David Hartanto Widjaya, an Indonesian high-achiever studying in Singapore, was found dead after allegedly attacking his dissertation supervisor with a knife. Indonesian commentators roundly rejected the suicide verdict delivered by the Singapore Coroner's Court, suggesting that David had been murdered to prevent him bringing state-of-the-art Singaporean knowledge back to Indonesia. When the Indonesian government did nothing to dispute the official Singaporean verdict, Indonesians experienced shock and despair at such apparent reluctance to seek justice for David and such seeming disregard not only for the wellbeing of the nation's most valuable human resources but also for the national futures that could be secured if their intellectual exchanges were conducted successfully. Such feelings were deeply consequential for Indonesians' political subjectivity, leading some to lose hope in the future and others to seek out dramatic forms of political alternative. Long's analysis thus broadens the scope of what 'an anthropology of intellectual exchange' should encompass by showing the need to examine the power of intellectual exchange as an ideal (rather than just a practice in and of itself): one that can be of immense significance and consequence even to those who are not directly involved in the intellectual exchanges.

As this discussion reveals, an anthropology of intellectual exchange can make important contributions to anthropology's ongoing endeavours to better understand various aspects of ethical life, including questions of 'the Good' and different communities' aspirations towards achieving it (on which, see Robbins 2013). Intellectual exchange can be reflected on and operate as an ideal to work towards (Long, this volume; see also Bayly 2009b) – an important point to recognize given the hitherto predominant focus on intellectual exchange as a practice. But equally, practices of intellectual exchange can form key means for striving towards varied conceptions of the Good (rather than function themselves as the Good), as we see in Copeman's chapter in this volume, which describes how exchanges of personal names can allow bearers to take on names capable of acting as models or ideals for assisting them in making of themselves the kind of people they wish to become (Laidlaw 2014b), and how the – sometimes intense – debates surrounding such name exchanges can allow a community of onlookers to not only appraise their success in doing so, but also allow the commentators themselves to performatively construct themselves as rightfully-minded advocates of whatever they believe their community most needs (more respect for Sikh tradition; more freedom of choice, and so on). Ethical subjects then may engage reflectively both *towards* intellectual exchange as the Good and *through* intellectual exchange towards other conceptions of the Good. Both ethical dimensions of intellectual exchange – as a practice of 'moral habituation' and as the subject of 'moral intellectual enquiry' (Yong 1996: 58) – centre on reflection and the aspiration to be certain kinds of person and thus form a privileged site for investigating moral experience and the dynamics of ethical life.

Indeed, one reason why intellectual exchange proves a fertile ground for such enquiry is because the pursuit of the Good via intellectual exchange is by no means always successful or straightforward. To understand why not, it is helpful to consider Hans-Georg Gadamer's observations, in *Truth and Method* ([1960] 2004), concerning the relationship between conversation and understanding. Gadamer rehabilitates prejudice and presupposition (or 'prejudgement') as the necessary ground of such engagements: without them we would simply be vacuous subjects to which conversations could reveal nothing (to paraphrase Mackenzie 1986: 44). He also notes, however, that conversational exchange 'is never completely under the control of either conversational partner, but rather is determined by the matter at issue' (Malpas 2018). As such, conversations – and intellectual exchange more broadly – involve high degrees of uncertainty, contingency and risk. Indeed, the possibility that an intellectual exchange might offer parties to it new insights and understandings hinges on its being able 'to assert its own truth against one's fore-meanings' (Mackenzie 1986: 44). Preconceived (and quite possibly cherished) notions may come under critical scrutiny, in ways that may allow subjects to advance towards the Good but may also unsettle established ethical projects and raise the spectre of moral peril.

Exchanges that pose some risk to one's fore-meanings need not precipitate their wholesale disintegration: we insist on the tenacity of subjects' capacity to discern amidst the unsettling winds intellectual exchanges can bring. In this volume, particularly compelling evidence of the durability of fore-meanings is provided in Christopher Goscha's account of French settlers living in Saigon at the time of the fall of French Indochina. Goscha's chapter explores this critical juncture in Vietnamese history from the perspective of French communities confronted with the end of empire, rather than the more widely-studied vantage point of Vietnamese nationalists. In terms of our enquiry into intellectual exchange, Goscha's study is fascinating for its portraiture of a community who 'disagreed vehemently that their time had come' even as their Vietnamese contemporaries argued that the age of colonization was over. Goscha cites the case of Jacques Le Bourgeois, the former director of *Radio Saigon*, whose memoirs betray an ongoing attachment to 'imperial time' and a conviction that Vietnamese nationalistic desire was 'entirely theoretical'. As Goscha notes, such a case resists easy theorization. It may be that Le Bourgeois's limited language skills hampered his understanding – a possibility that reiterates our earlier point about contingencies of interactional ecologies mediating the outcomes of intellectual exchange. Yet it also seems from Le Bourgeois's text that he was 'locked firmly in an imperial time warp', unable or unwilling to acknowledge the reality that surrounded him. Such cases are important for highlighting how intellectual exchanges are not automatically generative of new meaning but vulnerable to the dynamics of refusal (McGranahan 2016), while also showing that the forms of 'discernment' and 'active participation' with which people respond to intellectual provocations are not necessarily always characterized by careful sifting, selection and recombination of elements but can also involve inadvertent or fully wilful blindness (see Bovensiepen and Pelkmans 2020).

Nevertheless, although fore-meanings *can* be resilient in the face of intellectual exchange, this is not to be assumed. Goscha's case should be seen as occupying an extreme position on the spectrum of intellectual exchange outcomes, rather than being the default – for, if it were not possible for worldviews to be reshaped via processes of intellectual exchange, then the very institutions of education, research and learning that have led to this volume coming into being would be fundamentally unviable. The key point to take from Gadamer's work is that risk to fore-meaning is an inherent property of those intellectual exchanges that lead to critical scrutiny and examination of presuppositions. As such, contexts of intellectual exchange necessarily raise important questions about the durability or transformation of subjects' ethical commitments: an observation which means that intellectual exchange cannot be meaningfully understood aside from an engagement with its participants' and observers' ethical and moral lives. Here too, then, anthropology has much to contribute to the interdisciplinary conversations surrounding intellectual exchange, avowed as it is of a wide range of theoretical perspectives and tools designed to understand the contours, practice and experience of moral life (see, e.g., Faubion 2011; Laidlaw 2014b; Mattingly 2014; Zigon and Throop 2014).

Conclusion

With this introduction, we have not only introduced and contextualized the distinctive contributions made by the chapters in this volume, but established a case as to why anthropologists should take an interest, and get involved, in the growing multi-disciplinary intellectual exchanges regarding intellectual exchange. Given that intellectual life is a foundational aspect of human experience which represents a legitimate and fruitful (though by no means the only) point of departure for anthropological enquiry and analysis, there are many good reasons for the notion of 'intellectual exchange' to be front and centre of anthropological vocabulary. It is broad enough to encompass and bring into juxtaposition a wide variety of practices, while nuanced enough to avoid both the deterministic forms of power functionalism and the simplistic assumptions of incommensurability that have sometimes informed anthropologists' accounts of their interlocutors' intellectual lives. Intellectual exchange is thus a vibrant and fertile object of concern for contemporary anthropology.

Moreover, if one problem with much existing work on intellectual exchange has been its tendency towards particularist descriptivism, leaving its core concept 'undertheorized' (Merkel 2021), then anthropologists have much to offer the emergent conversations surrounding the term. While an attention to the complexities of scale, an open-mindedness regarding who or what should be encompassed within an account of 'intellectual exchange', and a critical attention to the cultural politics of the category 'intellectual' are not unique to anthropologists, they are all points on which anthropologists, by virtue of their training, are well positioned to make key contributions. We also highlight three further ways in which anthropologists are perhaps uniquely placed to invigorate the study of intellectual exchange: through their analytic attention to, and close ethnographic observation of, intellectual exchange's mediation by institutions, social structures, linguistic and interactional conventions and embodied topologies; by operationalizing an extensive disciplinary conceptual arsenal to capture diverse forms and logics of 'exchange' and recognize the differences and commonalities across them; and by embedding intellectual exchange within broader accounts of ethical life so as to better understand its consequences for self-making and to understand it not only as a practice, but as an ideal, or object of desire.

Clearly, this is only the beginning of what we hope will evolve into a productive and dynamic field of enquiry and debate: we make no claim to have offered an exhaustive account of all anthropological work related to intellectual exchange, nor to have advanced an all-encompassing anthropological theory of intellectual exchange. Instead, we offer readers from within and beyond anthropology a set of tools with which to think about these issues, and a collection of intriguing and compelling case studies in which to observe those tools at work. We hope that engaging with these writings will allow you, the reader, to gain new insights for your work, just as engaging closely with the work of Susan

Bayly has, in so many ways, inspired and informed the intellectual lives of each of the contributors. If it does not, then we hope that engaging with the volume will supply added clarity as to why you fortify your existing position. For if either outcome is achieved, then that in itself would be proof of the vibrancy, vitality and consequentiality of intellectual exchange – and of its deservingness of becoming a concerted focus of anthropological enquiry.

Acknowledgements

We would like to thank three anonymous referees for their supportive comments and insightful critiques on an earlier version of this introduction.

Nicholas J. Long is an Associate Professor of Anthropology at the London School of Economics and Political Science (LSE), where he works on the anthropology of Indonesia and on responses to COVID-19 in the UK and Aotearoa New Zealand. He won the 2019 Stirling Prize for Best Published Work in Psychological Anthropology for his article 'Suggestions of Power: Searching for Efficacy in Indonesia's Hypnosis Boom'.

Jacob Copeman is Research Professor, University of Santiago de Compostela, and Distinguished Researcher (Oportunius). His most recent monograph, co-authored with Dwaipayan Banerjee, is *Hematologies: The Political Life of Blood in India* (Cornell University Press, 2019). His most recent edited collection, co-edited with Mascha Schulz, is *Global Sceptical Publics: From Non-religious Print Media to 'Digital Atheism'* (UCL Press, 2022). He is principal investigator of the ERC-funded project 'Religion and Its Others in South Asia and the World: Communities, Debates, Freedoms'.

Magnus Marsden is Professor of Social Anthropology at the University of Sussex where he is also the Director of the Sussex Asia Centre.

Lam Minh Chau is Associate Professor of Anthropology and Chair of Social and Economic Anthropology at the College of Social Sciences and Humanities, Vietnam National University, Hanoi.

Joanna Cook is a Reader in Anthropology at University College London. She is the author of *Meditation in Modern Buddhism: Renunciation and Change in Thai Monastic Life* (Cambridge University Press, 2010), *Making a Mindful Nation: Mental Health and Governance in the 21st Century* (Princeton University Press, 2023), and the co-editor of *The State We're In: Reflecting on Democracy's Troubles* (Berghahn Books, 2016), *Detachment: Essays on the Limits of Relational Thinking* (Manchester University Press, 2015) and *Southeast Asian Perspectives on Power* (Routledge, 2012).

Notes

1. When writing of different intellectual 'traditions', we follow MacIntyre's definition of a tradition as 'an argument extended through time in which certain fundamental agreements are defined and redefined in terms of two kinds of conflict: those with critics and enemies external to the tradition ... and those internal, interpretive debates ... by whose progress a tradition is constituted' (1988: 12). Such traditions are deliberative. Though initially or ostensibly conflictual, interactions between them can produce rethinking, evaluation and examination by a tradition of its own practices and beliefs and lead to decisions to adopt, in their place, values and practices from rival traditions to live by (see also a similar line of argument developed with reference to religious traditions in Das 2014). Intellectual exchange, in this volume, is thus understood to be an emergent and constitutive property of nevertheless distinct traditions rather than something that takes place between already fully constituted self-enclosed universes in the form either of disintegration or mere encounter.
2. Of Bayly's own personal intellectual exchanges in Cambridge, it has always been clear how much joy her life in the Department of Social Anthropology gave her; while of her thirty-four-year marriage to the preeminent historian of India, the British Empire and world history Christopher Bayly (1945–2015), she has written that it was 'sustained and nourished by joyfully impassioned argument, and keen enthusiasm for one another's work' (Clark and Bayly 2018: xv).
3. However, see work by Gil (2010) and van der Geest (2018) exploring how interlocutors in the field may not only co-author or collaborate constructively but also engage in alternative modalities of intellectual exchange, such as refusal to cooperate, deceit, or the deliberate sabotage of one's project.
4. A striking recent example supporting this point is Brković's (2022) analysis of peer review practices in anthropology. For Brković, the effectiveness of peer review is undermined by the dominance of 'a "courtroom" model of an intellectual exchange' which foregrounds picking holes in authors' arguments and 'thinking against' them. While this can be stimulating, she argues, the stakes of publishing often render it a source of anxiety and grievance rather than intellectual pleasure; she instead advocates practices of intellectual exchange characterized by 'thinking with', 'imaginative identification' and 'intellectual accompaniment', modelled on the supervisor-doctoral student relationship.

References

Agrama, Hussein Ali. 2012. *Questioning Secularism: Islam, Sovereignty, and the Rule of Law in Modern Egypt*. Chicago: University of Chicago Press.

Alatas, Ismail Fajrie. 2020. 'Dreaming Saints: Exploratory Authority and Islamic Praxes of History in Central Java', *Journal of the Royal Anthropological Institute (N.S.)* 26(1): 67–85. https://doi.org/10.1111/1467-9655.13177.

Allen, Renee Nicole. 2021. 'From Academic Freedom to Cancel Culture: Silencing Black Women in the Legal Academy', *UCLA Law Review* 68(2): 364–409.

Anderson, John B. 1917. 'Religion and the Intellect', *The Biblical World* 49(1): 3–11. https://doi.org/10.1086/475673.

Assmann, Aleida. 2013. 'Civilizing Societies: Recognition and Respect in a Global World', *New Literary History* 44(1): 69–91. https://doi.org/10.1353/nlh.2013.0006.

Barth, Frederik. 1975. *Ritual and Knowledge among the Baktaman of New Guinea*. New Haven, CT: Yale University Press.

Bayly, Susan. 1989. *Saints, Goddesses and Kings: Muslims and Christians in South Indian Society, 1700–1900*. Cambridge: Cambridge University Press.
———. 1999. *Caste, Society and Politics in India from the Eighteenth Century to the Modern Age*. Cambridge: Cambridge University Press.
———. 2000. 'French Anthropology and the Durkheimians in Colonial Indochina', *Modern Asian Studies* 34(3): 581–622. https://doi.org/10.1017/S0026749X00003954.
———. 2004. 'Imagining "Greater India": French and Indian Visions of Colonialism in the Indic Mode', *Modern Asian Studies* 38(3): 703–44. https://doi.org/10.1017/S0026749X04001246.
———. 2007. *Asian Voices in a Post-Colonial Age: Vietnam, India and Beyond*. Cambridge: Cambridge University Press.
———. 2009a. 'Conceptualizing Resistance and Revolution in Vietnam: Paul Mus' Understanding of Colonialism in Crisis', *Journal of Vietnamese Studies* 4(1): 192–205. https://doi.org/10.1525/vs.2009.4.1.192.
———. 2009b. 'Vietnamese Narratives of Tradition, Exchange and Friendship in the Worlds of the Global Socialist Ecumene', in Harry G. West and Parvathi Raman (eds), *Enduring Socialism: Explorations of Revolution and Transformation, Restoration and Continuation*. Oxford: Berghahn Books.
———. 2013. 'Mapping Time, Living Space: The Moral Cartography of Renovation in Late-Socialist Vietnam', *Cambridge Anthropology* 31(2): 60–84.
———. 2014. 'How to Forge a Creative Student-Citizen: Achieving the Positive in Today's Vietnam', *Modern Asian Studies* 48(3): 493–523.
———. 2019. 'The Voice of Propaganda: Citizenship and Moral Silence in Late-Socialist Vietnam', *Terrain* 72. https://doi.org/10.4000/terrain.18881.
———. 2020. 'Beyond "Propaganda": Images and the Moral Citizen in Late-Socialist Vietnam', *Modern Asian Studies* 54(5): 1526–95. https://doi.org/10.1017/S0026749X19000222.
Bercovitch, Eytan. 1994. 'The Agent in the Gift: Hidden Exchange in Inner New Guinea', *Cultural Anthropology* 9(4): 498–536. https://doi.org/10.1525/can.1994.9.4.02a00030.
Berman, Elise. 2020. 'Avoiding Sharing: How People Help Each Other Get Out of Giving', *Current Anthropology* 61(2): 219–39.
Berreman, Gerald D. 1978. 'Scale and Social Relations', *Current Anthropology* 19(2): 225–45.
Bielo, James S. 2019. '"Particles-to-People...Molecules-to-Man": Creationist Poetics in Public Debates', *Journal of Linguistic Anthropology* 29(1): 4–26. https://doi.org/10.1111/jola.12205.
Bloch, Maurice. 2005. *Essays on Cultural Transmission*. Oxford: Berg.
Bohannan, Paul, and Laura Bohannan. 1968. *Tiv Economy*. Evanston, IL: Northwestern University Press.
Bohm, David. 1996. *On Dialogue*. London: Routledge.
Bovensiepen, Judith, and Mathijs Pelkmans. 2020. 'Dynamics of Wilful Blindness: An Introduction', *Critique of Anthropology* 40(4): 387–402. https://doi.org/10.1177/0308275x20959432.
Brković, Čarna. 2022. 'Introduction: "Thinking With" When Peer Reviewing', *PoLAR: Political and Legal Anthropology Review* (Emergent Directions) 16: https://polarjournal.org/2022/06/13/introduction-thinking-with-when-peer-reviewing/.
Brodkin, Karen, Sandra Morgen and Janis Hutchinson. 2011. 'Anthropology as White Public Space?', *American Anthropologist* 113(4): 545–56.

Burney, Shehla. 2012. *Pedagogy of the Other: Edward Said, Postcolonial Theory, and Strategies for Critique*. New York: Peter Lang.
Callon, Michel. 1984. 'Some Elements of a Sociology of Translation: Domestication of the Scallops and the Fishermen of St Brieuc Bay', *The Sociological Review* 32(S1): 196–233.
Carr, E. Summerson, and Michael Lempert. 2016. 'Introduction: Pragmatics of Scale', in E. Summerson Carr and Michael Lempert (eds), *Scale: Discourse and Dimensions of Social Life*. Berkeley: University of California Press, pp. 1–21.
Carrier, James G. 1995. *Gifts and Commodities: Exchange and Western Capitalism since 1700*. London: Routledge.
Carsten, Janet. 1989. 'Cooking Money: Gender and the Symbolic Transformation of Means of Exchange in a Malay Fishing Community', in Jonathan Parry and Maurice Bloch (eds), *Money and the Morality of Exchange*. Cambridge: Cambridge University Press, pp. 117–41.
Carter, David, and Arthur Spirling. 2008. 'Under the Influence? Intellectual Exchange in Political Science', *PS: Political Science and Politics* 41(2): 375–78.
Chakrabarty, Dipesh. 2000. *Provincializing Europe: Postcolonial Thought and Historical Difference*. Princeton, NJ: Princeton University Press.
Chen, Kuan-Hsing. 2010. *Asia as Method: Toward Deimperialization*. Durham, NC: Duke University Press.
Clark, Christopher, and Susan Bayly. 2018. 'Christopher Bayly and the Making of World History', in C.A. Bayly (ed.), *Remaking the Modern World 1900–2015: Global Connections and Comparisons*. Malden, MA: Wiley-Blackwell, pp. xiii–xviii.
Cole, Michael, and Sylvia Scribner. 1975. 'Theorizing about Socialization of Cognition', *Ethos* 3(2): 249–68. https://doi.org/10.1525/eth.1975.3.2.02a00110.
Comaroff, Jean, and John Comaroff. 1992. *Of Revelation and Revolution Volume 1: Christianity, Colonialism and Consciousness in South Africa*. Chicago: University of Chicago Press.
Cooper, Frederick. 2005. *Colonialism in Question: Theory, Knowledge, History*. Berkeley: University of California Press.
Csordas, Thomas J. 1994. 'Introduction: The Body as Representation and Being-in-the-World', in Thomas J. Csordas (ed.), *Embodiment and Experience: The Existential Ground of Culture and Self*. Cambridge: Cambridge University Press, pp. 1–26.
Das, Veena. 2014. 'Cohabiting an Interreligious Milieu: Reflections on Religious Diversity', in Janice Boddy and Michael Lambek (eds), *A Companion to the Anthropology of Religion*. Malden, MA: Wiley-Blackwell, pp. 69–84.
Ellen, Roy, Stephen J. Lycett and Sarah E. Johns (eds). 2013. *Understanding Cultural Transmission in Anthropology: A Critical Synthesis*. Oxford: Berghahn Books.
Ermarth, Michael. 1993. 'Intellectual History as Philosophical Anthropology: Bernard Groethuysen's Transformation of Traditional *Geistesgeschichte*', *The Journal of Modern History* 65(4): 673–705. https://doi.org/10.1086/244722.
Fatsis, Lambros. 2016. 'Becoming Public Characters, Not Public Intellectuals: Notes Towards an Alternative Conception of Public Intellectual Life', *European Journal of Social Theory* 21(3): 267–87. https://doi.org/10.1177/1368431016677977.
Faubion, James. 2011. *An Anthropology of Ethics*. Cambridge: Cambridge University Press.
Fennell, Lee Anne. 2002. 'Unpacking the Gift: Illiquid Goods and Empathetic Dialogue', in Mark Osteen (ed.), *The Question of the Gift: Essays across Disciplines*. New York: Routledge, pp. 85–102.

Freshwater, Dawn. 2007. 'Dialogue, Conversation and Discussion: Reflection Upon Languaging Relationship', *Journal of Psychiatric and Mental Health Nursing* 14(5): 431–32. https://doi.org/10.1111/j.1365-2850.2007.01140.x.
Frow, John. 1997. *Time and Commodity Culture*. Oxford: Clarendon Press.
Gadamer, Hans-Georg. [1960] 2004. *Truth and Method*, 2nd rev. ed., trans. Joel Weinsheimer and Donald G. Marshall. London: Continuum.
Garnett, Robert F. 2006. 'Paradigms and Pluralism in Heterodox Economics', *Review of Political Economy* 18(4): 521–46. https://doi.org/10.1080/09538250600915725.
Geertz, Clifford. 1973. *The Interpretation of Cultures: Selected Essays*. New York: Basic Books.
Gil, Gastón Julián. 2010. 'Ethnography among "Experts": Notes on Collaboration and Sabotage in the Field', *Qualitative Research* 10(1): 49–69. https://doi.org/10.1177/1468794109348682.
Glück, Zoltán. 2013. 'Between Wall Street and Zuccotti: Occupy and the Scale of Politics', in *Cultural Anthropology: Hot Spots, Fieldsights*. Available online at https://culanth.org/fieldsights/between-wall-street-and-zuccotti-occupy-and-the-scale-of-politics.
Gregg, Melissa, and Gregory J. Seigworth (eds). 2010. *The Affect Theory Reader*. Durham, NC: Duke University Press.
Gregory, Chris. 1982. *Gifts and Commodities*. London: Academic.
Groethuysen, Bernard. 1921. 'Lettres D'allemagne', *Nouvelle Revue Française* 8(97): 485–96.
Hamilton-Grierson, Philip James. 1903. *The Silent Trade: A Contribution to the Early History of Human Intercourse*. Edinburgh: W. Green.
Haven, Joseph. 1862. *Mental Philosophy: Including the Intellect, Sensibilities, and Will*. Boston: Gould and Lincoln.
Ho, Engseng. 2017. 'Inter-Asian Concepts for Mobile Societies', *The Journal of Asian Studies* 76(4): 907–28. https://doi.org/10.1017/S0021911817000900.
Honneth, Axel. 1995. *The Struggle for Recognition: The Moral Grammar of Social Conflicts*, trans. Joel Anderson. Cambridge: Polity Press.
Humphrey, Caroline, and Stephen Hugh-Jones. 1992. 'Introduction: Barter, Exchange and Value', in Caroline Humphrey and Stephen Hugh-Jones (eds), *Barter, Exchange and Value: An Anthropological Approach*. Cambridge: Cambridge University Press, pp. 1–20.
Jay, Martin. 1993. *Force-Fields: Between Intellectual History and Cultural Critique*. New York: Routledge.
Kenway, Jane, Elizabeth Bullen, Johannah Fahey and Simon Robb. 2006. *Haunting the Knowledge Economy*. London: Routledge.
Kundnani, Arun. 1999. 'Where Do You Want to Go Today? The Rise of Information Capital', *Race and Class* 40(2–3): 49–72. https://doi.org/10.1177/030639689904000205.
Kwon, Heonik. 2007. 'The Dollarization of Vietnamese Ghost Money', *Journal of the Royal Anthropological Institute (N.S.)* 13(1): 73–90. https://doi.org/10.1111/j.1467-9655.2007.00414.x.
Laidlaw, James. 2014a. 'Significant Differences', *HAU: Journal of Ethnographic Theory* 4(1): 497–506. https://doi.org/10.14318/hau4.1.032.
———. 2014b. *The Subject of Virtue*. Cambridge: Cambridge University Press.
Lambek, Michael. 2010. 'Introduction', in Michael Lambek (ed.), *Ordinary Ethics: Anthropology, Language, and Action*. New York: Fordham University Press, pp. 1–36.

Last, Murray. 1981. 'The Importance of Knowing About Not Knowing', *Social Science and Medicine* 15B(3): 387–92.
Latour, Bruno. 1987. *Science in Action*. Cambridge, MA: Harvard University Press.
______. 1996. *Aramis: Or, the Love of Technology*, trans. Catherine Porter. Cambridge, MA: Harvard University Press.
Leach, James. 2004. 'Modes of Creativity', in Eric Hirsch and Marilyn Strathern (eds), *Transactions and Creations: Property Debates and the Stimulus of Melanesia*. Oxford: Berghahn Books, pp. 151–75.
Lewis, Tania. 2004. 'Meaghan Morris and the Formation of Australian Cultural Studies: A Narrative of Intellectual Exchange and Located Transnationalism', *Cultural Studies ↔ Critical Methodologies* 4(1): 45–70. https://doi.org/10.1177/1532708603259446.
Long, Nicholas J. 2017. 'On the Islamic Authority of the Indonesian State: Responsibility, Suspicion, and Acts of Compliance', *Journal of the Royal Anthropological Institute (N.S.)* 23(4): 709–26.
______. 2018. 'Suggestions of Power: Searching for Efficacy in Indonesia's Hypnosis Boom', *Ethos* 46(1): 70–94. https://doi.org/10.1111/etho.12190.
______. 2019. '"Accept and Utilize": Alternative Medicine, Minimality, and Ethics in an Indonesian Healing Collective', *Medical Anthropology Quarterly* 33(3): 327–44. https://doi.org/10.1111/maq.12448.
Long, Nicholas J., and Henrietta L. Moore (eds). 2013. *The Social Life of Achievement*. Oxford: Berghahn Books.
Love, Bridget H., Emerald Templeton, Stacey Ault and Onda Johnson. 2021. 'Bruised, Not Broken: Scholarly Personal Narratives of Black Women in the Academy', *International Journal of Qualitative Studies in Education*: 1–23. https://doi.org/10.1080/09518398.2021.1984607.
MacIntyre, Alasdair. 1988. *Whose Justice? Which Rationality?* Notre Dame, IL: University of Notre Dame Press.
Mackenzie, Ian. 1986. 'Gadamer's Hermeneutics and the Uses of Forgery', *The Journal of Aesthetics and Art Criticism* 45(1): 41–48. https://doi.org/10.2307/430464.
Magnarella, Paul. 2003. 'Turkish-American Intellectual Exchange and Community Research in Turkey (1930–1980)', *The Turkish Studies Association Journal* 27(1/2): 69–89.
Malpas, Jeff. 2018. 'Hans-Georg Gadamer', in Edward N. Zalta (ed.), *The Stanford Encyclopedia of Philosophy. Fall 2018 Edition*. Available online at https://plato.stanford.edu/archives/fall2018/entries/gadamer/.
Marsden, Magnus. 2005. *Living Islam: Muslim Religious Experience in Pakistan's North-West Frontier*. Cambridge: Cambridge University Press.
Mathias, John. 2020. 'Sticky Ethics: Environmental Activism and the Limits of Ethical Freedom in Kerala, India', *Anthropological Theory* 20(3): 253–76. https://doi.org/10.1177/1463499619828128.
Mattingly, Cheryl. 2014. *Moral Laboratories: Family Peril and the Struggle for a Good Life*. Berkeley: University of California Press.
McGranahan, Carole. 2016. 'Theorizing Refusal: An Introduction', *Cultural Anthropology* 31(3): 319–25. https://doi.org/10.14506/ca31.3.01.
Merkel, Ian. 2017. 'Fernand Braudel, Brazil, and the Empire of French Social Science: Newly Translated Sources from the 1930s', *French Historical Studies* 40(1): 129–60. https://doi.org/10.1215/00161071-3686080.
______. 2021. 'Primer: Intellectual Exchange', *World History Commons*. Retrieved 20 December 2021 from https://worldhistorycommons.org/primer-intellectual-exchange.

———. 2022. *Terms of Exchange: Brazilian Intellectuals and the French Social Sciences*. Chicago: University of Chicago Press.
Miller, Daniel. 2000. 'The Fame of Trinis: Websites as Traps', *Journal of Material Culture* 5(1): 5–24. https://doi.org/10.1177/135918350000500101.
———. (ed.). 2005. *Materiality*. Durham, NC: Duke University Press.
Miller, Daniel, Elisabetta Costa, Laura Haapio-Kirk, Nell Haynes, Jolynna Sinanan, Tom McDonald, Razvan Nicolescu, Juliano Spyer, Shriram Venkatraman and Xinyuan Wang. 2019. 'Contemporary Comparative Anthropology: The Why We Post Project', *Ethnos* 84(2): 283–300.
Mosse, David. 2005. 'Global Governance and the Ethnography of International Aid', in David Mosse and David Lewis (eds), *The Aid Effect: Giving and Governing in International Development*. London: Pluto Press, pp. 1–36.
Murphy, Keith M., and C. Jason Throop (eds). 2010. *Toward an Anthropology of the Will*. Stanford: Stanford University Press.
Nash, David. 2019. 'Secularist History: Past Perspectives and Future Prospects', *Secularism and Nonreligion* 8(1): 1–9. https://doi.org/10.5334/snr.113.
Ní Bheacháin, Caoilfhionn, and Angus Mitchell. 2019. 'Alice Stopford Green and Vernon Lee: Salon Culture and Intellectual Exchange', *Journal of Victorian Culture* 25(1): 77–94. https://doi.org/10.1093/jvcult/vcz053.
O'Connor, Brendan H. 2020. 'Revisiting Americanist Arguments and Rethinking Scale in Linguistic Anthropology', *Journal of Linguistic Anthropology* 30(3): 284–303. https://doi.org/10.1111/jola.12280.
Parry, Jonathan. 1985. 'The Brahmanical Tradition and the Technology of the Intellect', in Joanna Overing (ed.), *Reason and Morality*. London: Tavistock, pp. 198–222.
Parry, Jonathan, and Maurice Bloch (eds). 1989. *Money and the Morality of Exchange*. Cambridge: Cambridge University Press.
Pine, Frances. 2002. 'Dealing with Money: Zlotys, Dollars and Other Currencies in the Polish Highlands', in Ruth Mandel and Caroline Humphrey (eds), *Markets and Moralities: Ethnographies of Postsocialism*. Oxford: Berg, pp. 77–97.
Reed, Adam. 2011. 'Inspiring Strathern', in Jeanette Edwards and Maja Petrović-Šteger (eds), *Recasting Anthropological Knowledge: Inspiration and Social Science*. Cambridge: Cambridge University Press, pp. 165–82.
Rivera, José Antonio Aguilar. 2000. *The Shadow of Ulysses: Public Intellectual Exchange across the US-Mexican Border*, trans. Rose Hocker and Emiliano Corrall. Lanham, MD: Lexington.
Robbins, Joel. 2013. 'Beyond the Suffering Subject: Toward an Anthropology of the Good', *Journal of the Royal Anthropological Institute (N.S)* 19(3): 447–62.
Robson, Eleanor. 2019. *Ancient Knowledge Networks: A Social Geography of Cuneiform Scholarship in First-Millennium Assyria and Babylonia*. London: UCL Press.
Schneider, David M. 1984. *A Critique of the Study of Kinship*. Ann Arbor: University of Michigan Press.
Scott, James C. 2009. *The Art of Not Being Governed: An Anarchist History of Upland Southeast Asia*. New Haven, CT: Yale University Press.
Shafir, Nir. 2014. 'The International Congress as Scientific and Diplomatic Technology: Global Intellectual Exchange in the International Prison Congress, 1860–90', *Journal of Global History* 9(1): 72–93. https://doi.org/10.1017/S1740022813000508.
Shah-Kazemi. 2002. 'Intellect and Religion: East and West', *The Ismaili United Kingdom* (45): 52–54.
Spiro, Melford E. 1997. *Gender Ideology and Psychological Reality: An Essay on Cultural Reproduction*. New Haven, CT: Yale University Press.

Spivak, Gayatri Chakravorty. 1985. 'Can the Subaltern Speak? Speculations on Widow-Sacrifice', *Wedge* (7–8): 120–30.
Stewart, Kathleen. 1996. *A Space on the Side of the Road: Cultural Poetics in an "Other" America*. Princeton, NJ: Princeton University Press.
Strang, Veronica. 2006. 'A Happy Coincidence? Symbiosis and Synthesis in Anthropological and Indigenous Knowledges', *Current Anthropology* 47(6): 981–1006. https://doi.org/10.1086/507196.
Strathern, Marilyn. 2004. *Partial Connections*, updated ed. Walnut Creek, CA: AltaMira Press.
Tindall, B. Allan. 1976. 'Theory in the Study of Cultural Transmission', *Annual Review of Anthropology* 5: 195–208. https://doi.org/10.1146/annurev.an.05.100176.001211.
Trento, Margherita. 2022. *Writing Tamil Catholicism: Literature, Persuasion and Devotion in the Eighteenth Century*. Leiden: Brill.
Trnka, Susanna, Nicholas J. Long, Pounamu Jade Aikman, Nayantara Sheoran Appleton, Sharyn Graham Davies, Antje Deckert, Edmond Fehoko et al. 2021. 'Negotiating Risks and Responsibilities during Lockdown: Ethical Reasoning and Affective Experience in Aotearoa New Zealand', *Journal of the Royal Society of New Zealand* 51(S1): S55–S74. https://doi.org/10.1080/03036758.2020.1865417.
van der Geest, Sjaak. 2018. 'Lying in Defence of Privacy: Anthropological and Methodological Observations', *International Journal of Social Research Methodology* 21(5): 541–52. https://doi.org/10.1080/13645579.2018.1447866.
Walzer, Michael. 1983. *Spheres of Justice: A Defense of Pluralism and Equality*. New York: Basic Books.
Yong, Patrick. 1996. 'Intellectualism and Moral Habituation in Plato's Earlier Dialogues', *Apeiron* 29(4): 49–61. https://doi.org/10.1515/APEIRON.1996.29.4.49.
Yue, Audrey. 2017. 'Trans-Singapore: Some Notes towards Queer Asia as Method', *Inter-Asia Cultural Studies* 18(1): 10–24. https://doi.org/10.1080/14649373.2017.1273911.
Zigon, Jarrett, and C. Jason Throop. 2014. 'Moral Experience: Introduction', *Ethos* 42(1): 1–15.

Part I

Bridging Worlds

1

Mapping Time, Living Space
The Moral Cartography of Renovation in Late-Socialist Vietnam

Susan Bayly

Introduction

This is a paper about the mapping of personal and official histories in contemporary Vietnam. Building on ethnographic fieldwork in Hanoi, my concern is with sites where both the nation and its citizens enact the divergent chronologies and spatial positionings of the late-socialist world. The activities explored here include divinatory grave-site searches and geomantic house-sitings, and occasions when families and individuals share narrative knowledge of working or studying overseas.

My focus is the ethical entailments of such activities, including those relating to the delineation of Vietnamese national space, and the astrobiological reckonings for which one commissions a geomancer. The cases I have in mind include that of Mr Toan, a teacher in my fieldsite who had received frustratingly inconclusive advice from ordinary jobbing seers about his family's health and money problems. 'I felt it a lot', he said. 'It was pain in my heart' (*ruột đau*). What hurt was his sense of moral deficiency, his failure to meet need. But he found relief from a specialist in the geomantic arts, a *thầy phong thuỷ*, who traced the cause of his family's troubles to a house extension undertaken by his father twenty years ago, without a sanctioning leave-seeking, a *xin phép*, from the house-plot's place-god, its *thổ địa*.

There is also my friend Mr Phong, who speaks elegiacally of the beauty of his father's work as a French-trained map-maker, recruited to draw maps for the Viet Minh revolutionary army that defeated the French in 1954. 'Đẹp quá!' he said about the maps, 'So beautiful!' Đẹp can mean good looks, but also spiritual beauty and moral harmony. Auspicious numbers are things of beauty too. People buy 'beautiful numbers' (*số đẹp*) for their mobile phones, i.e. a sim-card sequence in numerological resonance with the causal harmonies of earth and heaven. And specialists in the now actively revived science of *phong thuỷ* (geomancy) guide their clients in the selection of a house or tomb site with 'beautiful' geomantic properties, meaning an ideal placing between hills and flowing watercourses. For Mr Phong, both the act and the artefacts were beautiful. There was love and artistry like the icon-painter's dedicated spirituality in tracing out and bringing into view the beloved countenance of the national geobody (Winichakul 1994).

All cartography might, of course, be said to be both moral and political, as can be seen in accounts of the 'cartographies of power' (Clark 2003: 8) enacted in settings such as Stalin's Russia (Dobrenko and Naiman 2003). There are certainly objectifications of this kind in Vietnam, the most obvious instances being the ever-changing array of official posters and exhortation banners displayed in public spaces. These artefacts of the party-state at its most didactic project their messages in strongly cartographic terms, exalting love of homeland and of those who protect its frontiers, juxtaposing images of heroic soldier-citizens and flower-of-the-nation Youth Union (*Đoàn Thanh niên*) members with vivid representations of the national map.[1] One of the posters' recurring motifs is that of a gleaming industrial cityscape with grid-like streets and other tokens of topographic modernity, symbolizing national life as it should be lived by those embodying its values as disciplined spatial subjects. There are even special banners for display by designated 'spaces of modern civility' (*khu phố văn minh*), meaning neighbourhoods meeting exemplary standards of order and conduct.

Yet I believe the case of Vietnam shows that there is far more to cartography's ethical entailments than the projection of moralizing power/knowledge. Hanoians attach great importance to the ways actors and their affective collectivities engage with the world's mapped and mappable spaces, thereby showing themselves to be both achieving and ethically purposeful in the conduct of everyday life. Such modes of engagement include the ways demarcated space can be invested with meanings both intimate and exalting, as in the use of family photographs to recall and celebrate the traversing of near and distant revolutionary landscapes. And because calculation and exactitude in these matters have high value in Vietnam, the operations of geomancers and psychic grave-finders are also forms of moral cartography. These are widely esteemed as scientific pursuits in the value-laden sense in which positivistic modern science (*khoa học*) is understood in today's Vietnam.[2]

This is knowledge with distinctively moral entailments, of the kind deployed when clients use a chosen expert's skill and insight to make principled contact with a numinous and responsive geotemporal environment. My interest is thus in the importance of personal efficacy in the handling of spatial conditions and challenges; in the ethical reckonings made when cartographic skills are deployed for principled ends; and in the highly tangible ways such deployments reflect the intertwining of the temporal and geophysical.

The sites of these materializations include domestic ancestor altars and pagoda memorial walls, and other points where histories of kindred and nationhood interpenetrate in forms both exalting and painful for those involved. Moral cartography is a notion premised on precise methodologies, with a focus on actors' own perceptions of what it is morally creditable to strive for in a world of ever-challenging spatial and temporal knowledge, including contexts of commercial supply and exchange.[3]

This means that when Soviet-trained geologists or astronomers take up the geomantic arts in later life, those with a reputation for skill and honest dealing are regarded as bringing into fruitful resonance two distinct yet compatible realms of super-morality: that of hard-science positivism, and that of the open-ended world of numinous space and landscape. It is accepted that money will change hands when such arts are deployed. But this is not problematic if such earnings are used creditably, as when a geomancer's modest charges are ploughed back into 'research' (*nghiên cứu*, meaning the search for improved skill and knowledge).

Hanoians themselves attach value to their own and other people's modes of cartographic reckoning, and view the geotemporal sciences as fields of ethical practice drawing virtue from their Vietnameseness, and from the interactions they allow with the world's cosmic harmonies. Their geospatial knowledge is deployed for aims considered good and even exalting, not as a disciplining or act of control. This is moral agency conceptualized as the promptings of a feeling heart. The notion here is of attunement to what is good to do or aspire to that comes from the promptings of conscience (*tâm*) and natural sentiment (*tình cảm*), the all-important capacity to engage feelingly with living and ancestral others.[4]

This is what I believe Mr Phong the cartographer's son was expressing about his father's maps: the idea of his own loving sentiment, and of his father's use of skill and knowledge as an act of loving care. 'That is how I felt', he said, using the emotive idiom 'feel-perceive' (*cảm thấy*), not the much colder 'feel-think' (*cảm nghĩ*). He was speaking of something inherently fine and handsome: an honourable use of scientific knowledge for unimpeachably virtuous ends. The maps were tools of victory, constructive inscriptions of what he and his countrymen had brought into being: a tracing out of the nation's true features as a liberated land hitherto demeaned by the colonizers' inscription practices, that is, by denying its true name *Việt Nam*, proudly displayed on his father's maps in place of the hated foreign designation *Indochine*.[5] Far from being contaminated by association with colonial power/knowledge, the maps were infused by his father's patriotic heart with the beauty one ascribes to a loved one's radiant countenance.

The pursuit of cartographic imperatives can thus enhance as well as flatten and conventionalize the affective contours of a complex world, and cartography need not refer only to operations in Euclidean space. My idea of the moral cartographer is of someone like E.P. Thompson's co-participant in a moral economy. In Thompson's formulation, the moral economy was a domain of ethical life in time, its interactions principled and intensely felt, never coldly instrumental.[6] The living of morally cartographic life is also an active bearing of values, entailing purpose and sensibility even in mundane contexts such as the drawing of maps or the geomantic calculations involved in the auspicious positioning of tombs and house-plots. Cartography is therefore presented here as a matter of both temporal and geophysical siting, as in the deployment of skilled technique for the installation of the dead as an active presence on household ancestor altars. Such initiatives are often far from harmonious or gratifying, yet still expansive and ethically conceived. They also place strong emphasis on materiality in matters of geotemporal skill and knowledge, as in the case of ancestor altars and the pictures that furnish them.

Such objects act as connections or portals between different orders of past and present life. In so doing, they become far more than husk-like memory markers, in Pierre Nora's celebrated terms (1984). Yet, as I show below, Nora's *lieux de mémoire* (sites of memory) concept is still relevant to Vietnam. It is what the modern citizen knows the party-state has in mind as the proper way to regard a family ancestor altar or cemetery for the military war dead (*nghĩa trang*). Official ideology holds that such sites should be honoured and even sanctified, but not treated as points of access to responsive agency. Yet, as I show below, this is precisely what they have come to constitute, both in family life and in the party-state's increasingly sacralized celebrations of nationhood. Their existence in today's Vietnam thus throws up continual challenges for citizens whose lives as ethical agents entail a perpetual interplay of converging and contending cartographic imperatives.

Vietnam's Global Cartographies

With its record of rapid growth, high literacy and recent upgrading from 'developing' to 'middle income' in the World Bank's annual economic performance rankings, Vietnam is widely represented as second only to China among Asia's achieving late-socialist transition societies. Yet it has also been portrayed as a troubled 'country of memory' struggling with the unfinished business of its Cold War bifurcations and liberation wars.[7] Both versions of this transformation story prompt questions about time, maps and historicity. As citizens of one of the world's remaining Communist party-states, Vietnamese inhabit a world of multiple chronologies and spatial orders. It is from these interpenetrating sites and registers that they have negotiated the making and unmaking of what I have been calling the worldwide socialist ecumene (Bayly 2009).

Though much transformed in today's marketization era, the vision of a socialist ecumene in which Vietnam has played a role of heroic exemplification is still an active feature of collective and individual memory. Rather than focusing on official boundaries and demarcations, the idea of socialist ecumene focuses on notions of shared purpose and attainment, especially as manifested in the exemplary conduct and motivation of an achieving revolutionary citizenry. Its entailments are expressed in highly space- and time-conscious terms, as can be seen in personal and official accounts of the sites where Vietnamese men and women of science acquired and imparted the skills of socialist modernity, both within and beyond the old arenas of COMECON 'friendship' exchange.[8]

These positionings in time and space are not experienced as neatly demarcated layerings between a marketized present and high-socialist past, but as an entanglement of multiple temporal and spatial registers. Those to be explored here involve the markers and chronologies of at least three interacting time modes: revolutionary-socialist, historicist-national, and personal-familial. By connecting these with the notion of moral cartography, I hope to show that the ethical concerns of 'market socialism' are being negotiated in Vietnam not only in temporal terms, but through evocations of purposefully achieving life in space.

Hanoi people enact the cartographies that matter to them in remarkably varied ways. While there are undoubtedly pluralities of a similar kind in other global settings, those of particular resonance in Hanoi are the trajectories people focus on in relating their key affective collectivities to the spaces of a precisely delineated geohistory. This includes the national and personal narratives that connect Vietnam with the wider socialist ecumene.

The idea that their country's twenty-year marketization process has differed greatly from other post-COMECON market transitions matters greatly in Vietnam.[9] There is a strong affective dimension to portrayals of the country's marketization as self-wrought and moral, like its revolution and liberation wars, in sharp contrast to the disasters now afflicting its 'friends' of the former socialist ecumene.

Russia is a key case in point. Its terrain is still a hallowed space of socialist memory. Every Vietnamese schoolchild learns about the Odessa Steps and Stalingrad. But in the moralizing geohistories through which Hanoians so often narrativize their sense of familial and national life, present-day Russians are to be pitied and mourned for as the victims of toxic neoliberalizers and kleptocrats, a people demoralized and in stasis, without the temporal anchorings and trajectories that both challenge and animate today's Vietnam. There are also potent space and time narratives about relations with Vietnam's powerful socialist 'elder sister' China, to which I return below.

In my current fieldwork site, an inner-city residential area I call Hồ Tây (West Lake), residents are keenly aware of the massive changes engendered by market opening. Yet they do not speak of market transition as a state of undifferentiated simultaneity. Just as there are many states and conditions of post-coloniality, there are many forms and modes of post-socialism. These include spaces of dynamism, which is how Vietnamese like to describe their own homeland, as opposed to other spaces of the former COMECON world where momentum and directionality can be thought of as blocked or immobilized.

Of course, these are highly flattering self-images finding, not at home but in the ex- Soviet states and 'satellites', modernities stagnating or insecurely attained. The resulting sense of place is very different from what has been described in contexts where ex-revolutionaries have had to see other countries' socialist modernity as humiliatingly prior and superior to their own.[10]

The Vietnamese term for the marketization process is *đổi mới*, a 1980s neologism commonly translated as 'renovation'. It is not a term signalling the death or erasure of a discredited socialist past, but the revitalization of an enduring socialism: cosmopolitan, urbane and dynamic (Raman and West 2009). Yet today's renovation experience is also rooted in the ideas and practices of a moralized marketplace, as I explain below. Proclaiming the national roots of this space where needs are met and legitimate exchanges are enacted has become an important means of demonstrating that marketized Vietnam is not a mere dependent clone of its problematic 'elder sister', China.

The multiple time and space reckonings to be encountered in Hanoi include representations of Vietnam as a site of 'market-oriented' (*thị trường định hướng*), never 'capitalist', transformations. Even 'marketized' is unwelcome, suggesting outsiders directing the country's new course, rather than Vietnamese themselves setting the nation's chosen trajectory. Yet both official and personal time and space reckonings reflect the complexities arising from the country's confident but far from unproblematic engagements with today's wider world, especially the country's capitalist-tiger neighbours, where Vietnamese sojourners meet so many expressions of their ASEAN and WTO trading partners' capitalism-triumphant narratives.

The idea that the global capitalist order has displaced the great socialist trajectory of history unfolding progressively towards revolutionary end-time is clearly very different from the temporal reckoning still officially subscribed to in Vietnam. While energetically pursuing worldwide trade and diplomatic ties, the party-state continues to avow what the textbooks and state media call 'the everlasting vitality of Marxism'. There are also frequent exaltations of the grand landmarks and achievement markers of world Communism, both spatial and calendrical.

For Hồ Tây people, there are both tensions and intertwinings between these official sitings and temporalities and the lived experience of the personal and familial. So while certainly not suggesting any notion of unproblematic harmony between the pronouncements of state agencies and the geotemporal practices of community and family life, I do see a need to recognize the points where they meet and interpenetrate.

In pre-colonial times a typical peri-urban village with entrance gates and a community shrine-house (*đình*) for the local place gods, Hồ Tây is now a ward (*phường*) within one of the inner-city core-zones (*quan*). Most of its households descend from old West Lake fishing, market-gardening and craft-specialist lineages with strong connections to the Old Quarter market enclave.[11] Like other Hanoi neighbourhoods, Hồ Tây has undergone a feverish construction boom in recent years. Yet the relentless tearing down and in-filling are emphatically not a sign of detachment from place and roots: quite the reverse, even though West Lake is also a site of extensive in- and out-migration, with a markedly supra-local and mobile sense of what it means to be an urban villager enacting a life of shared familial landmarks and achievement.[12]

The old Hồ Tây families still live where their forebears resided, though no longer in the tiny clay-walled houses of a generation ago. The remarkable changes experienced within living memory are charted in terms far more complex than those of a simple before- and after-marketization timeline. 'We lost it in the wars', people say of old houses, family treasures, and knowledge of where ancestral graves are located, meaning both the 1946–1954 anti-French liberation war with its punitive raids and house-burnings, and the bombings and mass evacuations of the 1962–1973 anti-US War. And in contrast to wartime as a brutal paring-away of vital anchorings, people point to the high-socialist period as a critical first stage on the way to today's dramatically different Hồ Tây life.

This emphasis on gains achieved in the planned-economy years may seem surprising since the country's now precarious tiger-economy status is so widely thought of as a product of rupture with the socialist past. Yet for all its energy-sapping queues and shortages, the planning or 'subsidy' (*bao cấp*) period is recalled as a time of dynamic translocality generating work options very different from those of the sclerotic local fishing and craft collectives.

It took effort and a clean political dossier (*lý lịch*) to gain a much sought-after labour posting to one of the industrialized COMECON countries. People are not sentimental about those gruelling work stints, though there is pride at the memory of a father or youthful self getting to grips with technological modernity in an East German steelworks or Russian mining town. But what made the stays so keenly sought after was the chance to source items both portable and super-desirable in commodity-starved 1980s Hanoi. Electric fans and winter wear were particularly sought after, exchangeable on a largely cashless basis for tin roofing, indoor taps and window glass.

The stories of those forays into the subsidy-era grey economy are now much reflected on, their recounting an exercise in the sharing and transmission of a sense of purposeful action and achievement. They are not told as tales of wheeler-dealer canniness, but as moral narratives about brave traversings of the socialist ecumene, followed by a happy return to home and family with honourable gains in hand.

The emphasis on homes upgraded is of key importance in these accounts. To improve or construct a home is a resonant act in Vietnam, much spoken of in the nuanced language of Vietnamese achievement thinking as an instance of attainment, *thành quả*.[13] This is not the word for more ordinary accomplishments, even of a very positive kind. However ardently prayed for, a child's exam success or business deal profitably concluded is mere *thành tích*, the word for targets met and routine wins or gains. *Thành quả* is special, implying fruitfulness of an exceptional and important kind.

The construction or refurbishment of houses is achievement in this special sense because it is morally essential provision or 'family work' (*việc gia đình*). It is thus a manifestation of worth and capacity involving engagement with causal agency, both in the everyday sense of initiating consequential action in the mortal world, and in the wider sense of the material and non-material forces and agents shaping change and consequence in the interpenetrating realms of human, natural and cosmic reality.[14]

The awareness that human bodies, homes and graves are all critical sites of interface with the flows of causality in both agentive and unpersonified forms can now be openly acted on in Vietnam. This is done both practically and ritually: by means of careful geomantic siting and upkeep work at tombs and gravesites, and through acts of provisioning, such as the burning of paper votive goods (*vàng mã*) for the actively experiencing dead.

These are all important geotemporal actions. They bespeak a sense of what Mayfair Yang calls 'ritual territoriality' in her account of contested spatial use in China (2004). Yet the Vietnamese context does not present the same clear-cut division between the disenchanted spatialities of high-modernist state practice and what Yang calls the 'placeness' of families and rural communities. This reflects the extent to which both remembered and ongoing translocality pervades the processes of Vietnamese geotemporal life. When such actions are accomplished with spatial and calendrical precision in Vietnam, they suggest accuracy and care in a host of important ways, including those that can be proudly pointed to as embodiments of modernity and Vietnameseness. This entails a strong sense of 'our space and our sciences, not theirs', meaning most especially not those of the nation's ever-dangerous and difficult neighbour, China.

The fact that causality is legible to those with rigorous geotemporal knowledge is the essence of cartographic awareness in Vietnam (Kelley 2003). Death anniversaries and the phase-shift climacteric days of the waning and waxing moon (*ngày rằm*) are the key points of efficacy for engagement with those inhabiting the otherworld (*âm phủ*) where ancestral souls reside. Hồ Tây households ensure that the proper disciplining measures are taken for these important but risky interactions with the non-mortal world.[15] The realms of mortal and non-mortal life are thus spaces with boundaries and junction points that may be traversed by those performing appropriate ritual action in a manner correctly aligned with the flows and resonances of temporality.

For all the vigour of the high-socialist period's anti-'superstition' drives (*bài trừ mê tín dị đoan*), I do not know anyone in Hồ Tây who doubts that the world is numinous and suffused with responsive presence (*linh*: see Pham 2009; Kendall et al. 2010). They know it is important to choose an auspicious day and time when initiating excavation or building work. There is also *xin phép*, leave-seeking from the *thổ địa* (land gods), figures of vested authority with the power to punish those taking liberties with their terrain.

A key concern for many families today is the tracing of afflictions such as infertility to a specific geotemporal source. While the cause may turn out to be impersonally calendrical,[16] the source of bad occurrences will often be identified as the ire of an affronted *thần* divinity to whom reparations can be made with the help of a suitably qualified specialist. Many such practitioners now operate openly in Vietnam. There are famous specialist masters (*thầy*) with elaborate websites and celebrity client lists, and modest providers for everyday spatial rites and land-god problems. Such problems are typically both geospatial and temporal because place-deities are vested with power through time: those they have reason to punish can expect a long chain of consequences stretching forward from generation to generation as the outcome of an original misdeed.

But while cartographically legible to those with the right gifts and knowledge, the traces of such enactment can be painfully hard to decode, as in the case of those who have to decide again and again to seek out further expertise when a long-running grave-search or other distressing cartography problem remains stubbornly unresolved. This leads many households to consult a specialist in one or both of the key siting arts: calendrical calculus divination (*tử vi* horoscopy) and geomancy (*phong thuỷ*, cosmic energy-flow mapping). Both are widely practised; both have become strongly scientized fields rooted in complementary systems of geotemporal expertise.[17] Both are known to be Chinese-derived, though they are spoken of as having been given new life and distinctiveness in Vietnam, with a suggestion of valuable heritage lost and wasted in China under Mao. As a result, it fell to Vietnam to infuse their practice with scientific rigour while indigenizing them as caring arts deployed with a feeling heart.

For my friend Mr Toan, far from being a reversion to a pre-socialist world of 'traditional' lore and custom, or a rejection of high-socialist scientific modernity, the rites and knowledge to which he now has access are both fulfilment and enhancement of that modernity. 'We only knew about ghosts then [*ma*]', he says of the time when his father's earnings in socialist East Germany paid for their house extension, a time when people could do their best to provide for their families' needs but had to do so with only limited knowledge of the arts and sciences to which a caring provider now has much fuller recourse. 'Now it's different', he said. 'Now we can read books' – he has a large collection of horoscopy and geomancy texts – 'and we can talk to masters and learn from films' – he meant his DVDs and downloads from websites showing psychics (*nhà ngoại cảm*) and *Kinh dịch* diviners at work.[18]

This is a key instance of moral cartography in action. Mr Toan reads the world around him in terms of interacting cartographic norms and registers both official and unofficial, knowing that a fully ethical life involves many different forms of geotemporal provision. To fulfil his duty of loving care to living and ancestral kin, there must always be expenditure of money and effort. Now that efficacious knowledge and skill can be readily accessed by those in need, it behooves a man of conscience to do what he can himself – buying the appropriate divination and geomancy manuals and learning to use their techniques for ordinary daily needs, and paying whatever he can for the best available expertise in matters beyond his own capacity and skill.

The Moral Cartography of Provision

No-one says they made big money in the 'subsidy' years. 'It wasn't doing business' (*kinh doanh*), people say of their grey-economy dealings – 'not like the Dresdeners'. Dresdener is Hanoi shorthand for the COMECON returnees reputed to have amassed real riches through dealings on a scale far greater than anything my informants own up to.

Everyone recognizes the showy onion-domed trophy houses that are the hallmark of the COMECON new rich. But even the glossiest of today's new-money Hồ Tây houses are not thought of as a Dresdener's parading of excess. In Hồ Tây, the upgrading of homes to a hygienic and 'civilized' (*văn minh*) standard is a matter of enduring community pride. Even in the *bao cấp* ('subsidy') years, it was an achievement consistent with the hallowed ideal of Vietnameseness as the classic multi-generation household living harmoniously beneath a single roof. No-one would call such an existence 'feudal' or amorally 'familistic'. Indeed, for a whole locality to live such a life, its households residing in solid structures rather than huts and fishermen's lean-tos, is to epitomize both enlightenment and productive rootedness in the national soil.

These attainments of the planning years are therefore recalled as manifestations of an achievement ideal much celebrated in Vietnam, both in revolutionary narratives and in accounts of today's market-era good life. This is material provision in forms bringing *văn minh* (civility/culturedness) to a formerly 'backward' (*lạc hậu*) existence (Kelley 2003).

The moral cartography of such transformations is often traced out in narrative, as when West Lake people share accounts of the changes their COMECON work sojourns brought about for their homes and families. On such occasions, ex-contract workers display their workplace merit awards and productivity certificates, and recall the wares brought back for swap or resale from Prague or Eisenhüttenstadt. Their accounts often move seamlessly from this world to the next, from provision for children and household in the here and now, to their protection and nurture through engagement with the supra-mundane.

Such narratives almost always include accounts of the key cartographic preoccupation of finding lost family graves. But they often begin with the household's first daring installation of a domestic ancestor altar, this too a critical dimension of Hanoians' present-day moral cartography. Like a well-tended set of family tombs in the patriline's ancestral village (*quê*), a properly furnished altar (*bàn thờ tổ tiên*) is an active portal in time and space, hence a critical meeting point of divergent geographies and temporalities.[19]

An altar's all-important ancestral photographs are often copies of a loved one's old state identity-card pictures: many households were too poor before marketization for the luxury of family photos, or lost those they had in wartime. Everyone recognizes that this presence of party-state iconography on ancestral spaces represents geographies that are this-worldly and resonant of official regimens and disciplines. Yet they are resonant too as embodiments of meaningful life and attainment on the part of ancestral kin. There is no sense of incongruity when these and such state-issue items as regimental banners and workplace achievement certificates appear on household altars, often beneath brightly tinted oleographs of the Buddha in one of the numinous mountain landscapes where he is classically represented as eternal enlightener to all the world.

Equally prominent on many altars are portraits of the nation's quasi-sacralized founding father Ho Chi Minh (Malarney 1997). These are important images in the light of what the textbooks and state media now stress about Vietnam's current place on the world's geotemporal landscape, making much of its recent global attainment markers: the achievement of ASEAN, GATT and WTO membership; the securing of UNESCO listings for a growing number of natural and cultural heritage treasures. At the same time, the nation is still represented as being projected forward on a timeline framed in the evolutionist idiom of Marxist stage-theory, with Vietnam's history to be understood as a developmental trajectory from the feudal past to today's era of 'transition' (*thời kỳ quá độ*). Yet that march towards perfection need not be thought of as conflicting with what the markers of globalized attainment would appear to be saying about the nation's momentum in time and space. This is because it is humanized and Vietnamized through the exemplarship of Ho Chi Minh in his role as 'uncle' (*Bác*), elder kinsman of all the nation, a radiant maker and 'mirror' (*tấm gương*) of revolutionary morality and eternal nationhood, at once embodying and transcending all forms of mortal and progressive generational time.

In addition, both officially and in many families' home lives, there is also strong endorsement of what such altars' Buddhist iconography now signals. This is a composite of two interacting dimensional realms: one transcending mere mortal time; the other progressively salvationist, as widely expressed today through initiatives aimed at bringing the nation ever more fully into the fold of world Buddhism. These initiatives do not quite identify Buddhist belief as a fully-fledged national faith, but they do frame Vietnam's nationhood in terms of the decorously patriotic Buddhism now widely endorsed in public life. Such undertakings include the treatment of important Buddhist pagodas as hallowed national space, and the attendance of senior party-state officials at the installation of costly relics from the great overseas Buddhist holy places.[20]

Home Space and Geotemporal Provision

Within and beyond West Lake, household altars often have an even more complex geotemporal framing, their entwinings of globalized Buddhism and the party-state's iconography frequently enriched with yet another powerful presence. This is the stern-featured Trần Hưng Đạo, a real-life scholar-general exalted in the history books as the hero who repelled a thirteenth-century Mongol invasion force. But in Vietnam the national geobody is numinous as well as beloved, as are those who police its vulnerable margins and access points. So as deliverer and righteous orderer, Lord Trần is now revered as a saint-like *thánh* divinity with the power to possess (*nhập*) mortal hosts (Pham 2009). He is thus a key figure in today's globally framed spiritualization of national space and history, his temples lavishly upgraded at state expense, and his images on household altars revered as empowering points of access to the nation's archaic geotemporal life.

The worship of Lord Trần is popular in Hồ Tây. Many residents perform the arduous New Year pilgrimage to his 'homeland' (*quê*) temples where devotees scramble to receive his auspicious investiture seals. These replicate the royal decrees which confirmed the rank of pre-modern court officials; they are now much sought after as good-luck tokens for aspiring career achievers (Pham 2009). This side of the Lord Trần rites is officially frowned on, but the visits are still praised as fulfilment of the same cartographic imperative that the schools' morality texts exalt in regard to visiting one's familial 'homeland' (*quê*). Such visits are always 'returns' (*về*), occasions of renewal that nurture filiality and rootedness: far from inculcating parochialism, such communion with the essences of home and ancestry equips the achieving citizen to set forth boldly and productively into the wider world.

In the early marketization years, there were no public announcements that family altars (*bàn thờ*) could be safely erected, or votive offerings openly made to ancestors. People say they simply knew. They began to see ritual items and reissued ceremonial instruction texts in other people's homes, and on sale in the market. They say their new means and the novel idioms of change in the official media made it feel 'natural' and in tune with official 'cultured-family' (*gia đình văn hóa*) policy to make such provision for home and kindred. Yet it was hard, people say, to chart the boundaries between the permissible and impermissible. One's kin in the countryside might feel safe maintaining a discreetly placed ancestor altar when it was still too risky to do so in a Hanoi state-allocation flat (*khu tập thể*). And when a household first installed its altar, the safe thing to do was to make it look like a site of reverent memory in Nora's sense, rather than a point of interaction with the responsive dead. Families did this by minimizing the scale of their food offerings, and by burning their votive papers at night so neighbours could not see the dead being actively engaged with.

It is at this point that people's narratives often turn to their present-day moves to provide for kin, including activities for which homes are their base and jumping-off point: the commissioning of geomantic tomb-sitings and house-assessments and searches for lost family graves (*đi tìm mộ*: 'tomb seeking'), often again with a translocal dimension, there being so many soldier sons and fathers lost on a far-off battlefield. These are precisely the points at which divergent cartographic imperatives converge and contend, as for example when a diviner identifies a lost kinsman as residing in one of the graves of unknown soldiers located in painfully large numbers in the country's many military cemeteries.

It is a terrible thing for the dead and their living kin to lack a point of regular contact and interaction, so such finds are a welcome outcome of family grave searches. But they also require delicate negotiation, both with the authorities and the dead. While the site search itself is wholly creditable, a paradigmatic act of true feeling (*tình cảm*), seekers must not then signal that the moral maps they forge and enact as a family are superior to those created by the party-state in its own spirit of loving-duty (*nghĩa*) to the honoured dead. Their recovered kinsman must be asked, not told, about the journey his kin propose to make to bring the recovered remains back for burial in their ancestral village (*quê*).

Doing this – asking about his wishes with the aid of a reliable seer/psychic (*ngoại cảm*) – allows for the possibility that the lost son or father feels settled and content with the comrades he has been residing with. Raising this as a possibility shows that the family are sensitive and caring in their conduct of the search, that they have no selfish ends in view and do not think of the recovered dead 'superstitiously' as intercessors and boon-bringers, hence that they are modern and progressive people who recognize the big cartography of the patriotic nation, as well as that of their own familial spaces and trajectories.

Grave-seeking and geomantic house diagnostics are therefore key processes of emplacement through which householders must engage and bear witness to a very wide sense of cartographic morality as they engage the mesh of causality and temporal movement defined as *hạnh phúc*, happiness of a profound and far-reaching kind, not mere sensory gratification. West Lake people like to display their knowledge of the big-name grave-search and geomantic house-siting specialists. Those commanding particular respect are retired COMECON-trained physicists and geologists who have dedicated themselves in later life to what people speak of respectfully as 'research' (*nghiên cứu*) in the astrobiological fields, focusing on such key specialisms as horoscopy, geomantic calculation and *yin-yang* diagramming practices.

There are also psychic 'naturals' whose skills are in high demand. Those thought of as reputable, the sort of specialists a knowledgeable person can rightly be informed about, are adepts whose gifts have been subjected to forms of testing and scrutiny that they and their clients speak of as scientific and legitimating. This is an important context for the use of the term *nghiên cứu*, 'research'. What the word means in this case is the work of 'psy-capacity' specialists who usually do not have supra-normal powers themselves but are thought of as reputable experts with in-depth knowledge of psychic matters, hence the ability to spot cheats and frauds. Such expertise is often said to come from their scientific credentials and training in one of the former COMECON countries. It is widely known that paranormal research was a high-profile enterprise in old socialist scientific circles. Films of Soviet psy-power tests still circulate widely among Hanoians with an interest in the field of *tâm linh*, one of the key scientizing terms popularized in the early marketization years to denote spirituality in general, as well as the idea of engagement with non-corporeal forces and agencies in ways not smacking of superstitious trafficking in the black arts.

Cartographies of the Moralized Marketplace

So Vietnam is not straightforwardly post-socialist space, not only in relation to the mappings and temporalities still animating official discourse and iconography, but also in more personal and intimate contexts. For ordinary Hanoians too, the city is still a space of revolutionary and socialist tradition and memory, even in the midst of its profusion of new consumer-culture landmarks.

It is especially in domains of visuality that these interpenetrations are produced and experienced. In West Lake households, photographs are much employed as artefacts of critical memory, i.e. in practices of affective archiving enacted in the course of shared narrative occasions allowing for the pooling and transmission of family knowledge (Bayly 2007). Imparting and sharing such knowledge endows families with what such pictures refract and animate: their existence as affective moral entities, perpetually constituting and sustaining themselves through acts of enlightened provision and attainment.

To show how such enactments can embrace as well as transcend the times and spaces of the high-socialist era, I turn now to a set of fieldwork vignettes through which I shift focus from moral cartography as a broad conceptual field to the experiences of the individual moral cartographer.

'Ahhh... tradition! That's what we're losing! It's terrible – we're losing it all', said my friend Mr Chau, when we discussed a set of striking photographs of young Hanoi women taken in the Việt Bắc (the northern revolutionary warzone) in the early 1950s, during Vietnam's bitter nine-year anti-French resistance war. The photos are family treasures from the wartime period, when the women and their families had evacuated from French-occupied Hanoi to the 'liberated territories' under the authority of President Ho Chi Minh's Communist-led Viet Minh national liberation movement.[21]

In the pictures I showed Mr Chau, the women are in khaki battledress with guns on their hips, their hair cut short, looking to me quite unlike their elders, as seen in earlier photos of the young women's aunts and mothers in their super-respectable pre-war 1930s urban ladies' garb. So I had been thinking of the pictures as images of hyper-modernity narrativizing an amazing journey, both physically from Hanoi to the spaces of the new revolutionary proto-state, and morally, into the radically new world of the socialist ecumene.

Families' collections of such photos document their members' crossings and re-crossings of both national and supra-national space: their evacuations and returns during the French and anti-US wars; their wartime marriages, work and study stints in the states of the old socialist ecumene; their ambitious career moves in today's 'renovation' era. Their pictures are yet another instance of moral narrative projected onto a powerfully evoked geotemporal landscape. They too are enactments of moral cartography, narrativizations of a life lived with purpose: in the case of the women in khaki, that of a revolutionary future in the making. They show familial and national life conjoined, the act of traversing their homeland's liberated terrain itself a contribution to the nation's new life. This is socialist heritage of a very dynamic kind, fulfilled rather than overridden as a life of service and purpose in today's world of globalized mass-market consumerism.

That fulfilment can come at a high cost – even a sense of distress and loss of the kind Mr Chau was expressing in his lament for lost tradition. He went on to decry the cheap Chinese-made household goods now flooding Vietnam's booming consumer markets. Yet it would be easy to turn these images of frontiers breached and vulnerable into a simplistic decline-and-fall/end-of-history view of contemporary Hanoi life. This is why I want to stress the subtle interplays between different temporal and spatial orders, and connect these with the experience of a moralized marketplace.

There is much to learn about time and space cartographies from focusing on pictures used in ritual contexts. When displayed on ancestral altars, photos of the dead become instantiations and sitings, not just remembrances, of the active and conscious dead. Given the distinctive ways the living and the dead interact and co-reside in Vietnam, I think Vietnamese filmed images are a more convincing case of what Barthes claimed in *Camera Lucida* (1982) for photos in general. I have in mind his notion of 'death in person' as an expression of the photo's capacity to access someone absent as a radiant living presence of 'true being' (1982: 12–15). In his famous account of his dead mother's picture, the image is an agent actively conjuring her as an emanation of her former bodily presence, his gaze linking her to him through time and space, as if – he says – by an umbilical cord: not as a mirror or resemblance, but as a radiated reality with actual affective force (1982: 81).

This is very suggestive for the complex of ritual practices giving Vietnamese pictorial materials their capacity to animate plural temporalities, doing so in ways that do not entail a demoralizing narrative of ruptures and discardings. But it is not only photos that achieve this. Another critical class of image with this kind of interactive presence is that of paper gift items for the dead – *vàng mã*. They too are a kind of space-time umbilical cord. They include the mass-produced 'hell money' which Kwon has documented so compellingly (2007); but there are also replica houses and clothes, and wonderful prestige items with world-famous brand names: cars, karaoke machines, mobile phones, home and office furnishings.

Through burning, *vàng mã* items pass to the realm where deceased kin reside, making the afterlife look as though it has become an arena of spectacularly visualized consumer culture.[22] But unlike what Hanoians speak of as rampant amoral capitalist excess both at home and abroad, their own votive giving is conducted in a moral and moderate marketplace: nurturing provision, the meeting of loved ones' needs, not vulgar display or an indulging of greed.

Much of the care expended on *vàng mã* votive paper provision relates to its time and space dimensions: a brother who died near the Chinese border in a US bombing raid on a winter night complains of cold in his sister's dreams, so requires a new blanket on his death-anniversary day. Another kinsman reports in a dream that he is tired of the army uniforms he has received since his death in 1968, and calls for an updated wardrobe. He is still the young man who died on a distant battlefield in the far south; what the family now provide is the garb of today's twenty-year-olds.

So within and beyond the home, pictorial objects are used in two ways. One is as embodiments of the highly moral ways in which Vietnamese like to feel they are engaging with the crisis-hit world of marketization, as in the case of Mrs Kim, a retired kindergarten teacher who runs a small shop-house business selling votive paper items with her sister Mrs Lan. They dislike the idea of replica credit cards as a possible new product line. Replica cash is better in the afterlife, they say. They know about fraud and misused pin numbers: people know where they are making cash deposits in the Bank of the Dead. It is the way they like to run their own business: no website, no computerized accounts, not like the big businesses dealing in Chinese imports, unpredictably bouncing up and down in price and profitability; always the danger of fakes and frauds.

The big businesses running on that very different electronic-transaction basis include those dealing in other ritual goods such as the geomantic energy-concentrating spheres and amulets central to *phong thuỷ* (geomancy). Unlike these items and most non-ritual goods, paper votives are still Vietnamese-made, from known craft suppliers. Thus, as West Lake people see it, votive goods have nothing to do with the mad immoral world of Chinese and Taiwan-owned factories spewing out pollutants and poisoning the baby milk: the 2008 Chinese milk powder scandal is bitterly remembered.[23] Such iniquities kill both land and temporal order in terrible ways. Toxins leaching into the soil from unregulated factories stop bodies in their graves from decomposing: they mummify. When disinterred for secondary burial, they are still fleshed and unready, in painful stasis, so perhaps can never be moved on to the temporal and spatial sitings of proper ancestorhood.[24]

Paper votives are a produce line of which vendors often say, 'I sell by my conscience' (*có tâm; với cái tâm*, lit. 'with my feeling heart'). It is good for both sellers and purchasers that the goods and marketing outlets are simple, and that the selling takes place to meet need. Never for big profits, people say; the buyers always counselled to be caring yet abstemious; customers never pressed to buy two of something when they need only one because that's what the omen-dream said; paying suppliers in cash when they come with the new consignment, never on credit or electronically.

What is cheap in our world is transvalued into wealth in the cosmic beyond because of the special quality of the spaces and processes entailed in realm-to-realm movement (Kwon 2007). These are all respects in which buyers and sellers construct a moral cartography that is pervasive and valued in Vietnam: not in this case a matter of payment for refined geotemporal expertise, but a set of transactions in which the provision of replica brand-name goods for those residing in the death world takes place in a moralized marketplace framed as an exaltation of Vietnameseness: cosmopolitan and outward looking, yet still caring and morally sound.

The other way I see pictorial objects as makers and markers of moral cartography is in their channelling of movement between the spatial and temporal realms I am defining as revolutionary-socialist, historicist-national, and personal-familial. We can see this with paper votives, and with the photos of family members as a focus for offering and communication with the dead at sites where time and space come together in the key affective arenas of family and nation.

It is not just in home spaces that deceased kin are invited to travel from the afterworld to their kinfolk's ancestor altars, to be appealed to for protective intercession and reported to about family achievements in ways updating rather than denying or disconnecting from the complex of socialist and other temporal spaces the family has lived and acted in. There is also the placing of deceased relations' photos on the walls of Buddhist pagodas (*chùa*), ideally near the images of deceased monks: the deceased resides in the pagoda space, listening to the monks' sermons and benefitting from their exemplarship.[25] In some pagodas President Ho Chi Minh can be seen among these images, a presence both reverenced and reverencing in the company of the monk effigies.

What then about the man who said 'ah, tradition'? Mr Chau, whose lament for lost ways and mores was sparked by my photos of the women in khaki, is Hanoi-born, a Party member in his late forties. He is Soviet-trained in a technical field, one of the last of the Russian- and Chinese-speaking generation of intelligentsia to have been selected for the old high-socialist era career route to success in state service. He is also one of the first Hanoi high-flyers to have done an MBA at a famous US university. I met him through Hồ Tây friends who thought I should meet what they call a 'real Old Quarter family', people with the polished comportment that Hanoians like to point to as the hallmark of their distinctively cultivated and upright way of life.

This is not, as they see it, privileged distinction in Bourdieu's terms, but a distillation of the best kind of patriotic yet cosmopolitan Vietnameseness, modern and science-loving in outlook, yet honourable, scrupulously filial and heritage-conscious. People say Mr Chau's family embody all these virtues, especially his redoubtable trader mother, her goods the wares of homeland and authenticity, her trading the act of a selfless provider, definitely not a parasitical capitalist.

The Old Quarter market zone looms large in Hanoi moral cartography, both for the Hồ Tây people who have long been suppliers of traders like Mr Chau's mother, and more widely. It is hallowed revolutionary space, its shop-house streets a redoubt of freedom fighters in the 1946–1954 anti-French resistance war. That is what I feel Mr Chau was referring to when he reflected on the women in khaki: 'So traditional – it takes me right back to my childhood. I think of my mother, her sisters. That's what we've lost. We're losing it'.

His mother never wore a khaki uniform. But he was seeing in those pictures an Old Quarter heritage consistent with what the revolutionary war art depicts: the patriotic modern as both provider and consumer of wholesome homeland goods, in a world of virtuous cosmopolitanism embodied in both people and things, including the comportment of a moralized marketplace.

Like many other self-styled 'old Hanoians', Mr Chau often speaks of alien goods and values as corroding the legacy of his mother's world. But in recognizing what it is about contemporary life he and many other Hanoi people find so troubling, we can see what makes their perception of today unlike any simple 'end of history' idea of the death or displacement of socialism. The painful paradox of Vietnam's contemporary marketization experience is that the giant predator economy most powerfully acting as an unstoppable quasi-colonizer on its doorstep is not a capitalist ASEAN power, but 'elder sister' China, the greatest surviving socialist ecumene party-state.

Mr Chau is not nostalgic about his pre-marketization childhood, with its ration queues and commodity shortages, but he does deplore the new Hanoi of trashy foreign things and mores. What he found in my photos was 'tradition' – *truyền thống* – in the sense of Vietnameseness proudly exalted in the world those ardent young fighters were selflessly contributing to: a revolutionary nationalist order with ample room in it for people with his background, its socialism made moral rather than coldly forensic through its acceptance of properly conducted commercial life as a form of provision for family and nation.

These visions of a moralized marketplace have been vital to the development of Vietnam's revolutionary nationhood, and its renovation experience. Revolutionary message art portrayed market life as a space for the exercise of national and supra-national virtue, rather than an arena of competition and class exploitation, a site where, properly regulated by the party-state, patriotic moderns of every productive class – peasant, worker, intellectual, soldier, and the virtuous non-profiteering trader – connect with the virtuous essences of home soil, engaging selflessly with the wider world where Vietnam's productive socialist cosmopolitans make friends and meet others' needs.

These ideas are ideally suited to the spatial and temporal self-positionings of the 'renovation' era, but are much more than a recently devised variant of contemporary Singapore-style Asian-values ideology. They have a strongly Marxian bent, though one at odds with Soviet and other anti-market discourses: closer to Maoism with its emphasis on the mobilization of culture rather than class division as the engine of revolutionary change in a context of anti-imperialism.

Place and Space Morality

Hồ Tây families like me to meet elderly resistance survivors, including the celebrity heroines who distinguished themselves in the anti-French and anti-US wars. This includes amazingly vigorous octogenarians like Mrs Hoa, an officially designated Heroine Mother: still proudly a modern and a revolutionary, a Party member who has made her household altar a site of all the spaces and temporalities she connects with. In its place of honour is President Ho Chi Minh. Below it are pictures of her parents, and the parents of her patriot-martyr husband who died in the anti-US War. Her marriage story is a famous Hanoi resistance romance, as can be seen in her remarkable 1955 wedding photo: the bride with flowers, soldier-girl plaits and khaki uniform, standing shoulder to shoulder with her husband and their militia-boy comrades, a quartet of citizen-soldiers, in a space of unambiguous socialist temporality.

Like my elderly acquaintance Mrs Mai, in youth an iconoclastic Maoist and now an active lay Buddhist who regularly helps with installations of the dead on her pagoda's photo memorial wall, Mrs Hoa leads a much fuller ritual life than she had done in the high-socialist austerity years. Of such decisions, people do not say 'we're going back in time to a practice from our parents' day'. The photograph is modern and democratic, a progressive replacement for the use of the lacquered Chinese-calligraphy name-boards formerly used on ritual spaces, condemned as relics of 'feudalism' by the party-state.

Mrs Hoa keeps her altar 'warm', that is, active and dynamic, a place of interactive communion with the dead, but without a picture of her husband. He is one of the millions of war dead whose remains were never returned to their grieving families to be interred and resituated through secondary burial (Malarney 2001). It is an abiding sadness: he cannot come to co-reside within the altar space and partake of the food and other good things placed every day before her altar pictures. Yet he is still a presence. In place of his picture is his military death certificate. With its embossed seals and inscription of his rank, titles and status as a patriot-martyr, this artefact of the party-state at war provides a space for him in her daily act of *thắp hương* (incense-lighting), which connects and enacts her family's continuing trajectory through revolutionary-socialist, national and familial time.

One day, she told me, she and her daughters may commission a grave-finding (*đi tìm mộ*). But while grave-searches are very common now, they are not for everyone; there are many reasons why people hold off, why such 'family work' is invariably unfinished and ongoing. 'It was time', people say – 'my father came in a dream', 'I'd been yearning to do it'. But other family members may not share one's wish for deceased kin to live with the comforts they've now attained. My friend Chi and her widowed mother have relations in her father's ancestral village who have long resisted their wish to undertake a grave-site seeking for her war-martyr father. Important as such searches are in today's Vietnam, much discussed in families and the media as profoundly important fulfilment of both familial and national need, they can present problems of a highly painful kind.

The practice's complexities are strikingly reflected in the subtleties of language it entails. One speaks of 'tombs' (*mộ*) in contexts when foreigners might say either grave or 'site'. 'Never!' said a Hồ Tây householder, when I asked if people ever said they were looking for the 'place' where a lost kinsman's remains might lie, rather than seeking his 'tomb' as if there was already a marked and recognized burial place. 'We'd never say that, not even for a sailor drowned in the sea. It's never "place" (*chỗ*) or "burial-site" (*huyệt*) for dead people'. 'Place' (*chỗ*) is static and atemporal, conveying nothing of the care the dead receive, nor their active existence as experiencing agents. *Huyệt* has connotations of digging or scraping; its use would imply an uncoffined body put like rubbish in the dirt. The essence of care is structure and entombment, both for the dead and for the living who must also dwell in structured space, in a site made and acted on with all the feeling and art at one's command.

Another tricky dimension of tomb-searching is the expertise required to achieve a successful end, with the commissioning of psychics as paid site-seekers the most hotly debated aspect of these initiatives in today's Hanoi. Yet Chi said the problem was not that people might call her uncles superstitious (*mê tín*) for doing a grave-search. What they feared was looking shabby and ungenerous if their own fathers were not furnished with new tombs too. They were also worried about disturbing the existing tombs' auspicious geomantic sitings. In the volatile world of renovation-era market life, this was a case of one strand of a family's cartographic practice cutting across the very different geo-spatial trajectory being charted by another branch of the same patriline.

The seeking out and identifying of lost family remains can thus involve a whole host of reckonings and movements to do with the often fraught and contested chartings and inscription practices I have been referring to as moral cartography. The skills and knowledge used are no less personal and affective for being spoken of in terms people think of as scientific and rationalizing, whether manifested as the kinds of mapping used in Western-style geographical reckonings, or in the form of today's neo-traditional geomantic art.

The initiatives of family and lineage 'work' (*việc gia đình* and *việc họ*), purposeful initiatives undertaken on behalf of close and more distant kin, are both enacted and archived by means of imaging. During the grave-findings and reinterments, every step in the finding and resituating of the missing dead is filmed by those attending. Families thus have extensive household photo albums of such undertakings, even those taking place in the military cemeteries' sad precincts of unknown soldiers' graves. One such occasion was the attempt to find the remains of my friend Mr Hien's wife's younger brother, lost in battle in the anti-US War. Their album's grave-search sequence shows their diviner Mr Lam performing his site-quest by means of duck-egg divination, a kind of dowsing: the concentrated cosmic-energy flows from the deceased's remains make the duck egg adhere to an upended chopstick.

Mr Lam is one of the 'special-capacity' practitioners currently under study at the quasi-official Hanoi Human Capacity Research Centre.[26] I know a number of its clients and some of the researchers who work with its affiliated psychics (*nhà ngoại cảm*) and diviners. The clients I know greatly approve of its scientific ethos and avowed mission to make research on psychic powers and skills a credible Vietnamese enterprise, indeed a national resource.

The Centre's services include the commissioning of geneticists to perform DNA tests on the human remains unearthed in psychic grave-searches, giving families an accuracy test for the diviners' readings. Its work has been the subject of much controversy, with some fascinating blogging between defenders and hostile critics of its programmes of *tâm linh* (spirituality) research.[27] The sceptics meet vigorous ripostes from those arguing that *tâm linh* in the form of clairvoyance and divination is testable science, like traditional medicine as officially institutionalized in Vietnam and China. But it is central to the Centre's work to insist on the Vietnameseness of *tâm linh*, as manifested in practitioners' uncommercialized morals, as well as the scientifically verifiable nature of their work.

My friends the votive-sellers also have striking experiences of the spaces and moralities of the socialist ecumene and its painful afterlife. Showing me his pictures from a training stint in Moscow in 1992, their engineer brother Mr Duc told me about his research institute's secretary Natasha: 'Such a nice woman', he said, 'so well educated, so sad what happened to her'. It was the classic post-1989 Russian intelligentsia story: she had fallen into poverty as the value of her salary collapsed. His telling of the story made it a parable of familiality and the moral marketplace. Russians, he said – the old 'elder brothers' of the socialist ecumene – had lost or never learned the art of providing for kin and nation in a moralized world of trade. So he became the provider-brother, the rescuer and enlightener. When he found that Natasha's only idea of how to cope was by selling off her possessions one by one, he got her a job with one of present-day Russia's ultra-nationalist hate figures: a Vietnamese trader from the Cherkizovsky smuggled-goods market, itself a site of impassioned Russian cartographic moralizing, shut down by order of President Putin in 2009.[28]

'They were such a long time under their "subsidy" period', Duc said, meaning Russians. He spoke of them affectionately; he'd loved Moscow, never spoke of hostility on the streets or racist gang attacks. 'But so sad', he went on. 'They didn't know how to change their thinking – they couldn't catch up with modern life as fast as we did.'

So for Mr Duc there is both personal moral cartography and also profound moral meaning to be derived through an understanding of Vietnam's life, in relation to far richer and more powerful peoples and nations, in a world of profoundly different geospatial topographies and trajectories. He sees rescuing Natasha as a selfless meeting of need, and, I believe, a reason to take pride in what I am seeking to convey in this article. This is the idea of there being painful challenges but also profound advantages for those Vietnamese who have experienced, through engagements with an extraordinarily turbulent epoch of transformation, something I think they achieve and activate through the compelling and strongly visual cartographic regimens in which they all participate.

This is a sense of moral positioning in today's renovation life that is not post-socialist in any narrow or linear sense, and which instead entails the dynamics of what I have called a world of interacting temporalities and spatial sitings, embracing the ancestral past, the familial and national present, and even the uncertain and dangerous future. I have therefore sought to make a case for what I am calling moral cartography as a perspective to explore the ways Hanoi people perceive, negotiate and even creatively transform those challenging pluralities. In seeing cartography as engagement with both temporal and geophysical siting, focusing on issues of materiality, like the ancestor altars and pictures that furnish them as portals between different orders of past and present life, and on the efficacy and expertise that a family and nation can and should deploy to ensure the well-being of those in their care, I call attention to initiatives that are often far from harmonious or gratifying. Yet they are still expansive and ethically conceived as the projects of actively initiating agents, pursuing their ends in a world of demarcated space, in arenas where it is assumed and even gloried in that science and moral concerns will continually meet and interact.

I believe too that this perspective provides a language, not just for Vietnam, but for other contexts where being cartographically aware and active is a highly significant dimension of people's engagements with moral challenges and entailments. I have therefore tried to explore both the dilemmas and the satisfactions to be experienced in actors' exercise of efficacy and purpose in this world of mapped and mappable space and landscape. They do so as geotemporal agents negotiating terrain they know to be numinous, geomantically alive and bio-humourally dynamic, yet also responsive and amenable to scientific mapping and delineation.

Acknowledgements

For valuable comments, I thank Caroline Humphrey, James Laidlaw, Nikolai Ssorin-Chaikov and Nicholas Long; also Professor C. Hann, Dr K. Endres and colleagues at the Max Planck Institute, Halle. Fieldwork was funded by ESRC award RES-000-22-4632 in support of a joint project with Dr Long on 'The Social Life of Achievement in Indonesia and Vietnam'; for past awards I thank ASEASUK and the Cambridge University Evans Fund.

Susan Bayly is Professor of Historical Anthropology (Emerita) in the Cambridge University Department of Social Anthropology, and a Life Fellow of Christ's College, Cambridge. Her publications include *Asian Voices in a Postcolonial Age: Vietnam, India and Beyond*; and *Caste, Society and Politics in India from the 18th Century to the Modern Age* (both with Cambridge University Press). She has conducted extensive on-site fieldwork in both India and Vietnam, focusing most recently on projects aimed at bringing the insights of visual anthropology into conversation with the anthropology of morality and ethics. Her research interests also include Asian post-socialism; theories of historical change; the interface between history and anthropology; and colonialism and its cultural afterlife in South and Southeast Asia.

Notes

An earlier version of this chapter was originally published as Bayly, Susan. 2013. 'Mapping Time, Living Space: The Moral Cartography of Renovation in Late-Socialist Vietnam', *Cambridge Journal of Anthropology* 31(2): 60–84.

1. There are also real-life topography exercises, many of them connected with Vietnam's title claims over one of the most fiercely contested of the Asia-Pacific region's hot-spot island groups: as in the 2011 *Guinness Book of Records* bid by 1,500 Youth Union volunteers, massed in a giant seafront formation to create the world's largest ever human personification of a national map. See http://www.tinmoi.vn/ban-do-viet-nam-xep-tu-so-nguoi-tham-gia-nhieu-nhat-10980623.html (accessed 25 June 2013); http://tinngan.vn/print-347921-Teen-Viet-va-tinh-yeu-voi-Hoang-Sa-Truong-Sa.html (accessed 25 June 2013).
2. Modern empirical science, *khoa học*, has strongly positive connotations in Vietnam. Galileo, Darwin, Edison and Marie Curie are known to every child as classroom emulation models, as are the Vietnamese scientific luminaries whose stories are told as parables of truth seeking, allied to the noble ends of meeting need and relieving suffering. The idea of science as an expression of Vietnameseness reflects a long history of state-led indigenization initiatives such as the hospital-based professionalization of 'Eastern' (*Đông y*) medicine, and the fostering of key fusion specialities such as electric acupuncture.
3. Representing what is moral and ethical in Vietnam involves idioms relating to both feeling and principle. Notions of goodness/beauty (*tốt/đẹp*) and feeling/conscience (*tình cảm/tâm*) are much used for what is creditable and worthy. *Đạo đức* (lit. 'way of virtue') can mean both morality and ethics (Malarney 1997; Rydstrom 2003), but in the sense of codes and maxims, as in the parable-like schemas taught in the 'morals education' syllabus (*giáo dục* đạo đức). These are presented as absolutes, with no suggestion of dilemmas or ambiguity in the way the well-conducted citizen should feel and behave. Like other forms of classroom achievement, morals (*đạo đức*) teaching is subject to rigorous quantification: 'morality' marks are awarded for daily conduct (cleanliness, respectfulness, 'community spirit', etc.), and also catechismally – through exams calling for accurate replication of the schemas' key principles.
4. See Marr 2000. What should be awakened/kindled (*khơi dậy*) at home from earliest childhood is what must be felt – not just enacted – e.g. in relations with elders and the heartfelt tending of tombs and ancestor altars; also how a bride should conduct herself in her marital home – evincing sensibility (*tình cảm*), i.e. a true and proper 'feel' for such things as the right foods and votive goods to provide on death anniversaries; also how a husband should 'educate' his wife in such matters: gently coaxing (*dạy dỗ*), or more forcefully directing (*dạy bảo*) if she is slow or deficient. The same applies to matters of citizenship, e.g. the loving care of key figures of the nation's ethical landscape, notably Heroine Mothers, discussed below. To be attuned to sensibility in morally significant contexts, the heart must be 'fed' (*nuôi dưỡng*) to develop a girl's or boy's version of feeling/sentiment (Rydstrom 2003). One cannot do right as a matter of 'rule' (*lấy lệ*): the power of reason (*lý trí*) is essential to humanity, but its use must be heart-prompted to live the proverbial good life as *sống có tình có nghĩa* ('life lived feelingly/ dutifully-ethically').
5. See Winichakul 1994 and Goscha 1995.
6. Thompson's original account emphasized qualities of feeling and refined ethical sensibility in its conceptions of legitimate market practice (1971: 98–102).
7. See http://data.worldbank.org/news/dev-economies-increase-share-of-global-output (accessed 25 June 2013); and Hue-Tam Ho Tai 2001; Kwon 2006, 2008.
8. COMECON was the Soviet bloc's official economic alliance system. The notion of Vietnamese scientists as heroes and benefactors is closely connected with memories of the country's overseas 'friendship' initiatives to 'needy' African states in the high-socialist era (1975 to 1992). The story of Vietnamese science is thus told triumphally, not as

tutelage received from its colonizers and socialist 'elder siblings' (China and the USSR), but as the fruitful work of a dynamic self-modernizing achiever nation (Bayly 2007). The works on topography, space-time and spatial selfhood I have found particularly illuminating are those of Humphrey 1995 and 2006; Verdery 2001; Katz 2005; Ssorin-Chaikov and Sosnina 2009 and Ssorin-Chaikov 2013; also Gonzalez 1995 and Crang and Thrift 2000; and for the notion of ecumene Pollock 1998. And see Feuchtwang 1974 and Bruun 1996.

9. Not least in its understandings of attainment and success. On Vietnam's marketization see Fforde and de Vylder 1996; Chan et al. 1999; McCargo 2004; Dang Phong [Đặng Phong] 2003.
10. And their own home-grown versions of post-socialist transformation as deficient and unfulfilled (Donham 1999; West 2009). The idea of a clear divide between a dynamic marketized Vietnam and a wider world of faltering post-socialisms provides a welcome antidote to the fear that Vietnam may always be a geotemporal underachiever, held back in the global race for growth and productivity by the minority ethnic groups (*dân tộc thiểu số*) who predominate in the country's poorest provinces. These communities' characteristic land-use modes – both upland slash-and-burn and the canoe-dependent livelihoods of the deltaic south – are often represented as problematically archaic and un-Vietnamese (Taylor 2004).
11. Now a popular tourist venue, the Old Quarter is still much frequented by Hanoians seeking the traditional products still supplied by its trader-producers: herbal medicines; fruit preserves (*mứt*); ritual items, including second-burial coffins and ancestor altars.
12. As in the pride taken by the elders in charge of Hồ Tây's 'communal house' in their official twinning arrangement with one of Hanoi's major Buddhist pagodas.
13. As in China: see Wilson 1997.
14. All the more for Hồ Tây residents because of the community's fishing tradition, the lives of fisherfolk having been so widely stigmatized as marginal, asocial and backward, in contrast to the true Vietnameseness of those living the fully civilized life of a rooted terrestrial environment. One of the key moral acts of the nation as moral agent is to build houses of 'loving dedication' (*nhà tình nghĩa*) for Heroine Mothers as honoured recipients of its care and gratitude.
15. As at the lunar New Year (*ngày Tết*) when householders burn brightly coloured votive paper horses: these translocate to become steeds for the otherworld's *quan lại* (officers) as they patrol the *yin-yang* border zone, ensuring that the dead travel a properly directed route to their sites of annual sojourn in the living world. Installed temporarily on descendants' ancestor altars, the dead are a welcome and necessary presence, yet one needing proper 'management' so they do not stray, becoming unsited and lost, a danger to the living and a threat to cosmic order.
16. For example, the kind of persistent ill-luck that occurs in an inauspicious *xấu* (ugly) year. From birth date onwards, the temporal framework of a mortal life is its sequence of prevailingly good, neutral and *xấu* years. The use of an almanac and the services of a good astrologer can reduce the dangers of such conjunctures, as can the rite known as 'fate-cutting'.
17. By scientized, I mean such things as the coining of new academic and official terms to communicate the idea of a scientifically accredited domain of spirituality (*tâm linh*), recognized by experts as a 'natural' human need, and an exalting expression of cultural attainment. Such legitimating references to the voice of modern science have been central to the ritual revival trends accompanying marketization. I also have in mind the now widely held view that because the spiritual is a legitimate field for scientific study, Vietnamese scientists should conduct research on what Western scholars call the paranormal, meaning lab-based study of the 'special capacities' of those now widely known *nhà ngoại cảm* (psychic), a hard-science neologism offering a welcome alternative to the many terms signalling 'superstition' and fakery in the high-socialist period (e.g. *thầy bói*: 'seer/fortune teller'). Compare Humphrey 2006.

18. And in some cases having their capacities tested in lab-science settings: http://www.youtube.com/watch?v=wgLjIiI_pBo&feature=related (accessed 25 June 2013). *Kinh dịch* is the Vietnamese version of the ancient divination text widely known in the West as the *I Ching*.
19. It is before the household altar that one regularly performs the key act of incense-lighting (*thắp hương*), an essential precursor to ritual acts, though not itself a rite or ceremony (*lễ*) (Jellema 2007). There is no 'ritualized' way to enact *thắp hương*, beyond the expressive holding out of the glowing incense, its gleam the activating means to achieve connection with ancestors and other non-mortals, bringing them close (*gần*), meaning briefly but always repeatably translocated to our space of mortal existence from the non-mortal realms that adjoin yet are still distinct from our own.
20. Also rites of 'requiem' (*Lễ cầu siêu*) for the nation's war dead, conducted by Vietnamese and foreign monks including visiting dignitaries from the Dalai Lama's global network, now a regular feature of National War Martyrs and Invalids Day, an annual commemoration created in the revolutionary period: it is sometimes spoken of as a counterpart to the July *Tết Trung nguyên* ('ghost month') rites of succour for the unsited dead.
21. Reproduced in my book *Asian Voices* (2007) by kind permission of the Hanoi families with whom I conducted fieldwork, the photos provide rare glimpses of the personal side of Vietnamese wartime life.
22. As in Singapore and China where funerary offering is also widely practised (Feuchtwang 1993; Toulson 2012). The burning of death goods was yet another practice condemned as superstition (*mê tín dị đoan*) in the high-socialist period, though even Party members recall making comforts for the dead from old newspapers, burning them discreetly, out of the public eye.
23. See http://vnn.vietnamnet.vn/xahoi/2008/10/806682/ (accessed 25 June 2013).
24. This is a striking contrast to what modernity brings in Singapore, as documented by Toulson (2012): a speeding up, hence dangerous truncating, of the transformation process through which the unsettled recent dead become safely situated ancestors. In Vietnam, poisoned terrain has a toxifying effect with painful and malignant consequences for the living and the dead.
25. Money circulates in complex ways in these ritual contexts – clean unused currency for use on offering altars can be purchased at small outlets near pagodas, at an exchange rate of around twenty per cent. The donations required to install deceased kin on pagoda walls are logged by the volunteer congregants who perform such services in the fast-growing world of Hanoi lay Buddhist congregational activity (Soucy 2012).
26. *Trung tâm nghiên cứu tiềm năng con người*: see Schlecker and Endres 2011.
27. Given the vigour of this debate, and the importance of scientific validation to both sceptics and defenders of the *tâm linh* arts, one can dismiss any orientalist notion of Vietnam as a land of mystics where scientific modernity was never truly received or indigenized. This alliance between the divination arts and modern science is much approved of by those commissioning seers from the Capacity Centre, and a key feature of Hanoians' grave-seeking narratives is the rationality test, the moment when uncertainty is allayed through proof of the seer's powers: 'there really was a tree next to the road just as she said; we dug down and immediately found the bones'. Hence the attractiveness of the Centre as a place where modern science is harnessed to ensure that loving families can meet a need in ways that need not make a Hanoi modern ashamed or anxious, i.e. being in thrall to 'superstition' or gulled by fraud.
28. In Russian cartographic moralizing, the Cherkizovsky was a blot on the Moscow landscape, a nexus of every foreign-borne moral contaminant of the national geobody: Chechen mafia, Azeri oligarchs, East Asian drug traffickers.

References

Barthes, Roland. 1982. *Camera Lucida: Reflections on Photography*. London: Jonathan Cape.

Bayly, Susan. 2007. *Asian Voices in a Postcolonial Age: Vietnam, India and Beyond*. Cambridge: Cambridge University Press.

———. 2009. 'Vietnamese Narratives of Tradition, Exchange and Friendship in the Worlds of the Global Socialist Ecumene', in Harry G. West and Parvathi Raman (eds), *Enduring Socialism: Explorations of Revolution and Transformation, Restoration and Continuation*. Oxford: Berghahn Books, pp. 125–47.

Bruun, Ole. 1996. 'The Fengshui Resurgence in China: Conflicting Cosmologies between State and Peasantry', *China Journal* 36: 47–65.

Chan, Anita, Benedict J. Tria Kerkvliet and Jonathan Unger (eds). 1999. *Transforming Asian Socialism: China and Vietnam Compared*. St Leonards: Allen and Unwin.

Clark, Katerina. 2003. 'Socialist Realism and the Sacrilizing of Space', in E. Dobrenko and E. Naiman (eds), *The Landscape of Stalinism: The Art and Ideology of Society Space*. Seattle: University of Washington Press, pp. 3–18.

Crang, Mike, and Nigel Thrift. 2000. 'Introduction', in Mike Crang (ed.), *Thinking Space*. London: Routledge, pp. 1–30.

Dang Phong [Đặng Phong]. 2003. *Lịch sử kinh tế Việt Nam 1945–2000* [Economic History of Viet Nam 1945–2000]. Hanoi: nxb Khoa học xã hội [Social Science Publishing House].

Dobrenko, Evgeny, and Eric Naiman (eds). 2003. *The Landscape of Stalinism: The Art and Ideology of Soviet Space*. Seattle: University of Washington Press.

Donham, Donald L. 1999. *Marxist Modern: An Ethnographic History of the Ethiopian Revolution*. Berkeley: University of California Press.

Feuchtwang, Stephan. 1974. *An Anthropological Analysis of Chinese Geomancy*. Vientiane: Vithgna.

———. 1993. 'Historical Metaphor: A Study of Religious Representation and the Recognition of Authority', *Man (N.S.)* 29(1): 35–49

Fforde, Adam, and Stefan de Vylder. 1996. *From Plan to Market: The Economic Transition in Vietnam*. Boulder, CO: Westview.

Gonzalez, Jennifer A. 1995. 'Autotopographies', in Gabrial Brahm and Mark Driscoll (eds), *Prosthetic Territories*. Boulder, CO: Westview, pp. 133–50.

Goscha, Christopher E. 1995. *Vietnam or Indochina? Contesting Concepts of Space in Vietnamese Nationalism, 1887–1954*. Copenhagen: NIAS Press.

Hue-Tam Ho Tai (ed.). 2001. *The Country of Memory: Remaking the Past in Late Socialist Vietnam*. Berkeley: University of California Press.

Humphrey, Caroline. 1995. 'Chiefly and Shamanist Landscapes in Mongolia', in Eric Hirsch and Michael O'Hanlon (eds), *The Anthropology of Landscape: Perspectives on Place and Space*. Oxford: Clarendon, pp. 135–62.

———. 2006. 'The President and the Seer: A Case Study of Prophecy and Scientific Attitudes in Modern Political Life', in Rebecca Empson (ed.), *Time, Causality and Prophecy in the Mongolian Cultural Region: Visions of the Future*. Folkestone: Global Oriental, pp. 98–115.

Jellema, Kate. 2007. 'Everywhere Incense Burning: Remembering Ancestors in Đổi Mới Vietnam', *Journal of Southeast Asian Studies* 38(3): 467–92.

Katz, Cindi. 2005. 'Lost and Found: The Imagined Geographies of American Studies', *Prospects* 30: 17–25.

Kelley, Liam. 2003. 'Vietnam as a "Domain of Manifest Civility"', *Journal of Southeast Asian Studies* 34(1): 63–76.

Kendall, Laurel, Vũ Thị Thanh Tâm and Nguyên Thi Thu Hương. 2010. 'Beautiful and Efficacious Statues: Magic, Commodities, Agency and the Production of Sacred Objects in Vietnam', *Material Religion* 6(1): 60–85.

Kwon, Heonik. 2006. *After the Massacre: Commemoration and Consolation in Ha My and My Lai.* Berkeley: University of California Press.

______. 2007. 'The Dollarization of Vietnamese Ghost Money', *Journal of the Royal Anthropological Institute (N.S.)* 13(1): 73–90.

______. 2008. *The Ghosts of War in Vietnam.* Cambridge: Cambridge University Press.

Malarney, Shaun Kingsley. 1997. 'Culture, Virtue, and Political Transformation in Contemporary Northern Viet Nam', *Journal of Asian Studies* 56(4): 899–920.

______. 2001. '"The Fatherland Remembers Your Sacrifice": Commemorating War Dead in North Vietnam', in Hue-Tam Ho Tai (ed.), *The Country of Memory: Remaking the Past in Late Socialist Vietnam.* Berkeley: University of California Press, pp. 46–76.

Marr, D. 2000. 'Concepts of "Individual" and "Self" in Twentieth-Century Vietnam', *Modern Asian Studies* 34(4): 769–96.

McCargo, D. (ed.). 2004. *Rethinking Vietnam.* London: Routledge Curzon.

Nora, Pierre (ed.). 1984. *Les Lieux de Mémoire*, vol. 1, La République. Paris: Gallimard.

Pham Quynh Phuong. 2009. *Hero and Deity: Tran Hung Dao and the Resurgence of Popular Religion in Vietnam.* Chiang Mai: Mekong Press.

Pollock, Sheldon. 1998. 'The Cosmopolitan Vernacular', *Journal of Asian Studies* 57(1): 6–37.

Raman, Parvathi, and Harry G. West (eds). 2009. *Enduring Socialism: Explorations of Revolution and Transformation, Restoration and Continuation.* Oxford: Berghahn Books.

Rydstrom, Helle. 2003. *Embodying Morality: Growing Up in Rural Northern Vietnam.* Honolulu: University of Hawaii Press.

Schlecker, Markus, and Kirsten W. Endres. 2011. 'Psychic Experience, Truth, and Visuality in Postwar Vietnam', *Social Analysis* 55(1): 1–22.

Soucy, Alexander. 2012. *The Buddha Side: Gender, Power, and Buddhist Practice in Vietnam.* Honolulu: University of Hawaii Press.

Ssorin-Chaikov, Nikolai (ed.). 2013. *Topografiia Schastia: Etnografisheskie Karta Moderna* [The Topography of Happiness: Ethnographic Contours of Modernity]. Moscow: New Literary Observer Publishers.

Ssorin-Chaikov, Nikolai, and Olga Sosnina. 2009. Postsotsializm kak khronotop: postsovetskaia publika na vystavke 'Dary vozhdiam [Postsocialism as a Chronotope: Post-Soviet Public at the Exhibition of Gifts to Soviet Leaders], *Neprikosnovennyi Zapas* [Emergency Ration] 64(2): 207–26.

Taylor, Phillip. 2004. 'Redressing Disadvantage or Rearranging Inequality? Development Interventions and Local Responses in the Mekong Delta', in Phillip Taylor (ed.), *Social Inequality in Vietnam and the Challenges to Reform.* Singapore: Institute of Southeast Asian Studies, pp. 236–69.

Thompson, E.P. 1971. 'The Moral Economy of the English Crowd in the Eighteenth Century', *Past and Present* 50: 76–136.

Toulson, Ruth E. 2012. 'The Anthropology of a Necessary Mistake: The Unsettled Dead and the Imagined State in Contemporary Singapore', in Liana Chua, Joanna Cook, Nicholas Long and Lee Wilson (eds), *Southeast Asian Perspectives on Power.* Abingdon: Routledge, pp. 93–106.

Verdery, Katherine. 2001. 'Inequality as Temporal Process: Property and Time in Transylvania's Land Restitution', *Anthropological Theory* 1(3): 373–92.
West, Harry G. 2009. 'From Socialist Chiefs to Postsocialist Cadres: Neotraditional Authority in Neoliberal Mozambique', in Harry G. West and Parvathi Raman (eds), *Enduring Socialism: Explorations of Revolution and Transformation, Restoration and Continuation*. Oxford: Berghahn Books, 29–43.
Wilson, Scott. 1997. 'The Cash Nexus and Social Networks: Mutual Aid and Gifts in Contemporary Shanghai Villages', *China Journal* 37: 91–112.
Winichakul, Thongchai. 1994. *Siam Mapped: A History of the Geo-Body of a Nation*. Honolulu: University of Hawaii Press.
Yang, Mayfair Mei-Hui. 2004. 'Spatial Struggles: Postcolonial Complex, State Disenchantment, and Popular Reappropriation of Space in Rural Southeast China', *Journal of Asian Studies* 63(3): 719–55.

2

Worlds United and Apart
Bridging Divergence in Hanoi and Beyond

Susan Bayly

Introduction

Intellectual exchange is a bridging of worlds, not necessarily successfully or completely, but with at least the possibility of boundaries crossed and the generation of ties. When I was planning my article on moral cartography, my hope was that it would communicate something of the excitement I had experienced from learning about the many forms of world bridging I had encountered in the course of fieldwork in Hanoi. I decided to focus on the connections and crossings I had heard about in discussions with my interlocutors about the importance of geospatial knowledge in their daily lives. This includes the contemplation of national maps and other indicators of Vietnam's positioning in a world of interacting national geo-bodies, and what it is that gives people such a strong sense of gratification when they do so. It also includes the care they take in recounting family narratives of their elders' traversing of near and distant topographical frontiers.[1]

I was much intrigued by these responses to maps and their producers, so strikingly at odds with our widely held view of maps as instruments of subjugating power knowledge (Winichakul 1994; Ramaswamy 2002). I therefore came up with the notion of moral cartography as the article's framing idea, using it to explore both the anxieties and satisfactions my friends experience when they engage with the expertise of such people as map-makers, geomancers and psychic grave-finders, all of whom can be of great importance in the pursuit of a morally agentive life.

These observations were a spur to several of my subsequent research concerns, including an interest in notions of achievement in Vietnamese educational contexts (Bayly 2014), and an attempt to understand more about what Hanoians do to achieve a sense of themselves as ethically refined moral agents

(Bayly 2020). What I explore in this new chapter is how my moral cartography material relates to the volume's framing theme of intellectual exchange. In doing so, I present ethnography I have not used elsewhere, focusing on the ways my interlocutors have engaged with divergent traditions of knowledge in a variety of personal and familial contexts. My particular concern is with the experiences of those whose traversings of frontiers both tangible and intangible have taken place at points of interface between the domains of science and the supramortal, noting both the challenges and the gratifications that these encounters can entail.

Exchanging and Border Crossing

The processes of mapping and spatial positioning I explored in my moral cartography paper involve physical as well as intellectual border crossing, sometimes with pleasing outcomes, but often at considerable cost. These were dynamics I first began to recognize during my earliest research in Vietnam, when I was conducting fieldwork with interlocutors sharing a distinctive family heritage, that of *gia đình trí thức*: intelligentsia/intellectual families. I found that younger members of these lineages were keen to share family accounts of the life and times of their elders, taking particular note of the immense changes these older kin had learned to navigate in the years of their homeland's remarkable transition from the life of war and grim postwar high socialist austerity to the marketization era known as *Đổi Mới* (Renovation) that began in the early 1990s.

These family elders included both men and women who had amassed a sometimes dangerously diverse stock of cultural and linguistic capital from having been educated in early youth in francophone colonial *lycées*, and subsequently in universities and research institutes spanning the old East-West divide, such that a single lifetime could encompass training and work stints in Moscow, Warsaw or Beijing, as well as Harvard or the Sorbonne. Such traversings of national and supra-national space have been both celebrated and disparaged in Vietnam. To some, those participating in these perilous forms of globe-trotting were users of skill and learning for ignoble gain. Their detractors also tend to see the sciences as taught by foreigners as cold and mechanistic, hence destructive of the moral groundings of a Vietnamese sensibility. But engagement with other lands and knowledge systems has equally vehement defenders who see such borrowings as confidently dialogic, arguing that an outward-looking cosmopolitanism is the defining essence of Vietnameseness, and that one can learn what the wider world has to teach without any surrender of national values and identity.

Only in Vietnam, I was told, as I travelled with members of a lively Hanoi *trí thức*/intelligentsia family to the site of one of the psychic grave searches (*đi tìm mộ*) described in my moral cartography article, would I find someone like the eminent retired geologist with a PhD from a prestigious USSR university who had organized this occasion for his kin, and had kindly invited me to attend.

His post-retirement glissade from teaching science at a top Hanoi university to his more recently achieved local eminence as a master of the art of geomantic spatial reckoning (*phong thủy*: feng shui in Western parlance) was emphatically not seen by his relations as a repudiation of his earlier training in positivistic hard science, but as its fulfilment and ultimate realization.

It is a kind of life trajectory that is very familiar to my intelligentsia friends. They say that with dedication and loving care, a man or woman of rigorous mind can find points of synergistic interplay between seemingly incompatible domains, advantaging their loved ones and the world at large by melding the principles of the material and the auratic in the pursuit of virtuous goals. Doing so is especially commendable in cases like this one, where the goal is provision of care and comfort to the ancestral dead.[2]

Other Hanoians I know have also been dynamic participants in a world of bridging and exchange, including the people of far more modest backgrounds with whom I have worked in the inner-city neighbourhood I call West Lake, now my principal fieldsite. For many West Lakers, there were long periods of childhood relocation during the 1946–54 anti-French liberation war, followed by further dislocations and border crossings in the course of overseas work stints in the years during and after the 1962–73 US-Vietnam War. This entailed officially sanctioned sojourns in almost every region of what I have called the global socialist ecumene, including work stints in the Soviet Union and its so-called satellites, as well as aid work in Algeria, Guinée and the other decolonized lands that were also important participants in this world-spanning web of socialist and quasi-socialist 'friendship' ties.

There were some surprising exchanges in these far-flung settings. Our theories of ethically meaningful gifting are particularly relevant to the translocal bridgings they produced.[3] Beginning in the 1970s, medical aid workers from Hanoi introduced their Algerian counterparts to electric acupuncture (*châm cứu điện*), a home-grown fusion of 'Eastern' (*Đông y*) and international therapeutic practice that was also enthusiastically received in the Soviet Union, and is still hailed in Vietnam as one of the nation's great contributions to world science.[4]

This is a key instance of what the former aid workers like to say about their activities, which is that the aid providers' gifts of skill and expertise were a product of home-grown Vietnamese genius enriched through selective engagements with the wider world's sciences and knowledge systems. The picture painted here in regard to the Soviet Union is comparable to what my travelling companions said of their geologist kinsman Professor Đức: that there was mutual respect and benefits received on both sides, with the image of socialist 'elder siblings' enthusiastically learning from Vietnam providing a welcome counterweight to the knowledge of how dependent the country had been on Soviet and Chinese aid and tutelage in the 1946–54 and 1962–73 war years, and the straitened 1973–90 'subsidy' era (*thời kỳ bao cấp*) that preceded the onset of marketization. The welcome implication of this is that Vietnam has been as much a giver as a receiver of these frontier-crossing boons and benefits, rather than a perpetual junior in relations with its far richer socialist 'friends' and exchange partners (Bayly 2009). The former aid workers also like to stress that the care provided to the African countries they call 'undeveloped' was given freely and without expectation of return, thus not to be thought of as coldly instrumental, i.e. an exchange of conscripted intellectual labour power for monetary return.

In addition to these cases of Vietnamese gift-giving in faraway places, there were notable instances of intellectual gift-taking, as in the case of the pioneering Hanoi anthropologist Nguyễn Đức Từ Chi who first encountered the writings of Lévi-Strauss on the shelves of Guinée's National University library in Conakry, during his four-year posting as a pedagology teacher in the early 1960s. Từ Chi's discovery of Lévi-Strauss was of course a matter of serendipity. But I suggest that we can also see it as a matter of gift-giving, though the question that then arises is which of our varied models of gifting this might entail. At first glance, it may appear that it fits the model of the boon-like gift made by superiors to humbly deferential juniors in a scheme of top-down, asymmetrical gift provision. This would mean seeing the ideas Từ Chi found so exciting and revelatory as yet another instance of what I noted above in relation to the gifting of development aid, thus assigning Từ Chi to the unhappy role of humble junior receiving a top-down gift of enlightenment as an unreciprocating taker of intellectual largesse emanating from the 'developed' world.

But in fact I think something richer and more interesting can be made of this. On his return to Hanoi, Từ Chi held unofficial seminars in which he introduced students to the hitherto unknown methodologies of structuralism. These were tantalising novelties to a generation taught the social sciences from translated Soviet textbooks, and his young listeners debated what they heard in still-remembered exchanges around the café tables of the old student quarter in central Hanoi.[5]

Từ Chi also sought to build on Lévi-Strauss in his ground-breaking wartime fieldwork in the country's northern uplands, treading a dangerously fine line between the permissible and the transgressive in his daringly sympathetic accounts of ritual and spirituality among his ethnic minority Mường interlocutors (published under his pseudonym Trần Từ, 1996). In doing so he made his own reflective sense of structuralism, treating it as a source of insights to be made dialogically interactive with Vietnamese modes of thought, rather than a doctrine to be imbibed one-sidedly, without question or critical engagement. This too makes Hanoians who know about him think of the process as one in which Từ Chi was initially in the position of gift-receiver taking tutelage from a world of wider intellectual horizons than his own, but then rapidly proceeding to the status of provider and benefactor in his own right, as he shared his highly personalized version of this new learning with receptive juniors of his own.

For other Hanoians too, there were liminalities and exchanges to be navigated on home soil, most notably through experience of Vietnam's colliding and interpenetrating worlds of city and countryside, together with the giant revolutionary transformations of the pre- and post-Independence periods that brought the teachings of Vietnamized Marxism, Buddhism and Confucianism into furiously contentious conversation with the multi-stranded legacies of French colonial thought, and the output of Vietnam's own distinguished array of home-grown social theorists and moralists (McHale 2004). And both in the past and today, there is the mix of contrasts and intertwinings between the ancestral traditions that citizens are taught to revere, and the equally strong call to embrace high-tech ultramodernity as the nation's key ideal.

Bridging Science and the Supramundane

The form of bridging that is particularly relevant to my moral cartography concerns is that experienced in my friends' traversing between the domains of the scientific and the supramundane. It is their engagements with those seemingly disparate moral orders that the paper seeks to highlight. I learned a great deal about such fluidity from Professor Đức and his family, and much too from Mrs Lý, a redoubtable octogenarian whose grandson Binh is one of my principal West Lake interlocutors. There are features of Mrs Lý's life story that are notably similar to Professor Đức's, despite the very considerable differences in their backgrounds and career trajectories.[6] What they have in common are their confident traversings of knowledge realms that an outsider might think of as mutually antagonistic because they would seem to be based on radically conflicting views of human and cosmic nature. But in fact neither they nor my other friends regard the truths of science and the supramundane as incompatible or in rivalry as claims on the moral self. Both Professor Đức and Mrs Lý are longstanding Party members, and both evince wholehearted commitment to the principles of scientific materialism they were taught to embrace as the source of authoritative knowledge about the human and natural order. But as I noted in regard to Professor Đức and his family, there are challenges but not insuperable difficulties in aligning the insights of the scientist's reasoning intellect with those of the 'heart-mind' (*ruột* or *lòng*: literally 'gut') that provides access to the auratic and supramortal and is thus the seat of moral sensibility (Marr 2000).

In Professor Đức's case, we remain very much in the realm of science, *khoa học*, when we note his use of the knowledge practices of *phong thủy* (geomantic earth science). He regards his mastery of *phong thủy* as a further and higher level of the geology he learned from his Soviet professors and faithfully imparted to his students on his return to Hanoi, keen to inspire them with his own enthusiasm for the discipline's revelatory rigour.[7] Mrs Lý is equally passionate about the empowering truths of science, but her introduction to all she associates with the scientific cast of mind was very different from what Professor Đức experienced in the high-socialist 1960s. In his case this meant his life as a high-achieving pupil in the best of post-Independence Hanoi's selective 'gifted student' schools, followed by a long study stint in Moscow. This was a true glittering prize at the time, attainable by only a tiny minority of the country's ablest students, not least because of the need for an unimpeachably clean *lý lịch* (personal record), i.e. no suspect political ties or 'bad class' family background.

Professor Đức's parents were themselves Hanoi academics: committed revolutionaries of distinguished intelligentsia/*trí thức* ancestry. Mrs Lý's background is that of a very different Vietnam. Born into rural poverty in 1930, fifteen years before President Hồ Chí Minh's declaration of national independence and the launch of Vietnam's nine-year anticolonial resistance war, Mrs Lý was the first literate woman in her village, as well as its first female Communist Party member, and first entrant into the world of urban waged employment. Her husband Manh was one of the locality's earliest recruits to the Communist-led liberation force known as the Việt Minh. Following her husband's battlefield death in 1953, she was left to raise their daughter Huynh on her own, though of course with such help as her nine very poor siblings could provide, and with the benefit of the modest perks and entitlements allocated to the widows and children of officially designated *liệt sỹ* (war martyrs). 'Always hungry' is her terse comment on those years.

Today, although long retired from the last of her increasingly senior state service posts, she is still a dynamic presence in her daughter and son-in-law's household in the big port city where her grandson Binh was born. Mrs Lý's daughter is a late-career biology teacher at a top-ranked city secondary school; she is married to Cường, who also comes from a poor peasant family. Like Mrs Lý, Cường made a dramatic transition to a life of science and urban modernity, which in his case entailed selection for training as a practitioner of *Đông y*/'Eastern' medicine.[8] They live in modest comfort: good-quality motorbikes but as yet no car; a well-furnished house in a comparatively quiet inner-city neighbourhood.

The notion of life lived to a plan and of the sciences as the empowering source on which to draw in the forging of that plan is what Mrs Lý learned to embrace at the critical point in her life that I discuss below, and it has remained central to the conceptions of health and wellbeing that she still takes pains to instil in her younger kin. Her own day begins with the quiet chanting of Buddhist *sutras*. She does this in the early morning, seated before a cherished photo of her soldier-martyr husband. Like many other women of similar age and background, she embraced the daily disciplines of an active lay Buddhist devotee following her retirement from state service. She enjoys her role as informal advisor to family and neighbours on the correct placing of the food offerings and other items that belong on a properly tended household ancestor altar, so that its arrangement is effective in bringing the ancestral dead under the Buddha's compassionate care.[9]

For Mrs Lý and her family there is no conflict between her lay Buddhist lifestyle and her continued reverence for the Party and the humane scientism she regards as its moral core; the one has definitely not been a replacement for the other. She does make distinctions: she is not keen on the widely publicized occasions when officials forge partnerships with monks from regional pagodas for initiatives such as the provision of relief aid to flood victims. She has made it clear that she prefers relations with monks to be on a personal basis, by which she means teaching the Dhamma and performing life cycle rites in a family's home. Having been an official herself, Binh has told me, she believes it is for Party organizations such as the Vietnam Youth Union to define and meet citizens' material needs.

Mrs Lý's morning regimen continues with a brief but vigorous session of the balletic fitness exercises that are another widespread practice of the elderly in Vietnam; then a brisk reading from state media to her breakfasting kin. She always chooses the items for discussion and comment, favouring the venerable state daily *Lao Động* (Labour) because she likes its tips on health and bodily care, as well as its reports on developments in *khoa học*/science fields she considers good for human flourishing, such as advances in infertility treatments and neonatal care.[10]

That notion of a day mapped out in clock-time with regular intervals allocated to sleep, meals, work and recreation is one of the novelties she learned to embrace when she was in her early twenties, in the very different world she entered after her husband's death. There was a small quasi-industrial work unit in a locality several kilometres from her rural home, and she and one of her sisters took the bold step of saying yes when its recruitment team arrived in her village seeking young female volunteers to join its workforce.

This was the first of the great moments of transformation in Mrs Lý's remarkable life. The work was gruelling – the women's task was to tend the blazing outdoor vats in which old tyres and other rubber waste items were melted down for purposes that were never explained to her. With hindsight, her grandson thinks they were reusing the salvaged rubber to make new tyres for army porterage bikes, and probably soldiers' sandals as well. The unit's interior was where the male labour force worked, but at what exactly Mrs Lý says she never knew. 'For the army' is what she says she heard, which meant it was definitely not something to ask about.

All this may seem grim and dehumanizing, a kind of sub-industrial hell, yet Mrs Lý's accounts of her life at the site are strikingly elegiac. She speaks of her time there as a learning experience full of wonderful new inputs to her sense of the world and her place in it. Of course, I am bearing in mind that as she rose to senior service rank she would certainly have become well versed in the Party's narratives of empowering enlightenment conferred on an ever-grateful citizenry, its mass literacy campaigns and schooling in the ways of the modern industrial workplace to be applauded as triumphs of revolutionary developmentalism warmly welcomed by all (Malarney 2002).

But her grandson Binh, very much a cynic and quick to debunk everything he considers 'fake' in his highly formulaic Party history and ideology classes, says he has no doubt about the sincerity with which she speaks of her abiding gratitude towards those who shaped her new life at the site. The key figure in her stories is not another workmate or a work supervisor, but the youthful Party education officer she came to regard as a mentor, conforming to the time-honoured ideal of the caring village teacher selflessly nurturing the talents of the young, but in his case a revolutionary modern and thus eager to impart his learning to both male and female recipients of his care.

It was in the young officer's classes that Mrs Lý learned to read, filling her makeshift slate with the words and phrases of the day. And then came the revelatory new knowledge that she learned to call science, *khoa học*. What *khoa học* means to her is something she speaks of in wholly positive terms, and she too makes it clear that what she learned about its truths and principles was in no sense a refutation of the values and sensibilities she grew up with. Her notion of science is moral order, a vision of the world governed by the beauty of the truths and regularities of a benign and principled nature, with no call for the learner to renounce warmth and personal attachment, or to see the path of science as service to an abstract and depersonalized understanding of humanity or the nation.

The stories Mrs Lý tells of those times are thus of a very immediate and personal experience of her homeland's giant post-Independence leap from the immiseration of colonial rule to the wonders of revolutionary modernity that she narrativizes as the fruit of its citizens' hard work and sacrifice, given shape and momentum by the Party, with President Hồ Chí Minh as its guiding light and moral exemplar. And without directly disparaging the life of toil she had led on her family's tiny plot of unproductive farmland, she does make it clear that she feels her traversing of those few kilometres separating her natal village from her new life at the production site to have been an act of life-changing will and purpose, hence a move comparable to those I sought to relate to my notion of moral cartography.

What I think we can also see in Mrs Lý's life story is the way the idea of a morally cartographic dynamic in human life can be further enriched by relating it to a dynamic of intellectual exchange. Binh grew up on Mrs Lý's stories of how her teacher at the production site made science a realm of graspable truths to cherish and profit from. The teacher comes across in these accounts as the antithesis of the stereotypical Party modernizer hellbent on imposing a socialist version of the colonial *mission civilisatrice* on his rustic charges.[11] In Mrs Lý's accounts there is no suggestion that she was made to feel ashamed of her village ways, or that there could be any problem in finding points of interface between the truths of science and the knowledge of the 'heart-mind' she had brought with her into her teacher's open-air classroom. He showed the class the first bar of soap they had ever seen; she remembers her delight when he lathered his hands and made the bubbles float above their heads. It was a lesson on hygiene and orderly comportment, but there is nothing in the way she tells the story suggesting that the idea of regulating one's day by the principles of clock time and a formalized activity plan felt alien or dehumanizing to her, or that the lesson was delivered as a corrective to what a townsman might think of as a villager's backward ways. What Binh notes about her stories is that she speaks of the teacher's lessons as being angled towards what she cared about as the mother of a young child: the safeguarding of bodily health and the wellbeing of those in her care. This is what she still tells Binh about science: its truths are personal, resources to embrace in the pursuit of human flourishing.

She was certainly acquiring a new grounding and vision of the world and her place in it. 'He always explained', she says of the young teacher, and it clearly means much to her to be able to say that he took pains to provide a rationale for his lessons, rather than expecting mute compliance and regurgitation on command. When she speaks of the young education officer at her factory, she refers to him with respect and affection as 'my *thầy*', using the possessive pronoun to convey the notion of a warm bond between them, so the sense is something like 'my dear mentor/preceptor'.[12] Of course this is very much an idealized portrayal of the revolutionary enlightenment process, but even allowing for its likely elisions and omissions it is still very striking as a representation of intellectual exchange. She clearly wants her grandson and other young kin to see it as she does, a relation that was hierarchical, a male senior imparting revelatory truths to a female junior, but to be seen in terms of the naturalness and inherent virtue of such relations.

'Water flows downhill', people say. Binh uses this familiar proverb when we talk about these relationship issues. What it conveys to him and other Hanoians I know is that what is in nature, like the elements and their life-giving flows and energies, is morally sound. This includes the elemental truth that in human life, as in nature, it is right and proper for seniors to develop the minds and moral attunements of their juniors. And it is wholly unproblematic for those junior-senior relations to be those of a virtuously caring senior male and cheerfully deferential junior female.

What I am often told about these norms of everyday relational life is that their basis is the distinctiveness of the Vietnamese self, this being a nature that is predisposed to balance and harmony in dealings with mortal and non-mortal others because it is a form of selfhood innately rich in qualities of warmth and sensibility (*tình cảm*), hence distinctively equipped to constitute authority relations, including those that place men above women in orders of relational structure and status, as mutualities of love and exemplarship, not submission or subjugation. 'Up and down', people say, not 'top-down'. Indeed, the models most often called to mind are of planetary orbits, or a lodestone's magnetic pull; nothing rigid or ladder-like. So, while males and seniors are situated above women and juniors in relational contexts, as in the arrangement of photos on a household ancestor altar, the notions articulated are those of motility and the circuits of the heavens. The senior is thus the orbital heart and centre to which the junior's quickened sensibility will naturally orient itself.[13]

Again, there may well be much that is selective and idealized in Mrs Lý's account of her factory classroom experiences, intended to convey a moralizing message to Binh and her other kin about the virtues they should strive to uphold even though their circumstances and prospects are so very different from those of her own younger days. And there can be no doubt that in her later years Mrs Lý was well aware that there were Party ideologues who took a harsh and dismissive view of rustic conventions and mores. But when Party members speak or act in ways she finds problematic, her view is that although in her youth men and women of the Party were typically more virtuous than in today's Vietnam, it is the individuals who stray from its ideals and values who are deficient, not the Party itself as an enduring force for good.

I do not mean to suggest that these experiences of world-bridging were effortless or unproblematic for Mrs Lý. She makes it clear in looking back at her earlier life that there were many challenges to be faced as she sought to navigate between the truths of science and those of the auratic and the heart-mind. The first of these was the moment when she was told in her second year at the rubber melting site that her exemplary work and study performance had qualified her for a posting to one of Vietnam's few fully mechanized production units, a newly inaugurated Soviet-built canning plant in the big city I will not name in order to preserve her anonymity, where she would learn the skills of factory labour in its most excitingly modern form, as well as pursuing her classroom studies at a more advanced level. It was clear to her that this was a rare and wonderful opportunity that would vastly better her own prospects and those of her small daughter, for whom access to the high-quality schooling available only in the country's big cities would mean a future of career possibilities far better even than those for which Mrs Lý herself was clearly being groomed.

But there was still a difficulty to be faced. Mrs Lý was in no doubt that a life change of this magnitude required consultation with her departed husband. Without his knowledge and approval, she could not proceed. The post was a plum, but Binh says she could have turned it down; even in those far stricter times, a soldier martyr's widow of good repute could have said no to such a move. She would not have needed to say why, he assured me; it would have been assumed that she was reluctant to move too far from her husband's gravesite to be able to see to its care, and no official would challenge this virtuous expression of a wife's devotion and sensibility (*tình cảm*).

But in fact Mrs Lý did want the post, so long as she could be confident that her husband approved. So she returned quietly to the village to set the process in train. In the past as today, children learn from an early age that the ancestral dead are an aware and active presence in the affairs of the living (Jellema 2007; Endres 2018). It is a fundamental duty of the living to sustain and care for their departed kin, showing their loving remembrance (*biết ơn*) and respect (*kính trọng*) with gifts and offerings. This includes ensuring that the dead partake of the good things families share on key occasions such as their lunar New Year (*Tết*) gatherings; and communicating with them on a regular basis so they are informed about the doings of their loved ones and can provide what my interlocutors call 'support' (*phù hộ*) should they choose to intervene in times of need.

Today's practices allow for much more elaborate forms of provision and communication with the deceased than was possible in Mrs Lý's youth when, for example, there were no ancestor altars in people's homes of the kind Mrs Lý now warmly approves. But there is much about contemporary practices that she finds crass and unseemly. People today think they are entitled to make demands of the dead, she complains. This is ugly and unfeeling. No child should be brought up thinking it right to treat the ancestors as if they need to be cajoled and prodded into showing care for their kin. When performing incense lighting (*thắp hương*) at the family altar, one should say only 'my son has an exam tomorrow', or 'we hope to build our new house soon', and never turn such a report into an importuning; or, even more disgustingly, a transaction, as in 'I give you this offering, so please help me in return'.

Mrs Lý also disapproves of the staging of elaborate soul-callings (*gọi hồn*) of the kind that so often feature in the moral cartographies described in my paper. She sympathizes with those who arrange such occasions in order to facilitate grave searches, their aim being to end the pain of soldier-martyrs and other departed kin whose remains have been lost and therefore suffer because they have not been properly entombed. But she regards the process itself as invasive and hurtful, especially when performed by one of the many paid psychics (*nhà ngọai cảm*) who now offer their services as expert providers of contact with the non-mortal realm (the otherworld: *thế giới khác*). She thinks the *ngọai cảm* psychics use their 'special capacities' in a heartless manner that is disturbing and painful for the dead, and that the psychics are motivated by personal profit and fame rather than loving care for the departed (see Schlecker and Endres 2011; Fjelstad and Hien 2018).

Yet Mrs Lý has never concealed from her kin that she organized a *gọi hồn* calling of her own on that key occasion when she was offered the posting to the big port town. It is clear to her family, however, that it was a soul-calling quite unlike the *gọi hồn* procedures of today. She did arrange for an intermediary to make the necessary contact with her husband. But no money changed hands, merely the gift of a chicken as a gracious thank-you when the calling was done. And the soul-caller was a fellow villager, a woman who knew the family, not a hired practitioner like the unfeeling psychics of today. She uses the old-fashioned village term *bà đồng* (seer) for the provider, regarding *ngọai cảm* as a coldly scientized neologism used only by those who have professionalized and commodified their 'special capacities'.

Binh says he is sure that Mrs Lý would not have told her factory workmates or even her kindly teacher about the event. But she would not have considered it shameful or at odds with her commitment to the new socialist world she had so enthusiastically embraced. The outcome of the calling was favourable, and Mrs Lý did indeed take the new post, confident that her husband was supportive and at ease. And while she never again staged a soul-calling, she has never ceased to connect with her husband, doing so by means of the gentle communion that is set in train by the performance of *thắp hương*/incense lighting at one's household altar.

No one in the family would think of these engagements with the non-mortal realm as anything other than the normal acts of conscience (*tâm*) and moral sensibility (*tình cảm*) that are the essential underpinnings of a properly conducted Vietnamese life. They are certainly not thought to be in conflict with Mrs Lý's firm commitment to the Party and all she associates with its principles and values. When Mrs Lý speaks to her husband of family matters, she knows he listens with compassionate care. And he communicates with her, though not often, and not in words. There is a particular twinge of mild discomfort in her gut that she recognizes as an expression of his concern. And she knows there is something more seriously amiss when he appears to her in a dream, his face glimpsed in shadow but his expression recognizably one of warning and unease. When these contacts take place, she tells the rest of the family about them so they can discuss a likely cause and potential remedy. Perhaps there is an impending road journey for someone in the household and he foresees a danger and the need for extra care. Or he himself may be in distress, and they may need to check on his gravesite in the ancestral village in case it has been damaged in a recent storm.

Of course, Mrs Lý has known since those early years in her factory classrooms that the Party state is fiercely hostile to practices it defines as *mê tín dị đoan*, superstition (Malarney 2002; Schwenkel 2018; Endres 2020). It is a word she often uses, much as my other interlocutors do; always disparagingly, but referring to practices both she and they consider very different from their own. Officialdom says it is *mê tín* to traffic with seers and fortune tellers, but to my interlocutors this means practitioners of the malign black arts, not the reputable geomancers and other providers they and their families make use of for virtuous ends. The realm of *mê tín*/superstition also includes activities that Mrs Lý and my Hanoi friends regard as vulgar and excessive. So the burning of very large quantities of replica paper votive offerings (*vàng mã*) for the dead is *mê tín*/superstition. But the making of modest *vàng mã* gifts of a kind suited to the needs and tastes of departed kin is a loving act of care and reverence, thus wholly in keeping with the spirit of *tình cảm* (sensitive feeling for others), which is the bedrock of Vietnameseness (Rydstrom 2003).

The final stages of Mrs Lý's remarkable life trajectory began in the ten years that followed her move to the canning factory job. She was selected for Party membership, in those days an honour bestowed on those deemed outstanding contributors to national need. And she was once again recognized as a model worker and diligent learner, so was singled out for yet another plum: in this case a transfer to the city's Department of Education where she remained in post for the rest of her working life. Her duties were in the field of what the Party state calls ideology (*tư tưởng*), which was work assigned to particularly able and trusted Party members.

'Intellectuals', her grandson Binh told me, are of course the people qualified for actual teaching. Or if they work in administration, they are the right people to deal with the academic side of schooling and educational policy. But the head of the 'intellectual' is said to be filled with things like the chemistry or maths they had to master so as to qualify in their fields. Less so today, but certainly at the time when Mrs Lý was in post, the logic of this is that there must be reliable people like Binh's grandmother to complement the work of the academic specialists when key decisions must be made, such as which of a given cohort of the able young should be sent abroad for training in a field deemed important for the national interest.

'Reliability' in such cases meant someone coming to the work of educational decision-making from the factory floor, rather than the rarefied world of the scholar or 'brain worker'. And it was indeed one of Mrs Lý's key responsibilities to take part in the vetting of school leavers given provisional nomination for the joy of overseas study in the USSR or other Eastern bloc states. Of course, Binh explained, it was important for teachers and subject specialists to identify those pupils with the best academic qualifications for such placings. But vetting of the candidate's *lý lịch* ('background'/personal history dossier) by Mrs Lý's office was the crucial next stage in the approval process. The decisions could be harsh: a single 'bad class' grandparent could derail a brilliant student's otherwise unstoppable path to a university in the wider socialist world.

Even today, although such antecedents are no longer treated as a lifelong stigma, no one I know is puzzled about why such concerns were dealt with as matters of 'ideology'. Friends made clear to me that in official thought and language 'ideology'/*tư tưởng* is a capacious term. Of course, it is used in the familiar sense of a body of organized knowledge, and more specifically the ordering principles of the Party state, which the young are formally taught in their compulsory school and university classes on Marxism-Leninism and the thought of President Hồ Chí Minh. But it also denotes the work done by offices like Mrs Lý's, meaning the body of acquired insights and understandings that such units' staff would be assumed to have mastered through long years of work experience and Party training. So it was by virtue of rigorous 'ideology' training that someone like Mrs Lý would know that possession of a bright mind and disciplined study habits could not wipe away the stain of a youngster's 'bad class' antecedents.

Yet Binh speaks proudly of the instances Mrs Lý has told him about when her heart or 'gut' told her to 'do something' when such judgements were made.[14] What this meant was quietly finding a way to salvage a candidate's hopes by finding them a place in what was regarded as a second- or third-tier site of study: mechanical engineering or mining technology in a Polish or Romanian university, for someone ruled out on 'ideology' grounds for physics or maths in Moscow.

These were far from risk-free exercises in workplace moral cartography, but Mrs Lý clearly knew how to manage these delicate manoeuvres. It is clear that she too takes pride in what she did, feeling that she was serving the Party and her adopted city by ensuring that young people with talent were as well equipped as possible to contribute to its developmental needs. And while the life she knows her grandson leads as a rising star in his prestigious white-collar state service post is so very different from her own challenging life trajectory, there is no doubt that she rejoices in the material comforts as well as the job satisfaction that his achievements have brought him, while at the same time feeling in no doubt about the strength of the moral bonds that tie her life and values to his own.

Final Thoughts

I am profoundly grateful to the Editors for offering me this opportunity to revisit my moral cartography article, and to reflect on the ways its concerns connect with the notion of intellectual exchange as the framing theme for this volume. In doing so, I have found it intriguing to explore aspects of my interlocutors' experiences involving both literal and metaphorical acts of traversing and border crossing. What I wanted to highlight in this chapter is the remarkable mobility and translocality we can see in my interlocutors' life trajectories, both before and since the onset of the turbulent marketization processes known as Renovation/*Đổi Mới* in Vietnam, especially those involving their encounters with new and unfamiliar knowledge systems.

Although I believe my work with Hanoians from the city's distinctive intelligentsia/*trí thức* family networks to be of much interest for our topic, I did not want to confine my discussion to the case of multilingual globe-trotters like Professor Đức, who had to learn from early youth how to navigate the sometimes perilous intellectual and physical landscapes of what I have called the global socialist ecumene, often in situations where exchanges of skill and knowledge were represented in terms that were highly critical of those involved, despite attempts by their defenders to portray such relations as expressions of beneficence and dialogic gift exchange. But in order to extend my concerns beyond the world of the intelligentsias, I wanted to include something of the very different but equally challenging diversities of landscape traversed and made sense of by interlocutors from far less advantaged backgrounds, as exemplified by the redoubtable Mrs Lý. Yet my primary interest in both cases has been the mix of challenges and gratifications to be experienced at points of interface between the domains of science and the supramundane, especially as reflected on by my interlocutors from the vantage point of post-retirement, and in the presence of younger kin; and most particularly in situations where the truths of science/*khoa học* merge and interpenetrate with those experienced as truths of sensibility and a loving heart.

I know I still have much to learn about these and the many other processes of world-bridging and dynamic exchange that can generate both fulfilment and anxiety in today's Vietnam. As soon as the pandemic situation permits, I hope to return to Hanoi and am keenly looking forward to further fieldwork with my boundlessly patient interlocutors, whose friendship and willingness to share so much with me have been true highlights of my research career. For now, I hope that the material presented here provides a helpful grounding for my moral cartography paper, and that its reflections serve as an effective bridge to the theme my friends and colleagues have selected as the focus for this volume. I am deeply touched by their wish to mark my retirement in this enormously generous way, and I offer them my heartfelt thanks for doing so, and for the countless other kindnesses that have so wonderfully underpinned our many years of stimulating interactions across so many diverse areas of mutual interest and enthusiasm.

Acknowledgements

I am most grateful to the Editors for their insightful comments on earlier drafts of this chapter. My heartfelt thanks as well to my other friends and colleagues in Cambridge and beyond, especially those with whom I have learned and shared so much in Vietnam. I also owe much to cherished friends in India, which is where my research career began. And of course I have been sustained and inspired at every step along the way by the erudition and humanity of my dearly beloved late husband, Christopher Bayly.

Susan Bayly is Professor of Historical Anthropology (Emerita) in the Cambridge University Department of Social Anthropology, and a Life Fellow of Christ's College, Cambridge. Her publications include *Asian Voices in a Postcolonial Age: Vietnam, India and Beyond*; and *Caste, Society and Politics in India from the 18th Century to the Modern Age* (both with Cambridge University Press). She has conducted extensive on-site fieldwork in both India and Vietnam, focusing most recently on projects aimed at bringing the insights of visual anthropology into conversation with the anthropology of morality and ethics. Her research interests also include Asian post-socialism; theories of historical change; the interface between history and anthropology; and colonialism and its cultural afterlife in South and Southeast Asia.

Notes

1. This chapter is intended as a companion piece to my article 'Mapping Time, Living Space: The Moral Cartography of Renovation in Late-Socialist Vietnam' published in *The Cambridge Journal of Anthropology* in 2013 (31[2]: 60–84). My thanks to the journal's Editor and to the publishers Berghahn Books for permission to republish it here, and to the Editors of this volume for inviting me do so.
2. Also the relief of living kin who suffer because the loved one's remains have been lost or improperly interred, but the emphasis is always on the relief of the dead kinsman's suffering, not that of the mortals who seek to comfort them (Jellema 2007; Schlecker and Endres 2011).
3. I have in mind here the literature on the ethics of gift exchange that I engaged with in my work on the provision of development aid to African 'friendship' partners, for example when I sought to show that when official Vietnamese accounts represent these initiatives as acts of gift-giving, to be understood as cooperative interactions animated by feelings of selfless warmth, they are being portrayed as something akin to the 'empathetic dialogues' which Fennell (2002) says are generated out of the giving of 'illiquid', disinterested gifts between individual partners in exchange. See also Yan 1996; Laidlaw 2000, Venkatesen 2007; but also Copeman and Banerjee 2020. The language of the gift is widely used in official accounts of Vietnam's African aid schemes, and by the former aid workers themselves (Bayly 2009).
4. For more on these Vietnamese 'friendship' schemes that sent providers of development aid to socialist and quasi-socialist countries in north and sub-Saharan Africa from the 1970s to the early 1990s, see Bayly 2008 and 2009.

5. But as Dr L.M. Chau has been finding in his research on anthropology in mid-twentieth-century Vietnam, the university-based Hanoi anthropologists of this generation should not be seen as slavishly doctrinaire in the application of their textbook Marxist paradigms, and were far more intellectually adventurous and creative in the fieldwork they conducted in the 1970s and 1980s than has been assumed in the dismissive accounts provided by some scholars (Dr Chau, personal communication; Evans 1992; see also Truong Huyen Chi 2014).
6. Including the differences in their linguistic knowledge. Mrs Lý never learned a foreign language but is immensely proud of her grandson Binh's excellent English. Like his Soviet-educated contemporaries, Professor Đức learned Russian and Chinese at school, and gained working knowledge of German and Romanian during overseas postings in the 1980s. He taught himself basic English in the early Renovation years.
7. It is well known that the Party state was hostile to *phong thủy* (geomantic reckoning) in the decades before Renovation, but what I have been repeatedly told in discussions of these matters is that geomantic services were deemed 'feudal' (*phong kiến*) because they were costly and inaccessible to the 'masses', rather than because they belonged to the realm of *mê tín dị đoan*, superstition. This is a term still widely used in everyday speech (discussed later), and deployed in official contexts to identify such people as fortune tellers and spirit mediums (Endres 2011; Leshkowich 2014). For the Hanoians I know, *phong thủy* is definitely a science (*khoa học*). This is not the way they refer to knowledge of the supramortal and cosmological, and not a term they use loosely or for mere semantic effect. They define *phong thủy* as science/*khoa học* because, like physics and geology, it is systematic, ordered and textually based, employing procedures of calculation and measurement that they consider to be validated by the experimental hard sciences. Thus, I have been told that what physicists have determined about the harmful effects of electromagnetic waves on human tissue is precisely what the *phong thủy* expert makes known when employing the discipline's distinctive diagnostic techniques to detect an unfavourable flow of environmental energy (*qi*) impacting a home or business premises: 'same principle', one friend said; just a different application. Another friend told me what her secondary school history teacher had said during a classroom lesson in the late 1980s about one of the landmark events that is still central to the official narrative of Vietnamese revolutionary nationhood. This is the climactic moment in April 1975 that is celebrated every year as Liberation of the South Day (*Ngày Giải phóng miền Nam*), when the Communist North Viet Nam army's tanks smashed open the gates of the Presidential Palace in Saigon, formerly the capital of the US-backed South Viet Nam client regime. Of course, my friend said, the teacher told the class that the North's triumph was a product of 'our people's' valour and military skill, under the all-wise leadership of the Party. But the teacher also told the class something that is still widely recounted in Hanoi, which is that the strongman presidents who resided in the palace had failed to obtain proper geomantic expertise for its planning and layout, and in particular that the site's massive entry gates had been fatally misaligned in geomantic/*phong thủy* terms. My friend said the class had no trouble understanding why this was such a failure on the part of the Saigon leaders to those they claimed to hold in their care, hence so catastrophic for the regime. Even teenagers, she said, knew how much attention their elders paid to geomantic principles in the siting of a home's front door, or any other point of access to a space where there is a collective's wellbeing to care for, such as the gateway to a factory complex, or the gated entrance to a village or peri-urban residential neighbourhood (compare Harms 2012).
8. The Hanoi medical university where Cường trained also teaches Western-style medicine (*Thuốc Tây*), but towards the end of the 1962–73 anti-US War there was a major policy commitment to professionalize the traditional healing arts, and he was assigned to the university's *Đông y* teaching programme on his admission in 1970 (see Monnais et al. 2011; Wahlberg 2014).

9. There are many forms of Buddhism currently practised in Vietnam; so long as their adherents do nothing that appears challenging to the authority of the Party state, they are treated as valued partners in the national project (Soucy 2012).
10. This seems to me quite an agentive form of engagement with the government's didactic media organs, rather than a mere parroting of the Party state's official voice (Pettus 2004: 17).
11. Accounts of such figures in Vietnamese and other socialist contexts include Kipnis 1995; Fitzpatrick 1996; Donham 1999; Malarney 2002; Stone 2008.
12. Referring to someone as 'my *thầy*' signals a bond of reverence and warmth with the man who has taught them. Its use can also point to a real or quasi-parental tie, but more commonly denotes the status of a man who has acquired either traditional or modern disciplinary expertise through dedicated study.
13. Vietnam boasts impressive female educational performance and high levels of labour force participation, but also highly gendered divisions of labour and status in the home and workplace (see, e.g., Leshkowich 2006, 2014; Werner 2009; Bergstedt 2015; Rydstrom 2003, 2020). My friends of both sexes say they recognize how often their experience of the real world fails to live up to the vision of harmony and complementarity they see in the water proverb. But they also say it is still right to teach the young what the saying means: that there is righteous moral principle as well as a spirit of warmth and 'heart' underpinning the norms they grow up with. These include the modes of proper speech known as *xưng hô*, meaning use of the many familial-based me-you or 'person-reference' dyad idioms to be deployed in all conversational exchanges. The nuances of *xưng hô* are learned from early childhood, and its terminology is both gendered and hierarchical (Chew 2011; Hy Van Luong 1990; Sidnell and Shohet 2013). A sister is never a status-neutral 'I' to her elder brother's 'you'. Even in adulthood she must call herself *em* when speaking to him; this is the person-reference for a younger sibling, and its connotations are often warm, something like 'little one'. An elder brother He is always *anh*/senior male to her *em*. So too for husband and wife, regardless of their actual ages: she is *em*; he is *anh*. My friends insist that this is not 'etiquette' in the sense of the formalities foreigners learn by rote, but rather a bringing to verbal life of natural perceptions and sensitivities that are innate to the Vietnamese heart and spirit. They are therefore morally sound, as conveyed by the flowing water proverb. In the modern classroom the language of relational dyads is also differentially gendered: the pupil is *em*: his or her male teacher is *thầy*, while his female counterpart is *cô*. There is a gender-neutral word for teacher: *giáo viên*, a composite formed from *giáo*, which is the realm of teaching/education, and *viên*, a classifier term for the holder of a post or office. The way to specify male and female teacher is *thầy giáo* and *cô giáo*. *Thầy* is thus a term for males only and denotes someone with mastery of a specific field or discipline. In the case of *thầy giáo*, the master's field is that of teaching; the title is also used for premodern arts and skills, as in the case of *thầy số* (astrologer) and *thầy cung* (spirit priest), fields in which expertise is achieved under the tutelage of an established master. In contrast, the title for a woman teacher, *cô*, is specifically familial. It is used as the equivalent of Miss or Madam, but also has a definite kinship meaning: it is the *xưng hô* pronoun to use for a father's younger sister. And a woman who teaches is associated with one of the Party state's enduring iconographic traditions, still a feature of school textbooks and public message posters: a conventionalized representation of the female teacher gently guiding the hand of a young pupil as she takes her first steps towards the attainment of literacy. This is teaching as 'feeding' (*nuôi dưỡng*), people say, a word suggestive of the nurturing mother tenderly coaxing morsels of rice into the mouth of her infant child. Even in the case of a modern science teacher at secondary school level like Mrs Lý's daughter, much that is said about the *cô giáo*'s duties and ethos evokes this model of the womanly nurturer guiding her charges along the path of diligence and docile compliance. Something more inspiring and assertive is to be expected of her male counterpart, the *thầy*.

14. My interlocutors speak of compassionate feeling as profundity of heart *(tâm)*, and also as being sensitive to the promptings of *lòng*: lit. 'guts', the seat of true and heartfelt sensibility.

References

Bayly, Susan. 2008. *Asian Voices in a Postcolonial Age: Vietnam, India and Beyond.* Cambridge: Cambridge University Press.

_____. 2009. 'Vietnamese Narratives of Tradition, Exchange and Friendship in the Worlds of the Global Socialist Ecumene', in Harry West and Parvathi Raman (eds), *Enduring Socialism: Explorations of Revolution, Transformation, Restoration & Continuation.* New York: Berghahn Books, pp. 125–43.

_____. 2014. 'How to Forge a Creative Student-Citizen: Achieving the Positive in Today's Vietnam', *Modern Asian Studies* 48(3): 493–523.

_____. 2020. 'Beyond "Propaganda": Images and the Moral Citizen in Late-Socialist Vietnam', *Modern Asian Studies* 54(5): 1526–95.

Bergstedt, Cecilia. 2015. *Cultivating Gender: Meanings of Place and Work in Rural Vietnam.* Copenhagen: NIAS Press.

Chew, Grace Chye Lay. 2011. 'Politeness in Vietnam', in Daniel Z. Kadar and Sara Mills (eds), *Politeness in East Asia.* Cambridge: Cambridge University Press, pp. 208–25.

Copeman, Jacob, and Dwaipayan Banerjee. 2020. 'Actual and Potential Gifts: Critique, Shadow Gift Relations and the Virtual Domain of the Ungiven', *Anthropological Theory* 21(1): 28–49.

Donham, Donald. 1999. *Marxist Modern: an Ethnographic History of the Ethiopian Revolution.* Berkeley: University of California Press.

Endres, Kirsten W. 2011. *Performing the Divine: Mediums, Markets and Modernity in Urban Vietnam.* Singapore: NIAS press.

_____. 2018. 'Spirit Performance and the Ritual Construction of Personal Identity in Modern Vietnam', in Karen Fjelstad and Nguyen Thi Hien (eds), *Possessed by the Spirits: Mediumship in Contemporary Vietnamese Communities.* Ithaca, NY: Cornell University Press, pp. 77–94.

_____. 2020. 'From "Wasteful Superstition" to "Beautiful Tradition": Changing Assessments of Popular Ritual in Late Socialist Vietnam', in Christiane Brosius and Karin M. Polit (eds), *Ritual, Heritage and Identity: The Politics of Culture and Performance in a Globalised World.* London: Routledge, pp. 246–80.

Evans, Grant. 1992. 'Internal Colonialism in the Central Highlands of Vietnam', *Sojourn: Journal of Social Issues in Southeast Asia* 7(2): 274–304.

Fennell, Lee Anne. 2002. 'Unpacking the Gift: Illiquid Goods and Empathetic Dialogue', in Mark Osteen (ed.), *The Question of the Gift: Essays across Disciplines.* Abingdon: Routledge, pp. 85–102.

Fitzpatrick, Sheila. 1996. *Stalin's Peasants: Resistance and Survival in the Russian Village after Collectivization.* New York: Oxford University Press.

Fjelstad, Karen, and Nguyen Thi Hien (eds). 2018. *Possessed by the Spirits: Mediumship in Contemporary Vietnamese Communities.* Ithaca, NY: Cornell University Press.

Harms, Erik. 2012. 'Neo-Geomancy and Real Estate Fever in Postreform Vietnam', *Positions: East Asia Cultures Critique* 20(2): 405–34.

Hy Van Luong. 1988. 'Discursive Practices and Power Structure: Person-Referring in Colonial Vietnam', *American Ethnologist* 15(2): 239–53.

Jellema, Kate. 2007. 'Everywhere Incense Burning: Remembering Ancestors in *Đổi Mới* Vietnam', *Journal of Southeast Asian Studies* 38(3): 467–92.
Kipnis, Andrew B. 1995. 'Within and Against Peasantness: Backwardness and Filiality in Rural China', *Comparative Studies in Society and History* 37(1): 110–35.
Laidlaw, J. 2000. 'A Free Gift Makes No Friends', *Journal of the Royal Anthropological Institute* 6(4): 617–34.
Leshkowich, Ann Marie. 2006. 'Woman, Buddhist, Entrepreneur: Gender, Moral Values, and Class Anxiety in Late Socialist Vietnam', *Journal of Vietnamese Studies* 1(1–2): 277–313.
______. 2014. *Essential Trade: Vietnamese Women in a Changing Marketplace.* Honolulu: University of Hawai'i Press.
Malarney, Shaun Frederick. 2002. *Culture, Ritual and Revolution in Vietnam.* London: Routledge.
Marr, D. 2000. 'Concepts of "Individual" and "Self" in Twentieth-Century Vietnam', *Modern Asian Studies* 34(4): 769–96.
McHale, Shawn. 2004. *Print and Power: Confucianism, Communism and Buddhism in the Making of Modern Vietnam.* Honolulu: University of Hawai'i Press.
Monnais, Laurence, C. Michelle Thompson and Ayo Wahlberg (eds). 2011. *Southern Medicine for Southern People: Vietnamese Medicine in the Making.* Newcastle upon Tyne: Cambridge Scholars Publishing.
Pettus, Ashley. 2004. *Between Sacrifice and Desire: National Identity and the Governing of Femininity in Vietnam.* New York: Routledge.
Ramaswamy, Sumathi. 2002. 'Visualising India's Geo-Body: Globes, Maps, Bodyscapes', *Contributions to Indian Sociology (n.s.)* 36(1–2): 151–89.
Rydstrom, Helle. 2003. *Embodying Morality: Growing Up in Rural Northern Vietnam.* Honolulu: University of Hawai'i.
______. 2020. 'Disasters, Ruins, and Crises: Masculinity and Ramifications of Storms in Vietnam', *Ethnos* 85(2): 351–70.
Schlecker, Marcus, and Kirsten Endres. 2011. 'Psychic Experience, Truth, and Visuality in Postwar Vietnam', *Social Analysis* 55(1): 1–22.
Schwenkel, Christina. 2018. 'Religious Reassemblage and Late Socialist Planning in Urban Vietnam', *Journal of the American Academy of Religion* 86(2): 526–53.
Sidnell, Jack, and Merav Shohet. 2013. 'The Problem of Peers in Vietnamese Interaction', *Journal of the Royal Anthropological Institute* 19(3): 618–38.
Soucy, Alexander. 2012. *The Buddha Side: Gender, Power, and Buddhist Practice in Vietnam.* Honolulu: University of Hawai'i.
Stone, A.B. 2008. '"Overcoming Peasant Backwardness": The Khrushchev Antireligious Campaign and the Rural Soviet Union', *The Russian Review* 67(2): 296–320.
Trần Từ. 1996. *Người Mường ở Hòa Bình* [The Mường People of Hòa Bình]. Hanoi: Hội khoa học lịch sự Việt Nam [Vietnam Historical Society].
Truong Huyen Chi. 2014. 'The Margin Contextualized: Nguyễn Từ Chi (1925–1995) and an Alternative Ethnography in Socialist Vietnam', *Moussons.* Retrieved 20 April 2023 from https://journals.openedition.org/moussons/3116#quotation.
Venkatesen, Soumhya. 2007. 'The Social Life of a "Free Gift"', *American Ethnologist* 38(1): 47–57.
Wahlberg, Ayo. 2014. 'Herbs, Laboratories, and Revolution: On the Making of a National Medicine in Vietnam', *East Asian Science, Technology and Society: An International Journal* (8)1: 43–56.
Werner, Jayne. 2009. *Gender, Household and State in Post-Revolutionary Vietnam.* London: Routledge.

Winichakul, Thongchai. 1994. *Siam Mapped: A History of the Geo-body of a Nation.* Honolulu: University of Hawai'i Press.
Yan, Yunxiang. 1996. *The Flow of Gifts: Reciprocity and Social Networks in a Chinese Village.* Stanford, CA: University Press.

Part II

Asian Transformations and Complexities

3

Soviet-Style Apartment Complexes in Hanoi
An Intellectual Exchange in Architecture

Nguyen Van Huy and Nguyen Vu Hoang

Collective residential apartment complexes (*Khu tập thể*, KTT) have existed as a feature of Hanoi since the early 1960s. Although the new housing blocks, which became such a striking feature of the Hanoi cityscape in the high-socialist era, have been widely represented as a product of one-way knowledge transfers creating unhappy replicas of Soviet design and planning ideas, their construction involved a much more fluid process of interaction and exchange between Vietnamese architects and planners, and the foreign experts with whom they studied and worked. What our research uncovered in particular is a strikingly bold insistence by Vietnamese designers and builders that there were ways to benefit from the novel ideas about cities and urban planning that they were absorbing from their Soviet and other foreign consultants, while advocating the need to reshape what they were taught to fit the distinctiveness of their homeland's unique aesthetic and practical needs. This chapter attempts to elucidate some aspects of this international intellectual exchange that helped Vietnamese architects to become more mature and confident in the process of making residential blocks more relevant to the situation in Vietnam.

This architectural revolution is the result of a process of intellectual exchange between architects of the Soviet Union, North Korea, China and Poland with Vietnamese leaders, managers and particularly architects. Studying this process reveals a consistency with the key themes of the volume and brings a contribution to Susan Bayly's study on how Vietnamese intellectuals connected with Eastern European countries (Bayly 2004). While Bayly points out that Vietnamese intellectuals may possess different kinds of cultural capital, and some of these derived from the French colonial era, she argues that many people do not see it as part of their identities and they, during their employment as development experts in former French and Portuguese colonies in

Africa, leaned towards the relationship with peers from socialist countries in Eastern Europe.

The case of Vietnamese architects in this chapter shows that they actively learnt and creatively changed the acquired construction methods to suit the conditions of Vietnam, particularly the tropical climate and the shortage of building materials during the war (1955–75). With the close relationship between the two socialist countries, North Korea sent a delegation of architects to Hanoi to help make a masterplan for the city. The Korean experts also took the lead on the planning, design and construction of Kim Lien KTT. A team of Vietnamese architects, engineers and construction workers directly participated in this process. They learnt about and received the transfer of technology through many different forms. Moreover, over time, many Vietnamese architects who trained in the Soviet Union, China and Eastern European countries gradually returned. They were able to use the knowledge and methods they had acquired from their professors in different countries to build their home country. So, from the initial passive mode of receiving the new model of neighbourhood units, and the design and construction of Zone A and Zone B in Kim Lien, Vietnamese architects gradually progressed and took the initiative in the design of the residential apartment complexes. The revised plans consisted of four- to five-storey residential blocks, organized into smaller and self-contained apartments more suitable to the living conditions of Vietnamese families. They also used the large panel method of assembly to construct blocks that were more durable and quicker to build. This was the result of a process of exchange, learning, absorbing and creativity for the Vietnamese architects.

When talking about KTTs in Hanoi, many people take for granted that this refers to the Soviet-style apartment blocks. Many of these have been demolished in the last ten to fifteen years to make way for structures considered more modern and appropriate for the city's future. Yet the common view of them as 'Soviet' structures, and as the product of a one-way transmission of alien and inappropriate ideas about urban housing to a set of uncritical and passive Vietnamese recipients, is very far from the reality of how those actually involved in the building projects conceived of their work and aims. Each KTT has its own story that distinguishes it from the original concept. This chapter will explain the formation of KTTs in Hanoi and show how they have been the result of intellectual exchange between Vietnam and other socialist countries.

Background and Context: Housing in Hanoi

Until 1954, when President Ho Chi Minh's victorious liberation forces made Hanoi the capital of the revolutionary nation state, the Democratic Republic of Viet Nam (DRV), the city had been the French colonial government's administrative headquarters, with a comparatively small permanent population concentrated mostly in the densely populated commercial area called the Old Quarter. Thus, what the city urgently needed at the end of the nine-year anti-French Resistance War (1946–54) was residential accommodation for a growing wave of incomers from the countryside and the Viet Bac northern resistance zone, including young people recruited to serve as state officials and factory workers. Increasing numbers of both teachers and students also arrived as the city became a major centre for the country's fast-expanding educational initiatives. The DRV initially used requisitioned colonial-era residences for schemes of state-run allocation housing. But by the mid-1950s the idea of purpose-built, multi-storey apartment blocks became an increasingly attractive prospect for those engaged in these ambitious city planning initiatives. The first apartment blocks, called *nhà tập thể* and *khu tập thể*, were completed in 1956 on greenfield sites outside the Red River dyke embankment that had previously marked the outer boundary of the city.

From 1954 to 1955 the city entered a period of economic recovery, renovation and socialist construction. For the first time, North Vietnam, especially Hanoi, gradually transformed into a new socialist society. The important task for the development of Hanoi was to turn a city, with a low levels of production and service, into a political and cultural centre, balancing the development of industry and agriculture (Le Van Lan 2010: 33). In general, Hanoi at that time had formed two distinct zones with different architecture and lifestyles. First, the Old Quarter neighbourhood, located to the north of Hoan Kiem Lake, was formed. It was the place for people earning a living by trade, service and handicraft production to serve the lives of Hanoi residents and later the French. The houses in this neighbourhood were often built to have one or two storeys, with the first floor dedicated to streetside shops or manufacturing facilities. Second, the French Quarter (*khu phố Tây*), to the south of Hoan Kiem Lake, which stretched west to the West Lake, was formed at the end of the nineteenth century and was almost completed in the 1930s–40s. This area was planned, designed and built by the French during the colonial period (1884–1945) (Phan Phuong Thao and Nguyen Thi Binh 2017: 33–35). This was mainly an office area, where French officials and their families lived: upper-class Vietnamese, mandarins, officials working for the French, doctors, engineers, architects, physicians or emerging rich people. They lived in French-style villas, with gardens and fences, in neatly divided land plots, with each plot about 300–600 or 700 square metres (Phan Phuong Thao and Nguyen Thi Binh 2017: 36; Ta Thi Hoang Van 2017: 290). Shops, services and cultural institutions such as theatres, museums and galleries were built separately from residential areas. These two quarters were surrounded by villages and rice fields. Being the two main areas in the city, the Old Quarter and the French Quarter helped create the image of Hanoi until 1955.

The concept of collective apartment blocks was born in this period in 1955. The government had many ways to provide accommodation for the increasing number of cadres, workers and state employees. On the one hand, the state used abandoned villas whose former owners who had moved to the South, or houses that had belonged to the bourgeoisie, or large houses that had been distributed to officials. Many of these single-owner, one-family villas were turned into houses with many subjects and families living together. On the other hand, the city government started to build new residential areas separate from the Old Quarter and the French Quarter. The first collective apartment blocks were built in a space near the city centre, outside the Red River dyke. The Riverbank collective residential area (*khu tập thể Bờ sông*), designed by the architect Tran Huu Tiem (1912–84), was completed in 1956. These were two-storey blocks, all with large rooms, arranged in parallel to accommodate a group of people in a collective, or areas that were later divided between families (Dang Thai Hoang 1985). Each house had a common auxiliary area (kitchen, toilet, bathroom) separated by a yard (Le Van Lan 2010: 33–34). Nearby were one-storey collective apartment blocks on the banks of the Red River, in An Duong and Phuc Xa (north and northwest of Hanoi).

The period from 1959 to 1960 was the starting point for the construction of new-style urban centres in Hanoi. New collective apartment blocks (KTTs) were built on a larger scale in suburban areas. Some were small areas of about 3–6 hectares, and others were larger at about 40–50 hectares. The basics of the neighbourhood unit model in the Soviet Union as described in Buchli's and Humphrey's work can be observed in these buildings in Hanoi (Buchli 1998, 1999; Humphrey 2005). The process of implementing this model of housing subdivision lasted for four decades (1960–1990s). Under the command economy, the state implemented a subsidized housing policy for officials, workers and employees from the state budget. The construction of KTTs only ended when the renovation era (*Đổi mới*) began in 1986 (this era lasted until around 1990). The country then entered a new period, the period of socialist-oriented market economic development. The state also terminated the distribution of housing for officials and employees. KTT apartments owned by the state were gradually sold to tenants. The development of this type of housing subdivision basically came to an end at this point.

From the 1960s until 1990, Hanoi built about forty KTTs housing nearly two hundred thousand people (Duong Duc Tuan 2005: 4). These KTTs occupied an area of about 750 hectares in Hanoi city. In terms of living floor area, the total space of these apartment blocks was nearly five million square metres, roughly 50 per cent of the city's housing supply (Duong Duc Tuan 2005: 4). Most KTTs were planned for outside the core of the capital. During this period, a new, large and important space of the capital Hanoi was formed (Duong Duc Tuan 2005: 24). The KTT quarters became a new structural element of the city along with the Old Quarter and the French Quarter. The network of KTTs became the new residential areas, the new urban centres of Hanoi.

The following section will continue to unpack the concept of KTTs in Vietnam and shed light on the ways in which each KTT was constructed. First, the chapter discusses the way in which the KTT model was introduced into Vietnam and emphasizes the role of Vietnamese architects in the process of design and in exchanges with Soviet architects. It then moves on to discuss the transfer of a building method from North Korean experts to Vietnamese architects and engineers in the case of Kim Lien KTT. With diligence and proactiveness, Vietnamese architects invented new ways to produce prefabricated panels for quick construction. The new construction method helped to save time, money and labour, and also resolved the problem of housing in the 1970s–80s. The chapter ends with a section discussing how the KTT has been the product of intellectual exchange between foreign and Vietnamese experts.

Towards a New Architecture

In the years 1959–60, the issues of capital planning were raised frequently, but urban planning was a relatively new field for city officials and many architects. Therefore, the Government of Vietnam, for the first time, invited a delegation of Soviet experts from Moscow to help plan the city of Hanoi and a delegation of Chinese experts to help design the National Assembly house, following a new plan for the capital near the West Lake (Le Van Lan 2010: 49–50). The number of Vietnamese architects at that time was very limited. There were only eighteen architects in North Vietnam who had been trained in the French colonial period, fourteen of whom were working in Hanoi's Department of Architecture.[1] Four architects worked for the Section on Urban Affairs in this Department.[2] The architects of the department were assigned the task of drafting the plan for Hanoi. Architect Hoang Nhu Tiep (deputy head of the department) along with Ngo Huy Quynh, who belonged to the generation of French-trained architects (having graduated from the Indochina College of Fine Arts in 1943) and was also the first architect in Vietnam to earn a graduate degree from a university in the Soviet Union (1951–55), participated in the drafting of the central planning for Hanoi in 1959 with the help of Soviet experts (Ngo Huy Quynh 2020: 19). Because Vietnam was very inexperienced within the planning field, architect Demmetkovsky, the head of the Hanoi expert delegation from the Soviet Union, organized a training course for urban planning officials, leaders, architects and engineers of the Ministry of Architecture and Hanoi City. The concepts, principles and urban planning of the socialist system, the theory of neighbourhood units and sub-zones as a basic component in the urban structure, and experiences in the Soviet Union were widely introduced.[3] After a short period of close coordination between Soviet and Vietnamese architects, a draft plan for the capital's centre was presented to President Ho Chi Minh and other leaders in 1960 (Le Van Lan 2010: 46). In the same year, a draft plan was also created for the capital by the West Lake, chaired by architects Demmetkovsky and Ngo Huy Quynh, and a plan for Ba Dinh Square was developed by Ngo Huy Quynh and Le Van Lan (Le Van Lan 2010: 49). These plans became the foundation for the establishment of residential areas, industrial areas and river ports.

The birth and development of apartment buildings in Hanoi in the 1960s was greatly influenced by the theory of planning from the housing subdivision model or the neighbourhood unit. This was a completely new model of residence and housing that was different from the Indochina architecture during the French colonial period. While the French villas and the chessboard design of the streets were the key points of the French design in Hanoi in the early 1900s, the housing subdivision model was the predominant one from 1960 to 1990. At this time, the Soviet Union and other socialist countries were relying on this neighbourhood unit theory to implement the settlement of housing and urban development after World War II (Buchli 1998; Humphrey 2005). The neighbourhood unit theory was developed at the beginning of the twentieth century to create housing complexes consisting of many groups of houses gathered in one area and which contain essential social infrastructure facilities such as schools, playgrounds and shops. It created many subdivisions of urban settlements in a larger city. Clarence Perry was the person who put this model into practice in New York (USA) in 1929, and since then this model continued to be developed in European countries. In the 1950s, the Soviet Union absorbed and developed the theory of neighbourhood units from European countries and the United States and then expanded its application to China, Korea and other socialist countries (Tran Minh Tung 2016: 34). The model of housing subdivisions allowed millions of people to settle in the Soviet Union and other countries after World War II (Han Tat Ngan 1990: 32). Vietnam also received such assistance, and the planners, architects and engineers of the Soviet Union, North Korea, China and Poland worked and exchanged information with Vietnamese architects in Hanoi in the years 1958–60. KTTs or the collective housing complexes in Hanoi were born in such a context.

The idea of planning and building apartment complexes in the model of sub-residential housing was completely new to Vietnamese architects. However, in the process of learning and absorbing experience in planning and design from other countries, Vietnamese architects wondered how to build a new urban architecture while still maintaining some of the inherited architectural traditions of the nation. More than sixty years have passed, and only a few articles and documents have shared in detail how these concerns were handled while new construction plans were implemented in Hanoi. Fortunately, recently, the family of Ngo Huy Quynh, who participated in the planning of Kim Lien KTT, handed his personal files over to the Center for Heritage of Vietnamese Scientists (Ngo Huy Quynh 2020: 140). Studying these files revealed two valuable documents related to this situation.

The first of Ngo Huy Quynh's documents was the *Draft of Opinions Exchanged with Architectural Workers in Poland – Outline* (hereafter abbreviated to *Polish Outline*) of the Vietnamese Architectural Delegation for a trip to Poland before 1960. The trip was organized for a group of Vietnamese architects aimed at cultural exchange activities, mainly learning about experiences in planning and architecture. Studying the *Polish Outline* helps illuminate the thoughts of architect Ngo Huy Quynh in particular and Vietnamese architects in general on issues of planning and developing new urban areas. The *Polish Outline* also displayed the intellectual exchange with experts from socialist countries in creating a modern, socialist Vietnamese architecture. The surprise was that the author of the *Polish Outline* clearly identified the attitude of Vietnamese architects in exchanging knowledge with foreign experts, which was seen not as one-way, but more as 'critical' learning. The document demonstrates that it was a very open and equal way of working. This equal status was mentioned in Ngo Huy Quynh's words to the delegation: 'In general, [our] attitude is mainly to study modestly. But the examination of the problem and, above all, the application of the Polish cultural and artistic experience must be seen with a critical mind' (Ngo Huy Quynh 1960: 1). In the context of underdeveloped urban architecture and construction, Ngo Huy Quynh showed a very proactive attitude in exchanging knowledge and studying with colleagues abroad. He wanted to interact with the Polish architects by introducing 'the inheritance of the Vietnamese national architecture and draw[ing] lessons to help us create the new architecture, develop a new life, a new technology' (Ngo Huy Quynh 1960: 1)[4] 'as a basis for the initial discussion on the direction of new architectural creation in the architectural world in Vietnam' (Ngo Huy Quynh 1960: 8). He expressed his hope that in this dialogue, Polish architects would 'contribute more, give opinions on theory', and on 'how to use inherited capital in architectural and urban design work' (Ngo Huy Quynh 1960: 8).

Architect Ngo Huy Quynh expressed his support for a Vietnamese typicalization approach in architecture. The typicalization approach was understood as utilizing traditional methods to design and construct architectural work in Vietnam. He tried to argue that typical houses or same-styled houses did not always make the city look boring. He told the Polish architects that, 'With new construction, it is necessary to promote the tradition of typical construction' (Ngo Huy Quynh 1960: 6). Not only developing the concept, he also gave an idea of how to create an identity for the city when building typical types of houses with trees and water. Ngo Huy Quynh voiced a desire for a modern city in the future: 'Extensively using trees and water as factors not only creates a comfortable life in hot climate conditions but also makes the city more beautiful, having its own nuances of a tropical city' (Ngo Huy Quynh 1960: 8). This idea is shared by Ross King (2009) who discussed how architecture must adapt to the climate, and temperate conditions in Malaysia. Moreover, King also mentioned that *kampong* (the village) in Kuala Lumpur was seen as a dynamic part of the urban condition rather than something that was to be ignored. In fact, Ngo Huy Quynh's concept of typical design was later accepted widely, becoming a way to rapidly develop architectural works in urban areas in Vietnam. Architect Le Van Lan assessed the idea in the following way: 'The typical design work has contributed to speeding up construction significantly. Models of large slab houses, schools, kindergartens, cinemas ... have been built in many places' (Le Van Lan 1984: 15).

In the *Polish Outline*, Ngo Huy Quynh also emphasized the compatibility between architecture and people. From there, he made the following observations, which are in fact two very important orientations for Vietnam's urban architecture: '(1) Architecture with an intentionally largescale, frivolous design in an urban setting is not compatible with Vietnamese architecture. It can't be the way for new architecture and urbanism. (2) Vietnamese architecture is inseparable from nature, merging into the scenery of rivers, mountains and trees; renovating nature into a new setting for human life ... architecture uses rivers, mountains, trees (landscape) as an important part of architectural work' (Ngo Huy Quynh 1960: 7). His observations were crucial in discussions with Polish architects as it showed that Vietnamese architects did not passively accept the experience of international colleagues, but also had a critical view towards the global trends and the local, natural conditions in Vietnam.

The second document to explore is the outline of the talk on 'Nationality in Architecture and Urban Architecture' (hereafter abbreviated as *Hanoi Outline*) by architect Ngo Huy Quynh. He prepared this outline in December 1961 to present to Vietnamese architects. The *Hanoi Outline* consisted of only two pages but still showed the continuation of his thoughts and concerns about nationalism in modern, urban architecture. If the context of the *Polish Outline* was 'we had little experience in construction, not yet summed up', then at the end of 1961 the *Hanoi Outline* stated 'we have constructed quite a lot, there is merit in the new structures, but they do not demonstrate clear national characteristics'. What he hoped for was the development of a new kind of architecture for Hanoi that was both modern and recognizably Vietnamese in sensibility. Ngo Huy Quynh wanted to share with his colleagues the direction he envisaged in order to clarify 'the unclear national characteristics'. In this document, he specifically analysed the experiences of creativity in architecture in Vietnam, the Soviet Union and China. He pinpointed five aspects for thinking about national architecture: (1) The curved roof is a characteristic, but it is not the only one; (2) National characteristics can be seen in many other durable elements: climate, heat, cold, traditional aesthetics; (3) Nationality can be seen in the daily lifestyle of the people; (4) There is a fluid change on the surface/outside of national architecture; and (5) There is a need to avoid formalism, and the wasting of material. Still with a critical spirit, he not only mentioned successes but also pointed out some aberrations in architecture in other countries through the introduction and analysis with pictures, and at the same time pointed out the causes of the five points above (Ngo Huy Quynh 1961: 1). Unfortunately, we do not have the details of the specific analysis and criticism on record.

The last part of the talk focuses on a particularly important point that he wanted to make to the audience, which was suggestions for the direction of constructing a national architecture. In promoting the national spirit, he was particularly interested in three factors: '(a) Climate research to improve or adapt to the climate of houses and cities. (b) Using nature, trees, lakes and ponds, monsoons and sunshine. (c) Utilising previous experiences in houses, villages and ancient architecture' (Ngo Huy Quynh 1961: 2).

With the spirit of both learning and actively absorbing international experience, Ngo Huy Quynh wanted to 'adopt the achievements of the world's progressive architecture' (Ngo Huy Quynh 1961: 2). On the one hand, he called for a criticism of cosmopolitan architecture, constructivism, a form of architecture in the Soviet Union in the 1920s–30s, aiming to construct spaces for the creation of the new socialist utopia. On the other hand, he requested others to 'learn from experience in renovating and adapting to the climate in socialist countries, and tropical countries in Africa, and South America' (Ngo Huy Quynh 1961: 2). Ngo Huy Quynh's vision towards the future perspective of national architecture showed his interests in learning with a critical mind. However, it was not only Ngo Huy Quynh who had this vision; other Vietnamese architects also took this approach. In a newspaper interview, architect Le Van Lan made positive comments about the intellectual exchange between architects of the Soviet Union and other socialist countries and Vietnamese architects:

> Being Brother countries, first of all, the Soviet Union helped us design and build many buildings of important economic, political, cultural, and scientific significance. In general, the authors of the projects have made great efforts to understand the nature and people of Vietnam, expressing sincere feelings and responsibilities. Certainly, our colleagues also encountered many difficulties when solving architectural problems for a humid tropical area, approaching a series of problems about buildability, manageability, usage habits, and aesthetic tastes ... The most precious thing for us is that in addition to receiving great material and technical value, we have acquired relevant concepts, thoughts and methods to resolve issues boldly and resolutely; ingenious proportions in large and modern building scales; including the use of new materials and equipment. ... Through such support, the team of architects and technicians grew larger, more experienced, and able to use advanced computing and research tools. (Le Van Lan 1984: 17)

This section has shown an important aspect of intellectual exchange through the case of Vietnamese architects. It has demonstrated the attitude of early participants in training and learning sessions with foreign socialist experts, indicating that they considered themselves to be partners in a process of interaction and dialogue, rather than passive recipients of rules and inflexible models. The case of architect Ngo Huy Quynh has helped to point out the role of the French-educated generation in the postcolonial period in Vietnam. The point is that Ngo did not passively receive knowledge from the Soviet, Polish experts, but rather he actively contributed to the vision of both foreign and Vietnamese leading architects in promoting a vision of nationality when proposing architecture projects. The next section will examine the case of the Kim Lien housing complex, from which readers can see the stream of intellectual exchange between two socialist countries. It discusses how these perceptions were applied in the process to the actual construction of new housing complexes, showing that when the new initiatives got underway, there continued to be a dialogic process of exchange in what the planners and architects thought and did.

Apartment Blocks Built with North Korean Advice

As mentioned above, KTTs in their current form started to be constructed from 1959 to 1960. This opened a new era in terms of residential organization and lifestyle. The demand for quick construction of a series of buildings to meet the urgent need for accommodation raised many problems not only in planning but also in architectural design, construction techniques and building materials. Because Vietnam had no experience in constructing four- to five-storey buildings, President Ho Chi Minh and the Government of Vietnam invited North Korean experts to help design and build a residential housing complex in Hanoi to be called Kim Lien KTT. It was the first neighbourhood unit or subdivision to be constructed in Hanoi. The North Korean government sent architects, engineers and construction workers, led by Kim Pong Su, General Architect, to Hanoi to implement this task from 1959 to 1965. The North Korean group of architects and construction engineers worked mainly with Vietnamese architects from the Department of Urban and Rural Affairs, Ministry of Construction. At that time, the director was the engineer Nguyen Van Than, and the deputy director was the architect Hoang Nhu Tiep. Ta My Duat was in charge of the Hanoi team. This was the first group of foreign experts to help design a modern housing project in Hanoi and transfer the construction technique for building four-storey houses into the North of Vietnam. The case of Kim Lien KTT helps us to explore the ways in which Vietnamese architects acquired knowledge and technology from a socialist country.

The Kim Lien KTT area, which was originally the rice field of Kim Lien village on the outskirts of Hanoi, was about fifty hectares in size (Kim Lien People's Committee 2012). It is now located in Đống Đa, a central district of Hanoi. Korean experts and Vietnamese architects planned, designed and built the Kim Lien apartment complex. In 1959, architect Ta My Duat signed the planning document for the Kim Lien area.[5] According to the original design, this area consisted of 22 four-storey buildings/blocks. Several blocks were grouped into a neighbourhood divided into zones, named with the letters A to E. This area now has 67 four-storey buildings, of which Zone A has five buildings, Zone B twenty-five buildings, Zone C eight buildings, Zone D twelve buildings, and Zone E seventeen buildings.[6] It is said to be home to 2,600 households. The initial housing construction area was 84,400 square metres, and was arranged in the form of neighbourhood units, with residential apartment blocks, kindergartens, schools, stadiums, department stores and sewerage water systems (Le Van Lan 2010: 37).

North Korean experts directly designed and built the blocks in Zone A according to North Korean standards. The average distance between two blocks according to the original design is about 30 metres (Duong Duc Tuan 2005: 130). For the first time, a complete neighbourhood unit model, with functions including residential apartment blocks, canteens, department stores and schools, was transferred to Vietnamese architects. Thanks to the experience of designing and building Zone A with Korean experts, blocks in other zones of the Kim Lien area were redesigned by Vietnamese architects in Hanoi, forming a new urban face of the capital. Dao Ngoc Nghiem, former chief architect of Hanoi, commented, 'The architecture of the neighbourhood unit brought into play its strengths. Zone A, in particular, built entirely by Korean experts, had a spacious layout, a lot of greenery, creating conditions to build into the current Kim Lien hotel'.[7]

In 2012, Kim Lien People's Committee published a book entitled *Revolutionary History of the Party Committee and People of Kim Lien Ward* . It devoted a section to how Kim Lien KTT was built. It states: 'At first, officials and construction workers were very worried because their technical skills were still low and they had no experience in constructing multi-storey buildings by modern assembly methods' (Kim Lien People's Committee 2012: 29). Understanding the worries of the Vietnamese team, comrade Kim Pong Su, general engineer of the delegation of Korean experts, said: 'We were like you, but we had received technical help from the Soviet Union, so we knew how to assemble before you. But in order to have the assembly industry, we had to invest a lot of money for equipment. Therefore, we will share the technical factors, and the experience of North Korea and the Soviet Union, with all our Vietnamese comrades' (Kim Lien People's Committee 2012: 29). With the dedicated help of North Korean experts and the learning spirit of the command team and the site workers, in a short time a complete construction site was organized in the following manner: 'self-manufacturing material components on the spot and putting them into construction and installation right at the construction site, without having to buy them abroad or process them at other establishments; This is also the first pilot project of prefab construction in Hanoi' (Kim Lien People's Committee 2012: 29). The process of making prefabricated panels for Kim Lien KTT reflected the intellectual exchange between Vietnamese engineers and foreign experts. This issue will be discussed in the later section on large panel installation.

In our interview with Prof. Nguyen Quoc Thong, vice chairman of the Vietnam Association of Architects, he told us that Kim Lien KTT was the first complete model of apartment blocks designed by North Korea (personal interview, 21 April 2021). This model still exists in Pyongyang, North Korea. The Trung Tu, Nam Dong, Giang Vo, Thanh Cong and Thanh Xuan KTTs were later designed and built by the Vietnamese in the 1970s, incorporating certain improvements to suit the natural conditions, the climate and specific socio-economic conditions. In terms of planning, groups of residential blocks with kindergartens at the centre were designed to be more diverse in space, while paying attention to natural environmental conditions. For example, more buildings were constructed to be able to utilize the south or southeast wind; or there were different sizes of apartment to suit the diverse range of household sizes.[8] In certain conditions, a lake, a social communication space – as in the case of Giang Vo KTT – was deemed suitable for the climatic conditions and lifestyle of the residents, creating the characteristics of the urban area. In terms of interior architecture, the apartments with full facilities such as kitchens and bathrooms were diverse in size. The architecture of the blocks also changed. Vietnamese architects studied and contributed to the diversity and unique characteristics of each KTT (personal interview with Nguyen Quoc Thong, 24 April 2021).

Even in the present day, the residents of Kim Lien KTT often praise North Korea's architectural standards. They were especially impressed by the wide spacing between the blocks, considering it an important highlight left by Korean architects in Kim Lien. The Trung Tu area, built around the 1970s, designed by Vietnamese architects ten years after Kim Lien KTT, essentially kept the requirements for space between the blocks. The distance between the blocks was transferred from the Korean architects. Therefore, when looking from one block to another, it does not seem too close.

The case of Kim Lien KTT shows that the network of socialist countries was very effective in exchanging knowledge among intellectuals. Not only did Vietnamese intellectuals benefit from learning in universities and at convocational schools, but techniques, machines and other materials were also transferred. The Vietnamese architects were first the receivers of knowledge in Kim Lien KTT, but they actively applied this acquired knowledge to the particular conditions of Vietnam in the latter phase when building Trung Tu, Giang Vo and Thanh Cong KTTs. The next section delineates the struggle of Vietnamese architects for more privacy and convenience in these later KTTs.

Shared or Private Kitchen, Toilet and Bathroom: A Long-Term Struggle

Comparing the interior design of each apartment in Kim Lien KTT with other, later KTTs such as Trung Tu or Giang Vo, reflects the dynamic exchange involved in the planning and construction. For the living space in Kim Lien, according to the design of the Korean architects, on each floor there were two apartments on each side of the stairs. Each two-room apartment had a kitchen and a toilet, a bathroom separate from the living room in the entrance area. The area of each room was 18.2 square metres, with two large gable rooms, about 19.7 and 21.1 square metres (Dang Thai Hoang 1985: 39). The apartments were distributed by the state to officials, workers and public employees, initially according to salary and position, later taking into account the number of family members.[9] In fact, at that time only mid-level officials (department heads) could be allocated a two-room apartment, senior officials (deputy ministers) two apartments each, while the majority of officials and employees often lived together in shared apartments, or two families shared an apartment or even shared a room. In the early 1980s, the proportion of households sharing apartments/rooms in Kim Lien was about 61 per cent (Dang Thai Hoang 1985: 39). Certainly, single people living in the same room or apartment had to share kitchen, toilets and bathrooms. Many collective apartment blocks built later catered to the same lifestyle. This was the result of housing being built without fully considering the acceptable standard of living and actual usability. While many residents considered the KTTs to be desirable alternatives to the rural or urban accommodation they were familiar with, it was the sharing of bathrooms and kitchens, intended as a basis for the creation of a collectively-minded new socialist person, that were thought of as alien to the Vietnamese way of life with its emphasis on the values and virtues of the family. Consequently, this was widely resented and is still remembered as an unwelcome and problematic part of KTT life.

In 1968–69, during the anti-American war, architect Truong Tung and his colleagues were assigned the design of a new housing complex project for Hanoi. He and his team took the opportunity to insert a totally different plan for interior spatial design into the scheme. Drawing on Kim Lien KTT's experience, he did not design a space of four to five large rooms; instead he built an apartment with two small rooms, designed with its own private kitchen and bathroom. According to the design standards at that time, six square metres were allocated for the common kitchen, so when he designed six households with separate kitchens, toilets and bathrooms, the private kitchens were only one square metre. Truong Tung became a pioneer in creating the self-contained apartment with a separate kitchen, toilet and bathroom in KTTs. In our interview with him in 2021, Truong Tung explained that he was prompted to make this decision because he had actual experience of sharing a kitchen, toilet and bathroom, and understood the inconvenience for people who had to share ancillary facilities. He said that after gaining his doctoral degree in the Soviet Union, and returning home in 1966, for the first four years he lived in a three-storey block in the Van Chuong residential apartment blocks. He and his wife had one bedroom, sharing the kitchen and bathroom with four to five other households. Every morning he had to wait for someone else to finish cooking before he could take his turn; not to mention that he had to wait in line to use the toilet. He recalled: 'So at that time, I thought a lot, I just want to make separate kitchens, toilets and bathrooms for each family so that the people won't suffer' (personal interview, 29 July 2021). On the other hand, Truong Tung not only experienced self-contained apartments when he studied in the Soviet Union, but he also studied self-contained apartments in many other countries. He still keeps a very valuable file that he brought back from the Soviet Union, which includes twenty-one floor plans of prefab houses according to the different types of apartments. Most of the space layout drawings in these self-contained apartments are houses from towns or cities in non-socialist countries such as Rotterdam, the Netherlands (1934, 1949), Chicago, USA (1952), London, England (1953), Antwerp, Belgium (1954), Kember, England (undated) and Karacas, Venezuela (undated). Thanks to these diagrams, he persuaded Vietnamese leaders to try to popularize the advanced method of building prefab houses and organizing apartments. The design of a self-contained apartment with a separate kitchen, toilet and bathroom was built as an experiment in the Van Chuong collective area, then in Truong Dinh, Trung Tu and in many other areas.

Truong Tung's design of the self-contained apartments was not an easy process. Architect Trinh Hong Trien later summed it up: 'The road to the "self-contained apartments" suitable today was a long struggle of exploration, experimentation, summary, policy formulation, and developing standards' (Trinh Hong Trien 1984: 22). In fact, the design standards issued in 1969 still stated that two small apartments should share an auxiliary area (kitchen, toilet and bathroom). However, many designs from this period until 1976 included the private auxiliary area in large apartments.

After the pilot period, in 1973 in a housing design contest, the State Construction Committee and the Ministry of Architecture (now the Ministry of Construction) selected seven residential models in the style of 'independent apartments'. A year later, in 1974, this committee and the Institute of Construction Science chose six designs for households. Hanoi became a pioneer for the study and construction of housing complex projects (Tran Minh Tung 2016: 20). In 1977, the government officially introduced the design standards for housing construction in which 'each allocated family must have an individual kitchen and washroom' (Government of Vietnam 1977, Decree No. 150-CP).

The struggle for the inclusion of private auxiliary areas in an apartment for one household took about ten years. Architect Tran Minh Tung also considered it as the creative acquisition of Vietnamese architects in terms of adjusting the small area to suit the living standards in Vietnam. He pointed out that in the traditional space organization of the Vietnamese people, the kitchen, toilet and bathroom were secondary spaces, often arranged separately from the living space. In the beginning in the collective residential houses, therefore, this auxiliary zone was arranged separately from the main residential block. Later, it was integrated into the main residential block but still separated from the living space. Finally, the new kitchen, toilet and bathroom were included in the apartment, forming a self-contained apartment (Tran Minh Tung 2016: 21). In the process of dealing with the relationship between the living rooms and the space for the kitchen, toilet and bathroom, there has been a step-by-step change over several decades. This relationship clearly shows the transformation from the riverside collective houses to the Kim Lien, Nguyen Cong Tru and finally the Trung Tu and Giang Vo KTTs. Tran Minh Tung calls it the process of becoming 'more Vietnamese' or 'Vietnamization', and a move towards 'modern' apartments (Tran Minh Tung 2016: 20, 138). This process reflects the active role of Vietnamese architects and engineers in adapting an apartment design from foreign architecture to meet the needs and usage of Vietnamese people.

The Story of Large Prefabricated Panel Construction

The design of living space was not the only arena in which Vietnamese architects showed ingenuity; aspects of the construction process were also subject to inventive reformulation. This section will highlight the innovative ideas of

Vietnamese architects under the conditions of a country in wartime. It helps show the clever application of Soviet construction knowledge in Vietnamese conditions.

In 1960, the first four-storey house in Zones A and B of Kim Lien KTT was built with small prefabricated concrete panels, 20 cm thick load (Dang Thai Hoang 1985: 39). This was the first project to apply mechanized construction methods with the help of North Korean experts. The prefabricated structure was made of large-sized cinder-concrete wall blocks and reinforced concrete floor and roof panels. Meanwhile, four-storey houses in Nguyen Cong Tru KTT and other areas at that time were mainly built with brick walls and floors with reinforced concrete cast.

In 1970, nearly ten years after the first building of Kim Lien KTT, architect Truong Tung and his colleagues creatively applied the method of assembling large-panel houses with concrete frame slag. In 1966, Truong Tung had defended his PhD thesis entitled 'Design and Construction of Industrialized Houses in Hanoi' in Moscow, Soviet Union. At that time the Soviet Union was in a boom period of large-panel house assembly. The construction technology here was highly mechanized, manufacturing panels in the factory and assembling large-panel houses by mechanization. Truong Tung was able to intern in many concrete casting factories in Moscow and Kiev. When he arrived in Tbilisi, Georgia, he learned how to cast concrete at the site, on the ground, using the heat of the sun.

When he returned to Vietnam, many buildings including residential structures in Hanoi had been destroyed by American bombing raids. He said that if the government wanted to build quickly, they would have to use a prefabricated technique. However, construction in Vietnam was still being done by manual labour. He proposed and chaired the implementation of a pilot project for a two-storey building constructed from prefabricated concrete panels to be built on the campus of Hanoi's University of Science and Technology in Bach Khoa commune in 1970. Truong Tung said that he once went out onto the banks of the Red River and saw that people had thrown away excess coal slag from a power plant. He said: 'They throw away what I need!' (personal interview, 29 July 2021). He proposed making the panel out of concrete and slag. This new prefabricated slab combines concrete and slag concrete rather than only slag concrete, because a slag concrete slab could not withstand bombing. But how to make these large panels without a factory? He applied his experience from Georgia, taking advantage of the hot and humid climate in Vietnam to cast large slabs of concrete on the ground at the construction site, creating prefabricated structures that could be installed immediately. Truong Tung commented: 'Compared to the building panels that North Korea made for us in Kim Lien, our panels are much larger. We can build one room for every four panels. As for the North Korean way, they built large blocks of bricks into a room. They also made slag concrete, about 20 cm thick, while our concrete slab was only 10 cm thick, but very sturdy' (personal interview, 29 July 2021).

To assemble the large concrete slabs at that time, Truong Tung only had a wheeled crane used to salvage collapsed buildings after the war. This wheeled crane needs be anchored with a stone to keep the base heavy to prevent it from tipping over. After the completion of the house in Bach Khoa, this team started piloting in Van Chuong and then Truong Dinh, Trung Tu and many other places. In 1972, during construction of a two-storey house in Truong Dinh, the area was bombed by the US. The main area affected by the bomb was the second floor, but the house did not collapse. Truong Tung said: 'While we were cleaning the scene, people kept rushing in. I asked them, "What are you wanting to see?" They replied: "To see if the house is durable!"'.

Truong Tung's memories are supplemented with a document written at the time of the implementation of his projects. Fortunately, within the files from Professor Dr Nguyen Van Huong (1927–96), which are kept at the Center for Heritage of Vietnamese Scientists, there is a handwritten paper titled *The Problem of Building Housing for People and Officials in Hanoi.*[10] This paper was written by Professor Nguyen Van Huong to present at the National Assembly meeting on 24 March 1972. Professor Nguyen Van Huong at that time was Vice Rector of Hanoi University of Civil Engineering (1971–77), where architect Truong Tung was a lecturer. From 1969, Truong Tung was the head of the experimental research team on prefabricated houses in Hanoi, with close cooperation between the University of Civil Engineering and the University of Architecture. Professor Huong said that this team had 'the task of researching [everything] from building materials to the design and construction of houses and then setting out the industrial procedure for construction sites to construct a series of factories' (Nguyen Van Huong 1972).

This paper presented the methods for building new houses and ensuring that they could be constructed quickly as well as being durable and economical; this was what the research team of Dr Truong Tung had been implementing. It pointed out that if the experiment was successful, it would contribute to speeding up the construction of a modern city. Professor Huong assessed the situation: 'This is a modern method that is different from the usual pour-in-place method, allowing large batches of wall and floor panels to be cast at the construction site and then reassembled without the need for moulds and scaffolding at the site. It helped overcome the lack of materials such as wood and plank. The assembly was mostly done by mechanized methods, implementing lines and specialist techniques at some stages. As a result, it is possible to increase construction speed, which cannot be achieved by traditional methods, as well as reduce the time to train workers' (Nguyen Van Huong 1972). He pointed out that in Kim Lien KTT, with the help of North Korean experts, the blocks were built by small plate assembly. This was not as good as the new method.

In fact, after three years of piloting the new construction method that architect Truong Tung had brought back from Moscow and had applied creatively in Hanoi, the volume of housing in Hanoi increased significantly. Professor Huong reported that by early 1972, 'Hanoi had built 70,000 square metres of housing by this method. In 1971 alone, 40,000 m^2 was built, mainly prefab houses with 4–5 floors. The house style was also gradually improved from two floors to five floors. Each apartment was equipped with bathrooms, toilets and kitchens, which were convenient for living' (Nguyen Van Huong 1972).

Architect Trinh Hong Trien later also assessed the application of this new construction method: 'The large-panel assembly method has many creative applications suitable for the material and technical conditions of our country. This structural system with simple joints, which is easy to construct, has been tested through the American bombs in 1972 in Truong Dinh area. Five-storey prefab houses were built on a large scale in Giang Vo, Trung Tu, Thanh Cong, Quynh Loi, Vinh Ho, and Khuong Thuong KTTs in the years 1971–1980' (Trinh Hong Trien 1984: 22).

The story of architect Truong Tung and the application of the prefabricated construction method with large concrete slabs shows us the importance of knowledge exchange and sharing not only internationally but also within intellectual communities in Vietnam. This knowledge, in the case of architect Truong Tung, prompted a rapid change in the construction of apartment buildings in Hanoi, not only in quantity but also in quality.

Collective Residential Apartment Blocks: The Intellectual Exchanges

Exchanges on Planning and Design

The idea of the KTT was undoubtedly imported from abroad. In the planning and design process, Vietnamese planners and architects worked closely with experts from other socialist countries such as Russia, China, North Korea and East Germany. The research carried out by Christina Schwenkel (2020) in Vinh city also indicates that East German experts came to cooperate with Vietnamese architects in making a plan for rebuilding the city around 1973. Although Schwenkel's findings point out a variety of anecdotes/narratives on whose ideas contributed to the plans, it shows that the final master plan was the result of cooperation between the experts and Vietnamese architects and planners. Although the role of the stakeholders in this case could be viewed differently as the East Germans were mentors/trainers and the Vietnamese were mentees/trainees, both groups claimed their contribution to the master plan. Moreover, Schwenkel affirms that 'the exchange of planning knowledge was multidirectional and also included South-South exchanges, such as the training of Vietnamese architects in China and Cuba' (Schwenkel 2020: 142). Vinh city, therefore, was no different from the situation in Hanoi.

The role of Soviet expertise in the Hanoi master plan was affirmed by the studies of Lisa Drummond and Nguyen Thanh Binh (2020); Dinh Quoc Phuong (2019); and N. Hong and S. Kim (2020). The location of the KTTs was determined according to the Hanoi master plan, which was established by the government with the assistance of Soviet urban planners in the 1960s (Tran Minh Tung 2016). At that time, the plan was designed to expand the city's urban territory to the southwest from the city centre, ensuring the development of socialist industrial zones and universities with large-scale collective housing areas on the city's outskirts (Hong and Kim 2020: 603). However, none of these scholars mentioned above details the role of Vietnamese architects in the planning process. While discussing the planning of Hanoi in the 1960s, Lisa Drummond and Nguyen Thanh Binh focused on the case of Nguyen Cong Tru KTT. As mentioned in the previous section of this chapter, Nguyen Cong Tru KTT was the first multi-storey KTT to be built in Hanoi, followed by Kim Lien KTT, Giang Vo KTT and Trung Tu KTT. One reason for this was that its first design planned this area 'simply as a high-density solution to the pressing demands for housing supply' (Drummond and Nguyen Thanh Binh 2020: 73). By 1963, after its construction was complete, Vietnamese officials began to discuss the design principles of the Soviet concept of the *microraion*, or micro-district (Drummond and Nguyen Thanh Binh 2020: 73). According to the *microraion* concept, an urban residential complex is a self-contained neighbourhood unit, meaning that it includes not only residential buildings but also basic services and amenities for daily life. Nguyen Cong Tru KTT was then expanded with a canteen, primary school and kindergarten. Dinh Quoc Phuong (2019) argues that Nguyen Cong Tru KTT, together with other KTTs in Hanoi, 'represent an important layer of Hanoi's architecture' (Dinh Quoc Phuong 2019: 313). In fact, Hanoi's KTTs display a link to the Soviet-style architecture.

Hong and Kim point to the construction of KTTs as a solution to the rapid urbanization and the shortage of housing in Hanoi. They write: 'The KTTs model in Vietnam was a localization of the micro-district and contributed to Hanoi's transition into a socialist city. The idea of socialist collective housing was conceived not only to cope with the rapid urbanization but also to realize an ideal socialist society with modernized and standardized collective living. Under this approach, the state actively built the KTTs in the peri-urban areas of Hanoi from the 1960s onwards' (Hong and Kim 2020: 603).

The cases of Ngo Huy Quynh and Le Van Lan in this chapter help show the vision of Vietnamese architects in the process of making the Hanoi master plan in the 1960s. Ngo Huy Quynh not only contributed to the plan but also brought his thought to the socialist world when presenting his paper in Poland in 1960. While many scholars focus their analysis on the influence of Soviet style in the KTTs in Hanoi, this chapter points out the opinions of Vietnamese architects in applying Vietnamese knowledge to the plan, particularly within the ideas around the tropical climate and traditional vernacular architecture. One such application was the south/southeast-facing building in order to take advantage of the most favourable wind in the hot climate of Hanoi (Nguyen Phu Duc 2011). Even in the present day, this standard is still applied in construction work. This case suggests that the KTTs in Hanoi were the product of exchange between intellectuals of both Vietnam and the socialist world.

Exchanges on Building Methods

Four-storey KTTs of Nguyen Cong Tru were the first mid-rise buildings to be constructed in Hanoi after 1954. Before this time, people in Hanoi were only familiar with French-style villas and urban tube houses in the Old Quarter. Therefore, in order to build a Soviet-style apartment complex, Vietnamese engineers and architects needed to rely on the building methods and technology of the socialist countries. The exchange of construction methods in this period deserves significant discussion. China, East Germany, North Korea and Russia were still the advisers for methods and donors of technology for KTT constructions. The anthropologist Christina Schwenkel also points out that the authorities understood that to build a future-oriented Vinh city, 'it was necessary to establish a building materials industry that could construct public works over the long term' (Schwenkel 2020: 155). To keep up with the pace of construction, the building materials industry and mechanization technology needed to be prioritized. The same view was demonstrated in Hanoi with Nguyen Cong Tru KTT and Kim Lien KTT in the early 1960s. Drummond and Nguyen Thanh Binh indicate that Nguyen Cong Tru KTT was built using 'the building materials and technologies employed under the colonial regime: brick load-bearing walls, tiles roofs and concrete panel floors. It was built to be sound and permanent' (Drummond and Nguyen Thanh Binh 2020: 72). However, the building methods and materials were not the same in all KTTs. Each one was built by different methods due to the approval of the city authorities and the available materials. Therefore, while Nguyen Cong Tru KTT was built with bricks, Kim Lien KTT was approved to be built using prefabricated materials (Drummond and Nguyen Thanh Binh 2020: 72).

Discussing the building materials for Kim Lien KTT in Hanoi, this chapter has pointed out the role of architect Truong Tung in applying Western technology in order to create large panel prefabs in the climate of Hanoi. While Drummond and Nguyen Thanh Binh (2020) acknowledge the different building materials between Nguyen Cong Tru KTT and Kim Lien KTT, the role of Vietnamese architects and engineers is overlooked. Hong and Kim (2020) as well as Dinh Quoc Phuong (2019) also seem to take for granted that prefabricated materials were merely imported from Soviet countries. The case of Truong Tung here suggests that technology and methods should be seen as moving in a progressive direction in which the successors have continuously contributed to their predecessors' work. Without the invented slag-concrete prefabricated slab method in the 1970s, the later KTTs such as Giang Vo and Trung Tu may not have been built at such a quick pace. This example also demonstrates the active attitude of Vietnamese engineers when dealing with the shortage of materials. These practices helped Vietnam overcome the fact that material donations to the 'Third World' were 'second hand', and 'already obsolete', as mentioned in the case of Quang Trung KTT in Vinh city (Schwenkel 2020: 157).

Exchanges on the Idea of Building a Socialist Country

Finally, the idea of building KTTs as part of creating a socialist society is shared among the published work on KTTs in Vietnam. While Dinh Quoc Phuong (2019) points out the influence of the Soviet socialist ideology on Hanoi's urban fabric, Hong and Kim (2020: 602) argue for a localization of the *microraion* (micro-district) concept introduced by the Soviet Union. During the Vietnam War (1955–75), a principal policy was that houses and land were under the control of the Vietnamese government. Therefore, Hanoi's government implemented subsidized public housing schemes for its employees and staff. Housing construction also reflected the ideological orientation of Vietnam, which supposed that the state would provide and control all aspects of everyday life – including work, consumption and residence. Although the idea of socialist collective housing was conceived not only 'to cope with the rapid urbanization but also to realize the ideal socialist society with modernized and standardized collective living' (Hong and Kim 2020: 603), it is also criticized for being built unilaterally without any resident participation (Drummond and Nguyen Thanh Binh 2020: 84).

The result of the implementation is that although it provided housing for thousands of people, many problems were reported by, and among, residents soon after they moved in. Drummond and Nguyen Thanh Binh point out that Nguyen Cong Tru KTT residents complained that the shared kitchen and bathroom among the multiple households on every floor created tension among the residents (Drummond and Nguyen Thanh Binh 2020: 74). While some people wanted to keep them clean and tidy, others failed to maintain them in good condition. Moreover, the living environment became crowded, dirty and smelly, with chicken coops being housed there and pigs being raised in the bathroom. The same situation was reported in Kim Lien KTT. Our respondents in Kim Lien KTT shared a number of narratives on how raising chickens and pigs in the shared space helped them overcome economic hardship during the difficult economic period of 1976–86.

However, the shared auxiliary space in KTTs ceased to exist in later KTTs such as Van Chuong, Giang Vo and Trung Tu. This was the result of the diligent work of Truong Tung, as shown earlier in this chapter. Recognizing the irrationality of the shared space among the apartments, Truong Tung, together with his colleagues, succeeded in designing and persuading the authorities to approve the new model. The self-contained apartments then became the standard and resolved the tensions among residents. However, as shown, it was the process of Truong Tung's learning from Western countries such as the Netherlands, Belgium and England together with his determined efforts when struggling with the leaders of the Ministry of Architecture of Vietnam that enabled the KTTs to be built. The example also adds to the main argument that a one-size-fits-all model cannot be applied to different societies. Insiders with their experience and acquired knowledge can effectively contribute to the improvement of this housing.

Today, KTTs continue to be a symbol of the influence of the Soviet-supported period. But everything in KTTs has changed since the Government of Vietnam changed its policy in 1986. The market economy gradually expanded through its economic and social policies. People in KTTs quickly took these opportunities to change their livelihoods, to earn more money for their families and to make their life better. Adapting to the new economic policies, the residents of KTTs directly changed the architecture of the buildings and the space of each of these areas. First-generation, second-generation and new owners were the main agents that began to erase the old face of KTTs, creating a new appearance that even the people who made the rules and the architects who designed them could not have imagined. These changes were not the dreams of architects and social managers, but met the needs of residents living in the KTTs.

Conclusion

The case of the Hanoi KTTs is such a striking instance of intellectual exchange partly because these mass housing projects have been so widely thought of both within and beyond Vietnam as passively accepted features of Soviet Union influence. However, this chapter has shown that the opposite is true: the Vietnamese demonstrated agency within the scientific modernism deployed and embraced the opportunities of the postcolonial context. This chapter has shown multiple aspects related to the establishment of Soviet-style apartment complexes in Hanoi since the 1960s. The materials indicated that although the idea of constructing KTTs fitted in with the socialist building ideology, its implementation proved that KTTs in Vietnam were not a model copied from other socialist countries. Instead, the various styles of KTTs were the result of a negotiation process among architects, engineers and planners at multiple levels across decades. Vietnamese people were not only students in this field but also became experts and were able to apply their acquired knowledge from abroad to create a solution to the housing shortage in Hanoi. Their diligence and determination helped them recognize the problem of the Soviet-style KTT model and then propose a change in both construction methods and the designation of the living environment. These Vietnamized version of KTTs indicated that Vietnamese intellectuals not only applied the Eastern European training and knowledge to their practice but also actively responded to the worldwide architectural and engineering discipline. The examples in this chapter help to advance Bayly's ideas around the cultural capital of intellectuals in socialist countries.

Acknowledgements

This research is funded by the Vietnam National Foundation for Science and Technology Development (NAFOSTED) under grant number 602.08-2020.03.

Nguyen Van Huy is the founding director of the Vietnam Museum of Ethnology (1995–2006), the innovative exhibitions of which have earned national and international acclaim. He is now the director of the Nguyen Van Huyen Museum (Hanoi) and consultant on issues of ethnicity, culture and education in Vietnam.

Nguyen Vu Hoang, Ph.D. in Anthropology at the University of Toronto in 2017, is currently a faculty member in the Department of Anthropology, University of Social Sciences and Humanities, Hanoi. His interests include urbanization issues, diaspora, homeland, and ethnicity in Vietnam.

Notes

1. This later became the Department of Urban and Rural Affairs, then the Institute of Urban and Rural Planning Design, Ministry of Construction.
2. See https://www.viup.vn/vn/Lich-su-int23.html. Information about the Vietnam Institute for Urban and Rural Planning.
3. See https://moc.gov.vn/vn/tin-tuc/1184/8591/nua-the-ky-vien-quy-hoach-do-thi--nong-thon.aspx. Information about the Vietnam Institute for Urban and Rural Planning on the website of the Ministry of Construction.
4. Ngo Huy Quynh refers here to the vernacular architecture in Vietnam.
5. See https://www.viup.vn/vn/Lich-su-int23.html. Information about the Vietnam Institute for Urban and Rural Planning.
6. However, according to architect Đào Ngọc Nghiêm, this area consisted of 38 four-storey blocks and some public buildings with the capacity for 2,600 households, and the standard for eight square metres per person. See https://vnexpress.net/dau-an-trieu-tien-trong-khu-tap-the-60-nam-o-ha-noi-3887895.html.
7. See https://vnexpress.net/dau-an-trieu-tien-trong-khu-tap-the-60-nam-o-ha-noi-3887895.html. Information about the Remarks of North Korea in Kim Lien KTT in Hanoi after 60 years.
8. In Vietnam, a house facing the south or southeast is most favoured.
9. See https://m.thuvienphapluat.vn/van-ban/lao-dong-tien-luong/thong-tu-529-ttg-quy-dinh-tam-thoi-che-do-nua-cung-cap-hien-nay-21668.aspx and https://m.thuvienphapluat.vn/van-ban/bat-dong-san/quyet-dinh-150-cp-tieu-chuan-phan-phoi-dien-tich-lam-viec-dien-tich-o-17679.aspx. Information about two legal documents: Circular No.529-TTg of Prime Minister in 1958 on Temporary Regulations on Distribution Policy; Decision No. 150-CP of the Government of Vietnam in 1977 on promulgating standards for distributing living space and working space.
10. Nguyen Van Huong was a member of the 4th National Assembly (1971–75); see Nguyen Van Huong (1972).

References

Bayly, Susan. 2004. 'Vietnamese Intellectuals in Revolutionary and Postcolonial Times,' *Critique of Anthropology* 24(3): 320–44.

Buchli, Victor. 1998. 'Moisei Ginzburg's Narkomfin Communal House in Moscow: Contesting the Social and Material World,' *Journal of the Society of Architectural Historians* 57(2): 160–81.

_____. 1999. *An Archaeology of Socialism*. London: Routledge.
Dang Thai Hoang. 1985. *Kiến trúc nhà ở Hà Nội thế kỷ 19-20* [Architecture of Houses in Hanoi in the Nineteenth and Twentieth Centuries]. Hanoi: Hanoi Publishing House.
Dinh Quoc Phuong. 2019. '(Re)Developing Old Apartment Blocks in Hanoi: Government Vision, Local Resistance and Spatial Routines', *Journal of Asian Architecture and Building Engineering* 18(4): 311–23.
Drummond, Lisa, and Nguyen Thanh Binh. 2020. 'The Rise and Fall of Collective Housing: Hanoi between Vision and Decision', in Lisa Drummond and Douglas Young (eds), *Socialist and Post-Socialist Urbanisms: Critical Reflections from a Global Perspective*. Toronto: University of Toronto Press, pp. 69–88.
Duong Duc Tuan. 2005. 'Cải tạo không gian kiến trúc – Tái khai thác khu chung cư cũ tại Hà Nội đáp ứng điều kiện tạm cư và tái định cư tại chỗ' [Renovation of Architectural Space – Renovating Old Housing Complexes in Hanoi to Fit in the Temporary Residence and Resettlement], Ph.D. dissertation. Hanoi's University of Architecture.
Government of Vietnam. 1977. *Quyết định ban hành tiêu chuẩn phân phối diện tích làm việc và diện tích ở* [Decree on Standard for Working and Living Space], Decree No.150-CP, June 10.
Han Tat Ngan. 1990. 'Quanh vấn đề tiểu khu nhà ở' [On the Issues of Residential Subdivisions], *Tạp chí Kiến trúc* [Vietnamese Journal of Architecture] 3(29): 32.
Hong, N., and S. Kim. 2020. 'Persistence of the Socialist Collective Housing Areas (KTTS): The Evolution and Contemporary Transformation of Mass Housing in Hanoi, Vietnam', *Journal of Housing and the Built Environment* 36: 601–25.
Humphrey, Caroline. 2005. 'Ideology in Infrastructure: Architecture and Soviet Imagination', *Journal of the Royal Anthropological Institute* 11(1): 39–58.
Kim Lien People's Committee. 2012. *Lịch sử cách mạng Đảng bộ và nhân dân Phường Kim Liên* [Revolutionary history of the Party Committee and people of Kim Lien Ward]. Hanoi: Politics and Administration Publishers.
King, Ross. 2009. *Kuala Lumpur and Putrajaya: Negotiating Urban Space in Malaysia*. NIAS Press.
Le Van Lan. 1984. 'Nâng cao hơn nữa chất lượng sáng tác kiến trúc, đáp ứng yêu cầu xây dựng Thủ đô trên những chặng đường mới' [Improving the Quality of Architectural Creation, Fitting in the Requirement for Building the Capital in the New Era], *Tạp chí Kiến trúc* [Vietnamese Journal of Architecture] 3.
_____ (ed.). 2010. *55 năm kiến trúc Hà Nội* [55 Years of Hanoi Architecture]. Hanoi: Times Publishers.
Ngo Huy Quynh. 1960. *Dự thảo ý kiến trao đổi với những người làm công tác kiến trúc ở Ba Lan - Đề cương* [Draft of Opinions Exchanged with Architectural Workers in Poland – Outline], archived at the Center for Heritage of Vietnamese Scientists, accessed in 2021.
_____. 1961. *Đề cương bài nói chuyện về 'Tính chất dân tộc trong kiến trúc và kiến trúc đô thị* [Nationality in Architecture and Urban Architecture], archived at the Center for Heritage of Vietnamese Scientists, accessed in 2021.
_____. 2020. *Kiến trúc sư* [Architect]. Hà Nội: Hong Duc Publishers.
Nguyen Phu Duc. 2011. 'Điều tiết quy hoạch xây dựng trên đất khu tập thể cũ ở Hà Nội' [Regulating the Construction Planning on the Land of Old Collective Apartment Complexes in Hanoi], available online at: https://ashui.com/mag/tuongtac/phanbien/5022-dieu-tiet-quy-hoach-xay-dung-tren-dat-khu-tap-the-cu-o-ha-noi.html (accessed May 2022).

Nguyen Van Huong. 1972. 'Vấn đề xây dựng nhà ở cho nhân dân và cán bộ ở Hà Nội' [The Problem of Building Housing for People and Officials in Hanoi], conference paper presented at the National Assembly on 24 March 1972; archived at the Center for Heritage of Vietnamese Scientists, File number 2015/444/32.3.

Phan Phuong Thao and Nguyen Thi Binh. 2017. 'Nhận diện "khu phố Tây"/"khu phố Âu" ở Hà Nội thời Pháp thuộc: Khái niệm và địa giới' [Identifying the "Western Quarter"/"European Quarter" in Hanoi during the French Colonial Period: Concepts and Boundaries], in Phan Phương Thảo (ed.), *Khu phố Tây ở Hà Nội: Nửa đầu thế kỷ XX qua tư liệu địa chính* [The Western Quarter in Hanoi: The First Half of the Twentieth Century through Cadastral Documents]. Hanoi: Hanoi Publishing House, pp. 33–54.

Schwenkel, Christina. 2020. *Building Socialism*. Durham, NC: Duke University Press.

Ta Thi Hoang Van. 2017. 'Kiến trúc đô thị kiểu Pháp ở Hà Nội nửa đầu thế kỷ XX' [French Urban Architecture in Hanoi in the First Half of the Twentieth Century], in Phan Phương Thảo (ed.), *Khu phố Tây ở Hà Nội: Nửa đầu thế kỷ XX qua tư liệu địa chính* [The Western Quarter in Hanoi: The First Half of the Twentieth Century through Cadastral Documents]. Hanoi: Hanoi Publishing House, pp. 243–338.

Tran Minh Tung. 2016. *Chân dung một Hà Nội-Quá độ trong chuyển đổi các dạng thức quy hoạch đô thị Hà Nội* [A Portrait of Hanoi: Transition in the Change of Urban Planning in Hanoi]. Hà Nội: Construction Publishing House.

Truong Tung. 1966. *Design and Construction of Industrialized Houses in Hanoi*, PhD Dissertation, Moscow State University of Civil Engineering (MGSU).

Trinh Hong Trien. 1984. 'Hà Nội xây dựng nhà ở' [Building Houses in Hanoi], *Tạp chí Kiến trúc* [Vietnamese Journal of Architecture] 3.

4

Intellectual Exchanges in Muslim Asia
Intersections of History and Geography

Magnus Marsden

Introduction

'The Alan question' shaped intellectually the year I spent writing up my PhD thesis in Cambridge under the supervision of Susan Bayly and the following period during which I converted it into a book. Susan Bayly and I used 'the Alan question' to refer to a simple yet powerful question posed to me by Alan MacFarlane during a seminar held in Cambridge in February 2002. Addressing the emphasis I placed in the talk on the significance of critical debate to the living of a Muslim life in Chitral, northern Pakistan, he asked, 'Is what you are describing particular to Chitral or generalizable to other parts of the Muslim World?'[1] The question was a variation on a theme for anthropology – a discipline in which the relationship between 'the general' and 'the particular' has long been a central concern. Never having been especially confident in Cambridge's seminar culture, I gave an incomplete answer. My lacklustre performance on the day, nevertheless, resulted in years of animated discussion between Susan Bayly and myself: what wider implications, we discussed, did my work on Muslim life in Chitral have for the anthropology of Islam?

My thesis concerned what I had come to see as being the distinctive way in which Chitral Muslims set to the task of leading a Muslim life (Marsden 2005). At the time, I regarded Chitral as being a 'relatively remote' district in northern Pakistan. Chitral's population largely comprised Khowar-speaking Sunni and Shii Ismaili Muslims who collectively distinguished their society from that of the Pashto or Pakhtu-speaking majority of what was known at the time as Pakistan's North West Frontier Province.[2] I documented the strenuous lengths to which Muslims in Chitral's villages and small towns went in order to cultivate emotionally rich and intellectually vibrant lives. I focused ethnographically on the important role played by the arts of debate and discussion in villagers' understandings of 'the life of the mind' – a term that captured the importance that my friends in Chitral placed upon the active and ongoing cultivation of their mental faculties, the vocal exercise of critical thought and the sensitive deployment of emotional intelligence. I also emphasized the extent to which my informants in Chitral led culturally rich existences that revolved around music, dance and poetry. The medium of these cultural forms and genres was Khowar (an Indo-Persian language spoken by approximately 250,000 ethnic Chitrali or Kho people). Chitrali poetry also drew, however, upon a vast repertoire of Persian Sufic poetry. Building on anthropological discussions of the relationship between 'the intellect' (*'aql*) and the 'carnal soul' (*nafs*) in the leading of Muslim lives, my research addressed the ways in which local practices of debate and critical discussion rendered Chitral's villages not simply the passive recipients of forms of Islamic reformism emerging from urban centres but sites of intellectual exchange and significance. I was also interested in the role village intellectuals in Chitral – from musicians to poets and religious scholars – played in ongoing interactions between the region's local culture and that of the wider 'Persianate world' – most broadly defined as the great parts of the Eurasian continent over which Persian has had a linguistic and cultural influence (Green 2019).

I emphasized these facets of Muslim village life in Chitral at a time during which Islamizing processes that were national and transnational in shape and scope were influencing the region. Many of the Sunni and Shii Ismaili Muslim villagers with whom I lived in Chitral were critical of reform-minded Muslims, especially those who advocated strict and rigid understandings of Islam's legal code, the sharia. Villagers of both 'doctrinal clusters' told me that they regarded reform-minded Muslims in Chitral and in 'down Pakistan' (the term used by Chitralis to refer to Pakistan's southern regions) as advocating narrow-minded (*tang nazar*) forms of religiosity. The Taliban – an Islamic movement comprising a heady mix of madrassa students and militants that came to power in Afghanistan in 1995 in the wake of the country's protracted conflict following the collapse in 1992 of the Soviet-backed government – maintained an office in Chitral. Indeed, some of the region's most influential religious figures (known in Khowar as the *dashmanan*) vocally supported the Taliban's aims and goals. The world of village and small-town Islam that I sought to describe and analyse was not secular. Nor were its people poorly informed about Islamic knowledge and ethical principles. Indeed, the 'ordinary Muslims' (Peletz 1997) with whom I spent much time did not seek to 'resist' reformist Islam in any simple sense. I documented, rather, a more multi-layered range of responses to the forms of faith and religiosity emerging from urban centres in Pakistan and Afghanistan. Some of Chitral's mullahs and 'men of piety' were themselves renowned in the region for displaying their own creative and independent thought. Individual *dashman* openly contested the sharia-centred forms of religiosity associated in the minds of many Chitrali Muslims with 'down country' reformists and gained respect locally for doing so. Likewise, individuals active in Islamist political parties – including the Jama'at-i Islami – achieved fame and repute in Chitral by writing love poems (*ghazals*) and attending musical gatherings (*mahfil*; *ishtok*) that were scorned in Friday sermons given by hardline *dashmanan* in Chitral's mosques.[3] The region's people were critically responsive to a wide range of ways of thinking about Muslim faith and experience with which they were familiar. These included various iterations of Islamic reformism that historians and anthropologists had tended to regard as exerting a homogenizing influence on 'local' modes of being Muslim.

In this chapter, I reflect on both my fieldwork in Chitral and my subsequent experiences in connected regions of Afghanistan, Tajikistan and beyond; I do so with the aim of making two specific contributions to the anthropology of intellectual exchange. At one level, the chapter addresses the varying forms of intellectual exchange that have shaped and transformed my understanding of Muslim life in Asia. These include my discussions with Susan Bayly, engagement with historical scholarship on Islam, and intensive interactions with a diverse range of interlocutors in the various fieldsites in which I have worked. At another level, I seek to theorize the character and direction of intellectual exchange in Muslim Asia. My central argument is that a great deal is revealed about Muslim intellectual exchanges in Asia if these are investigated in contexts at which multiple geographical and temporal scales intersect.[4] Research conducted at contexts characterized as intersecting points of space and time illuminates the way in which Muslim intellectual exchanges are shaped by overlapping yet distinct 'knowledge ecumenes', multiple 'critical' geopolitical events (Das 1996), and deeper historical processes 'sedimented' in society and culture (Koselleck 2018). In the connected parts of Central and South Asia in which I have worked, intellectual exchanges involving Muslims are best considered not only in relationship to 'the Islamic tradition' (Asad 1986) and the 'Turko-Persian ecumene' (e.g. Canfield 2002), but also to the 'global Cold War' and its ongoing social, political and geopolitical legacies (Kwon 2010). Much recent scholarship has argued that Muslim thought and identity is rarely helpfully understood in relationship to static categories such as 'local' and 'global' or 'traditional' and 'reformist'. At the same time, however, it is also unhelpful to think of the intellectual life of Muslims as being shaped either by specific knowledge ecumenes or distinct ethical traditions. The context in which the people with whom I have worked set to the task of being Muslim is an expansive arena that transgresses the boundaries of regional studies, 'culture areas' and nation states. It is an arena both affected by and influential within multiple geopolitical processes, from European imperialism to the Cold War and, most recently, competing projects of regional 'connectivity'. Each of these processes, I show, has ongoing implications for shaping the forms of intellectual exchange in which Muslims in the arena participate and the range of normative and political stances they adopt in relation to these.

Conceptualizing 'the Islamic': Between Anthropology and History

The ways in which Chitralis identified with Persian and Persianate heritage, literary genres and knowledge illustrated the problems of using one-dimensional temporal frames such as those of 'local' and 'global' Islam to understand contemporary iterations of Muslim identity. At the time, anthropological studies focusing on connections between Muslims living across complex spaces tended to be framed in relationship to transnationalism or globalization and – in the Muslim world – mostly studied by way of explorations of particular Islamic organizations. As Engseng Ho has noted, such work tended to be 'historically thin' (Ho 2006). The decade following the 2001 attacks was, indeed, one of especially critical significance for the anthropology of Islam.[5] A series of studies emerged that were concerned with the 'piety movement'. Largely based on research conducted in the Middle East, especially in Cairo (Hirschkind 2006; Mahmood 2004), these studies built upon Michel Foucault's later work on the significance of disciplinary practices of self-fashioning for the leading of ethical lives. Ethnographically, they demonstrated the way in which Muslim men and women involved in 'piety movements' actively and consciously cultivated their selves in a manner that reflected ethical principles historically sedimented within 'the Islamic tradition'. Another body of scholarship emerged that identified its focus as being on 'everyday Islam' rather than piety-minded forms of Islam deriving from Islam's textual tradition. Work on 'everyday Islam' brought attention to the inconsistencies and ambiguities of Muslim moral universes in the context of everyday life and questioned the ethnographic depth of studies of the piety movement that emphasized ethical coherence (for example, Schielke 2009; Soares and Osella 2009).

Both the piety-minded and everyday Islam approaches to the anthropology of Islam shared a focus on 'Muslim selves' (individual or collective) and the ways in which these related to 'the Islamic tradition'. The most fascinating aspect of my experiences in Chitral, however, had been the degree to which the thinking and identities of Chitrali Sunni and Shii Ismaili Muslims needed to be considered in relationship to a range of cultural genres and practices of importance at multiple geographical and historical scales. Irfan Ahmed (2017) has noted that literature on 'the Islamic tradition' tends to focus almost exclusively on the significance of the Qur'an and the Hadith as textual cornerstones. My informants regularly interspersed their daily conversations, however, with quotations from Rumi's Mathnawi, a text that some referred to as 'the Qur'an in Persian'. The range of modes of identification open to my informants were not limited to a choice between 'local' and 'global Islam' or a form of 'the Islamic tradition' that was unmediated by a specific cultural context. Likewise, the distinction between pious and everyday Islam did not do justice to the complex interactions between different forms of Muslim thought and identity in the settings in which they lived. Deploying either of these categories to analyse the vast range of modes of behaviour and religiosity I observed in my fieldsites would have erased a great deal of what was important to my informants' experiences. Of more significance, rather, was their awareness of their place within a transregional setting informed by Persianate culture.

Exploring Chitrali Muslim thought and identity in terms of its relationship to the wider 'Persianate' world revealed dense webs of historical connectivity between northern Pakistan and neighbouring regions of Afghanistan and Tajikistan. Hitherto anthropologists had largely viewed these connections from the prism of the flight of refugees and the activities of 'jihadi' organizations in Afghanistan and Pakistan (for an important exception, see Kreutzmann 1998). Addressing such longue durée connections from a broader perspective that incorporated actors including traders, development workers and musicians presented an opportunity to historicize both the anthropology of local Islam and of globalization (Marsden 2008). Connections between Muslims in adjacent settings illuminated 'the Islamic' as a lived realm of thought, agency and relationality forged through movement and the exchange of knowledge, people and experience in multiple, overlapping and expansive arenas.

While anthropologists debated the merits and demerits of understanding Muslim thought and identity through the lens of 'piety' or 'the everyday', historians developed a more expansive approach that conceptualized 'the Islamic' as an inherently flexible field that is the outcome of ongoing human agentive assertion. This approach made possible a closer consideration of the relationships and intellectual interactions between diverse forms of Muslim thought and identity. A rich body of work by historians that challenges reified understandings of both Islamic chronology and geography has played an especially important role in the development of the study of thought and agency in Muslim Asia. Several scholars have recently argued that Islamic history has traditionally been 'presented as pegged to a straight timeline that begins with the life of Muhammad and continues to the present in (post)modern transformations' (Bashir 2014: 520). According to Shahzad Bashir, this reified understanding of Islamic history has had a range of negative consequences for the historical and sociological study of Islam. Most evidently, it has resulted in an 'overemphasis on the Arab Middle East', the tendency to interpret the 'evolution of ideas and practices as part of a predetermined or natural cycle … without reference to material circumstances', and the 'undervaluation of the role of human agency in creating "time" within Islamic social, cultural and religious contexts' (Bashir 2014: 521). In place of reified understandings of Islamic chronology, Bashir and other historians writing in a similar vein have advocated that in the study of Muslim societies time should be considered as 'an ideological and narrative product that is forever being made and remade within Islamic perspectives' (Bashir 2014: 521). In this regard, recent historical scholarship builds on early work in anthropology that was critical of the reification of Islam and advocated, instead, for an approach that identified multiple 'islams' (el-Zein 1977; cf. Gilsenan 1982). It goes beyond such approaches, however, by arguing for the ongoing relevance of 'the Islamic' as a category of analysis when it is conceptualized as an 'aspect of human agentive assertion' that can 'accommodate internal diversity' and is 'characterized by fluidity rather than stasis' (Bashir 2014: 512; cf. Ahmed 2015; Henig 2016, 2020).

Understanding 'the Islamic' as a field produced by Muslim agency in time and space has important implications for conceptualizing the geographic contexts in which Islam is studied. For Bashir, conceptualizing 'the Islamic' in this way requires scholars to appreciate not only 'the internal projection of universalism' but also 'the incessant traffic of ideas and people' within particular and often expansive arenas (Bashir 2014: 522). In terms of geography, Shahab Ahmed's work has been especially influential in challenging the overemphasis of 'the Middle East' in the study of Islam (Ahmed 2015).[6] Ahmed deploys the transregional category of 'Balkans-to-Bengal complex' to refer to the lands of Islam that stretch between present-day Bosnia-Herzegovina, Turkey, Iran and Central Asia, down and across Afghanistan and North India to the Bay of Bengal. For Ahmed, between 1350 and 1850 CE, this expansive arena shared a powerful commonality in terms of the influential and overarching role played by Sufi ideas and values, often expressed in poetry written in both Persian and Turkish. From the 1850s onwards, modern nationalism and the rise of reformist Islam with the emphasis it placed on texts and codified versions of Islamic law weakened these interconnections and the forms of self-understandings with which they were implicated.[7] Focusing on an intermediary, transregional scale of identity and experience in Muslim Asia offers multiple insights into these cross-cutting intellectual debates involving anthropologists and historians. The points at which geographical and temporal scales interact help to reveal the ways in which Muslims mediate between interacting geographies and histories by way of actively participating in various forms of exchange, ranging from the intellectual to the political and the economic.

Transregional Muslim Identities

Chitral shares a long border with Afghanistan and in places is only a few miles from Tajikistan, a formerly Soviet Muslim-majority Republic in Central Asia. During my research in Chitral, I had spent much time with small-scale traders from northern Afghanistan. These men had lived in Chitral since the early 1980s when they fled regions of the country (especially Panjshir and Badakhshan) that had been subject to Soviet bombing campaigns; they mostly ran businesses in villages and towns, largely making a living as butchers and bakers. Several men from Tajikistan also lived in the Chitrali village in which I stayed having fled the civil war in their home country (1992–97). After the 2001 defeat by US and allied forces of the Taliban, several of the Afghan families I knew returned to Afghanistan. Others stayed in Chitral while sending a family member to open a business in the country, mostly in Kabul and Kunduz (Marsden and Hopkins 2012). Spending time with such actors, I explored the ways in which mobile people mediated Chitral's position in a transregional context.

Working with mobile Muslims in a transregional arena raised two intellectual concerns. First, there had been a tendency for social scientists interested in 'transnational' and 'global' Islam to focus attention on participants in worldwide movements of Islamic reform and purification (e.g. Mandaville 2001). Fewer studies engaged conceptually, however, with the dynamics of transregional Muslim identities and the types of cultural influences and knowledge ecumenes that shape these.[8] In a recent book, Nile Green has distinguished between 'global' and 'world' Islam. For Green, global Islam 'refers to the versions of Islam propagated across geographical, political and ethnolinguistic boundaries by Muslim religious activists, organizations, and states that emerged in the era of globalization'. By contrast, 'world Islam refers to the older versions of Islam that developed and adapted to different local and regional environments during the millennium before the onset of globalization' (Green 2020: 8). In the transregional arena in which I work, a great deal of attention has been paid to the actors involved in the propagation of 'global Islam', but alongside these it is also important to recognize the significance of identify formations formed as a result of a historically durable process of exchange across transregional arenas. Such forms of 'world Islam' constitute a growing field of exploration for historians of Islam, yet most anthropological and sociological work on Islam remains focused on modern expressions of global Islam.

Second, my fieldwork in Chitral had made me aware of the rigid boundaries that anthropologists and historians tended to erect between scholarship on different 'areas'. Working on the connections between northern Pakistan, Afghanistan and Tajikistan afforded the opportunity of nuancing rigid approaches to area studies, and, in particular, bringing greater recognition to the vital nature of connections between South and Central Asia. The emerging anthropology of Central Asia focused almost exclusively on life in the five former Muslim majority states of the Soviet Union.[9] I found the boundaries between different areas problematic because the Chitrali Muslims with whom I had lived were intimately aware of their historic connections to Central Asia. Not only did many speak Persian, they also imagined the forms of Islam they practised in relation to a broader Central Asian geography, often telling me, for example, of how in past generations their family members had studied in centres of Islamic learning in the great Islamic city of Bukhara (cf. Pickett 2020).

As I embarked upon a connective historical ethnography of Muslim life in a transregional arena in inland Asia, scholarly interest in Persianate cultural forms largely remained the preserve of historians of the pre-modern Muslim world. Marshall Hodgson (1963) had developed the term 'Islamicate' to refer to cultural forms visible across 'the Eurasian Islamicate oecumene' – a space he identified as being one of 'Muslim dominion' but in which non-Muslims also played critical and vital roles. In regional terms, historians of pre-modern India, Muzaffar Alam and Sanjay Subrahmanyam's (2007) study of the traditions of Persian-language travel writing that had been popular in India during the highpoint of the Mughal Empire was a source of inspiration. Anthropological approaches deployed the term 'Turko-Persian' in order to emphasize the interactions between Turkish and Persian literary traditions and knowledge systems in Central Asia (Canfield 2002). Yet ethnographic accounts of Persianate dynamics were limited largely to accounts of the role played by historic Persian texts in the teaching of Islam and ethics in Afghanistan (Shahrani 1984, 2001). My fieldwork experiences questioned the inevitable salience of the boundary between pre-modern and modern history (Shryock and Smail 2011) and highlight parallels between ethnographic and historical work on the region.

Historical scholarship on the category of Persianate has become increasingly sophisticated, especially in terms of understanding the relationship between Islam and geography. Early work in the field associated Persian with the territories of modern-day Iran and India (e.g. Cole 2002). Newer scholarship explored Persian's role as a trans-cultural and trans-religious language of significance in a vast Eurasian terrain stretching from the Balkans to the Bay of Bengal (e.g. Ahmed 2015; Green 2019; Sood 2015). Mana Kia, indeed, highlights the importance of relationality to live in Persianate settings, arguing that 'to be a Persian was to be embedded in a set of connections with people we today consider members of different groups' (Kia 2020: 12).

Persian's relationship to Islamic history is now also the focus of considerable scholarly scrutiny. The religious dynamics of the Persianate world have been poorly understood when considered in relationship to the traditional field of Islamic history. As Ahmed noted, this work focused on law and gave little significance to the importance of cultural genres, such as poetry and related forms of cultural expression (Ahmed 2015). For other scholars, the relationship between Persian and Islam is itself not straightforward. If 'Islam permeated the beings of Persian-speakers in multiple settings', then it did not do so in any 'totalising fashion': 'Persians', rather, 'could profess other faiths, or even be hostile to Islam, without necessarily being outside of it' (Kia 2020: 214). Historical debates about Islamic and Persianate geographies more than anthropological work on either pious or everyday Islam illuminated my fieldwork on border-crossing forms of mobility that involved people crossing a transregional Muslim geography.

In order to generate insights into lived experiences of life in a Persianate arena, I worked with a range of actors who regularly crossed the borders between Pakistan, Tajikistan and Afghanistan. While the mobile people with whom I spent time exerted great energy into crossing the national borders of the countries across which they lived, they adapted to life in the settings to which they moved with relative ease. I also discovered how during their travels they were able to re-activate older connections of kinship. Such ties of kinship pre-existed the boundaries of the nation state. In particular, notable families of religious authority had close ties of kin that had been regularly reaffirmed over decades through marriage. While connections remained in the aftermath of the creation of Pakistan in 1947, the increasingly rigid nature of the boundaries during the Cold War period until the invasion of Afghanistan by the Soviet Union in 1979 reduced connections between the three regions (cf. Kreutzmann

2015). After 1979, refugees who came to Chitral from neighbouring Badakhshan were able to trace their distant relatives in the region's small villages.

During fieldwork, I saw how people reinvigorated kinship connections in the context of the mobility that arose from Tajikistan's civil war and the conflict in Afghanistan (Marsden and Hopkins 2012). In addition, people also emphasized the shared cultural forms important to their lives, especially those they depicted as arising from their knowledge of Persian. One especially vital cultural form was the very practice of travel itself. My informants engaged in various forms of travel – from local 'tours' to more extensive boundary-crossing journeys (Marsden and Hopkins 2012). My informants thus talked about these forms of mobility as having critical implications for their self-identifications and social relationships – travel provoked reflection on 'the strange and wonderful' (*ajeeb u gharib*), and also allowed individuals to test and assess one another's trust – aspects of *safarnama*s (travel journals) that had been studied by Alam and Subrahmanyam (2007). This finding was important because it enabled me to see how the Persian cultural forms so cherished by my Chitrali friends were also an important aspect of the manner in which connections were built and ideas exchanged across national boundaries. Far from being a 'relatively remote' region of northern Pakistan, I now recognized that Chitral was part of an interconnected arena informed by shared Persianate cultural forms that shaped and directed the nature of intellectual exchanges.

It was not only in relationship to specific cultural forms that I was able to conceptualize Chitral as part of a wider arena that challenged the relevance of national and ethno-linguistic boundaries to understanding all aspects of daily life. I was conducting research in a setting in which sharia-centred and piety-minded forms of Islam occupied a critical and important place in everyday life, as well as in national and local legal and political structures. As in Chitral, so too in the contexts in Afghanistan and Tajikistan in which I worked, I discovered that debate and discussion occupied an important part of the everyday lives of my informants. This was as important among active members of movements of Islamic piety and Islamism as it was for Muslims whom my informants in Chitral would refer to as 'open-minded'. In the new settings in which I was working, such folk, however, had been active participants not only in Islamist but also in socialist movements and political organizations. I was now spending time not only with the 'religious-minded' but also with former members of Afghanistan's leftist political organizations – most notably but not exclusively the People's Democratic Party of Afghanistan. Doing so illuminated aspects of being Muslim in the region that had not been evident in the anthropology of Islam (given its focus on everyday expressions of Muslim personhood and practices of ethical self-fashioning) or in Chitral (a context in which the influence of forms of reformist Islam left little if any space for leftist politics).[10]

In Afghanistan, daily discussions about the importance of macro-political and geopolitical processes to people's religious identities wove themselves into the fabric of daily conversation. As Osella and Soares have argued (2020), work on piety-minded forms of Islam illuminates the micro-politics of such movements (especially in terms of their relationship to women's agency) yet rarely addresses the connections between such movements and macro-political dynamics. This tendency reflects the ways in which initial studies of piety-minded Islam challenged work (often in political science) that focused on the socio-economic causes of support for 'political Islam' while denying the ethical and religious aspects of such modes of faith and identity. In both Afghanistan and Tajikistan, however, an important aspect of my fieldwork was spending time with people who were not merely sceptical about the religious activities of reform-minded Muslims, but rather critical of the role played by Islam in their social, political and moral worlds. I had not encountered this type of Muslim voice in Chitral. The closest my Chitrali friends came to talking about religion in this way was in sharing rumours that one or another of their professors at the university was a 'communist'. Spending time with individuals with a history of participation in leftist movements, both in Afghanistan and subsequently in its diasporas, provoked me to question the assumption evident in work across the anthropology of Islam that religion was necessarily always at stake in the thinking and identities of people of Muslim background (Marsden and Retsikas 2014). I also came to see at first hand in Afghanistan that close political and social relationships existed between communist and Islamist-affiliated political figures. The forms of Muslim thought and identity I was now encountering arose in the context of a transregional Muslim arena shaped by an expansive Persianate culture. At the same time, it was impossible to understand Muslim identity and intellectual exchange in the region without taking into account the afterlife of the global Cold War. As I now explore, this wider geopolitical context also shaped the region's inhabitants' modes of intellectual exchange.

Islamism and Identity in Northern Afghanistan

I conducted fieldwork in the northern Afghan town of Kunduz between 2007 and 2009 and spent many hours participating in debates and discussions about Islam. The intellectual exchanges I participated in were informed by a Persianate heritage similar to that I had encountered in Chitral, but the context in which they took place was markedly different and this context shaped the character of such exchanges. The context in which I was now working was shot through with the afterlives of the Cold War, and this illuminated the degree to which understanding the intellectual exchanges I observed required a consideration of a wider geopolitical context and not simply one defined in relationship to a single, culturally defined knowledge ecumene.

Discussions in which I participated in Kunduz took place in a range of settings from petrol pumps (*tonk-e tel*) to bookshops (*kitab furooshi*) and in the midst of great picnics (*mela*) organized by politicians and business people. The social milieu in which I circulated in the town was highly shaped by the affiliation of my informants to the anti-Soviet mujahidin, especially the factions that were affiliated with the Islamist Jamiat-e Islami Party. In the 1990s, the party had played a prominent role in the government of Afghanistan, and its leadership continued to engage in 'resistance' (*muqawmat*) against Taliban rule until 2001 (see Roy 1992). After 2001, these figures and those affiliated to them played a major role in the governments that were established after the military defeat by the US and its local and international allies of the Taliban.

My informants in Kunduz were mostly pious people (*mardum ha ye ba taqwa*) – including many who had fought alongside the mujahidin in the anti-Soviet war in the 1980s, others who had instructed fighters in Islamist thought, and several who identified as 'Salafi' and would eventually become active members of the Taliban.[11] Yet they discussed a range of topics. Their conversations were interspersed with the poetry of Persian poets such as Hafez. A young man I had known and taught English to in Chitral, for instance, was an avid reader of Islamic reformist literature, and active in a friendship circle that identified itself as Salafi: he would go on to become an active participant in the Taliban movement in Kunduz before being killed in a night raid by US forces. This young man followed the work of Salafi thinkers and told me that he dreamed of marrying an educated Egyptian rather than a 'traditional' (*sunnati*) and 'uneducated' (*besawaad*) Afghan woman. At the same time, however, he enjoyed spending his evenings playing a game in which men sequentially recited the verses of the fourteenth-century Persian poet, Hafez. The discussions I witnessed in this group and others were serious and often animated but they were also interjected with joking and humour. My Salafi friend enjoyed making men laugh in the midst of conducting their prayers so that they would have to repeat the ritual.[12] The pious Muslims with whom I spent time in Kunduz did not all think in a positive manner about the category of 'open-mindedness'. In a discussion with two friends of my Salafi informant, rather, I was told in no uncertain terms that being *rawshan fikr* merely meant having been influenced by the West (*gharb zadagi*).

One man I came to know especially well in Kunduz was a former ideologue in the Hezb-e Islami Party led by Gulbudin Hekmatyar.[13] By the time we met, however, he had switched his allegiance to the Jamiat-e Islami Party (besides being regarded as more moderate in terms of its approach to Islam, this party largely also represented the political interests of ethnically Tajik Persian-speaking people). In subsequent years, the man achieved a degree of fame across Afghanistan for admitting on national television to the mistakes made by the mujahidin in their period of government in Kabul between 1992 and 1995 (though he also pointed towards the lengths to which secular regimes had gone across the Muslim world to disempower Islamist parties). In his everyday social relationships, however, the man was known to all for being above all else '*ijtimaaye*' (social), meaning that he was able to 'sit with anyone, big or small'. His son once told me how his father never forced his opinions about Islam on anyone, not even Afghan communists, among whom he counted many friends and never asked them to reform their behaviour in line with Islamic principles, preferring instead to encourage them to change through his own behaviour.

Importantly, while being a committed Islamist, this man was also the descendant of a religious family in northern Afghanistan that had for a long time earned repute for its position of authority within a Sufi brotherhood (*tariqa*), the local lodge (*khanaqah*) over which family members had presided. A combination of factors – including perhaps most importantly the role his family has long played as social mediators – had drawn this man to an ethics of exchange that consciously emphasized pluralism. His embrace of this position contrasted him to others in the town (including the Salafi men discussed above) who regarded open commitment to intellectual pluralism as inherently un-Islamic and a reflection of Western influence.

The Islamists of northern Afghanistan with whom I interacted were a world away from depictions by anthropologists of Islamist ideologues and piety-minded Muslims (Bayat 2007). They were educated and well versed in both Persianate and reformist expressions of Islamic thought. In terms of knowledge, they were fluent in the teachings of the Qur'an and the Sunna. They also placed high moral value on deep knowledge of the corpus of Persianate Sufi poetry. And they established relationships with people of varying backgrounds, not infrequently taking advice from individuals with very different understandings of Islam than their own. With regards to questions of personal morality, they adapted flexibly to the different situations they faced in the countries across which they moved and emphasized their ability to cultivate and maintain relationships with people regardless of their levels of religious commitment or political dispositions.

Muslim intellectual exchange in this part of Asia needed to be analysed in relation to broader political, cultural, historical and geopolitical dynamics and processes. Several visits that I made to Badakhshan between 2005 and 2011 underscored this. Until the end of the nineteenth century, Badakhshan was a khanate in Central Asia ruled by a Mir who had close relationships with neighbouring political entities, including the state of Chitral, and the court of Kabul, and the Emirate of Bukhara.[14] After that point, Badakhshan was incorporated into the structures of the Afghan state; in the first decades of the twentieth century, the region was divided along the River Pyanj between Afghanistan and the Soviet Republic of Tajikistan. Chitral and Badakhshan had hitherto been closely connected to one another through trade and the circulation of commercial, religious and official personnel, as well as sustained patterns of intermarriage. The family with whom I had lived in Chitral claimed descent from a notable religious family in Badakhshan, and, during my stays, I was able to visit their distant relatives, many of whom had lived in Chitral during the Afghan civil war in the 1980s and 1990s.

A visit I made to Badakhshan in 2011, however, alerted me not only to the region's interactions with South Asia but also to its connections to the world beyond. Staying in the Afghanistan-Tajikistan border town of Ishkashim, I made friends with a butcher (Rasul) from the neighbouring region of Panjshir. In addition to butchery, Rasul also traded in precious stones on the weekly border market (*bazaar-e mushtaraq*) that takes place in no-man's land between

Tajikistan and Afghanistan. He invited me to visit a nearby village with him in order to meet a person he thought I would find of interest. The village was an hour's drive along the rough road from Ishkashim in the direction of Faizabad (the administrative headquarters of Afghan Badakhshan) and miles from a district (Warduj) in which the Taliban were active and that friends had told me not to visit. On arriving in the village, my friend told me that he would introduce me to a committed Talib who was also a Shii Ismaili. I assumed my friend was joking – in Chitral the very concept of an Ismaili Talib would not have made sense given the overwhelmingly Sunni composition of the Taliban and a perception of it being hostile to Shii Muslims. A few minutes later, however, a bearded man in clothing resembling that generally worn by the Taliban walked in our direction and greeted us. After the traditional exchange of greetings, I joked that I had never heard of an Ismaili being a Talib. The man responded that he had been an active member of the Taliban until the early 2000s and maintained close ties with the organization. He soon told me his path to becoming a Talib. In the final years of Afghanistan's pro-Soviet government, he had been awarded a scholarship by the Afghan government for military training in Ukraine. On his return to Afghanistan in 1992, President Najibullah had relinquished power, diverse mujahidin groups had taken control of the country, and a civil war had subsequently erupted. As a result of the change in political leadership, he was not appointed to position in the country's military. Unlike many other Soviet-trained Persian-speakers from northern Afghanistan who joined mujahidin groups largely made up of Sunni ethnic Tajiks, my new acquaintance told me that he had not wished to serve alongside mujahidin leaders because of the harsh manner in which its fighters had treated Ismailis in his home region. He chose to leave Afghanistan and live in Chitral where he met individuals belonging to the Taliban. As a result of his opposition to the mujahidin fighters and leaders in government in Afghanistan at the time, he decided to join the Taliban. Aware that he was an Ismaili, the Taliban were nevertheless keen to incorporate him into their networks and structures: the technical knowledge he had acquired in Ukraine was something they and their movement needed.

My interaction with the man offered insights into the pragmatic nature of relationships in Afghanistan's political culture and structures. In the context of Afghanistan, an attempt to address the nature of piety-minded Islam without addressing national and geopolitical dynamics is entirely unsatisfactory. Anthropological work on piety-minded Islam addressed the concerns held by many anthropologists and scholars in related disciplines about the US-led 'War on Terror' and the modes of representing 'good' and 'bad' Islam with which it was connected. In the context of Afghanistan, however, the activities of the Taliban movement are intimately connected to Cold War dynamics but also to the state of Pakistan and other actors in the region – in the 1990s the Gulf States, and today China, Russia and Iran. Ethnographically, then, my conversations with interlocutors in Badakhshan and Kunduz were a constant reminder of the need to understand all forms of collective self-identification – including those of pious Muslims – in relation to local, national and transregional political and geopolitical dynamics. There was the scope for not only diversity but also varying normative positions about intellectual exchange and pluralism– some of which arose from ethical and others from pragmatic imperatives. Importantly, there was no simple correlation between the position an individual took about the ethical status of intellectual pluralism and their affiliation to a particular political or religious organization.

In the transregional arena of Muslim connectivity I was investigating, it was too simplistic to assume that the ethical and ideological dynamics of movements of Islamic piety were inevitably shaped in relationship to the Islamic discursive tradition. A research trip I made to Kabul in 2017 resulted in further insights into the internal complex relationship between ethnicity, religion and geopolitics. During the course of the trip, I visited a notable figure from Badakhshan who had served in various levels of government during the mujahidin and post-Taliban regimes. Affiliated with the Jamiat-e Islami and from a family of religious notables tied by kin to Chitral, I had known his family members in Pakistan and spent time in his home village in Badakhshan in the summer of 2010. On this occasion, he was hosting a gathering of influential politicians from across Afghanistan's political spectrum. They had been invited by the figure to interact with Afghan men and women whose names had recently been submitted by the country's president to the parliament for approval for ministerial appointments. During the evening, the ministerial candidates would have the opportunity to persuade the sitting MPs that they were worthy of their support in an upcoming vote in the parliament. MPs in Kabul often used such occasions to request gifts from the candidates in return for pledging to offer them their votes.

Rather than have myself sit between senior figures in Afghanistan's government, I was beckoned next to the man who my host joked was also English (*inglis*), presumably on account of his fair skin and light hair colour. My new companion transpired to be a Shughni-speaking Ismaili from Badakhshan.[15] Having undergone training in the Soviet Union, he had served in the security services of the Afghan state in the 1980s. At the time of our meeting, he was living with his family in Tajikistan's Badakhshan border town of Khorog, while also seeking the support of the notable figure from Badakhshan in whose garden we were sitting for securing employment in the Afghan Ministry of Defence. After briefly chatting over a sumptuous meal of kebabs and rice cooked with meatballs and pulses and glasses of green tea, we shared our phone numbers and agreed to meet the next day in the historic Bagh-e Babur – the burial place of the Mughal Emperor Babur. Walking around the gardens – restored in the 2000s by the Aga Khan Trust for Culture – the man told me that during the pro-Soviet government of Dr Najibullah, he had served in the presidential bodyguard.[16] After the fall of Najibullah's government, he had maintained a position in the presidential guard during the period of mujahidin rule, during which time Professor Burhanuddin Rabbani, a Cairo-educated Islamist from Badakhshan, had been Afghanistan's president. My newly made friend then went on to explain how during the era of the Taliban he had continued to serve in the country's security and intelligence services. Being Ismaili, he did not pray alongside the Taliban. Yet he was able to avoid the attention of their morality police (*amr bil maruf*) by growing a beard and vocally remonstrating with people he met on the street who had not offered their prayers (*namaz*). Later in the evening, we took a taxi to the exterior gates of the house of one of Afghanistan's most influential political figures. Having whispered a code (*fish*) to a bodyguard and handed over a small bundle of cash, a bottle of locally brewed alcohol (*sharaab watani*) was handed over to my friend, which we consumed that evening with kebabs. Interacting with individuals active on the fringes of the Taliban illuminated the problems of anthropological work on both piety-minded and everyday Islam that overlooks the significance of political dynamics and pragmatism.

Self-reflexive discussions about the nature and ethics of intellectual exchange formed an important aspect of the discourses of the Muslims in northern Afghanistan with whom I worked. Informed both by ethical and pragmatic concerns depending on the backgrounds and situations of individuals and communities, the nature and character of normative positions about intellectual exchange were shaped by the Cold War and its ongoing geopolitical legacies. If a shared Persianate heritage was evident in continuities in the nature of intellectual exchange in Chitral and northern Afghanistan, the significance of the Cold War to life in the latter context had also resulted in significant ruptures and differences in the parameter, consequences and nature of such intellectual exchanges.

Khorasan and the Reconceptualization of the Nation State

Attempts by scholars to conceptualize the Persianate world and transregional forms of Muslim thought, identity and agency are mirrored in debates among intellectuals and politicians from the region about their collective history and identity. As I now explore, these debates build both on historical scholarship arising in Western universities and from the work of intellectuals from Afghanistan and the wider region, many of whom lead mobile and diasporic lives, and, critically, have participated in formal higher education programmes in diverse geopolitical contexts.

During my research visits to Afghanistan, I interacted with many different actors who identified themselves in relation to a history that they counterpoised to the boundaries of the modern nation state. Many of my Persian-speaking informants from northern and western Afghanistan routinely reject the identity category 'Afghan'. They argue that in Afghanistan's Persian-speaking communities the term *Afghan* – locally pronounced *awghan* – refers specifically to Pashto-speaking peoples. On entering the Panjshir valley – a Persian-speaking region that was the base of the anti-Soviet and anti-Taliban fighter Ahmad Shah Massoud (d. 2001) – graffiti inscribed on a large river boulder reads '*ma afghan nistim* (we are not Afghans)', the title also of a popular song sung by a young musician from the region. Some of my interlocutors argue that the term 'Afghanistani' better identifies their identity (*huiyat*) than 'Afghan'. Afghanistani, they say, identifies citizenship as defined by the state of Afghanistan rather than membership of a particular ethno-linguistic group.

Others, however, are critical of the notion of Afghanistan itself. They reject not only the ethnonym 'Afghan', but also the geographical and cultural categories with which the term is now entwined. These actors promote the use of categories that, they argue, more closely reflect their historical and cultural backgrounds. Most regularly, for instance, the term Khorasan is deployed by Persian-speakers in Afghanistan to refer to the territories within and beyond Afghanistan with which they identify.[17] Advocates of this cultural geography include not only intellectuals but also influential political figures who refer to '*Khorasan zamin*' (the land of Khorasan) in their speeches, published books and articles, and in widely read and circulated social media communications. Such intellectual trends and debates are also materialized in the broader community and its social institutions. Restaurants owned by traders from Afghanistan named 'Khorasan', for instance, indicate the political viewpoint of their owners, as well as their active participation in political and intellectual debates about culture and identity in Afghanistan. Such discourses are enriched by debate and discussion with intellectuals – often based in the country's diasporas – who both conduct independent research on the region's history and maintain close relationships with political figures, sometimes as paid advisors (*mushawar*), but mostly from within friendship circles.

The use of the term Khorasan in Afghanistan is highly controversial and if transregional connections are an important aspect of life in the wider arena this in no sense means that the boundaries of the modern nation state are insignificant. Those who use such terminology are widely accused of treachery (*khiyaanat kardan*) by political figures who promote autochthonous forms of nationalism. According to such forms of national identity, Afghanistan's indigenous (*bhumi*) population are distinct ethno-linguistic groups (notably Uzbeks and Tajiks) that are depicted as having migrated to the country from Central Asia in the wake of the Bolshevik revolution. A former ambassador of Afghanistan to a country in the MENA region told me that critiques of dominant discourses of Afghan nationalism were largely repressed until the emergence of greater intellectual and political space in the country following the defeat of the Taliban by international forces and their local allies in 2001. The ambassador, a trained religious scholar, argued that support for the Taliban among the country's political elites arose from a desire to crush such discourses and their attempts to rethink national identity in Afghanistan. Meanwhile, an intellectual active in developing the concept of Khorasan in the 1980s told me that influential figures from northern Afghanistan who in later years had widely used the concept in their speeches had initially been critical of him because they regarded his use of the term as indicating his disloyalty to Afghanistan and his tacit promotion of ethnic separatism.

In the 2000s, a group of Persian-speaking 'Afghanistanis' from a range of settings across northern Afghanistan who were based in London established an organization that held talks and produced publications about Khorasan's history. Speakers at events included both students from Afghanistan studying in UK universities and scholars in Europe and North America with an interest in the study of the history of Afghanistan. The general aim of the group's activities was to illuminate the effect of the modern Afghan nation state on the historic identities of the regions of Afghanistan with which they identified. This group of scholars also emphasized the historic significance of the Hanafi School (*maslak*) of Islamic jurisprudence to the identity of Muslims in Southwest and Central Asia.[18] In this respect, while emphasizing the broad historical and cultural geography of which modern-day Afghanistan is a part, some of these actors depict non-Hanafi forms of Sunni Islam (e.g. Salafism) and Shii Islam (including the Twelver and Ismaili clusters) as being external to the region's culture and therefore a source of disunity (*fitna*). Some members active in the organization had been officials in former Afghan governments – being aligned both to communist and left-wing movements (several having also studied for degrees in the Soviet Union) and to the mujahidin-led administration of the 1990s (of whom some had studied for degrees in Islamic studies in universities run by Afghan Islamist organizations in Pakistan). Still more were the sons of influential Afghan political and intellectual figures from a variety of backgrounds and had recently studied various aspects of Afghan history at British universities. Over the course of the following decade and more, several members of the organization and participants at the events it had held travelled to Afghanistan in order to take up positions in the government, mostly working as senior advisors for politicians from the north of the country. In turn, on their visits to the UK, influential politicians from northern Afghanistan gave speeches focusing on the idea of Khorasan to large audiences assembled by diaspora organizations.

There is diversity in terms of the ideas that the members of different organizations hold about the cultural content of the idea of Khorasan. A range of different cultural organizations have been established in the UK. One of these, for example, does not merely emphasize the transregional aspects of northern Afghanistan's history, they also emphasize in their activities the region's pre-Islamic history, arguing that Islam was imposed upon the region forcibly by Arabs. Proponents of this approach to Khorasani geography and history and of its relevance to modern identity took active steps to distance particular aspects of their self-identifications from Islam, most usually by changing their given Arabic names for pre-Islamic Persian names, at least informally.

A form of diaspora politics and identity that focuses on ethnic boundaries informs the notion of Khorasan. At the same time, however, the geographical category of Khorasan enables the articulation of an imagined geography rooted in an alternative history to that of the modern nation state of Afghanistan. This is because the key historic urban centres of contemporary Afghanistan (especially Herat and Balkh) were of great significance in the eastern Islamic lands in the mediaeval period. Cultural organizations in Afghanistan are active in promoting and articulating scales of identity, culture and geography alternative to those of the modern nation state. One Afghan think tank, for instance, active in the country until its takeover by the Taliban in August 2021, organized its flagship conferences in the historic city of Herat (rather than the country's capital of Kabul) in order to celebrate the city's mediaeval position in a wider geography. Rather than subsuming this to the logic of modern Afghanistan, the think tank addressed wider transregional aspects and dimensions of the issues facing Afghanistan and used its events as a platform to promote regional dialogues with neighbouring countries including Iran, Uzbekistan and Tajikistan. As with the UK-based organizations, the think tank also hosts speakers and conducts research that challenges the singular role of Islam in the political culture of Afghanistan. It organized events and publications focusing on religious diversity in historic Khorasan, initiating discussion in Herat and beyond, for example, about the role played by Jews in the urban dynamics of the city and the wider Khorasan region. Leading figures within the think tank regard Khorasan not as a template for a new nation state but rather as facilitating the presentation of a different image of Afghanistan to the wider world. In addition, according to their interpretations, the culture of Khorasan is crystallized in terms of connections between multiple traditions and geographies, meaning that it carries the possibility of promoting cultural and historic relations between Afghanistan and countries in West and Central Asia. As with many other politicians and intellectuals active in debates about Khorasan, he argues that such relations have been marginalized by the focus of both Afghan nationalists and Western policy-makers on the country's close relationship to Pakistan. In this context, the idea of Khorasan being a historically inclusive cultural realm is part of a project of the imagination produced and sustained by intellectuals, cultural elites, diaspora figures, international finance organizations and regional governments.[19]

Politically, however, Khorasan is not simply a way of referring to the geographic location and cultural composition of Afghanistan in relationship to the notion of the transregional. It also reflects the significance of language and ethnicity to Afghanistan's political dynamics. Identifying with the notion of Khorasan often indexes a distinction between Persian-speakers (referred to in Afghanistan as Persian-speakers or *farsiwan*), as well as those identifying as Turkic-speakers (*turk tabaar*), and Pashto-speaking Pashtuns – the latter being widely, if problematically, represented in those advocating for Khorasan as dominating the country's political structures.[20] In terms of ethnicity, the vast majority of people who identify themselves as 'Khorasani' regard themselves as being ethnic 'Tajiks', though Uzbeks are also active in attempts to define the concept.

Afghanistan's position in the Cold War is also imprinted in powerful ways on the genealogy of the idea of Khorasan in modern Afghanistan. Leftist movements and organizations in northern Afghanistan played a critical role in influencing discussions about the relationship of ethnicity to the state in the country and also in shaping the imagination of alternatives to it. Building on the theories of national identity important in the Soviet Union, leftist thinkers, notably the Badakhshan-born Tahir Badakhshi (1933–79), interpreted their revolutionary struggles in relation to ethnic and regional political struggle. Badakhshi's 'Revolutionary Organization of the Toilers of Afghanistan' argued that a socialist revolution would only be possible in the country after the end of the 'national oppression' of minority ethno-linguistic groups by the Pashtun political elite (see Nunan 2016).

Within the geopolitically divided Persianate realm, the notion of Khorasan also enables types of expansive geographical imaginations that are not subordinate to the regional political ambitions of powerful nation states in the region, notably Iran. This is especially important in the context of Afghanistan given the hierarchical relationship of the country to Iran and the degree to which Afghan nationalism has historically sought to distinguish the form of Persian spoken in the country (officially referred to as Dari since 1958) from that spoken in Iran.[21] Indeed, autochthonous nationalist movements in Afghanistan depict communities that have ties to adjacent regions of Iran and Central Asia through marriage and kinship as inauthentic Afghans. The leaders of such movements regularly depict individuals, movements and organizations that emphasize the importance of transregional connections and histories to their identities as pursuing the geopolitical agendas of neighbouring states, especially Iran but also Tajikistan, and therefore as being disloyal to Afghanistan.

Conclusion

'The Alan question' contrasted the particular with the general, and the local with the global, in a manner that narrowed the scope for considering the ways in which the Muslims with whom I worked mediated between different yet interacting scales of history and geography. Using this framework made it difficult to conceptualize the ways in which life at the intersections of these scales had important implications for understanding the thinking, agency and identity formations of a wider and inherently transregional context. Far from being exceptional, the forms of Muslim thought and identity I encountered in Chitral were nestled in an expansive arena that transgressed the conventional boundaries of culture areas and nation states (cf. van Schendell 2002).

This chapter has sought to make a contribution to this volume's focus on intellectual exchange in two major ways. First, I have sought to reflect on the ways in which my ethnographic work on Muslim thought and identity has been shaped by multiple forms of intellectual exchange over the past two decades and more. Of particular importance have been my attempts to engage with historical scholarship on Islam, and with my diverse and varied interlocutors in the field. Both of these axes of intellectual exchange build on the key themes of Susan Bayly's work (see the Introduction). Second, the chapter has also contributed to the anthropology of intellectual exchange in Muslim societies by arguing that in addition to recognizing the significance of the Persianate ecumene and the Islamic ethical tradition, geopolitical processes also play a powerful role in shaping the character and direction of intellectual exchange in complex transregional arenas in Muslim Asia.

Across the specific arena in which I have worked, 'the Islamic' articulates in a complex manner with linguist, ethnic, national and sectarian identity markers. Various manifestations of modern and global Islam, notably those labelled as reformist and Salafi, also compete for space and influence. The people with whom I work are also fluent in a range of practices from travel to poetry and music that reflect and sustain a shared Persianate history. On reflection, my initial work on Chitral was insufficiently bold in challenging conceptualizations of Islam as a religion that revolves around legal and ethical prescriptions. Chitrali Muslims did not, as I had argued, merely cherish a form of Islam shaped by Persianate culture and criticize reformist Islam. Rather, in the wider region in which they lived, 'the Islamic' was best defined in terms of its capaciousness and ability to incorporate multiple and often contradictory aspects (Ahmed 2015). As I have shown in this chapter, such contradictions are enfolded in the lives of pious Muslims as much as they are evident in the field of 'everyday Islam'. Historians have tended to equate the rise of the modern era with the demise of 'world Islam'. My fieldwork points, however, towards the ongoing relevance of historic expressions of world Islam, even in a context that has been shaped powerfully by reformism, the modern nation state and multiple geopolitical projects. The expressions of the Islamic that I have studied have been formed in the context of intense and ongoing intellectual interactions and exchanges in multiple and overlapping domains of life. They are evident in the activities of villagers, small-town people, urban intellectuals, religious scholars, political leaders and movements, as well as merchants and long-distance traders. The modes of Islam with which they are attached continue to occupy an important yet dynamic aspect of the thought, identities and experience of Muslims in this arena.

The chapter has also explored the ways in which the intellectual exchanges that permeate everyday life in connected regions of South and Central Asia are shaped in relationship to transregional forms of Muslim thought and agency. In order to understand the direction and nature of intellectual exchanges involving the region's diverse Muslim population, these need to be analysed in relation to geopolitical events and processes of significance to the region's people, notably those emerging in the context of the global Cold War. Approaching intellectual exchange in relation to these overlapping contexts enables an understanding of their significance in the production of a diverse range of imaginations and identity formations that hold political, cultural and religious significance in the region.

Data Statement

This study was based on data collected for three projects: 'The Afterlives of Urban Muslim Asia: Alternative Imaginaries of Society and Polity' (grant number AH/V004999/1); TRODITIES, 'Yiwu Trust, Global Traders and Commodities in a Chinese International City', European Research Council under the European Union's Horizon 2020 research and innovation programme 669 132; and 'Islam, Trade and Citizenship on the Frontiers of Central and South Asia', funded by the Leverhulme Trust. Due to the politically sensitive nature of the research, some the data analysed in this article cannot be made openly available. Data relevant to parts of the article is available at https://protecteu.mimecast.com/s/W9kTCg2QrT1Dp3KfN0rtN?domain=doi.org.

Acknowledgements

The research upon which this article is based would not have been possible without funding from the Arts and Humanities Research Council, United Kingdom, for the project entitled 'The Afterlives of Urban Muslim Asia: Alternative Imaginaries of Society and Polity' (grant number AH/V004999/1). The article analyses data gathered in the context of research funded by the European Research Council under the European Union's Horizon 2020 research and innovation programme 669 132 – TRODITIES, 'Yiwu Trust, Global Traders and Commodities in a Chinese International City'. It also builds on fieldwork conducted for a project entitled 'Islam, Trade and Citizenship on the Frontiers of Central and South Asia' that was funded by the Leverhulme Trust. I am grateful to David Henig for his critical comments on an earlier version of the article, three Berghahn anonymous reviewers, and the book's editors.

Magnus Marsden is Professor of Social Anthropology at the University of Sussex where he is also the Director of the Sussex Asia Centre.

Notes

1. Alan MacFarlane was a longstanding member of the Department of Social Anthropology at Cambridge who also acted as Susan Bayly's 'mentor' after her appointment to Lecturer in Social Anthropology in 2000.
2. The North West Frontier Province was renamed Khyber Pakhtunkhwa in 2010.
3. The Jama'at-i Islami is Pakistan's most established Islamist party founded by the politician-ideologue Mawlana Mawdudi (d. 1979). See Nasr 1994.
4. I follow Nile Green and deploy the broad concept of 'Muslim Asia' as a 'collective shorthand for Asia's Muslim-majority population zones' (Green 2016: 275).
5. It was hard as a young anthropologist writing about Islam at the time not to be affected by an environment in which depictions of Islam in general and Pakistan in particular focused almost inevitably upon brainwashed madrassa students, violent insurgents and

the ultra-orthodox forms of sharia embraced by the Taliban. To challenge such stereotypes by depicting another side of Muslim life in Pakistan, however, came with its own pitfalls. Such work ran the risk of reproducing the simplistic discourses of many public intellectuals and policy-makers at the time who categorized Muslims in terms of their being either 'good' or 'bad' (Mamdani 2004).

6. For one especially critical discussion on the concept of 'the Middle East', see Green 2014.
7. For a detailed discussion, see Marsden and Henig 2019.
8. For a notable exception, see Henig 2016.
9. For an overview, see Marsden 2012.
10. On the experience by the region's people of the Cold War, see Nunan 2016 and Kirasirova 2011.
11. The term 'Salafi' referred to Muslims who advocate a return to Islamic 'first principles' as laid out in the Qur'an and the Sunna. See Farquhar 2016.
12. On the historical significance of humour to debate in the region, see Subtelny 1984.
13. On the Hezb-e Islami, see Edwards 1993.
14. On the history of northern Afghanistan, see Lee 1996 and Noelle-Karimi 1997.
15. Shughni is an Indo-Iranian language spoken in the Shughnan districts of both Afghanistan and Tajikistan.
16. The Aga Khan Trust for Culture is an organization working within the broader remit of the Aga Khan Development Foundation – a development organization founded by the leader of the world's Shii Ismaili Muslims, the Aga Khan.
17. Khorasan is generally used to refer to a region that today comprises the eastern part of Iran, the west and north of Afghanistan, and those parts of formerly Soviet Central Asia that lie on the southern banks of the Amu Darya (Oxus River). Most of the people with whom I interact deploy a broader usage that incorporates Persian-speaking regions of modern-day Tajikistan and Uzbekistan. The term dates back to sixth-century Sassanian Iran, but it was also used by a variety of political entities and empires in the region after the arrival of Islam in the seventh century. On the shifting geography of Khorasan in the early modern period, see, for example, Noelle-Karimi 2014.
18. The Hanafi School of jurisprudence (*fiqh*) is named after Abū Ḥanīfa an-Nu'man ibn Thābit, an eighth-century CE Muslim jurist of Persian ancestry whose family is regarded by many in northern Afghanistan as originally hailing from present-day Charikar, a town to the north of Kabul.
19. See also Anderson's (forthcoming) discussions of the ways in which his informants from Aleppo argue that people from the city are the heirs of a unique 'Eastern Spirit'.
20. On the problematic narrative of 'Pashtun domination' in the history of Afghanistan, see Hanifi 2011.
21. On such attempts to bind according to nationality different forms of Persian, see Green 2019.

References

Ahmed, Irfan. 2017. *Religion as Critique: Islamic Critical Thinking from Mecca to the Marketplace.* Chapel Hill: University of North Carolina Press.

Ahmed, Shahab. 2015. *What Is Islam? The Importance of Being Islamic.* Princeton, NJ: University Press.

Alam, Muzafar, and Sanjay Subrahmanyam. 2007. *Indo-Persian Travels in the Age of Discoveries, 1400–1800.* Cambridge: Cambridge University Press.

Anderson Paul. 2023. *Exchange Ideologies and Merchant Politics in Post-Baathist Aleppo.* Ithaca, NY: Cornell University Press.

Asad, Talal. 1986. 'The Idea of an Anthropology of Islam', *Occasional Paper Series*. Washington, DC: Center for Contemporary Arab Studies, Georgetown University.
Bashir, Shahzad. 2014. 'On Islamic Time: Rethinking Chronology in the Historiography of Muslim Societies', *History and Theory* 53(4): 519–44.
Bayat, Asef. 2007. 'Islamism and the Politics of Fun', *Public Culture* 19(3): 433–59.
Bayly, Christopher. 1989. *Imperial Meridian: The British Empire and the World 1780–1830*. London: Routledge.
Canfield, Robert L. (ed.). 2002. *Turko-Persia in Historical Perspective*. Cambridge: Cambridge University Press.
Cole, Juan. 2002. 'Iranian Culture and South Asia, 1500–1900', in Nikki Keddie and Rudi Matthee (eds), *Iran and the Surrounding World: Interactions in Culture and Cultural Politics*. Seattle: University of Washington Press, pp. 15–35.
Das, Veena. 1996. *Critical Events: An Anthropological Perspective on Contemporary India*. Delhi: Oxford University Press.
Edwards, David. 1993. 'Summoning Muslims: Print, Politics, and Religious Ideology in Afghanistan', *The Journal of Asian Studies* 52(3): 609–28.
Englund, Harri. 2007. 'Pentecostalism beyond Belief: Trust and Democracy in a Malawian Township', *Africa* 77(4): 477–99.
Farquhar, Michael. 2016. *Circuits of Faith: Migration, Education, and the Wahhabi Mission*. Stanford, CA: Stanford University Press
Gilsenan, Michael. 1982. *Recognising Islam*. London: Croom Helm.
Green, Nile. 2014. 'Rethinking the "Middle East" after the Oceanic Turn', *Comparative Studies of South Asia, Africa and the Middle East* 34: 556–64.
———. 2016. 'The Demographics of Dystopia: The Muslim City in Asia's Future', *History and Anthropology* 27(3): 273–95.
———. 2019. 'Introduction: The Frontiers of the Persian World (ca. 800–1900)', in Nile Green (ed.), *The Persianate World: The Frontiers of a Eurasian Lingua Franca*. Berkeley: California University Press, pp. 1–71.
———. 2020. *Global Islam: A Very Short Introduction*. Oxford: Oxford University Press.
Hamid el-Zein, Abdul. 1977. 'Beyond Ideology and Theology: The Search for the Anthropology of Islam', *Annual Review of Anthropology* 6(1): 227–54.
Henig, David. 2016. 'Crossing the Bosphorus: Connected Histories of "Other" Muslims in the Post-Imperial Borderlands of Southeast Europe', *Comparative Studies in Society and History* 58(4): 908–34.
———. 2020. *Remaking Muslim Lives: Everyday Islam in Postwar Bosnia and Herzegovina*. Champaign: University of Illinois Press.
Hirschkind, Charles. 2006. *The Ethical Soundscape: Cassette Sermons and Islamic Counterpublics*. New York: Columbia University Press.
Ho, Engseng. 2006. *Graves of Tarim: Genealogy and Mobility across the Indian Ocean*. Berkeley: University of California Press.
———. 2017. 'Inter-Asian Concepts for Mobile Societies', *Journal of Asian Studies* 76(9): 907–28.
Hodgson, Marshall. 1963. 'The Interrelations of Society in History', *Comparative Studies in Society and History* 5(2): 227–50.
Kia, Mana. 2020. *Persianate Selves: Memories of Place and Origin before Nationalism*. Stanford, CA: Stanford University Press.
Kirasirova, Masha. 2011. '"Sons of Muslims" in Moscow: Soviet Central Asian Mediators to the Foreign East, 1955–1962', *Ab Imperio* 4: 106–32.

Koselleck, Reinhart. 2018. *Sediments of Time: On Possible Histories*, trans. and ed. Dean Franzel and Stefan-Ludwig Hoffman. Palo Alto, CA: Stanford University Press.

Kreutzmann, Hermann. 1998. 'The Chitral Triangle', *Asien Afrika Lateinamerika* 26: 289–327.

———. 2015. *Pamirian Crossroads: Kirghiz and Wakhi of High Asia*. Wiesbaden: Harrassowitz Verlag.

Kwon, H. 2010. *The Other Cold War*. New York: Columbia University Press.

Lee, Jonathan. 1996. *The 'Ancient Supremacy': Bukhara, Afghanistan and the Battle for Balkh, 1731–1901*. Leiden: Brill.

Levi, Scott. 2020. *Bukharan Crisis: A Connected History of 18th-Century Central Asia*. Pittsburgh: University of Pittsburgh Press.

Mahmood, Saba. 2004. *Politics of Piety: The Islamic Revival and the Feminist Subject*. Princeton, NJ: Princeton University Press.

Mamdani, Mahmoud. 2004. *Good Muslim, Bad Muslim: America, the Cold War and the Roots of Terror*. Ranikhet: Permanent Black.

Mandaville, Peter. 2001. *Transnational Muslim Politics: Reimagining the Umma*. London: Routledge.

Marsden, Magnus. 2005. *Living Islam: Muslim Religious Experience in North-West Pakistan*. Cambridge: Cambridge University Press.

———. 2008 'Muslim Cosmopolitans? Transnational Life in Northern Pakistan', *The Journal of Asian Studies* 67(1): 213–47.

———.2012. 'Southwest and Central Asia: Comparison, Integration or Beyond?', in Richard Fardon (ed.), *The Sage Handbook of Social Anthropology*. London: Sage, pp. 340–65.

———. 2016. *Trading Worlds: Afghan Merchants across Modern Frontiers*. London/ New York: Hurst/Oxford University Press.

———. 2021. *Beyond the Silk Roads: Trade, Mobility and Geopolitics across Eurasia*. Cambridge: Cambridge University Press.

Marsden, Magnus, and David Henig. 2019. 'Muslim Circulations and Networks in West Asia: Ethnographic Perspectives on Transregional Connectivity', *Journal of Eurasian Studies* 10(1): 11–21.

Marsden, Magnus, and Benjamin D. Hopkins. 2012. *Fragments of the Afghan Frontier*. London: Hurst.

Marsden, Magnus, and Kostas Retsikas. 2014. 'Introduction', in M. Marsden and K. Retsikas (eds), *Articulating Islam: Anthropological Approaches to Muslim Worlds*. Dordrecht: Springer, pp. 1–31.

Nasr, Seyed Vali Reza. 1994. *The Vanguard of the Islamic Revolution: Jama'at-i Islami of Pakistan*. London: I.B. Tauris.

Noelle-Karimi, Christine. 1997. *State and Tribe in Nineteenth-Century Afghanistan*. Richmond: Curzon Press.

———. 2014. *The Pearl in Its Midst: Herat and the Mapping of Khurasan (15th–19th Centuries)*. Österreichische Akademie der Wissenschaften. Veröffentlichungen zur Iranistik 74/Denkschriften der philosophisch-historischen Klasse, 463. Band. Vienna: Verlag der ÖAW.

Nunan, Timothy. 2016. *Humanitarian Invasion: Global Developments in Cold War Afghanistan*. Cambridge: Cambridge University Press.

Osella, Filippo, and Benjamin Soares. 2020. 'Religiosity and Its Others: Lived Islam in West Africa and South India', *Social Anthropology* 28(2): 466–81.

Peletz, Michael. 1997. '"Ordinary Muslims" and Muslim Resurgents in Contemporary Malaysia: Notes on an Ambivalent Relationship', in Robert W. Hefner and Patricia

Horvatich (eds), *Islam in an Era of Nation-States: Politics and Religious Renewal in Muslim Southeast Asia*. Hawaii: Hawaii University Press, pp. 231–73.

Pickett, James. 2020. *Polymaths of Islam: Power and Networks of Knowledge in Central Asia*. Ithaca, NY: Cornell University Press.

Roy, Olivier. 1992. *Islam and Resistance in Afghanistan*. Cambridge: Cambridge University Press.

Schielke, Samuli. 2009. 'Being Good in Ramadan: Ambivalence, Fragmentation and the Moral Self in the Lives of Young Egyptians', *Journal of the Royal Anthropological Institute* 15(S1): S24–40.

Shahrani, Nazif. 1984. 'Causes and Context of Responses to the Saur Revolution in Badakhshan', in Nazif Shahrani and Robert L. Canfield (eds), *Revolutions and Rebellions in Afghanistan: Anthropological Perspectives*. Berkeley: University of California Press, pp. 139–69.

______. 2001. 'Pining for Bukhara in Afghanistan: Poetics and Politics of Exilic Identity and Emotions', in Timur Kocaoglu (ed.), *Reform Movements and Revolutions in Turkistan 1900–1924: Studies in Honour of Osman Khoj*. Haarlem, Netherlands: SOTA, pp. 369–91.

Shryock, Andrew, and D.L. Smail. 2011. *Deep History: The Archaeology of Past and Present*. Berkeley: California University Press.

Soares, Benjamin, and Filippo Osella. 2009. 'Islam, Politics, Anthropology', *Journal of the Royal Anthropological Institute* 15: S1–23.

Sood, Gagan. 2016. *India and the Islamic Heartlands: An Eighteenth-Century World of Circulation and Exchange*. Cambridge: Cambridge University Press.

Subtelny, Maria Eva. 1984. 'Scenes from the Literary Life of Tīmurīd Hērāt', in R. Savory and D.A. Agius (eds), *Logos Islamicus: Studia Islamica in Honorem Georgii Michaelis Wickens*. Toronto: Pontifical Institute of Mediaeval Studies, pp. 133–75.

van Schendel, Willhelm. 2002. 'Geographies of Knowing, Geographies of Ignorance: Jumping Scale in Southeast Asia', *Environment and Planning D: Society and Space* 20(6): 647–68.

Wimmer, Andreas, and Nina Glick Schiller. 2002. 'Methodological Nationalism and Beyond: Nation-State Building, Migration and the Social Sciences', *Global Networks* 2(4): 301–34.

5

Super Singhs and Kaurageous Kaurs
Sikh Names, Caste and Disidentity Politics

Jacob Copeman

Susan Bayly (Chapter 2, this volume) writes of intellectual exchange as 'a bridging of worlds, not necessarily successfully or completely, but with at least the possibility of boundaries crossed and the generation of ties'. Naming practices can be employed as means of doing both precisely this and its opposite. Names frequently bridge (families, cultural forms, times), but bridges, and name-bridges too, may be burned – most dramatically in cases of 'toponymic cleansing', typically after regime changes, when the renaming of streets, places and monuments can remove unwanted associations in enactments of symbolic retribution (Azaryahu 2011), but also in cases where the composite religious connotations of boundary-crossing names are expunged in favour of singular onomastic signage (Copeman 2015; see also Bayly 2004; Banerjee 2008). In this chapter, 'name exchange' principally refers to the straightforward substitution of one personal name for another. However, reflecting anthropological work that shows how names and titles can form political, ritual or economic resources exchangeable between specific exchange partners (Codere 1950; Harrison 1990), the chapter also considers attempts to restrict certain personal names from exchange (Weiner 1992), even the mode of exchange that is an exchange *for* rather than an exchange *between*, thereby causing such names to resemble a form of intellectual or cultural property comparable to protected brand names (Hayden 2011) or proper names as used in commercial trademarks (Harrison 1999). Name exchange is thus a particularly layered instance of exchange, because while a name can in itself form a bridge or tie between worlds, exchanging one name for another also involves sometimes controversial displacements, assertion of boundaries and disputation concerning ownership and use rights. It is therefore unsurprising that such name exchanges frequently both arise out of and prompt charged debates and *intellectual* exchanges.

The foundational exchange of names on which this chapter is based took place in 1699 when Guru Gobind Singh, the tenth and final living Sikh Guru, enacted the birth of the Khalsa (order of initiated Sikhs).[1] It was then, in Anandpur, that the guru, 'through a dramatic hoax, demanded the ultimate test of loyalty to his person as a holy man' (Gold 1987: 21). Asking for volunteers to offer him their heads in a test of faith, he secretly substituted goats for the five disciples who stood up ready to sacrifice their lives. It was here also that the famous five distinctive symbols that identify Sikhs as Sikhs were adopted – *kesh* (long hair), *kara* (bracelet), *kangha* (comb), *kirpan* (sword) and *kacha* (underclothes). At the same time, in a template meant to be followed, each of the disciples exchanged his family and community (caste) name in favour of 'Singh', a name typically used by the prestigious Rajput caste, which is associated with martial, lordly ideals and claims Kshatriya descent. One of the four major *varnas*, or caste groupings, of 'idealised human callings', Kshatriyas are 'usually associated with rulers and warriors, but also includ[e] seigneurial landed groups' (Bayly 1999: 8). The exchange thereby entailed taking the symbolic form of a prestigious name from one zone of the culture and moving it to another.[2] 'Distinctions of caste, class, and family profession are therewith abolished', says Nikky-Guninder Kaur Singh (2005: 56), and 'a new egalitarian and kindred identity announced in the new family name of Singh'. However, while the resounding importance of the 'five K' identity markers has received sustained and illuminating scholarly attention (e.g. Uberoi 1991), and so has the ideal-typical Sikh body that bears them (e.g. Axel 2001), analysis of the guru's act of renaming and its consequences remains comparatively insubstantial. This insubstantiality is puzzling given how richly resonant and imbued with meaning the name Singh and names more broadly are for many if not all Sikhs. The equivalent caste-obviating name for a Sikh female, Kaur, is equally as resonant and meaningful as the male Singh with which it forms a pair in a multilayered symbolic complex. At the same time, Kaur and Singh each possess their own specific histories, values and connotations.

This chapter explores the tensions as well as creativity in the ways Sikhs both in India and the diaspora use, change and debate what to do with those apparently innocent male and female identity markers, Singh and Kaur. It aims to provide a composite portrait of these names – ethnographically and historically informed, but far from complete – through discussion of a series of condensed accounts of Sikh 'name exchanges' in which one name is exchanged for another. These name exchanges both emerge from and precipitate intellectual exchanges. Further, they generate forms of exchange value. If, classically speaking, exchange value is the value acquired when objects are exchanged for one another, expressed in money and price, the exchange of names produces a different kind of exchange value, one that is qualitative rather than quantitative. For instance, the foundational name exchange enacted by Guru Gobind Singh, as classically understood, aimed to mix the four castes into one and fashion Singhs as one family and thereby to instil the value that all were equal in race and creed (K. Singh 1952). It follows that Kaur/Singh are as much *disidentity* as identity markers, undoing identity on one level while remaking it on another – a reminder of solidarity's entwinement with estrangement and disidentification (Stasch 2009). These names, alongside the five Ks, allow Sikhs to present – to be treated, or counted – as 'one thing, something that, before it was thus unified or counted, was neither unified nor particular' (Hallward 2003: 5; Badiou 2006).

The meanings, values and uses of the names Singh and Kaur are far from fixed and have been discussed and debated for centuries. These debates have particularly focused on their non-use, re-use, or over-use, and the name exchanges presented here must be understood as set within and precipitative of further orders of (intellectual) exchange in the form of critique and counter-critique. To reiterate, vibrant debates and intellectual exchanges both give rise to and in turn are precipitated by practices of name exchange. Such debates and exchanges are not solely cerebral but grounded in strong and potentially volatile affects, alerting us to how emotions are intertwined with the more reason-oriented aspects of intellectual exchange, supporting the latter by 'providing [them] with salience and goals' (Blom and Lama-Rewal 2020: 3). These affects and desires are linked to identifications, which must be understood with reference to broader historical processes and structures as well as the emotive force and impact they bring to such debates. Caste is one such salient identification. The most frequently heard complaint concerning Kaur/Singh among both orthodox Sikh reformers and the 'ordinary' west Delhi Sikhs I have spent time with[3] is that their disuse is strongly linked to a resurgence of caste identities. The concern is that Guru Gobind Singh's exchange of names at the birth of the Khalsa is being reversed, with caste names increasingly reinstalled and Kaur/Singh dropped: the value of equality thereby is lost and that of caste affiliation enhanced through this reversal of the founding exchange of names.

Yet concerns over the nature and use of these names go beyond their vexed relationship with matters of caste, even as caste logics remain difficult to withstand. Following this, a key focus of the chapter is on the role of government agencies, not caste, in suppressing Singh and Kaur due to their almost limitless recurrence and consequent inability unambiguously to individuate their bearers. Unable to countenance such common and therefore 'improper' names (Deseriis 2015) – which from an orthodox Sikh standpoint is precisely the point of them – schools or passport agencies demand alternatives, which often take the form of caste names. Forming a striking modern parallel with colonial censuses, which scholars have widely argued 'inscribed identities', especially ones of caste, 'that their subjects were behoved to fulfil' (Bhogal 2014: 283), use of caste names apparently is rising among Sikhs, but not necessarily due to a resurgence of 'caste mentalities'. Further, orthodox Sikh parents I know in Delhi bemoan their children's distaste for Singh and Kaur, which they consider archaic and embarrassing. Connectedly, debates precipitated by particular instances of name exchange focus on the ability of Kaur and Singh to act as simultaneous bridge and border with Hinduism and bulwark against moral degradation. Naming practices and concerns about naming practices therefore participate in what has been described as a larger 'crisis' of Sikh identity (Duggal 2015), itself the subject of a series of ongoing and highly emotive intellectual exchanges. However, counterpoised to such exchanges, and apparently in contrast with the opening up of these names at the birth of the Khalsa, is another set of arguments about who can be permitted to use them. Intellectual exchanges here centre on whether baptism is a formal requirement for eligibility to bear these names and their status as a kind of cultural property, and whether they should be disbarred from use by non-Sikhs or those who engage in behaviour considered to reflect badly on Sikhism. Attempts to police their usage show how debates and exchanges centring on names can switch easily from concerns about these names not being used enough to their being used too much or by the wrong kind of person.

Like the Japanese cherry blossoms analysed by Emiko Ohnuki-Tierney (2002), Singh and Kaur are symbols with a very large field of signification that is neither frozen in culture nor a linear progression through time from one meaning to the next (282). Some of these meanings compete and are logically incompatible with one another – in which case fierce debate and argument can and does arise. Understood as instruments of equalization, they have been viewed as capable of challenging the normative order, offering new possibilities (ibid.: 57). However, viewed as Sikh possessions, perceived instances of their misuse can provoke feelings of impugned honour and moves towards their policing. Connectedly, many Sikhs see their main value as providing distinct identity markers – helping to distinguish Sikhs from and defend against the influence of Hindus and thereby maintain (separate) community. Others still see their primary importance as means for instilling and displaying self-respect and martial prowess.

The relative salience of these different meanings and values crystallizes in acts of name exchange at particular moments in time. To exchange one name for another reflects, enacts and produces value(s) and value judgements (Lambek 2008). This chapter is arranged through description of such exchanges as a means of illuminating the role of names in the formulation and reformulation of Sikh values. We shall see how, in addition to being the subject of exchanges, names may also be withheld from them and act as bulwarks against undesired cultural exchanges. They also engage in forms of exchange with their bearers, affecting and being affected by them. Writing of the fictional works of Israeli author S.Y. Agnon, Shira Hadad (2012: 5) finds that names are encountered in his texts 'at moments of extreme failure or distortion'. Among the exemplary name exchanges considered in this chapter we find ones that provoke accusations of distortion, failure and inauthenticity – disuse of Sikh/Kaur is often understood, for instance, as a failure to commit to being fully visible as a Sikh. But the exchanges, taken together, suggest that concealment of one's Sikh-hood via naming practices is never simply concealment. Rather, practices of concealment entail becoming visible in other forms – for instance, as a Hindu, or as a unique individual visible to bureaucratic apparatuses, or as a caste-bearing person visible to one's caste brethren, or as fashionably visible within spaces of modernity. However, the chapter is equally concerned with moments of 'coming home' to Sikh/Kaur to become fully visible as Sikh once more. Here, then, rather than a singular equation with failure, it is more helpful to think of moments of name exchange in terms of newness and decision. A new name is a record and consequence of a decision (not necessarily made by oneself) about the self that one wants to be, or that one wishes another person to be (for instance, one's child). Such decisions, as noted, reveal and produce value(s). The decision-event (Humphrey 2008) of a name exchange produces value in its providing a name capable of mediating between who one is and who one feels one should be.[4]

Those who engage in the affectively charged dialogues, encounters and interactions prompted by instances of name exchange include but are certainly not restricted to Sikhs understood as intellectuals or intelligentsia. The varied interpretations and values of Kaur/Singh described here are debated in the mode of 'reasoned passion' and 'passionate reason' (Carsten et al. 2018: 8) in Sikh periodicals, magazines and online forums of both Indian and diasporic origin – a kind of 'virtual *sangat* (congregation)' that holds particular interest for bypassing traditional authority structures (Jakobsh 2014a: 224) – and also within and around the west Delhi *gurudwaras* (Sikh places of worship) where I have conducted ethnographic research since 2012, and the chapter draws on data from all these sources.

Historical Background

Although Sikhism is widely thought of and often spoken of by Sikhs themselves as a casteless religion, it is nonetheless common for members of the community to think and speak of themselves and others using the caste terms 'Sikh Jats', 'Sikh Khatris' and so on, and especially to retain an awareness of who is and is not of Dalit/ex-untouchable descent. Sikh naming practices lie at the heart of the religion's ambivalent and paradoxical attitude to caste. The relationship of Singh/Kaur with caste was ambiguous from the beginning, for as has been widely noted, the pre-existing association between the title 'Singh' and Rajputs makes it possible to view the initial baptism ceremony as being less a move towards putative castelessness than one towards martial 'Rajputization'. An educational tract on 'Sikh Castes' explains that the convention by which Sikh men take on the name Singh and women Kaur 'is an extension of the Hindu Rajput or Kshatriya tradition into Sikhism in addition to some other aspects of Rajput martial culture like "Jhatka" [single blow animal killing], "Shastar Tilak" [weapon carrying], etc. which are preserved in the traditions of Nihang and Hazoori Sikhs to this day' (Singh 'Panthi' n.d.).[5] But even so, the tract explains, this was not to devalue the other three *varnas*. Entrants into Guru Gobind Singh's new Khalsa order were to embody idealized versions of all four of them, but since 'fighting for both one's life and faith was the greatest need in era of Gurus ... the Kshatriya part of Sikh's identity got more highlighted in Sikh society' (ibid.). Obviously, embodying the best aspects of each *varna* suggests less the destruction of caste than a kind of enfolding or sublation of it, and historians and Sikh thinkers continue to weigh up whether the correct Sikh attitude to caste is to adopt the position that castes do exist but are equal (i.e. caste*ism* should not exist), or conversely that castes are not to be recognized at all and therefore all caste markers must be removed (i.e. caste itself should not exist). Moreover, the association, already mentioned, between 'Singh' and Rajputs lends Sikhism an air of Rajputism, notwithstanding the diversity of the caste makeup of adherents. I point to these different understandings simply to show that prior to present-day debates about the use of caste names by Sikhs, there were already ambiguities concerning Sikh approaches to caste, not least in respect of the name Singh: the very name which some see as levelling caste has been viewed by others as a marker of Rajputization.

However, Singh and Kaur are historically meaningful in further ways besides that do not strictly relate to caste. As already suggested, the conferral of Singh and Kaur is remembered to have been not only a means of caste-elision in accord with drinking from a common bowl but also an act of 'nominative uplift', for the name 'Singh' means 'literally a lion, and metaphorically a champion or warrior' (Cunningham 1918: 73), and 'Kaur' princess – a Punjabi equivalent of the Rajput term 'prince' (*kanwar*) (Jakobsh 2014b: 597). They are designed to be – and have been experienced as – powerful, vitalizing names: names that have life in them (Prytz-Johansen 2012: 114). This is how a Sikh woman in her twenties explained to me the importance of the foundational exchange of names:

> When the Sikhs were fighting the Mughals we had small-small names like Billu, Tillu, Kalu, Neela, Peela – not impressive names like the Mughals. A [Mughal] name like Bakhtavur Khan is very impressive and intimidating. Guruji said: How can we fight the Muslims when our names are small but theirs are great, very big names? *You* should also have heavy and good names. Then at the Khalsa he created Kaur and Singh and his name was changed from Gobind Rai to Gobind Singh. Now, if someone listens to the name, it is heavy, it is Singh. With big, heavy names your strength becomes more.

Other Sikh friends also used the word 'heavy' (*bhari*) to refer to the properties of Singh and Kaur. Meanwhile, complementing the exchange of these titles for divisive caste-title suffixes, 'little' first names such as Billu, Tillu and Kalu were to be replaced by weightier, grander-sounding first names. Indic connotations of 'heavy' include mass, density and energy (White 1984: 56). Bestowing the heaviness and density of 'Singh' was to imbue the *panth* (Sikh community) with a martial impermeability and reminder of the need for courage.

A politically active Dalit Sikh in his thirties also spoke to me of the transformative effect on Sikhs in the seventeenth and eighteenth centuries of the guru's granting of Singh and Kaur. The new name imbued Sikhs with what he termed 'name spirit': 'the name Singh gave them strength, that "I am a lion" kind of spirit'. He even went so far as to couple together the sword and the name as comparably important acquirements for readying Sikhs for coming battles: 'He [the guru] has given the sword, He has given the name'. A further significant aspect of this new name spirit was the unrestrictedness of its uplifting effects: 'In Indian history, Dalits [former untouchables] cannot use this name "Singh". Someone has a very derogatory name; [but] suddenly his name is *this!*', he exclaimed. One can see why for a Dalit activist such an opening up or making democratic of a prestigious name was worthy of note. 'The most common of the distinctive names in use among Rajputs' (Cunningham 1918: 73), 'Singh' was now no longer exclusively for use by this caste. This opening up of the name could also be viewed as a means of borrowing 'name spirit' from Rajputs (or as Rajputization) even as the name no longer becomes associated only with this community. But from the viewpoint of my Dalit respondents, use of 'Singh' suggests less the aping of a distinctively Rajput name than its subversion and it being made to open up beyond itself. As Opinderjit Kaur Takhar (2005: 94) writes of the new initiation ceremony, 'they shared *amrit* from a common bowl: something highly alien to the Hindu caste system. Eradication of *zat* [sub-caste] names in favour of Singh and Kaur meant that an individual's *zat* could no longer be distinguished by one's *got* (family name). Thus, initially at least, Sikhism appealed very much to the lower castes who underwent initiation via *khande-di-pahul* [baptism] and became Sikhs'. Sikhs thus transferred to themselves, via the name-titles Singh and Kaur, some of the charisma of the Rajput. Further, if the title affects the initiate (conferring on them its 'name spirit', a sense of nominative uplift and appreciation of equality), the initiate affects the title – its connotations begin to extend well beyond the Rajput: the title and the people who bear it emerge hand in hand (Hacking 1986).

If taking on Singh and Kaur was meant to de-differentiate internally within the *panth* by downplaying caste distinctions between Sikhs, they were – in part, and in conjunction with other symbols – meant externally to differentiate by distinguishing Sikhs from non-Sikhs. One produces the other: Sikhs must not be individuated (nominatively) so that Sikhism can be so. The name, then, was a key aspect of the guru's marshalling of the corporate imagination in both the external (differentiating) and internal (de-differentiating) senses just noted. Specifically in respect of de-differentiation, Guru Gobind Singh is reported to have said that with the new name-titles and five K symbols, 'never again would Sikhs be able to conceal their identity as they had done when his father was executed' (Fenech and McLeod 2014: 8).[6]

The origin of the use of Kaur is less clear, but probably also connected with the imperative of external differentiation. Cunningham (1918) mentions many Sikh females named Kaur, but says nothing about the significance or provenance of the name-title. In this, Cunningham's history shares features with early Sikh prescriptive texts that focused on male ritual codes and identity and 'are either highly contradictory or silent about women's inclusion into the Khalsa' (Jakobsh 2014b: 596). Doris Jakobsh (2003, 2014b) provides helpful clarity here, noting that concern with the male 'Singh' completely eclipsed the matter of female Sikh names in the early days of the Khalsa. If the injunction that Sikh men must always use their full names (i.e. not omit the suffix 'Singh') is quite clear, so far as female names are concerned there is silence – Sikh women are referred to simply as 'Sikhnis' or 'Gursikhnis' (2014b: 596). It is in the nineteenth century that 'Kaur' starts to become visible as part of an effort by the Sikh reform movement, the Singh Sabha, to rewrite history and construct religious boundaries (Oberoi 1994).[7] Presenting evidence of the historical convention of using Devi as a suffix of Sikh female first names, as was also the case for Hindu women and which had actually received sanction in the Prem Sumarg,[8] Jakobsh (2014b: 598) shows how Singh Sabha reformers took to recording the name of one of Guru Gobind Singh's wives, previously known as Sahib Devah, as Sahib Kaur, before finally in 1950 the order was included in the Sikh code of conduct (*Reht Maryada*) that Kaur should suffix the given name of all female infants, just as Singh should suffix all male given names. 'Devi', evidently, was too Hindu-inflected. Consequently, if 'Kaur' is elusive in historical accounts of the formation of the Khalsa, there is a good reason for this.

Meanwhile, in *The Birth of the Khalsa* (2005: 55–56), Nikky-Guninder Kaur Singh states, with revealing elusiveness, that in addition to the guru's hailing of Sikh men at the foundation of the Khalsa as 'Singhs', 'Sikhs also mention that on that day Guru Gobind Singh gave the name "Kaur" to Sikh women'. In a later work she states that, just as 'men received the surname Singh, women received the surname Kaur', but also that 'the exact historical origins of this tradition [regarding Kaur specifically] are obscure' (N-G. K. Singh 2011: 52). This ambiguity results from Singh's desire to read a feminist message into the conferral of 'Kaur' as the guru's gift of freedom from the lineage of fathers and husbands (2011: 106; 2005: 187), an argument that is hampered by a lack of supporting historical evidence. This is not to criticize Singh, who is clear that her analysis is at the level of mythos and the recovery of lost potentials. What is important here is less historical certitude regarding whether or not the guru gave the name Kaur to Sikh women, or the intentions of the Singh Sabha innovators who assert that he did, than the fact that contemporary Sikh feminists hold a powerful understanding of Kaur as a key asset in their framing of the Sikh faith as one that is particularly progressive in its approach to sex/gender precisely because 'as "Kaur," a woman retains her identity for her whole life … [s]he does not have to adopt the name of her father at birth nor that of her husband at marriage' (N-G. K. Singh 2011: 106). Yet we must note the ambiguity of the freedom that this name confers: if it frees its bearer from patriarchal and caste norms, it does so even as it binds her to a particular religious faith. The 'inaugurative power of name-giving' (Humphrey 2006: 173) is not excised but relocated.

However, the interpellation is not straightforward. Sikh religious boundary construction remains an ongoing project subject to an array of challenges, contradictions and ambivalences both reflected in and accentuated by personal naming practices. The Shiromani Gurdwara Prabandhak Committee (SGPC) is the Sikh *panthic* body that manages *gurudwaras* in Punjab and Haryana and formal custodian of the *Reht Maryada* or Sikh code of conduct. In her work on

Sikh group formations, Takhar (2005: 27) discusses this code's provision that 'Boys are to be given the name Singh and girls the name of Kaur'. If the code is applicable to *amritdhari* Sikhs, namely Sikhs who have been initiated into the Khalsa, Takhar asks, what of those Khalsa Sikhs who do not consistently follow the code's prescriptions? Equally, what of those outside the Khalsa fold who *do* follow them?[9] Consider the case of names among the Ravidasis, Dalit (usually Ramdasia[10]) followers of the outcaste saint Ravidas (c. 500) whose works feature prominently in the *Adi Granth*, the principal Sikh scripture. Some Ravidasis bear names characteristic of Hindus (e.g. Anita Devi, Ram Lal) while many more bear Singh and Kaur – yet Ravidasis are neither Hindu nor Sikh in any straightforward sense, and are certainly not *amritdharis*: 'It is interesting to note that though many Ravidasis retain Kaur and Singh in their names, these same individuals emphatically claim they are not Sikhs but Ravidasis' (ibid.). Conversely, self-identifying Sikhs may well not bear Singh or Kaur, which is one of the key problematics addressed in this chapter. This can confound others' attempts to define and stabilize religious identities. For instance, not bearing these names has the potential to count against Sikhs in the event of their seeking refugee status, with Australia's Refugee Review Tribunal in 2005 having sought clarification on precisely this question, asking: 'Would someone whose name is not Singh and who does not exhibit any external signs of Sikh religion (e.g. uncut hair) plausibly be a Sikh?'[11] Such cases remind us that the names Kaur and Singh are not and never have been failsafe indicators of their bearers' religious identities. But still, and as we will see below, certain mainstream Sikhs lay claim to these titles as a special class of intellectual property or 'inalienable possession' (Weiner 1992) as if they were theirs alone. Full of shifting significances, Singh and Kaur are names that Sikhs have borrowed but that are also, and significantly, theirs.

We have seen, then, how the ceremonial exchange of Singh for caste names at the birth of the Khalsa was at the same time an exchange of a single caste name in place of several: the internal levelling of identity took place under the sign of the Rajput whose values the exchange was designed creatively to appropriate. The values displayed and advanced by the exchange included formal equalization within the *panth*, separation from non-*panth* elements, novel access to a prestigious name for those whose caste backgrounds were usually associated with demeaning ones, and elevated martial density and courage. The later exchange of Kaur for Devi might initially have reflected a will to differentiate, but the exchange has since accrued further (progressive feminist) values.

It is values such as these that disuse of Kaur and Singh threatens. With such disuse, complains Sikh commentator G.P. Singh (2003), it appears that people 'want to hide their Sikh identity'. This 'hiding' – as we will see in this chapter – can take many different forms across different scales. G.P. Singh himself connects this 'disturbing trend' with the 1947 partition of India and particularly the anti-Sikh violence that followed the assassination of Indira Gandhi in 1984. He is right that many Sikhs in present-day Delhi can cite examples of family, friends and acquaintances who in 1984 changed both their names and appearance. Several Sikh army officers at the time are said to have changed the 'Singh' they bore to the similar but more Hindu-sounding 'Singha' or 'Sinha': at least one of them continues to bear the altered surname, though for others the dropping of Kaur/Singh and shorn hair were only temporary. 'They came again as "Singh" and "Kaur" when it was safe to do so', an elderly female respondent told me. Other respondents spoke about the violence of partition and 1984 as tests of commitment separating the wheat from the chaff: those who, in the face of mortal danger, cut their hair and changed their names – especially those who continued to cut their hair and use their new names after the immediate danger had passed – are considered to have failed these tests. In this way, these tragic episodes caused certain 'unripe' ones to be 'shed' (*kache pille*). It is not clear, however, that the cause identified by G.P. Singh for disuse of Kaur and Singh is as salient now as it was in the 1980s and 1990s. This chapter suggests other reasons for such disuse. I turn now to more recent episodes of name exchange set within the give and take of interchanges about names and identity in the contemporary Sikh world.

Exchange 1: Avtar Singh for Mr Makkar

In 2005, in a minor twenty-first-century reproduction of the foundational name exchange enacted at the birth of the Khalsa, an individual known as Mr Makkar was renamed Avtar Singh, with his caste name dropped for the non-caste-disclosing Singh. Insofar as the drift towards disuse of Kaur/Singh and take-up of caste names had encouraged the creation of a countervailing movement towards renewal of Sikh identity, there was nothing especially unusual about the exchange. Koonal Duggal (2022) discusses the case of the Punjabi pop singer Vinaypal Buttar whose music videos have depicted the co-implication among Sikh youth of loss of identity markers such as unshorn hair and a slide into moral degeneracy typified by consumption of alcohol and weakened commitment to communitarian practices such as *seva*. In one video Buttar's own personal journey of restoration is depicted as he moves from '*gunahgar*' (sinner, transgressor) to a process of contemplation, finally to full identity and identifiability as a reformed Sikh subject. Marking the transition, the now turbaned singer took to introducing his live performances with the declaration: '*Vinaypal Buttar siga ji main, hun Vinaypal Singh ban gaya*' ('I was Vinaypal Buttar, now I am Vinaypal Singh') (ibid.: 7).

Buttar/Singh is particularly scathing of the spiritual backsliding of the *panth*'s principal authority figures, or *jathedar*s, whose power and corruption is markedly prevalent within the very institutions meant to uphold its moral precepts. Indeed, the reason I foreground the exchange of Singh for the caste name Makkar is precisely because the exchange took place on the occasion of Makkar/Singh's appointment as head of the Shiromani Gurdwara Prabandhak Committee (SGPC). Recall that the SGPC is the custodian and guarantor of the *Reht Maryada* (Sikh code of conduct). On the face of it, the exchange of names simply showed him obediently complying with the rules of the organization he now headed. At the same time, that the head of the same body that devised the *Reht* should need to enact self-reform invited reflection. Why was he even considered let alone elected to such a position of authority if the quality of his adherence was so evidently suspect? For the reforming Sikh youths in Delhi whom I know, what was particularly noticeable was the apparent reluctance with which Mr Makkar (as was) dropped his caste surname, suggesting that it was precisely the many newspaper advertisements offering him congratulations the day after his appointment, which addressed him simply as 'Avtar Singh', that forced his hand. The notices of congratulation were pointed: to (re)name him was to correct his name. For many of my Sikh acquaintances in Delhi, the apparent hesitance of the head of one of the highest of the Sikh temporal authorities to abide by such a basic teaching was depressing but not surprising – after all, they said, such appointments had long been reduced to the politics of influence and wealth. At the same time, the episode was recalled to me with sadness and regret for its exemplification of the larger condition of the tradition: if figures within the very lofty institutions tasked with upholding the teachings of the gurus cannot be trusted to abide by such a basic one as that concerning the bearing of names, it merely hints at the scale of the degeneration elsewhere.

The critique is not altogether recent. A contribution to the monthly journal *The Sikh Review*[12] titled 'Caste among Sikhs: Dichotomy between Belief and Practice' (Lal 2000) cites a letter written to the journal in 1978 from a correspondent named Ganda Singh, which refers to a 'disease of separateness' in the land that has 'not only adversely affected the Muslims and Christians, but has also spread in a worst form among the Sikhs, who were expected to uproot it altogether. Guru Nanak had condemned caste-ism as *phakkar*, or nonsense. To abolish all caste and sectarian differences, Guru Gobind Singh had given to his followers the common surname of Singh, and desired them to recognize the entire mankind as one caste – *manas ki jat sabh ekai pahchanbo*. But the baneful influence of Brahminism in this respect is so strong in the country that caste-ism is also penetrating into the reformist sections of the Sikhs, the Singh Sabhaites, the Akalis [Sikh politicians], the Chief Khalsa Diwanists[13] and the members of the SGPC, and other Sikh institutions' (ibid.: 11). The disease of separateness – separation within the fold (in the form of resurgent caste names and therefore, presumably, 'caste mentality') – implies the unwanted opposite 'outside' of it: a collapsing of the boundaries (so laboriously constructed over previous decades and centuries) between the Sikh fold and Hinduism, the paradigmatic locus of 'caste mentality'. This is not only because the former comes to share characteristics with the latter, but also because the basis of affiliation becomes insecure: caste names cut across the two folds; a Dhillon, Arora or one of many other caste names may equally belong to a Hindu or a Sikh. To whom, then, is one affiliated most closely? Do caste allegiances interfere with, supersede or override religious ones? For some Dalit Sikh activists they certainly do, as we shall see now, with an exchange of names signifying an exchange of allegiances.

Exchange 2: Chokha Mukta for Bhupinder Singh

It is a commonplace to note that the act of naming a child symbolically transforms bare human life into personhood, that is, an individual with a history.[14] But which history? The answer may not be straightforward. In India the information conveyed by personal names tends to be that of the caste and/or religious backgrounds of their bearers; place of origin, too, might be communicated. However, if Hindu names normally disclose both caste and religion, the case of Sikh names is different. Correct use of Kaur and Singh – their use instead of rather than as well as caste names – elides caste identity. For most Sikhs I know in Delhi, that is their main purpose. In its ideal form, a Sikh's name discloses religious but not caste lineage. Some individuals of Sikh background, however, find reason to made visible in their names a different identity. This is most striking in the case of Sikh-background Dalit activists. A naming episode recounted by Manpreet, a male Dalit activist who hails from Uttarakhand but now lives in Chandigarh, vividly demonstrates this. He told me:

> There was a lot of struggle when our son was born. My parents said we will take his name from the Sikh rituals, from the *Guru Granth Sahib* [involving the random opening of the book for the first letter of the name]. My father went to the *gurudwara* [to get the name], and the name was such a disgusting name. It was Bhupinder Singh. This was the name that was given. I did not go to the *gurudwara*, I did not perform anything. I said I will not accept it at all. My father said you have no rights on this issue.[15] I rejected it. My wife and I had already decided we would give him the name Chokha [short form of Chokhamela]. Chokhamela is not a Sikh name at all. Chokhamela was a Dalit poet.[16] He is a role model. Before Guru Gobind Singh, before Guru Nanak, there was Chokhamela. A great Dalit poet. We thought, if he [will be] a boy, we will give him this name. We had to struggle hard. My mother, father, mother-in-law, sisters and brothers were all angry with me: 'What is this name?' 'This is not a Sikh name at all'. I said, 'He is our role model. I want to revive my memories of him; it will always remind me, you know, which community I am from'.

In rejecting the possibility of a Sikh name for their son, the boy's parents prioritize caste over religious lineage. Not only is this exchange a reversal of that enacted as a template at the birth of the Khalsa, it also reverses the more common strategy of Dalits exchanging their own caste-revealing name for either a generic surname (such as Kumar) or a nominally upper-caste one (such as Sharma) in order to 'pass'. The reasons for this are understandable. Names that convey the Dalit backgrounds of their bearers may be derogatory (Paik 2011) and/or count against them in job applications (Thorat and Attewell 2010). Dalit educational or labour migration to a city where one is unknown can become an opportunity to exchange names in this way. However, forming part of a wider countervailing activist strategy of prideful assertion (Gorringe 2010), Chokha's parents do the opposite: they foreground Dalit identity in their child's name to 'remind' them of 'which community' he is from in the singular.

But the name Chokha both is and is not a caste name; it has its own condensed history that is irreducible to a singular identity despite the intentions of Chokha's parents. On the one hand, in disavowing the Khalsa template, Chokha's parents reverse the originary name exchange and reinstitute visible caste. But on the other, while Chokha was indeed a figure from a marginalized community, the name is in fact fashionable among upper-caste and -class cosmopolitans, and the surname they gave him – Mukta – which Manpreet himself had adopted while a university student, is not a caste name. Rather, Manpreet adopted Mukta, which means 'liberation', after reading Ambedkar as a teenager in order to signal his freedom from caste and religion (rather than release from rebirth as in more conventional usages). Evoking South Asian paradigms of renunciation, rationalist and progressive figures have drawn on an imagery of freedom in bestowing names. The daughter of noted Maharashtrian rationalist Narendra Dabholkar was also named Mukta in the sense of 'freedom from superstition'. This is similar to the process that led Independence leader Maulana Kalam Azad to adopt the pen name 'Azad'. As he wrote (1959: 3–4): 'I passed from one phase to another and a stage came when all the old bonds imposed on my mind by family and upbringing were completely shattered. I felt free of all conventional ties and decided that I would chalk out my own path. It was about this time that I decided to adopt the pen name "Azad" or "Free" to indicate that I was no longer tied to my inherited beliefs'. Connectedly, several Sikh-background atheists I know choose to bear caste names rather than Kaur or Singh. This can seem counter-intuitive, since atheist activists loudly proclaim their anti-caste fight, with many declining to use caste names (Copeman 2015). These Sikh-background atheists, on the other hand, faced a progressive naming dilemma, finally choosing, like Manpreet Mukta, caste names over ones that draw a veil over caste but are 'religious'.

In light of this, we can see how the name Chokha Mukta condenses two different phases in Dalit thought and activism. Manpreet describes his own earlier adoption of Mukta as 'childish' and 'romantic'. It was a conscious attempt to build bridges via naming; a means to go beyond 'community thinking', especially caste: 'that "everyone should be an Indian first" sort of feeling'. Though he is nostalgic about this phase in his life and sees his adoption of Mukta as 'not a stupidity', he now holds the strong opinion that 'any effort of hiding caste cannot lead you anywhere. I think you should be very vocal that I belong to this community – either you like me or dislike me, it's your wish. I don't care'. Not dissimilar to larger global trends in which racial colour blindness is considered passé and separate identity asserted as the basis for political mobilization (or 'social justice'), Manpreet says it is better for Sikhs to 'have history in their names'. Referring to Jat and Khatri Sikhs – the former typically dominant-caste cultivators of Punjab-Haryana, the latter prosperous traders – he goes on: 'It should be in the public domain what these people are and that they have this cultural capital. Maybe now they become sensitive and want to use only Singh, but that history should be there. I have looted the resources and suddenly I am saying I have left all these things' (rolls his eyes). The name Chokha Mukta thus enfolds two key but very different strategies that a single individual adopted at different historical moments: one of seeking to overcome divisions of identity – now seen as ill-equipped for a newer phase of assertion – and another of acknowledging and reinstituting them.

The case is illustrative of the broader Dalit Sikh activist response to the reformist effort to revivify Kaur/Singh. To such activists, the effort is too close to – indeed, can be understood as the Sikh variant of – the broader effort over decades to combat caste discrimination through policies of caste blindness, an approach they consider to be obsolete and discredited. Indeed, Satish Deshpande, whose work finds a strong reflection in the views of the Dalit Sikh activists I know, is quite clear that state programmes of caste blindness and social justice are 'conflicting policies' (2013: 32). As Jasminder, one of Manpreet's colleagues, told me: 'Singh and Kaur were given to us Sikhs with good intentions but the need of the hour is different. Those who are trying to bring them back may also have good intentions ... [But] caste is a tool for me to fight – if I don't have that then where I will go?' That is to say, Dalit activism requires 'conspicuous caste' not caste blindness, and this overtakes the Sikh reformist attitude to naming practices.

The Dalit Sikh activist critique of the Sikh reform effort can take on a sharper edge still. Reformers, they say, hardly ever practise inter-marriage among the Sikh castes; indeed, endogamy is still the norm. If they were serious, according to this line of thinking, they would not only drop their caste names, they would go beyond this and marry outside their own caste communities.[17] Indeed, several activists used the word 'alibi' in reference to the Sikh reform agenda's approach to names. Eliminating caste names in favour of Kaur/Singh allows reformers to show or claim adherence to the egalitarian spirit of Sikhism while continuing to enact the exclusion that continues to mark Dalit Sikhs' experience of the religion; 'They don't see us as true Sikhs', I was repeatedly told (or as one Dalit Sikh quoted by Kalra and Purewal (2020: 123) put it: 'Though I can recite all the verses of the Guru Granth Sahib, they would still not count me as one of them. Sikhism has been captured by the *jats* (non-*dalits*)'). The suggestion is that it would be less hypocritical for such reformers to keep, not drop, their caste surnames, and further that the reform attempt is well in keeping with a religion whose 'ideological self-image [as] without caste' (Jodhka 2004: 172) notoriously is not matched by practice. For this reason, while many Dalit Sikhs continue to see an extraordinary egalitarian potential in the ideology of Sikhism (Hans 2016), the activists I know who maintain links with it do so with much ambivalence.

The exchange of the name Chokha Mukta for Bhupinder Singh thus marked an exchange of allegiances that produced value for Manpreet Mukta in terms of its capacity to remind him of his community (notably in the singular) and coherently map onto a wider movement of Dalit assertiveness. But it is important to note that Sikhism and Punjab have their own rich and varied histories of striving for versions of 'blindness' to community distinctions, quite apart from post-Independence governance and urban middle-class strategies to stop caste coming into the public sphere and thereby having to negotiate over its position. This tradition ranges from Guru Nanak's mystical attempts to move beyond socially named selves in statements such as 'There is no Hindu nor Muslim' (Bhogal 2007: 107) to Sufi singer Abida Parveen's invocation of Sufi poet and philosopher Baba Bulleh Shah's (1680–1757) desire to 'go to that place where everybody is blind where none knows your name or caste' ('*Chalve Bulleya othe chaliye jithe saare anne na koi saddi zaat pichane na koi sanu manne*') (Duggal 2015: 4) to revolutionary fighter Udham Singh's adoption of the name Ram Mohammad Singh Azad, 'a name that invoked the three major religious communities of the Punjab – Hindu, Muslim, and Sikh – as well as his anticolonial sentiment' (Mir 2010: 2–3). It is this tradition as much as the post-Independence one criticized by Deshpande and others (e.g. Jodhka and Shah 2010) that Manpreet Mukta displaces in his exchange of names.

Another significant constituency of Sikh background individuals who frequently make visible in their names an identity other than, or in addition to, Sikhism is the Jat caste grouping of cultivators and landholders in Punjab and Haryana. As with Dalit Sikh activists, the reason for this is assertion. But it is assertion of a very different kind in that its starting point is from an already existing position of strength. Considered by Sikh Dalits, Khatris and others to have 'captured' Sikhism, Jat dominance extends to other areas of Punjabi life besides, with their existing socio-economic ascendency having enabled them to reap the successes of the Green Revolution of the mid to late 1960s. Celebration of Jat identity is an utterly mainstream element of popular culture in both Punjab and the Sikh diaspora; for instance, it is a central ingredient of pop music (Dhanda 2009; Duggal 2015). In light of what has been described as 'the Jat insistence on marking caste over religious, linguistic, regional, or other identities' (Mooney 2013: 315), it is of course unsurprising that if Punjabi Jats bear Singh and Kaur at all it is predominantly as middle names followed by caste surnames. Consequently, non-use of a caste surname in Punjab tends to signify either that one is a highly diligent Sikh, such as a professional *ragi* who is held to higher religious standards than others (Kaur 2011), or indeed a Dalit 'with something to hide'. The London-based Sikh influencer Jagraj Singh, who before his early death in 2017 had amassed a large following for his explanatory YouTube videos, described the problem as 'Sikhi[18] vs. Punjabism', with the culture of the state – dominated by Jats – militating against the ideals of the religion founded there. Though strongly encouraging use of Kaur/Singh and disuse of caste names, Jagraj Singh's position was moderate: for him, knowledge of one's caste background or *gotra* should be maintained in order to avoid marriages between inappropriately close kin; it was not caste but merely caste pride that must be extinguished.

Exchange 3: Ramit Bains for Ramit Singh

Jat diaspora *bhangra* star Jazzy B, though he does not use a caste name, conforms to the above description in his non-use of Singh. Though the hypermasculinity exhibited in Jazzy B's persona and music videos is perfectly congruent with the celebration of Jat identity in pop music just mentioned, his name nevertheless shows how Sikhism can be de-emphasized by itself without a caste identity necessarily being reinstituted in its stead or causing that de-emphasis in the first place. Jazzy B was clearly the inspiration for a cartoon character named Jazzi C who featured on pedagogical posters displayed on *gurudwara* walls in Punjab and Delhi in the mid 2010s (Figure 5.1). Referencing the Punjabi taste for global travel and relocation, the cartoon is set in a visa-passport office (a pivotal location of the name's corruption, as we will see below). The white desk worker who greets the young Punjabi male is a picture of confusion ('????' as the speech bubble has it) because, though wearing a turban and therefore seemingly identifiable as a Sikh, his customer has a trimmed beard (he is also wearing sunglasses and holding a *tabla* and miniature sitar). 'Hello Mr. Singh, what is your name?' 'My name is Jazzi C', is the response. The desk worker's assumption that the youth's surname is Singh is incorrect: his confusion deepens. A boy wearing a topknot, a witness to the scene and representative here of a more devout strain of Sikh youth, turns to the viewer to make explicit the cartoon's didactic message: 'In making us "Singhs", the guru transformed us from cowardly hyenas into lions. But now, not only have we left behind our Sikh appearance, we're also removing "Singh" from after our [given] names'. Caste is neither mentioned nor insinuated, and indeed, no caste name has been added; it is simply Singh that has been dropped. For the fashion-conscious Sikh-background male, the cartoon

Figure 5.1. 'In making us "Singhs", the guru transformed us from cowardly hyenas into lions'. © Jacob Copeman.

suggests, Singh stands for that which is embarrassingly outmoded. The spatio-temporal dimension of this requires emphasis: in Punjab, in particular, the fate of a person's name can be foregrounded in narratives of rural-urban migration and loss of roots, as in the lyrics of a well-known Punjabi pop song sung by Satinder Sartaj: 'On reaching the city the village boy turned urbane ... See how the youth of today has gone astray. They no longer take pride in the gurus' glory. "Gurmeet Singh" has turned "Garry." ... Sit down and think: ... why have the leaves become the enemy of the branches?'

'Now it is the fashion [*riwaaz*] not to have Singh-Kaur; the youth especially, they abbreviate their names. We don't have *phechan* [identity] like that anymore....' I was told this by a Sikh male in his mid sixties in Delhi and it can stand for the many reasonings I heard that imputed disuse of these names not to caste sensibility but to something else: the desire to be modern. Nonetheless, caste still enters the picture in the form of the names that tend to be used to replace those that are discontinued; and since the displaced names are markers of Sikh identity, they become a site of anxiety concerning the proximal influence of Hinduism. In addition to expressing sorrow concerning an increase in beard trimming among Sikh males, one Sikh writer complains that 'Many Sikhs now feel shy to use "Singh" or "Kaur" in their names. You come across names like Harjit Soni, Birinder Kohli, Gurdeep Gill, and so on, without using "Singh" or "Kaur". It appears they want to hide their Sikh identity. This defeats the very purpose and the spirit in which Khalsa was created as one brotherhood' (G.P. Singh 2003). What is more, according to many understandings I encountered, one's name and one's moral conduct are not isolates: a negative change to one might negatively affect the other, as we shall see.

Contemporary embarrassment about Kaur/Singh is of course the reverse of the origin story of the names, according to which their conferral by the guru produced powerful vitalizing effects that raised much-needed self-respect. For many Sikh-background youths their connotations are now very different. In France, argues Baptiste Coulmont (2014), soon after lower-class parents start mimetically to give middle- and upper-class associated names to their children, they lose their value as signs of distinction for their original upper- and middle-class conferrers, and the cycle begins again. Naming practices thus exhibit marked fashion dynamics. In an era in which the Indian prime minister wears an exorbitantly expensive suit emblazoned with hundreds of iterations of his own name, and business signboards loudly proclaim their owners' names where they might once more modestly have featured the names of their grandfather or father (Pinney 2004; Shukla 2013), Singh/Kaur can seem to offer the very opposite of distinction.[19] Coulmont also suggests that a primary motivation for name changes in France is to take on a 'younger' name. French name changers change names associated with earlier generations: 'they take a first name that implicitly signifies their belonging to a younger generation (compared to the generation implied by their previous first name)'. If, in France, this 'allows one to be perceived as younger than before', for Sikh name changers the concern is to signify belonging to the current generation via discarding the onomastic residue of an earlier one. It is another way of attempting to be perceived as younger than before.

It is not only Sikhs who do this. Notaries I have accompanied in west Delhi report that the most common reason for changing a name, apart from marriage, is to acquire a more tasteful, less 'backward'-sounding one. But a further possible contributing factor for Sikhs is the widely popular middle-class tradition of Sardarji (or Sant Banta) jokes – decades long but strongly revived in the era of social media – which ridicule the inability of Sikhs to negotiate modern mores adequately, with Sardarjis the 'spatio-temporal foil' through which tellers disclose their own successful negotiation of them (Hall 2019: 499). Often sexualized, and featuring linguistic mishaps due to the imputed inability of Sikhs to command modern admixtures of English and local languages, Sikhs – and Sikh men in particular – are invariably situated in them as simple, rustic and outside of discourses of modernity (ibid.: 497). Many such jokes play on phonetic misunderstandings of 'Singh': a turbaned man climbing over a fence is asked, 'Why are you trespassing?' 'I am not Trespa Singh, I am Jaswanth Singh.' Beach settings feature prominently in such jokes as globalized, English-dominant leisure spaces open to misreading by the rustic Sardarji (ibid.: 500): an uncomfortable-looking turbaned man walking on a beach is asked by tourists in swimwear, 'Sir are you relaxing?' 'No, I am Zail Singh.' While Sikh intellectual and humourist Khushwant Singh's own telling of the jokes is often posited as an alibi by current tellers, almost all the Sikhs I know in Delhi intensely dislike them. Some experienced them as part of wider patterns of bullying while at school. While their effect on use and disuse of Singh/Kaur is difficult to gauge, it is notable that when a Sikh lawyer asked India's Supreme Court to ban Sikh jokes in 2016, she not only equated the jokes with racial abuse but also said: 'My children are humiliated and feel embarrassed', they 'do not want the "Kaur" and "Singh" tag with their names'.[20]

A Delhi Sikh male in his late forties, a property dealer, recounted to me how his two sons, now in their mid twenties, stopped using Singh during their college years because, they told him, it made them feel 'backward'. It was they, not their parents, who took the initiative in resuscitating their caste name (Bains) as a 'family surname'. Though their use of the term 'backward' suggests a possible caste dimension to their actions, their father insisted to me that their dropping of Singh was simply a matter of modern style – their wish to be onomastic moderns (even some of the teenagers I spoke with who attended Singh Sabha schools expressed embarrassment about having to use Kaur and Singh, implying that were it not for strict parents and school policy they might be inclined to shed them). Style is an overdetermined word: it is frequently invoked as code for moral degradation (Cohen 2011), and this is exactly what the pained father suggests has been the consequence of his children's name change: 'Those who believe in Sikhism keep the name Singh, but those who don't believe in it, they think [that] to name [should be] according to their own freedom. They say to keep [the names Kaur/Singh] is fundamentalist. They think they should have a modern style. If Ramit [one of his sons] remains "Singh" he can't smoke and take liquor'. He turned to English to express his point with a poetic flourish: 'If he doesn't have the name then he also doesn't have the shame [of drinking and smoking]'. For Ramit's father, then, the name is understood connectedly as both a binding force and as a prophylactic against modern excesses: bowing to modern nominative style by ceasing to use Singh is a stepping stone towards ceasing to adhere to a code of acceptable behaviour. Being shed, the name spirit of Singh can no longer perform its sentinel function in the sense of an 'ought' identity to aspire to.

Yet personal names seem to weigh more heavily on their bearers than in the sense of a mere linguistic or semiotic 'ought'. Consider the narratives of Sikh parents who, when their children were small, did not insist that they took Singh and Kaur and later express their regret at this, noting its fateful consequences. One woman in her late fifties told me she sincerely regretted not giving her two children, one girl and one boy, 'Kaur' and 'Singh'. If she had done so, she is sure they would not have cut their hair and, in her words, 'practically become Hindus'. Rather than 'substance-code' – the term employed by McKim Marriott (1976) and others to highlight how in South Asia exchanges of substance (food, water, bodily materials) govern behaviour and affect personhood (see also Sarbadhikary, this volume) – we find understandings of a kind of 'name-code', with name-sign and bearer exchanging properties and forming a dynamic whole. Kaur and Singh are thus sentinel presences that provide a kind of immunity to Hinduism. In consequence, their removal can lead to 'immunodeficiency' (reduction in connective force among and towards the *panth*). To quote just one impassioned chatroom debater on the topic: 'I'm not saying other faiths are lower or not spiritual. I'm saying if people don't choose to have [Kaur or Singh] in their name, they will stray away from Sikhi, which is happening a lot'.[21] That other faith almost always is Hinduism as both cause and effect: its influence causes disuse, or else 'practically becoming Hindu' is cast as the eventual effect of such disuse, even in cases where 'fashion' is advanced as the primary cause.

Exchange 4: Jasmeet Kaur for Jazz

If names are folded together with commitment, action and conduct, the onomastic reform effort comes to appear particularly urgent. As we have seen, however, traditional reformist organizations such as the SGPC are suspect due to politicking and their domination by Jats. Youth dissatisfaction with these structures, particularly in the diaspora, has led to the creation of entities such as the US Jakara Movement, which organizes student conferences (Jakobsh 2014a). Also of note is the International Institute of Gurmat Studies' (IIGS) yearlong programme of Sikh youth camps across the world, whose camp registration forms state, rather admonishingly, 'Applicant's Name: Sardarni/Sardar (Just the name, NO Castes Please) ________'. Explicitly addressing matters of pride and fashion, the Mr Singh International Turban Pride Fashion Show, held annually in Amritsar in the form of a male 'beauty contest' with contestants competing in fitness, talent, attire and 'correct manners and knowledge of tradition', pointedly refers in its title not only to the major visible accoutrement of the *panth* but also the name Singh.[22] Meanwhile, the Bollywood blockbuster *Singh is Kinng* (2008) received praise for its celebration of Sikh values and foregrounding of the 'name spirit' of Singh, even if some commentators frowned on the trimmed beards it featured;[23] and the popular Sikh clothing company, 1469, which sells cultural products that mark an 'ethnicized selfhood' (Comaroff and Comaroff 2009: 139), similarly valorizes the name Kaur in its line of 'Kaurageous' t-shirts.

Sikh film festivals have also been a notable means of responding to fears concerning dilution of Sikh identity, including the rejection of Kaur/Singh as a question of fashion. Of particular interest here is a short film titled *Karizmaa of Kaur*, submitted to a 2013 festival of Sikh film, which depicts both the fashionable denigration of Kaur and its recuperation as a vital bearer of name spirit (or 'karizmaa'). Directed by Ravneet Kaur, it is set where it was produced, in Mumbai. First we meet a turbaned woman, the turban an unmistakable sign that she is a Sikh and not ashamed of it.[24] She drives to work in a high-end Mercedes, with *kirtan* (Sikh devotional songs) playing on the stereo. She arrives at a modern office building where she enters a room of company directors. As she takes her seat serenely at the head of the table, the titles announce that she is 'Satnam Kaur, Managing Dir., Adhamang Pvt. Ltd'. Pointedly, her first name, Satnam, means 'true name'. Clearly, she has reached the highest rung of the ladder not in spite of the discernible signs of Sikhism that she bears, but in large measure because of the strength and grace they afford her.

Another female employee – heavily made-up and clearly bored by the proceedings – comes into view. In the office she is known simply as 'Jazz'. But Satnam Kaur turns to her: 'Jasmeet, I would like you to personally monitor this project'. As her (clearly Sikh) name is voiced, Jasmeet is a picture of squirming embarrassment. Later, on a balcony and in private, away from the meeting, Jasmeet is still upset: 'I'm so irritated. I mean how could she. I still can't believe it. She called me Jasmeet. That, too, in front of everyone. *Kissi ko bhi mera yeh nam nahi pata ta aur ab pure office me phel gaya hai* [No-one knew this name of mine and now it has spread through the whole office]. You know, I feel so embarrassed. *Mujhe to ghin aa ti hai is naam se* [this name makes me feel disgusted]. It's so outdated'. Her boyfriend Rahul approaches and teasingly asks: 'So, how's my Jasmeet darling?' 'Shut up Rahul', she replies. '*Tum bhi*? [You too?]'. Rahul: 'Oh my god. You are taking it so seriously!' Jasmeet: 'If I don't get serious what else should I do? So much embarrassment in the office. And at home, my great sister [*meeri mahan sister*] Tejbir Kaur Khalsa. All the time she's lecturing me. "Go to *gurudwara*, do *simeran* [remembering God]"'.

One of Jasmeet's friends says to her: 'When I was coming to the office today there was a big crowd outside the *gurudwara*. Is there a festival of you Sikhs today?', in response to which Jasmeet shrugs. 'My psycho sister was forcing me to go to *gurudwara* today. She goes and does the *porcha* [i.e. performs service, or *seva*, in this case mopping] like a servant, ugh. We are young. We shouldn't be like our CEO ... even in the office *Ram-Nam* [repetition of God's name] continues'. Meanwhile we see the MD on the cover of *Entrepreneur* magazine, and a scene featuring Satnam in the roles of good mother and daughter-in-law as she assists her mother-in-law in telling her son stories about the guru the day's festival will glorify. The child says: 'Like the *sahibzadas* [sons of the final living Sikh guru, Guru Gobind Singh], I will love my Sikhism, and bring glory to the name of my mama and papa [*nam roshan karna*]'. After Skyping her husband on her iPad, Satnam Kaur listens to *kirtan* while getting ready to attend the *gurudwara* where she will humbly serve food; Jasmeet by contrast is applying her makeup to a soundtrack of loud music for a different kind of evening out. Gazing at herself in the mirror, her intimacy with her truncated name is apparent: 'Jazz, you are looking gorgeous. Muah'.

Later we see her drinking beer at a disco. On leaving with her boyfriend Rahul, some male youths pretend to help her open the car door. 'Oh Madam Ji. Shall we help you? You were having a lot of fun inside. Have some fun with us.' At this sexually threatening behaviour, Rahul simply runs away. Surrounded by the youths, her sister's pious voice comes into her head. 'Only God's name will save you when everyone else abandons you.' She starts to pray. The two charismatic Kaurs thus combine: first, her sister's advice to pray, and then – apparently in consequence – Satnam Kaur, having left the *gurudwara*, arrives on the scene. Her formidable charisma causes the youths to quickly depart in fright. Jasmeet is grateful and contrite: 'Today I realize why Guru sahib has given us this form [*swaroop* – i.e. the turban] and the sword'. Satnam replies: 'We are Sikhs and Sikhs are always learning, and from today you have learned how to live'. Having asked for forgiveness in the *gurudwara*, and now back at work in a headscarf, her hair in a plain pony tail, Rahul asks her: 'Jazz, what has happened to you? And I'm sorry *yar*. If I stuck around yesterday those people would have killed me'. Jasmeet responds: 'Someone who can't protect himself, how can he protect me? And by the way my name is Jasmeet Kaur. Don't ever call me Jazz again'. Finally, a textual reminder is emblazoned on the screen: 'Don't forget your real identity. Only a real Kaur can be: charismatic, brave, and complete in all aspects', and Satnam – true name – Kaur is momentarily depicted in each of the multiple roles that the name Kaur appears to lubricate and finesse: daughter-in-law, mother/wife, *sevak*, worshipper and CEO. It is a parable of names: she whose name is 'true name' combines with God's true name (contiguous with – the very form of – God himself in Sikhism and parts of Hinduism) at a time of danger to return Jazz to the names Jasmeet and Kaur. Satnam's son's wish to bring glory to the name of his parents stands as a metaphor for the larger story of which it is a fragment: the name of the Sikh inheritance can only be glorified if its adherents continue to bear its name(s).

The film thus depicts how 'Kaur', far from being a mark of backwardness, is an asset for flourishing within modernity. Satnam's professional success, technological skill, charisma and bravery are not hindered by her name and 'complete' Sikh identity, quite the opposite. Conversely, Jasmeet's concealment of name and identity – her shedding of Kaur and disfigurement of a conventional

Sikh first name – stands, like the case of Ramit, for a corrupted engagement with modernity. But the film is recuperative, the name re-enlivened as 'Jazz' becomes 'Jasmeet Kaur'. The name spirit or charisma of Kaur works a kind of sympathetic magic, both saving and being (re)adopted by Jasmeet. The exchange value generated by substituting Jasmeet Kaur for Jazz lay in its revelation of Kaur as embodying an inherent compatibility between Sikhism and an ability to flourish in modernity. Here the name offers something more than an ideal to aspire to. A notion of name-code better captures the sense of names' capacity to act on code, transforming and engendering transformation (Hadad 2012: 5). But the process is not one-way. We now consider cases that provide a stark contrast with those considered so far, since rather than encouraging use of Kaur, Sikh authorities here seek to discourage its use by those they consider unfit to bear it – precisely because of the fear that code might act on the name, sullying it.

Exchange 5: Hard Kaur for Taran Dhillon

In 2018 the successful Canadian-origin Bollywood actress Sunny Leone released a biopic series based on her life story titled *Karenjit Kaur – The Untold Story of Sunny Leone*. Controversy immediately arose, with Sikh leaders demanding the biopic's title be changed to remove 'Kaur'. The problem, for protesters, was Leone's former career as an adult film star. As tweets sent by Delhi's SGPC head put it: 'Kaur is a surname that has been given to Sikh girls and women by Guru Sahibs. To use it for publicity stunt and depict the porn-life of a celebrity is derogatory for Sikhs all across the world. If the title of the series is not changed, we will be forced to take our protest to @ZeeTV offices and take a stern stand against the team behind the series'.[25] Her former career meant she didn't 'deserve to share "Kaur" with the other pious women of the Sikh community'.[26] While not strictly an exchange – she continues to use Sunny Leone as her stage name – her sudden striking onomastic assertion of the little-known fact of her Sikh heritage precipitated attempts to police the name Kaur as a kind of cultural property, with rights of usage restricted to those determined by authorities to be legitimate bearers. Yet Leone also had many defenders within the Sikh fold – why, Sikh feminists asked, does Punjabi rapper Yo Yo Honey Singh, whose lyrics glorify violence and male chauvinism, not encounter similar attempts to police his bearing of Singh? A case centring on perceived misuse rather than disuse of a Sikh name, it exemplified how group conflict may arise over the use or ownership of religious symbols (Harrison 1999: 249), raising questions concerning honour, misogyny, the name as a form of possession, and the vulnerability of names.

These matters had also come to the fore a few years earlier when the Punjab-origin UK hip hop artist Taran Dhillon began to gain recognition in the early 2000s. Her case differed from Leone's in that it was her stage name – Hard Kaur – not her 'real' name, that caused offence. Here the profaning of the sacred name had a double character. As with Leone, the behaviour of its bearer was considered to sully the name (Dhillon's documented liberal use of expletives, open consumption of alcohol, sexual frankness, immodest dress and so on); but in addition, Dhillon's coupling of Kaur and 'hard' produces not only a connotation of 'tough Sikh female', which she undoubtedly is,[27] but also one of hardcore pornography.

A petition launched on the Change.org website demanded that Dhillon remove the suffix Kaur from her stage name. Signatories dwell in their comments on her alleged unworthiness to bear the name as encapsulated in the offensive incongruence between its *ought*-ness and the *is* of her behaviour: 'She does not deserve to class herself as a Kaur with the behaviour she puts up'; 'Her actions are not living up to gracious name of Kaur'; 'Her behaviour, her abusive language, her dress code is an absolute disgrace ... The surname Kaur is given to us by our 10th Master, meaning Princess, Lioness representing high morals, ethics and living by the *[Reht] Maryada*. Hard Kaur does not represent any of this ... rather the opposite'; 'If you want to use Kaur your moral standards should be royal, e.g., language, wearing clothes...'[28]

Recalling our earlier discussion of the ability of code to act on name, other comments bemoan the reputational damage to the name Kaur and Sikhism more generally by Dhillon bearing it: 'She has continuously behaved inappropriately and put up a bad name for all Sikhs all around the world'; 'She is tarnishing our name!'; 'Misguides public and media as to what a Kaur stands for'. Other key words repeated in the comments include 'mockery', 'hurtful', 'filthy', 'abusing', 'insult', 'disrespect' and 'shame'. We find an echo here of the classical Brahmanical understanding that forms of exalted language – words, text and other sound-forms – are as vulnerable to pollution as bodies if uttered, read or borne by the unfit (Parry 1985; Lamb 2002).[29]

Overlaid in the responses just cited are themes of desecration, reputational damage, honour, shame and vulnerability. Veena Das (2015) explains how names are sites of vulnerability on account of their iterability: a personal name is 'both mine and out of my control' (ibid:. 3). The doomed bids to wrest back control of Kaur in the cases of Leone and Dhillon suggest something of this vulnerability. For brand names, vulnerability comes from the mimetic ability to copy the name and use it for an inferior product, or to take a similar sounding name and thus to steal a part of the name and the market share (Das and Copeman 2015: 11). Kaur/Singh are similarly vulnerable in that their status and function as both personal names and sacred objects that participate in the entities they represent seems to give them a particularly heightened potential to cause injury, if 'misused', to the larger collectives they stand for. In Annette Weiner's famous schema, inalienable possessions are 'imbued with the intrinsic and ineffable identities of their owners which are not easy to give away' (Weiner 1992: 6); indeed, such items may be held back from circulation. If we think of Kaur as a kind of inalienable possession for Sikhs, the problem is that, as a name, it is one that cannot easily be kept out of circulation and away from unsanctioned bearers. The fear, of course, is that illicit associations arising from the use of Kaur – as a personified form of cultural property (Kaneff and King 2004: 14) – by improper bearers might in time compromise or even overcome its sanctioned associations.

This begs the question: is Singh as much of an inalienable possession as Kaur? It is true that Singh seems less subject to attempts to constrain its usage than its female counterpart, thus suggesting at least the possibility of a misogynistic double standard. As was noted earlier, visual aspects of Sikh identity have tended to receive far more scholarly attention than linguistic ones. In the case of Taran Dhillon, the two thematics converge, since her 'immodest dress' and eschewing of the traditional Indian headscarf (*dupatta*) of idealized Jat female style, which connotes modesty, respect and humility (Mooney 2011), is counted as one of the ways in which she dishonours Kaur. Honour is a marked cultural value among Punjabi Jats and, as elsewhere, women far more than men are tasked with maintaining it. Following this, perceived breaches that cause shame are far more likely to be concentrated on the bodies and persons of Jat Sikh women (Jakobsh 2015). Something of this is seen in the responses to both Leone's and Dhillon's uses of Kaur discussed above. However, outrage is not the only Sikh reaction; rather, Kaur finds itself at the centre of 'competing communities of interpretation' (Chidester 2018: 13), with progressive Sikhs – often, though not exclusively located in the diaspora and well aware of the gendered nature of Jat honour codes – providing a starkly contrasting mode of commentary. Comments accompanying a 2007 interview with Dhillon on the Sikhchic website – popular in the diaspora, particularly among young Sikhs – demonstrate this. One, from a male Sikh in Malaysia, states: 'Grow up, babe. The word "Kaur" doesn't belong to you to get you on stage. You are obviously using it to attract attention'. A second comment, from a male Sikh based in Birmingham, UK, contests this interpretation: 'Wow, the level of misogyny is incredible. The amount of Sikh singers who get on stage with the name "Singh" doesn't attract any comment. As soon as an independent woman expresses herself she gets abuse from insecure sexists'. But not only male Sikhs object. I quote a UK-based Sikh woman: 'As a Kaur myself, I would rather she didn't denigrate my name, the meaning of which I am rather proud of. I am the equal of my brothers in all that we do. But that does not give me or any Sikh woman the right to tarnish our good name, given to us by our Guru Sahib. Respect it, or don't use it!' Note the phrase 'my name', reflecting once again Kaur's inalienability and consequent ability to reflect back (positively or negatively) on its common owner. The progressive voice of the moderator responds: 'So, we as Sikhs have the right to demand others who we consider "bad" to change their names? How about all the non-Sikhs in India who use the name "Singh" and also live lives far short of our ideals? You may need to think this one out a bit'.

The moderator rightly asserts that an existing gendered honour code is extended to the name Kaur in a way that is not seen in the case of Singh. But Singh and Kaur are not absolute equivalents. As the moderator asserts, many non-Sikhs use Singh. This is much less true of Kaur. Singh is very much a Sikh name but everyone knows it is not only a Sikh name but the surname for an array of individuals and groupings – Rajputs, various 'OBCs' (Other Backward Classes), Dalits who have taken it on in place of derogatory names, and so on. Kaur, on the other hand, is a much readier identifier than Singh of Sikh-hood. While some non-Sikhs use Kaur, this is far less the case than with Singh. This is not, of course, to justify attempts to exert control over Kaur that are absent for Singh, but to seek to understand why there might be an additional felt imperative to do so in the case of Kaur that is not ipso facto reducible to a sexist double standard.

A further way some Sikhs seek to place restrictions on usage of Kaur and Singh is disclosed in one of the comments attached to the petition demanding that Dhillon cease using the name Kaur, which states: 'Kaur should only be used when *amrit* has been administered.' According to this view, Kaur/Singh should be assumed only after one has undergone the baptismal ritual (which features the ceremonial imbibing of sacred nectar, or *amrit*) and joined the Khalsa. While it is true that *amritdhari* Sikhs are bound more scrupulously to wear the five Ks, and that Khalsa identity has a normative influence on mainstream Sikhism, vast swathes of non-Khalsa Sikhs bear these names, and experience no contradiction or pushback in doing so (Takhar 2005). During fieldwork in Delhi, neither Khalsa nor non-Khalsa Sikhs thought the issue an important one – far from restricting usage, the primary effort was to encourage take-up of Kaur/Singh, as we have seen.

However, increasingly influential online constructions of Sikh identity, Jakobsh suggests, have contributed to an inflationary enlargement of claims to purity and exactitude (2014a: 232). Jakobsh is writing in respect of female take-up of the turban in the diaspora, but the observation also applies to viewpoints concerning usage of Kaur/Singh. For instance, far from encouraging participation in these names, young Italian Sikhs claim that *amritdhari* Sikhs alone are 'true' Sikhs and 'Singh' is reserved for this group: 'If you aren't "baptized" you can't ... even let other people call you "Singh" ... you aren't even a "Sikh" (Balginder, 23-year-old *amritdhari* male, born in India, in Italy since he was nine years old)' (Bertolani 2015: 215). Rajvir K., a nineteen-year-old *amritdhari* girl (born in India, in Italy since she was ten years old), is equally strident: '[In ancient times], everybody had his family name before being "baptized" ... and people adopted the name "Singh" only after being "baptized" ... Only nowadays the children of a "Singh" receive the name "Singh" ... only nowadays! Therefore, in my opinion a person who is not "baptized" can't have the name "Singh"' (ibid.). The problem, in this view, is that what properly are titles earned through initiation have been devalued via their routine inheritance as family names. If they are markers of equality at all, this can only be so within, not outside, the Khalsa. Their main function, instead, should be to mark the exclusivity of 'full' Sikh-hood – a condition, as was noted earlier, that is usually equated with bodily markers, but which I suggest also possesses an important linguistic component.

I focus now on a debate between UK-based Sikhs in an online discussion forum that once again follows on from an instance of name exchange.

Characterized by both reasoned argument and affects and desires, we see how one woman, Divneet, responds to such claims of exclusivity, describing her recent adoption of Kaur (presumably in place of a caste surname) using a passionate rhetoric of empowerment. 'I have Kaur in my name, but did not before. I had added [it] myself. Are you saying I don't deserve it? Try stopping me from keeping it ... How on earth are people going to get close to Sikhi, if you going to say they don't deserve it ... At least it's better than not having it and being confused as to what faith we belong to. Some people go and convert to other faiths if they don't have in their name, coz *gwacheo hunde* [they are lost]. With Singh or Kaur in [their names] they will be grounded to stay where they are, somethin is better than nothing'. But a stern reply states: 'What is a name without the significance of carrying it, but just a false label? You can stick a Ferrari badge on your Fiat but it ain't a Ferrari ... When someone is introduced as XYZ Singh/Kaur, I need to be able to rely on them to hold the values of Sikhi ... The name is not something that one "deserves," that is a very egotistical view. The name is a responsibility'.[30]

In this view, Kaur and Singh must function as transparent signs of initiated Sikh-hood. Divneet, on the other hand, understands the bearing of Kaur in a less exalted manner as an aid for embarking on a path towards a fuller expression of her Sikhness. 'Kaur' provides a quiet sense of oughtness and affinity with the identity she seeks to bring herself closer to. She replies: 'I feel good that I have [Kaur] in my name now ... Now I have it, I want to know more about Sikhi ... If Waheguru [God] wants they will bless me with Amrit, if they don't they won't, but at least I am taking steps towards it, and my putting Kaur in my name is a great start I think for myself'. If the name has injurious effects – a theme that has preoccupied a number of poststructuralist theorists[31] – here they are apparently focused less on the bearer than on the witness whose demand for a kind of 'dogmatism of the signifier' (Jameson 2005: 180), according to which the meanings of Kaur and Singh would be fixed, stable and assigned definitive content, is unmet. The answer is to restrict usage of the titles to Khalsa Sikhs – a proprietorial stance that of course obscures Sikhs' own borrowing of the names from Hindu Rajputs. Divneet, conversely, sees Kaur not in Bourdieu's (1991) terms as a name that informs her in an authoritative way of what she is and must be, but as a self-chosen guide and reminder of her heritage and what she can be in relation to it – the name's inaugurative power is desired and taken on voluntarily as part of an attempt to make of herself a certain kind of person, because it is as such a person that, on reflection, she thinks she ought to live (Laidlaw 2002: 327). This is the value produced through adoption of Kaur for Divneet, one that is hardly congruent with the depthlessness of a 'false label'. Meanwhile, if those who for the sake of purity would restrict Kaur/Singh only to Khalsa Sikhs are successful, the result, almost certainly, would be to increase the use of caste names in their place. Indeed, this is what tends to happen when such restrictions are put in place, as we shall see in our final set of exchanges.

Exchange 6: Sathnam Sanghera for Sathnam Singh

Classrooms, and school registers in particular, are classic onomastic 'scenes of instruction'. With teachers intervening to make student names fit certain requirements (most frequently of legibility but also sometimes purity), students can come to learn, frequently for the first time, the connotations of their own and others' names, and thereby about the broader operation of names as identifying marks which, 'by the application of a rule, establish ... that the individual who is named is a member of a preordained class (a social group in a system of groups, a status by birth in a system of statuses)' (Lévi-Strauss 1966: 181). Manuela Ciotti's Chamar[32] informants recounted to her how when Babasaheb Ambedkar's father first took him to school he was asked to write the child's name on the register.[33] 'At that moment, people came to know that the child was a Chamar [Dalit]. Ambedkar was abused and sent back home with the excuse that studying was sin for him' (Ciotti 2006: 905). In schools in the Sundarbans, schoolteachers may remove Islamic elements from student names that had formerly possessed both Islamic and Hindu associations (Jalais 2010). No longer an onomastic indicator of composite religiosity or 'the bridging of worlds', the purified name becomes an artefact of exclusive religion.

Young Sikh adults I know in Delhi recounted to me a different 'pedagogy of the name'.[34] On the very first day they had attended their orthodox Singh Sabha school, their teachers had refused to countenance the caste surnames they had gained admission with, writing only Kaur or Singh on the school register. The subtractions were not superficial. Having left school, they continued to bear the names their teachers had insisted on; moreover, some recalled how at the time their parents had followed suit and discarded their caste names as well. Smiling, they explained to me how, as a consequence of the teacher's purifying elimination of caste surnames, class registers might contain four Gurpreet Kaurs – distinguished in the register as Gurpreet Kaur 1, Gurpreet Kaur 2, Gurpreet Kaur 3 and Gurpreet Kaur 4 – plus three similarly differentiated Jasmeet Singhs, for instance. Former classmates often still think of each other in these numeric terms!

As a Sikh-run school, the teachers in this case had some licence to 'correct' their students' names by making them accord with orthodox Sikh requirements. Sikh experiences in mixed schools in Delhi or the diaspora can be just as onomastically pedagogical, but with very different – indeed opposite – outcomes. In his poignant comic memoir of growing up in Wolverhampton in the 1980s, Sikh-background author Sathnam Sanghera recounts his own first day at a school which, though mixed, mainly comprised Indian-origin students. As the teacher takes the register, she begins to despair at the number of Kaurs and Singhs: 'Oh dear, oh dear, oh dear ... This won't do at all. Now then ... Can those of you called Kaur or Singh provide me with a surname, please?' Most other students could provide a surname in the form of a caste name, but Sathnam could not.

'Sath-nam? Is that how you say it?'

'Yes, miss,' I lied.

'Your surname?'

'Singh, miss.'

'Come on now, don't be a silly sausage.' A ripple of giggles across the room. 'Everyone has a forename – mine, for example, is Hyacinth ...' More giggles. 'Most people have a middle name ... mine, for example, is Edna ...' Open laughter now. 'Yours is Singh. And you should also have a surname or family name. Like *Jones*?'

Sathnam agrees to go home and ask his parents what his surname is. His mother resists: '"Your surname is Singh," she said eventually... "It means lion. A name shared by every Sikh man and a name to be proud of... Don't you remember the story I told you?"' In response, Sathnam decides to press his point 'by exploiting my mother's instinctive and total respect for authority. "My teacher says I must have a family name," I ventured.' His mother finally tells him to ask his elder sister who must herself have gone through a similar experience when she began school. In this way he eventually learns his 'family surname', Sanghera, which he has to practise saying on his way to school the next day. In the process, Singh apparently becomes not even the middle name his teacher suggests it really is, but is lost altogether in favour of Sanghera, a caste name. Far from the removal of caste names we saw in the case of the Singh Sabha school (an echo of the same process enacted at the founding of the Khalsa), here use of caste names is reinstituted in the classroom.

The episode is recounted humorously and without rancour. However, it points towards a different means of policing Kaur/Singh than those discussed earlier – one that is institutionally and bureaucratically driven. We encounter two conflicting 'rights': the 'right to control one's name' versus the right of the state to identify its citizens (Coulmont 2014: 503). The 'becoming legal' (Deseriis 2015: 23) of the proper name is of course central to the story of the modern state. The institutionalization and fixing of surnames by colonial governments saw the name enter 'a whole network of apparatuses (demographic records, criminal records, tax records, voting records, immunization and health records) through which the state can both identify an individual and deploy a series of calculations and operations whose domain and target is the population' (ibid.). Specifically in India, the colonial complaint was that family surnames were too recurrent, contributing to a native propensity for impersonation (Singha 2000).

Indeed, to exchange numbers for caste names in the Singh Sabha school was implicitly to acknowledge precisely the problem of recurrence, but as a specifically Sikh rather than pan-Indian difficulty. The complaint finds many forms of expression. The reviewer of a book featuring numerous Sikh protagonists might complain of confusion caused by the number of Singhs (e.g. Cannell 2018).

Owen Cole (1994) observes that despite the prized ability of Singh/Kaur to elide caste, 'a glance at a London telephone directory with its many columns of Singhs, or reading an article by "Harbans Singh" in a Sikh newspaper (there are at least six theologians or journalists who share the name, to my knowledge)' quickly reveals the disadvantages. 'Consequently, many Sikhs will use the *got* [subcaste or clan] name.' Cole's final remark reflects both Sathnam Sanghera's experience and the standard argument I heard in Delhi, namely, that uptake of caste names among Sikhs is not the result of some sinister resurgence of caste pride but simply a solution to a bureaucratic problem.

Sikh temporal authorities recognize the difficulty but for obvious reasons are unwilling to endorse use of caste names to remedy it. They propose as an alternative the addition of a place name as an individuating suffix to Singh/Kaur. Such toponymically adjusted personal names may feature the name of a village, neighbourhood, town, state or even country from which the bearer hails, as in the names of senior Akali Dal politician Parkash Singh Badal (Badal is a village in Punjab), Manjeet Singh GK (after the Greater Kailash colony where he lives in Delhi), and Akali leader Jasjit Singh UK (who had previously lived in the UK). This, then, is the theologically sanctioned solution to the problem. But its use among Sikhs as a solution to the problem of 'name concentration' (Pina-Cabral 2012) is far rarer than the reinstitution of caste names.

Exacerbating the difficulty is the Punjabi taste for travel and relocation that precedes, but has also been accelerated by, intervals of intense persecution of Sikhs in the country. As was noted earlier, visa and passport offices are known to be key sites of the 'problematization' of Kaur/Singh. This came dramatically to light in 2007 when it was revealed that the Canadian immigration service had refused to accept Kaur and Singh as surnames for the previous ten years. As a 2007 *Toronto Star* news report stated:

> [Finally] one of the most common surnames in Canada, imbued with religious significance for millions of Sikhs around the world, is now, after yesterday's reversal of a 10-year policy, deemed acceptable by the Canadian government. For the past decade, Indian immigration applicants with the surname Singh or Kaur were told by the Canadian High Commission in New Delhi that their names, too common to process quickly, would have to be changed ... It's not known how many people have been affected. Liberal MP Ruby Dhalla (Brampton-Springdale) says in the past three years she's received about 500 complaints from constituents whose family members were told to change their names when applying to immigrate... [A]ccording to statements from the department, the policy asking for a different name was meant to help speed up applications and prevent cases of mistaken identity due to the commonness of Singh. It said its New Delhi visa office had reported 'very few complaints' about the request and explained that most Singhs or Kaurs often have an additional family name, even if it is not often used, that can be easily added to their passport. 'If you have to change your name to come here, we have to ask ourselves, "Are we really celebrating all the great things that are hallmarks of this multicultural country?"' said Dhalla.

The episode, placed alongside similar reports from the United States and Sanghera's experience in a UK school, shows how migration and diaspora have often increased the visibility of caste in Sikh names. But it is not only diasporic administrations that take issue with the generality of Kaur/Singh. Scores of Delhi-based Sikhs I spoke with reported taking up a caste surname only after finding that the Indian passport authority refused to countenance Singh or Kaur as family names. The process becomes self-fulfilling: on hearing of their fellow Sikhs' name-related difficulties in the passport office, they pre-emptively make the change themselves. Strongly implied, once again, is that it is not pride but the mundane demands of officialdom that cause the (re)adoption of a caste name.

It is difficult to determine whether the bureaucracy-led visibilization of caste in Sikh names causes its substantialization. The evident ability of a Sikh passport applicant to call on a caste title as a means of 'solving a bureaucratic problem' demonstrates well enough that prior processes of making caste onomastically invisible barely if ever caused Sikhs to become unaware of it.[35] In light of wider processes of caste assertion and the 'unfashionableness' of Kaur and Singh for some young Sikhs, bureaucratic aggravations might provide welcome cover for some Sikhs to alter their names in a way they already secretly wanted.

The dynamics described here recall longstanding bureaucratic exercises involving the caste-wise enumeration of local populations, particularly the colonial census beginning in the nineteenth century, which scholars argue was not simply referential but, in fact, generative (Peabody 2001: 821). Though debate persists about the effects of such numerical collection of data on caste (Bayly 1999), it is a widely shared view among scholars of South Asia that by means of nomenclature and census, the British inscribed identities that it was incumbent on their subjects to fulfil (Bhogal 2014: 283). While people do not simply become the labels attached to them (Biehl and Locke 2010) – Sikhs bureaucratically pressured to use caste names may refuse to identify with them, or otherwise redefine or redeploy them – the parallel with the colonial census is nonetheless striking. Administrative demands for surnames other than Kaur/Singh, similar to the census, cause what may be unelaborated categories to become more 'pronounced and visual' (Sengupta 2018: 67), an outcome starkly at odds with the orthodox Sikh aspiration of not wanting to 'sort themselves out'.[36] For bureaucratic agencies, homonymy is a pathology, a personal name worthless if it does not individuate (Pina-Cabral 2012: 18). Guru Gobind Singh's foundational name exchange, on the other hand, sought to produce a kind of value – disidentification – that bureaucracy computes only to the extent that it knows its task is to 'correct' it. To return to Cole's point about the disadvantages of 'six Harbans Singhs': for my Sikh friends in Delhi, this multiplicity is precisely the point; the scope for prideful egoism is diminished via the multiplicity of the single name versus the multiplicity of different names desired by visa and passport authorities. The Canadian immigration service backpedalled, as we have seen, and demands for onomastic distinction made by equivalent authorities elsewhere are uneven. Together, however, such agencies have forced many ordinary Sikhs to make difficult decisions concerning their names.

Conclusions

A key concern of Susan Bayly's multifaceted work on intellectual exchange has been to nuance (and frequently to contest) reductive characterizations of colonial and postcolonial intellectual exchanges as 'mere exercises in power-knowledge, conceived solely as a means of dominating voiceless Asian Others' (2009: 192). My concern here has been different but complementary. First, the chapter has sought to show how the exchange of names generates for Sikhs both different forms of exchange value and significant intellectual exchanges. Focused on cherished identifications, these intellectual exchanges are frequently both reasoned and emotive, cerebral and volatile. While the role of visa and passport offices in the revival and objectification of caste names brings to mind existing scholarly treatments of the colonial census, name exchanges more typically take place on the basis of active reflection and decision, with new names value-producing instruments for mediating between what one is and what one might hope to be – whether this entails a movement towards esteemed Sikh values or not. Second, we come to see how such active bearing of names can call into question pervasive depictions of them as merely dominating or forming instructions to their bearers.

What is exchanged when one name is taken on in place of another are ideas, values and allegiances. We have seen how name exchanges can both bridge worlds and also burn such bridges. We have also seen their ability not only to mark but also produce, challenge and negate value(s). In the case of bureaucratically enforced name changes, an exchange value is generated (unambiguous individuation) that can only come at the cost of the negation of traditional Sikh values of caste-elision and being 'counted-as-one'.[37] Passport and visa authorities compel a decision between two forms of visibility. To be fully visible as a Sikh is to enact a form of concealment from bureaucratic authority. To become visible to bureaucratic authority forces a form of concealment of one's Sikhness. Indeed, an appreciation of concealment as something more than itself – as a process of becoming differently visible – crosscuts the exemplary name exchanges discussed in the chapter. This important theme goes back to the founding of the Khalsa. 'The point of the five Ks', writes Cynthia Mahmood, 'was to ensure that Sikhs would not be able to shirk their duty to defend their faith by blending unnoticed into a crowd' (1996: 44–45). Since the founding of the Khalsa, becoming fully visible as Sikh has tended to involve the onomastic concealment of one's caste origin, while making visible one's caste origin has been to run the risk of concealing one's Sikh-hood. These concerns form points of discussion within impassioned yet reasoned debates about both bureaucratically-driven and fashion-induced name exchanges, with orthodox commentators expressing anxiety that concealment of Sikh markers, including but not limited to names, causes Sikhs to become visible as Hindus. Fashionable disuse of Kaur/Singh is thus far from being a frivolous matter.

This chapter has examined reasons why young Sikhs in particular might consider bearing Kaur and Singh an unattractive proposition (their perceived archaism, discordant relationship with individualism, association with the rustic Sardarji of Santa Banta jokes, etc.), but also some of the means employed to recuperate them as indispensable sources of dynamism and charisma in 'an achievement-conscious society' (Bayly 2014: 496). Both dynamics are visible in the 2017 Punjabi movie *Super Singh*, which features a protagonist, Sajjan Singh, who uses the name Sam to fit in more easily with his friends in Canada, where he has moved to study. His 'inauthentic' deviation from Sikh values and signifiers is embodied in his wish to marry Kathy, a white Canadian woman, and especially his willingness to cut his hair to please her. Meanwhile, on a visit home to Punjab he discovers he has superpowers. At the hairdresser – an emotionally charged space in the Sikh imagination – it is revealed, once he takes it off, that it is his turban that is the source of his powers. He comes more fully to realize that Kathy's expectations of him demonstrate disrespect of his Sikh culture and values. In consequence, he doesn't cut his hair after all and, as with the exchange of Jasmeet Kaur for Jazz discussed earlier, he 'comes home' to the name Sajjan Singh, discarding its inauthentic anglicized variant while also deciding to 'help others to realise who Singhs are and thus to become [like him] *Super Singhs*'.[38] In this way the film not only participates in an effort to rehabilitate pride in Sikh markers in the face of 'Indian jokes featuring Sikhs as the punch line' and Bollywood depictions of 'bumbling Sikh sidekick characters',[39] but enacts the dramatization, replete with humour, sadness, indignation, shame and pride, of a key line of thinking within the intellectual exchanges that we have seen are generated by name exchanges.

While it is notable how quickly debates can seem to switch from concerns about these names not being used enough to their being used too much or by the wrong kind of person, these seemingly different imperatives are not necessarily contradictory: it is important to take up these names, but in the right way. Here, too, visibility and concealment arise as key thematics. Certain responses to the use of Kaur by Taran Dhillon and Sunny Leone imply that perceived 'bad Sikhs' should indeed conceal their Sikhness. To attempt to force them to cease bearing Kaur is to treat it as a form of intellectual property as if it had not been borrowed from elsewhere; the earlier exchange is hidden or denied (Bercovitch 1994; Rio 2007). In the case of debates about restricting rights of usage only to those who have undergone baptism, non-baptised bearers of Kaur/Singh are accused of generating a problematic opacity that compromises an onlooker's ability properly to discern Khalsa Sikh-hood. However, such a view of their value forms but a fragment of their strikingly plural significance, a significance that is in constant motion and that continues to accrue resonances and to display and produce value(s) – both in specific instances of onomastic exchange but also as the dynamic focus of a broader give and take of vibrant intellectual exchange within the worldwide Sikh community.

Acknowledgements

This chapter is based on research generously supported by an Independent Social Research Foundation Early Career Fellowship and a British Academy Mid-Career Fellowship. It has particularly benefited from generous and incisive engagements by Susan Bayly and Doris Jakobsh. For valuable comments and suggestions I also warmly thank Lam Minh Chau, Nick Long, Arkotong Longkumer, Bjørn Ola Tafjord, Koonal Duggal, Hugo Gorringe, Nathaniel Roberts, Neelabh Gupta, Neerja Pathak, Johannes Quack, Mascha Schulz, John Hagström and Amelie Blom. Thanks also to Bhuvi Gupta and Prasannanshu for inspiring discussions of naming practices more broadly.

Jacob Copeman is Research Professor, University of Santiago de Compostela, Distinguished Researcher (Oportunius) and Senior Researcher at the Centro de Investigación Interuniversitario en Paisaxes Atlánticas Culturais (CISPAC), Santiago de Compostela. His most recent monograph, co-authored with Dwaipayan Banerjee, is *Hematologies: The Political Life of Blood in India* (Cornell University Press, 2019). His most recent edited collection, co-edited with Mascha Schulz, is *Global Sceptical Publics: From Non-religious Print Media to 'Digital Atheism'* (UCL Press, 2022). He is principal investigator of the ERC-funded project 'Religion and Its Others in South Asia and the World: Communities, Debates, Freedoms'.

Notes

1. 'Over time, "Khalsa" and "Sikh" have become synonymous terms, and even though only a minority of Sikhs are formally initiated into the Khalsa order, all Sikh men and women trace their personality, name, religious rites, and prayers – what they do, what they wear, how they identify themselves – to this liberating Baisakhi [Punjabi harvest festival] of 1699' (N-G. K. Singh 2005: xi). See also Copeman and Banerjee (2019: chapter 6) on this pivotal event and the iconography associated with it.
2. A paraphrase of Greenblatt (1995: 229).
3. A mix, mainly, of *khatri* (stereotypically trader), *jat* (stereotypically cultivator) and Dalit (former untouchable) Sikhs.
4. See Laidlaw (2014). In this, names as intellectual exchange objects perform a function somewhat similar to exemplars, as described by Robbins (2018).
5. Nihangs are an armed Sikh warrior order.
6. Guru Gobind Singh's father, the ninth Sikh guru Guru Teg Bahudur, was executed on the orders of Mughal Emperor Aurangzeb in 1675. I note that some Sikhs see the reformist focus on names and external symbols as being at odds with Sikh teachings. 'According to the gurus' thoughts [*sikhi sikya gurvichar*]', one devout Sikh woman in her sixties told me, 'what matters is inside [the devotee] – their thoughts and their faith. We should not

be bothered about labels and symbols'. Scholars, too, have observed how the predominant focus on external symbols – hair, names, swords and so on – inaugurated at the birth of the Khalsa led to a tension between it and countervailing teachings that seek a movement beyond such things (Fenech and McLeod 2014: 8; Bhogal 2007: 107; Takhar 2014: 352).

7. The Singh Sabha, a Sikh revivalist movement founded in the nineteenth century, sought to remove Hindu influences from Sikhism.
8. An eighteenth-century manual elaborating a 'Sikh way of life'.
9. For instance, the Namdharis and Nirankaris (see S.K. Singh 2017: 21; Copeman 2009: chapter 4), who are otherwise controversial among mainstream Sikhs for continuing to revere living gurus.
10. 'A Sikh of the Chamar (leather-working) caste; an Outcaste Sikh' (Fenech and McLeod 2014: 259).
11. Refugee Review Tribunal Australia – RRT Research Response (Number: IND17527). Country: India. 26 September 2005: http://www.refworld.org/pdfid/4b6fe2090.pdf.
12. *The Sikh Review*, begun in 1953 and published by the Sikh Cultural Center, Kolkata, and whose content occupies a borderland between the academic and the popular, features contributions from Sikhs in both India and the diaspora.
13. The Chief Khalsa Diwan, which oversees various branches of the Singh Sabha, is primarily a Sikh educational and cultural body.
14. A paraphrase of Paul Carter (1987: xxiv).
15. In many Indian traditions, elders choose the names of newborns. See Jhumpa Lahiri's *The Namesake* (2003).
16. See Zelliot (1981) on Chokhamela.
17. Reformist efforts here might be taken more seriously were it not for Dalit Sikhs' continued exclusion from numerous *gurudwaras*, key Sikh leadership positions, inter-caste violence, prohibitions on inter-marriage and so on (the very things that at least in part explain the striking growth of less exclusionary *deras* in Punjab and Haryana – see Takhar 2005; Duggal 2015; Kalra and Purewal 2020). See Bayly (1999: 18–19) on caste in casteless religions.
18. 'Sikhi' is an informal term, which tends to be used by adherents rather than non-Sikhs, for the Sikh religion.
19. *Firstpost*, 28 January 2015.
20. *Business Today*, 26 April 2016.
21. For a 2013 discussion on 'Sikhs not using Singh and Kaur as their last name', see https://www.sikhsangat.com/index.php?/topic/70467-sikhs-not-using-singh-and-kaur-as-their-last-name/page/3/.
22. *Daily Mail*, 12 December 2012.
23. Review of *Singh is Kinng*, available at: http://rajeevmasand.com/admin/reviews/our-films/singh-is-kinng-review.
24. See Jakobsh (2015) on female Sikhs and the turban.
25. See collection of related articles and comments on Twitter, available here: https://twitter.com/i/moments/1018828931934380032?lang=en.
26. *The Wire*, 18 July 2018.
27. For details of her difficult upbringing, see sikhchic.com/article-detail.php?id=336&cat=4.
28. Comments on the Change.org petition: 'HARD "Kaur" – Real Name: Taran Dhillon: Remove the Suffix "Kaur" from Her Stage Name'. See https://www.change.org/p/hard-kaur-real-name-taran-dhillon-remove-the-suffix-kaur-from-her-stage-name/c?source_location=petition_show.
29. A corollary of which is the capacity of certain names to cause pollution to their utterers or viewers (Banerjee 2008; Jaoul 2008).
30. It is commonly understood that while Khalsa Sikhs should take on Singh/Kaur, there is also no bar to non-Khalsa Sikhs using them.

31. Most notably, Judith Butler and Jacques Derrida.
32. A Dalit, traditionally leather tanning community.
33. Ambedkar, though a Dalit, was in fact a Mahar.
34. This phrasing draws on an earlier article by the author that similarly sought to unpack the pedagogical implications of personal naming practices (Copeman 2015).
35. Though in Sanghera's account it appears that the bureaucratic push towards a family name other than Singh may have thwarted the chance he had to be ignorant of his.
36. At least, within the *panth*. After Bowker and Star (1999).
37. After Badiou (2006); see also Humphrey (2008).
38. Review of *Super Singh*, available at: https://www.cinestaan.com/articles/2017/jun/17/6474.
39. Review of *Super Singh*, available at: https://www.thestar.com/entertainment/movies/2017/06/20/super-singhs-star-diljit-dosanjh-says-its-the-less-dark-knight.html.

References

Axel, Brian Keith. 2001. *The Nation's Tortured Body: Violence, Representation, and the Formation of a Sikh Diaspora*. Durham, NC: Duke University Press.

Azad, Abdul Kalam. 1959. *India Wins Freedom: An Autobiographical Narrative*. Delhi: Orient Longman.

Azaryahu, Maoz. 2011. 'The Critical Turn and Beyond: The Case of Commemorative Street Naming', *ACME: An International E-Journal for Critical Geographies* 10(1): 28–33.

Badiou, Alain. 2006. *Being and Event*, trans. Oliver Feltham. London: Continuum.

Banerjee, Mukulika. 2008. 'Introduction', in Mukulika Banerjee (ed.), *Muslim Portraits: Everyday Lives in India*. Delhi: Yoda Press, pp. xii–xv.

Bayly, Susan. 1999. *Caste, Society and Politics in India from the Eighteenth Century to the Modern Age*. Cambridge: Cambridge University Press.

———. 2004. 'Conceptualizing from Within: Divergent Religious Modes from Asian Modernist Perspectives', in J. Laidlaw and H. Whitehouse (eds), *Ritual and Memory: Toward a Comparative Anthropology of Religion*. Walnut Creek, CA: Altamira Press, pp. 111–34.

———. 2009. 'Conceptualizing Resistance and Revolution in Vietnam: Paul Mus' Understanding of Colonialism in Crisis', *Journal of Vietnamese Studies* 4(1): 192–205.

———. 2014. 'How to Forge a Creative Student-Citizen: Achieving the Positive in Today's Vietnam', *Modern Asian Studies* 48(3): 493–523.

Bercovitch, Eytan. 1994. 'The Agent in the Gift: Hidden Exchange in Inner New Guinea', *Cultural Anthropology* 9(4): 498–536.

Bertolani, Barbara. 2015. 'Young Sikhs in Italy: A Plural Presence for an Intergenerational Dialogue', in Knut A. Jacobsen and Kristina Myrvold (eds), *Young Sikhs in a Global World: Negotiating Traditions, Identities and Authorities*. Aldershot: Ashgate, pp. 209–30.

Bhogal, Balbinder Singh. 2007. 'Text as Sword: Sikh Religious Violence Taken for Wonder', in John R. Hinnells and Richard King (eds), *Religion and Violence in South Asia: Theory and Practice*. London: Routledge, pp. 101–29.

———. 2014. 'Postcolonial and Postmodern Perspectives on Sikhism', in Pashaura Singh and Louis E. Fenech (eds), *The Oxford Handbook of Sikh Studies*. Oxford: Oxford University Press, pp. 282–97.

Biehl, João, and Peter Locke. 2010. 'Deleuze and the Anthropology of Becoming', *Current Anthropology* 51(3): 317–51.
Blom, Amelie, and Stéphanie Tawa Lama-Rewal. 2020. 'Contentious Emotions: An Introduction', in Amelie Blom and Stéphanie Tawa Lama-Rewal (eds), *Emotions, Mobilisations and South Asian Politics*. Abingdon: Routledge, pp. 1–34.
Bourdieu, Pierre. 1991. *Language and Symbolic Power*. Cambridge: Polity Press.
Bowker, Geoffrey C., and Susan Leigh Star. 1999. *Sorting Things Out: Classification and Its Consequences*. Cambridge, MA: MIT Press.
Cannell, Christopher. 2018. 'Review of *The Tartan Turban: In Search of Alexander Gardner* by John Keay', *Scottish Affairs* 27(3): 397–99.
Carsten, Janet, Sophie Day and Charles Stafford. 2018. 'Introduction: Reason and Passion: The Parallel Worlds of Ethnography and Biography', *Social Anthropology* 26(1): 5-14.
Carter, Paul. 1987. *The Road to Botany Bay: An Essay in Spatial History*. London: Faber and Faber.
Chidester, David. 2018. *Religion: Material Dynamics*. Oakland: University of California Press.
Ciotti, Manuela. 2006. 'In the Past We Were a Bit "Chamar"': Education as a Self and Community Engineering Process in Northern India', *Journal of the Royal Anthropological Institute* 12(4): 899–916.
Codere, Helen. 1950. *Fighting with Property: A Study of Kwakiutl Potlatching and Warfare 1792–1930*. New York: J.J. Augustin.
Cohen, Lawrence. 2011. 'Style', in Raka Ray (ed.), *Handbook of Gender*. Delhi: Oxford University Press, pp. 249–68.
Cole, W. Owen. 1994. *Sikhism: An Introduction*. London: Hodder and Stoughton.
Comaroff, John L., and Jean Comaroff. 2009. *Ethnicity, Inc.* Chicago: University of Chicago Press.
Copeman, Jacob. 2009. *Veins of Devotion: Blood Donation and Religious Experience in North India*. New Brunswick, NJ: Rutgers University Press.
______. 2015. 'Secularism's Names: Commitment to Confusion and the Pedagogy of the Name', *South Asia Multidisciplinary Academic Journal* 12.
Copeman, Jacob, and Dwaipayan Banerjee. 2019. *Hematologies: The Political Life of Blood in India*. Ithaca, NY: Cornell University Press.
Coulmont, Baptiste. 2014. 'Changing One's First Name in France: A Fountain of Youth?', *Names* 62(3): 503–30.
Cunningham, Joseph Davey. 1918. *History of the Sikhs from the Origin of the Nation to the Battles of the Sutlej*. Oxford: Oxford University Press.
Das, Veena. 2015. 'Naming beyond Pointing: Singularity, Relatedness and the Foreshadowing of Death', *South Asia Multidisciplinary Academic Journal* 12.
Das, Veena, and Jacob Copeman. 2015. 'Introduction. On Names in South Asia: Iteration, (Im)propriety and Dissimulation', *South Asia Multidisciplinary Academic Journal* 12.
Deseriis, Marco. 2015. *Improper Names: Collective Pseudonyms from the Luddites to Anonymous*. Minneapolis: University of Minnesota Press.
Deshpande, Satish. 2013. 'Caste and Castelessness: Towards a Biography of the "General Category"', *Economic and Political Weekly* XLVIII(15): 32–39.
Dhanda, Meena. 2009. 'Punjabi Dalit Youth: Social Dynamics of Transitions in Identity', *Contemporary South Asia* 17(1): 47–64.
Duggal, Koonal. 2015. 'Crossing Religious Boundaries: Representation, Caste and Identity in Contemporary Punjab', Ph.D. dissertation. English and Foreign Languages University, Hyderabad.

———. 2022. 'The "Vexed" Status of Guru Images: Visuality, Circulation and Iconographic Conflicts', *South Asian Popular Culture*. doi:10.1080/14746689.2022.2047457.
Fenech, Louis E., and W.H. McLeod. 2014. *Historical Dictionary of Sikhism*. Lanham, MD: Rowman and Littlefield.
Gold, Daniel. 1987. *The Lord as Guru: Hindi Sants in North Indian Tradition*. New York: Oxford University Press.
Gorringe, Hugo. 2010. 'Resounding Rhetoric, Retreating Rebels: The Use and Impact of Militant Speeches in Tamil Dalit Movements', *Contemporary South Asia* 18(3): 281–92.
Greenblatt, Stephen. 1995. 'Culture', in Frank Lentricchia and Thomas McLaughlin (eds), *Critical Terms for Literary Study*. Chicago: Chicago University Press, pp. 225–32.
Hacking, Ian. 1986. 'Making Up People', in Thomas C. Heller, Morton Sosna and David E. Wellbery (eds), *Reconstructing Individualism*. Stanford, CA: Stanford University Press.
Hadad, Shira. 2012. '"A Thousand Names They Called Him": Naming and Proper Names in the Work of S.Y. Agnon', Ph.D. dissertation. Columbia University.
Hall, Kira. 2019. 'Middle Class Timelines: Ethnic Humor and Sexual Modernity in Delhi', *Language in Society* 48(4): 491–517.
Hallward, Peter. 2003. *Badiou: A Subject to Truth*. Minneapolis: University of Minnesota Press.
Hans, Raj Kumar. 2016. 'Making Sense of Dalit Sikh History', in Ramnarayan S. Rawat and K. Satyanarayana (eds), *Dalit Studies*. Durham, NC: Duke University Press, pp. 131–51.
Harrison, Simon. 1990. *Stealing People's Names: History and Politics in a Sepik River Cosmology*. Cambridge: Cambridge University Press.
———. 1999. 'Identity as a Scarce Resource', *Social Anthropology* 7(3): 239–51.
Hayden, Cori. 2011. 'No Patent, No Generic: Pharmaceutical Access and the Politics of the Copy', in Mario Biagioli, Peter Jaszi and Martha Woodmansee (eds), *Making and Unmaking Intellectual Property: Creative Production in Legal and Cultural Perspective*. Chicago: University of Chicago Press, pp. 285–304.
Humphrey, Caroline. 2006. 'On Being Named and Not Named: Authority, Persons, and Their Names in Mongolia', in Gabrielle vom Bruck and Barbara Bodenhorn (eds), *The Anthropology of Names and Naming*. Cambridge: Cambridge University Press, pp. 157–76.
———. 2008. 'Reassembling Individual Subjects: Events and Decisions in Troubled Times', *Anthropological Theory* 8(4): 357–80.
Jakobsh, Doris R. 2003. *Relocating Gender in Sikh History*. Delhi: Oxford University Press.
———. 2014a. 'Offline Politics/Online Shaming: Honor Codes, Modes of Resistance, and Responses to Sikh Gurdwara Politics', *Diaspora* 17(2): 220–38.
———. 2014b. 'Gender in Sikh Traditions', in P. Singh and L.E. Fenech (eds), *The Oxford Handbook of Sikh Studies*. Oxford: Oxford University Press. doi:10.1093/oxfordhb/9780199699308.013.005.
———. 2015. 'Feminizing the Khalsa: Text, Narrative and Image within the Virtual Realm', *Sikh Formations* 11(1–2): 190–209.
Jalais, Annu. 2010. *Forest of Tigers: People, Politics and Environment in the Sundarbans*. Delhi: Routledge.

Jaoul, Nicolas. 2008. 'The "Righteous Anger" of the Powerless: Investigating Dalit Outrage over Caste Violence', *South Asia Multidisciplinary Academic Journal* 2. Retrieved 20 April 2023 from https://journals.openedition.org/samaj/1892.
Jameson, Frederic. 2005. *Archaeologies of the Future: The Desire Called Utopia and Other Science Fictions*. London: Verso.
Jodhka, Surinder. 2004. 'Sikhism and the Caste Question: Dalits and Their Politics in Contemporary Punjab', *Contributions to Indian Sociology* 38(1–2): 165–92.
Jodhka, Surinder, and Ghanshyam Shah. 2010. 'Comparative Contexts of Discrimination: Caste and Untouchability in South Asia', *Economic and Political Weekly* 45(48): 99–106.
Kalra, Virinder S., and Navtej K. Purewal. 2020. *Beyond Religion in India and Pakistan: Gender and Caste, Borders and Boundaries*. London: Bloomsbury Academic.
Kaneff, Deema, and Alexander D. King. 2004. 'Introduction: Owning Culture', *Focaal–European Journal of Anthropology* 44: 3–19.
Kaur, Inderjit N. 2011. 'Sikh Shabad Kirtan and Gurmat Sangit: What's in the Name?', *JPS* 18(1–2): 251–78.
Lahiri, Jhumpa. 2003. *The Namesake*. Houghton Mifflin Harcourt.
Laidlaw, James. 2002. 'For an Anthropology of Ethics and Freedom', *Journal of the Royal Anthropological Institute* 8(2): 311–32.
______. 2014. *The Subject of Virtue: An Anthropology of Ethics and Freedom*. Cambridge: Cambridge University Press.
Lal, Harbans. 2000. 'Caste among Sikhs: Dichotomy between Belief and Practice', *Sikh Review*, April.
Lamb, Ramdas. 2002. *Rapt in the Name: The Ramnamis, Ramnam, and Untouchable Religion in Central India*. New York: SUNY Press.
Lambek, Michel. 2008. 'Value and Virtue', *Anthropological Theory* 8(2): 133–57.
Lévi-Strauss, Claude. 1966. *The Savage Mind*. Oxford: Oxford University Press.
Mahmood, Cynthia Keppley. 1996. *Fighting for Faith and Nation: Dialogues with Sikh Militants*. Pennsylvania: University of Pennsylvania Press.
Marriott, McKim. 1976. 'Hindu Transactions: Diversity without Dualism', in B. Kapferer (ed.), *Transactions and Meaning: Directions in the Anthropology of Exchange and Symbolic Behaviour*. Philadelphia, PA: Institute for the Study of Human Issues, pp. 109–42.
Mir, Farina. 2010. *The Social Space of Language: Vernacular Culture in British Colonial Punjab*. Berkeley: University of California Press.
Mooney, Nicola. 2011. *Rural Nostalgias and Transnational Dreams: Identity and Modernity among Jat Sikhs*. Toronto: University of Toronto Press.
______. 2013. 'Dancing in Diaspora Space: Bhangra, Caste, and Gender among Jat Sikhs', in M. Hawley (ed.), *Sikh Diaspora: Theory, Agency, and Experience*. Leiden: Brill, pp. 279–318.
Oberoi, Harjot. 1994. *The Construction of Religious Boundaries: Culture, Identity, and Diversity in the Sikh Tradition*. Oxford: Oxford University Press.
Ohnuki-Tierney, Emiko. 2002. *Kamikaze, Cherry Blossoms and Nationalisms: The Militarization of Aesthetics in Japanese History*. Chicago: University of Chicago Press.
Paik, Shailaja. 2011. 'Mahar–Dalit–Buddhist: The History and Politics of Naming in Maharashtra', *Contributions to Indian Sociology* 45(2): 217–41.
Parry, Jonathan. 1985. 'The Brahmanical Tradition and the Technology of the Intellect', in J. Overing (ed.), *Reason and Morality*. London: Tavistock, pp. 200–25.

Peabody, Norbert. 1991. 'In Whose Turban Does the Lord Reside? The Objectification of Charisma and the Fetishism of Objects in the Hindu Kingdom of Kota', *Comparative Studies in Society and History* 33(4): 726–54.
______. 2001. 'Cents, Sense, Census: Human Inventories in Late Precolonial and Early Colonial India', *Comparative Studies in Society and History* 43(4): 819–50.
Pina-Cabral, João. 2012. 'The Functional Fallacy: On the Supposed Dangers of Name Repetition', *History and Anthropology* 23(1): 17–36.
Pinney, Christopher. 2004. *'Photos of the Gods': The Printed Image and Political Struggle in India*. London: Reaktion Books.
Prytz-Johansen, Jørgen. 2012. *The Maori and His Religion in Its Non-Ritualistic Aspects*. Chicago: Hau Books.
Rio, Knut. 2007. 'Denying the Gift: Aspects of Ceremonial Exchange and Sacrifice on Ambrym Island, Vanuatu', *Anthropological Theory* 7(4): 449–70.
Robbins, Joel. 2018. 'Where in the World are Values?', in J. Laidlaw, B. Bodenhorn and Holbraad (eds), *Recovering the Human Subject: Freedom, Creativity and Decision*. Cambridge: Cambridge University Press, pp. 174–92.
Roberts, Nathaniel. 2016. *To Be Cared For: The Power of Conversion and Foreignness of Belonging in an Indian Slum*. Oakland: University of California Press.
Sanghera, Sathnam. 2012. *The Boy with the Topknot: A Memoir of Love, Secrets and Lies*. London: Penguin.
Sengupta, Papia. 2018. *Language as Identity in Colonial India: Policies and Politics*. Houndmills, Basingstoke: Palgrave Macmillan.
Shukla, Rakesh. 2013. 'Agent Provocateur Par Excellence', *Himal South Asia*, 4 December.
Singh, G.P. 2003. 'The Sikh Identity', *Sikh Review*, June.
Singh, Khushwant. 1952. *A History of The Sikhs*. Delhi: Penguin.
Singh, Nikky-Guninder Kaur. 2005. *The Birth of the Khalsa: A Feminist Re-memory of Sikh Identity*. New York: SUNY Press.
______. 2011. *Sikhism: An Introduction*. London: I.B. Tauris.
Singh, Santosh K. 2017. 'Deras as "Little Fiefdoms": Understanding the Dera Sacha Sauda Phenomenon', *Economic and Political Weekly* LII(37): 20–23.
Singh 'Panthi', Baldev. n.d. 'Sikh Castes: An Academic Perspective', https://www.sikhcastes.com/.
Singha, Radhika. 2000. 'Settle, Mobilize, Verify: Identification Practices in Colonial India', *Studies in History* 16(2): 151–98.
Stasch, Rupert. 2009. *Society of Others: Kinship and Mourning in a West Papuan Place*. Berkeley: University of California Press.
Takhar, Opinderjit Kaur. 2005. *Sikh Identity: An Exploration of Groups among Sikhs*. Aldershot: Ashgate.
Takhar, Opinderjit Kaur. 2014. 'Sikh Sects', in Pashaura Singh and Louis E. Fenech (eds), *The Oxford Handbook of Sikh Studies*. Oxford: Oxford University Press, pp. 350–59.
Thorat, Sukhadeo, and Paul Attewell. 2010. 'The Legacy of Social Exclusion: A Correspondence Study of Job Discrimination in India's Urban Private Sector', in Sukhadeo Thorat and Katherine Newman (eds), *Blocked by Caste: Economic Discrimination in Modern India*. Delhi: Oxford University Press, pp. 35–51.
Uberoi, J.P.S. 1991. 'Five Symbols of Sikh Identity', in T.N. Madan (ed.), *Religion in India*. Delhi: Oxford University Press, pp. 320–32.
Viswanath, Rupa. 2013. 'The Emergence of Authenticity Talk and the Giving of Accounts: Conversion as Movement of the Soul in South India, ca. 1900', *Comparative Studies in Society and History* 55(1): 120–41.

Weiner, Annette B. 1992. *Inalienable Possessions: The Paradox of Keeping-while-Giving*. Berkeley: University of California Press.
White, David Gordon. 1984. 'Why Gurus are Heavy', *Numen* 31(Fasc. 1): 40–73.
Zelliot, Eleanor. 1981. 'Chokhamela and Eknath: Two Bhakti Modes of Legitimacy for Modern Change', in J. Lele (ed.), *Tradition and Modernity in Bhakti Movements*. Leiden: Brill, pp. 136–56.

6

Retrieving the Muted Subject in the Early Socialist Ecumene

The Example of the Mongolian Scholar Mergen Gombojab

Caroline Humphrey

'Is that fire smoking?' said Horace Lamb.

'Yes, it appears to be, my dear boy.'

'I am not asking what it appears to be doing. I asked if it was smoking.'

'Appearances are not held to be a clue to the truth,' said his cousin. 'But we seem to have no other.'

—Ivy Compton-Burnett, *Manservant and Maidservant*

In November 1924, a group of young Mongolians made their way across the steppes from the Mongolian capital, Niislel Hüree, to the border with the Soviet Union. Here, at the Russian border town of Kyakhta, they could find no transport for their onward journey. One of them later recalled that their leader, Mergen Gombojab[1] with a person called Petrov,[2] had to undergo the highly annoying – especially for a Mongolian used to riding – disruption of walking on foot several times back and forth the six kilometres to the Russian military garrison of Troitskosavsk in order to hire horses and two carts to carry them and their luggage.[3] After a rough cart journey over several days through snow and wind, the group reached Verkheneudinsk where they could catch the Trans-Siberian train to Moscow, and then take another train on to their final destination. These young people had just become students, sent by their new socialist government to Leningrad. There they were to study a range of subjects and become the first generation of Mongolians educated in the methods of modern European sciences and humanities. I mention the halting, laborious and unevenly speeded journey as an analogy for the path of the transformation they were making in their lives. Gombojab (1906–40) was a particularly vivid case in point: he was leaving behind a childhood as an aristocrat and the inheritance of a high post in a hierarchical Buddhist theocratic state. Only two years earlier he had made the radical decision to reject this status and embrace the vision of an egalitarian socialist future for himself and his country.

This chapter aims to contribute to the understanding of the 'international socialist ecumene', to use Susan Bayly's felicitous phrase. Most of the literature on this theme has been written by historians, and Bayly's work (2004, 2007, 2009) is notable for her anthropological approach that examines contrasting and interacting moral traditions and the importance of memory and affect in transnational movements. Much of her work concerns Vietnamese students in the USSR and the ways in which their enlightening experiences impacted on their lives after they returned to Vietnam and were remembered by their descendants. This chapter will perforce have to adopt a different focus, however. This is because the Mongolians and Buryats I discuss were involved in international education at an earlier and far more brutal period, the 1920s–30s rather than the 1960s–70s, and because many of them, including Gombojab, were to fall victim to the Stalinist purges. Gombojab, an extraordinarily precocious, gifted youth, was only thirty-one when he was arrested in 1937; he had no old or even middle age in which to reminisce to descendants. Furthermore, much key documentation, such as his culminating academic work and correspondence, has disappeared. He was among an important group of scholars and national activists whose names for decades could not be mentioned in public; their contributions to Mongolian culture were silenced. Although a substantial literature has now appeared around the most prominent Buryats, Gombojab remains a subject more difficult to trace, as can be seen from two collections of articles about him (Tamir and Aira 2016; Khishigt 2017) in which he is glimpsed through gaps and shadows and by brief notes and traces he left behind. The intellectual exchange in which such subjects engaged can be perceived only indirectly. Nevertheless, I believe Gombojab's story is significant. By tracking the passage of one man through utterly dissimilar politico-ideological 'imperial' situations – the Mongolian theocracy and early Soviet radicalism – this chapter shows the distinctive demands that each made on its subjects. It attempts to trace how this man, as an example of one trans-political subject, represented *in and through his own person* the effects of the contradictory intellectual currents that swept back and forth at the time.

In respect of anthropology, this story epitomises a particularly sharp series of ideological transformations and reversals experienced by transcultural actors inspired by socialism at this epoch-changing time. The problem is the muting that enveloped people such as Gombojab. In what follows, I have chosen not to discuss his interrogation reports, although they contain lengthy statements he is alleged to have made, because they were composed by the investigator and signed by him under duress.[4] Rather, I adopt the approach suggested long ago by Jean and John Comaroff (1992) when they debated how anthropologists can write about the silenced subjects of European colonialism. They wrote:

> For the poetics of history lie also in mute meanings transacted through goods and practices, through icons and images dispersed in the landscape of the everyday. ... At its best, anthropology has never been content to equate meaning merely with explicit consciousness.[5]

The opening up to social mobility across Eurasia brought about by the demise of the Chinese Qing Empire in 1911, the downfall of the Russian Tsarist Empire in 1917 and the neo-imperial advances of the Japanese in the same period has been extensively studied. The Mongolian cultural region, which found itself embroiled in all three processes, also has its own large literature. Apart from general histories (Bawden 1968), this includes studies of international relations (Kotkin and Elleman 1999), new forms of post-imperial governance (Sablin 2016), the political role of Mongolian and Buryat intellectuals (Rupen 1964), close-grained border history (Urbansky 2020), ethnicity, nationalism and intellectual life (Tolz 2008, 2009), biographies of Buryat Soviet spies (Atwood 1994) and accounts of ethnic political leaders (Ulymzhiev and Tsetsegma 1999; Sablin 2022). These works mention the multiple travels of individuals and groups in relation to the themes mentioned above, but few of them make this cross-Eurasia journeying central to their discussions. An exception is an important paper by Vera Tolz (2015), who brings to attention the theme of 'transcultural mobility', which she discusses in relation to the influence of nationalist political ideas held by Buryat intellectuals from colonized Siberia, above all the well-known activist Jamtsarano, on the imperial cosmopolitanism of the Russian intelligentsia.

It is the suggestion of this chapter that the idea of transculturality could nevertheless do with further examination in relation to the practices and structures of power at the time. To what, indeed, does the term refer?[6] Is transculturality to be seen as movement, influences, exchange and so on taking place between 'cultures' seen as separate wholes; or as Stephen Greenblatt (2010) maintains, are cultures themselves to be understood as inherently changeful, such that 'cultural mobility' is a constituent element of life in any case? Greenblatt argues that cultures, however they have come to be made up of inherited and in-mixed elements, at any one time are almost always nevertheless apprehended by those inside them as local and rooted. Mobility is often seen as a threat to traditions, convictions and rituals and therefore is frequently hidden or downplayed in the public discourse about 'us'. What needs to be studied are the literal exigencies of travel, the physical, infrastructural and institutional conditions of movement; only then will it be possible to grasp 'the more metaphorical movements: between center and periphery, faith and scepticism, order and chaos, exteriority and interiority' (2010: 250). Greenblatt's manifesto argues for the need to account in new ways for the tension between individual agency and structural constraints. He also calls for attention to be given to the ways in which cultures, ignoring the mobility inherent to them, take pleasure in the localness, in '*this* way of doing something (cooking, speaking, making love, dancing, wearing a headscarf, etc.) and not *that*' (2010: 252). If one adopts this view, 'transcultural mobility' can no longer be imagined as a vague vision of freely circulating travellers. Here I attempt to describe the actual conditions of early socialist international movements, how they were conceptualized by the actors involved, and what these considerations imply for these actors' political subjectivity.

Piecing together the episodes of Gombojab's short life is instructive in this regard. It lays bare the specific arrangements that operated within the 'international socialist ecumene', which I suggest can be considered as itself something like a globalized political 'culture' that extended to socialist enclaves within capitalist countries (Goebel 2015; Fowler 2007). Although Gombojab's adult life was dominated by these early socialist imperatives and control of mobility, as a person he also traversed between and within cultures in the more usual 'rooted' (ethnic, linguistic, cultural) sense referred to by Greenblatt. He could hardly have been more mobile. His almost incessant journeys spanned from his homeland in the far reaches of the Mongolian steppes to Leningrad, Shanghai, Ulan-Ude and Paris. This chapter aims to examine mobility and self-transformation between and within 'cultures' imagined in these two ways, the political-ideological and the ethnic-national. Caught between them, Gombojab repeatedly had to remake himself, to take up cultural elements with which to represent himself in public, but also to decide on one or two that presented himself for himself.

Moving between Disbanded Empires

Most of the people who crossed the Russia–Mongolia–China borders in the early twentieth century were undocumented refugees fleeing from revolution and civil war, but a few who also left Siberia were well-educated and politically adept Buryats – a people who were citizens of the Russian Empire but linguistically and culturally part of the Mongolic world. Buryat ways of life had become considerably Russianized, the diverse groups combining in various ways Mongolian-type transhumant pastoralism and Buddhism, indigenous shamanism and ritual customs with Russian patterns, such as settled farming, conversion to Christianity, interaction with the Tsarist administration, and education (for a few) in Russian-language schools. In other words, the Buryats were long since multicultural by reason of their geo-political location and imperial incorporation. In the 1920s, they were the first people sought to be guides and interpreters for Russian political activists and the trade, military and scientific expeditions going into Mongolia, or to be sent as spies into Mongolian regions of China. Several talented and energetic individuals among them became major national intellectuals and political leaders in the 1920s, only for almost all of them to perish in the Soviet purges of the late 1930s. Mergen Güng Gombojab was more simply an academic who shared that tragic fate, but his life shifts were far more sharply drawn than those of the Buryats. He was brought up in a remote and rural Mongolian homeland and he chose to throw over its entire apparatus of political status, social hierarchy and cultural and religious habitus in favour of a vision of a life as a scholar in a progressive, modern, urban society.

This personal transformation happened at a time of massive political and cultural turmoil. But it would be a mistake to assume that civil war and the military incursions into Mongolia from China and Russia meant abandonment of old governmental practices for control of the population. After a 'people's' Mongolian government was established in 1921,[7] new Soviet procedures were added by incoming Buryat politicians in the following years as increasing attempts were made by Comintern and other Soviet agencies to impose their policies on Mongolia. Before long, the politics of this era morphed again: the crucial leftist 7th Party Congress of 1928 ousted the gradualist and religiously tolerant Mongolian ruling elite and soon the somewhat independent, class-based, post-national vision of global socialism promoted by Comintern was also to falter as the organization became ever more directly a tool of Russo-Soviet foreign policy (Sablin 2016). Mongolians found they had escaped from Manchu-Chinese imperialist-colonialism only to fall by the late 1920s into the grip of Soviet revolutionary imperialism. Not all of the earlier Russian habits of governance were abandoned after the Soviet agencies superimposed their vision of modern society and honed new techniques of governance in Mongolia. As regards mobility, these techniques included the record of official domicile and property, the passport, the visa, the official travel assignment (*komandirovka*), numerous registration forms (*anketa*), and the accounting and reporting procedure (*otchet*) for those travelling. To these can be added the interrogation (*dopros*) of suspicious individuals by guards of internal borders and security services. The combination of these strictures – or Soviet cultural practices – dictated, but also limited, and thus provided an infrastructure for, the experience of mobility in the early socialist ecumene.

In the case of scholarly international travel, the operation of these state-imposed techniques was mediated in practice by the flexible and varied social relations of those involved. True, these relations were invariably ranked, with academic directors, expedition leaders, professors, and heads of delegations assigned charge of 'assistants', 'students', 'guides', 'interpreters' and 'ordinary members' of groups, but the relationships could nevertheless be very varied. The leader or professor not only relied on the practical help of assistants and students but in some instances owed important discoveries or essential academic tools to them, which might or might not be acknowledged. Sometimes, the people became close and dear friends whatever the hierarchical distance between them. One observation made here is that such complex relations obtained not only in the cases that are more widely studied, the exploration-cum-scientific expeditions sent from metropolitan Russia to Mongolia (Shearer 2019), but also in the groups travelling in the reverse direction: in the cohorts of 'students' or 'assistants' who were dispatched out of Buryatia and Mongolia to work with professors in the academies of the capitals.

This chapter does not attempt anything like a fully fleshed out biography of Gombojab, for reasons mentioned earlier. In the confines of a short chapter, it is only possible to address a few of the 'transcultural situations' in which he was involved. I have chosen to focus on two of them: the brief period in 1923–24 when Gombojab transformed himself from a hereditary duke to a student dispatched to Leningrad, and the phase in 1926–30 when he experienced life in Western Europe only to be sent back to a suddenly more oppressive socialist environment. After a thumbnail sketch of Gombojab's life, the chapter first describes the governmental techniques that framed his travels and then discusses the ways in which we can begin to perceive the personal metamorphoses of a man whose voice we will never hear.

Mergen Gombojab: An Outline of His Life

Figure 6.1. Mergen Gombojab. Courtesy of the descendants of Mergen Güng Gombojab.

Gombojab was born in 1906, the eldest son of Mönh-ochir, who was the Mergen Güng ('Wise Duke'[8]) and ruler of the Banner (domain) of the same name in Sain Noyon Khan Aimag in northwest Mongolia.[9] The family's noble status of *taiji* was documented from the seventeenth century, but Mönh-ochir traced descent from the Golden Lineage (*altan urag*) of Chinggis Khan, a far older ancestry. Around 1912, the new theocratic ruler, the Jebtsundamba Hutugtu, awarded him with the hereditary titles of Güng (duke) and Mergen (wise), as well as the privilege of wearing a one-eyed peacock feather on his hat, in recognition of his sagacious, loyal and efficient rule (Tamir and Aira 2016: 18). Gombojab's well-educated father sent the young boy to study with the best minds of region, including the famous and progressive-minded reincarnate lama, Darba Bandid. The precocious boy learned to read Mongolian, Tibetan and Manchu, and by the age of ten was also studying Chinese. However, Gombojab was to become an orphan, as his mother died when he was only ten and his father a few years later. In 1920, when he was fourteen, a marriage was arranged for him with Tuvaansüren, daughter of a neighbouring aristocrat. She was already pregnant, and the couple were soon to have further children in rapid succession. By the age of twenty, Gombojab was the father of five children.

Just before Mönh-ochir died, he transferred the duke title and the post of Banner ruler (*zasag noyon*) to Gombojab. Soon a revolutionary People's Party cell was founded in the main monastery of the Banner with the progressive Darba Bandid's blessing. Gombojab joined it, took part in debates and committees and was elected a representative of his Banner. He then took the opportunity to be sent as a delegate to Niislel Hüree (present Ulaanbaatar) for a meeting of the Youth Revolutionary League. Once in the capital, he was so active in Party and League politics that he had no time for the usual life of a young man (Tamir and Aira 2016: 36). In 1924 he was one of only two Mongol nobles to renounce his title, seal of office, and post of Banner ruler (Batbold 2015: 211).

Gombojab also became a pupil (in Mongolian, a disciple, *shabi*) of Tseveen Jamtsarano, the Buryat intellectual who was Managing Secretary of the new Scientific Committee[10] that was later to become the Mongolian Academy of Sciences. Jamtsarano was an extraordinary and brilliant scholar but also a pan-Mongolian nationalist activist. For this reason, he was shunned by the government in the USSR, but he became an important political actor in Mongolia, 'commanded' there by Comintern as their Far Eastern Secretary (Khamaganova 1998). With Jamtsarano's encouragement, Gombojab was sent in 1924 to Leningrad to obtain a general higher education. Being evidently very talented, he soon established good relations with Russia's leading orientalists, such as Boris Vladimirtsov and Nicholas Poppe. His wife Tuvaansüren again became pregnant and went back to Mongolia. But Gombojab stayed, and from Leningrad he took part in expeditions to photograph and collect ethnographic materials in Buryatia and Mongolia. In this period, the Mongolian Scientific Committee also sent him to Hohhot, Beijing and Shanghai in China to collect manuscripts for the new state library. In 1927, the Committee sent him to Paris, via Germany, to study with the well-known orientalist Paul Pelliot. In 1929, however, following the 'left turn' in the USSR, the 7th Party Congress demanded the recall of all the Mongolian students in Western countries. Gombojab was forced to return to Mongolia without finishing his studies. He is recorded as having 'nothing', no property at all at this time; he became a student under the aegis of the Scientific Committee. At the same time, Jamtsarano, being a national-minded moderate, lost his leading role in Mongolia and was exiled[11] to the Soviet Union as a lowly scholar in Leningrad. Gombojab, as a known associate, was exiled in 1929 to Ulan-Ude, the capital of Buryatia. Here he worked as assistant to the Buryat scholar Bazar Baradiin. He was the main compiler of a Buryat orthographic dictionary, which aimed to clarify how the language should be written in the 'new' (Latin) script, and a primer for learners (Khishigt 2017: 19). He also accompanied the Russian linguist and ethnographer Poppe on trips to various parts of Buryatia to collect oral texts and document shamanic rituals (Poppe 1983: 98–101). In 1933 Gombojab was called back to Ulaanbaatar to work on translations of Russian and world literature into Mongolian and take part in a commission working on an explanatory terminological dictionary that aimed to help clarify translations between radically different languages and cultures (Poppe 1983: 24).

In Ulan-Ude Poppe had learned in 1930 that a purge was impending in academic circles in Leningrad, and he did not want to be away during such a critical event. As an important professor he must have been able to arrange for a transfer back to the city. His memoir (1983) details the difficulties of his lengthy journey from Siberia and the harrowing purge of academicians that soon followed. In 1934, Gombojab, who had remarried to Oyun-Bilig, a progressive-minded young Buryat scholar, was sent to Leningrad a second time, now as a research student to work under Poppe's supervision (Khishigt 2017: 16). He was assigned the task of editing, translating and analysing the 'White History' (*Tsagaan Teüke*). This was an immense and responsible task, as the manuscript was not only one of the most important of early Mongolian religious histories, said to have been composed at least in part by Emperor Hubilai, but it was also full of disputed passages, additions and redactions. Over the next few years Gombojab accomplished most of the work and even had a signed contract with a publisher. But the book never saw the light of day and Gombojab's text was lost or destroyed.

In 1937, Gombojab was arrested and accused of belonging to a Japanese-sponsored anti-Soviet, Buryat nationalist and spying conspiracy headed by Jamtsarano. He was interrogated and signed a report admitting the numerous charges. His mentor Jamtsarano meanwhile suffered a parallel fate and similarly signed a confession. Both men were imprisoned while cases were prepared against them, and around a year and half later were interrogated again. This time, they separately denied their earlier confessions, which they said had been signed under conditions of torture, deprivation of sleep and physical beating. The denials were not accepted. Gombojab was condemned to eight years' imprisonment, and he died in 1940 in, or on the way to, the Sevvostlag camp in far north-eastern Siberia.[12] His second wife, Oyun-Bilig, was exiled from

Leningrad with their two young children. After many travails she ended up living in the Bashkir area on the Volga, and many years later she went to live in Mongolia (Poppe 1983: 89). Gombojab was posthumously rehabilitated in 1956.

The *Komandirovka:* Travel Assignment in the Socialist Ecumene

In this section I focus on the travel assignment (*komandirovka*), which was specific to Russian and Soviet governmental practice and may be unfamiliar to some readers. It took the form of an authoritative order document that could extend its jurisdiction beyond Russia's borders. Inherited from Tsarist practice, it became a universalized and Sovietized version of the same procedure, now employing an 'international' rather than 'imperial' language. The *komandirovka* became the key to the organization of official travel, both within and beyond the country. A Soviet citizen designated for a foreign *komandirovka* had to obtain a formidable range of attestations beforehand, without which they could not travel.[13] When the order was finally issued, a bureaucratic sequence would follow: the advance of funds, the foreign passport, the visa, the residency questionnaire (*anketa*) and the accounting report (*otchet*). Discussion of the *komandirovka* enables me to disarticulate generalizing and flattening terms, such as 'traveller' or 'migrant', as well as 'native assistant' and 'student', and to show how mobile persons were pegged to state and party institutions, assigned ranks, and thereby differed among themselves.

It was by means of the *komandirovka* that appointees, instructors, agitators, spies and research workers flowed out from Moscow, 'the Red Capital of the Great Bolshevik Republic', and delegates, cadres and students travelled in the other direction to attend congresses and receive education and instructions (Fowler 2007: 63). They would come to join new schools, such as the Sun Yat-sen University of the Toilers of China, renamed in 1928 Communist University of the Toilers of China, or the School of Living Languages of the East in Leningrad, to which Gombojab was sent in 1924. The system extended far beyond the USSR to all the regions of Comintern activity. It was the infrastructure that made possible the emergence of revolutionary and communist nodes in the far reaches of the socialist ecumene.

The Soviet action-category of *komandirovanie* can be translated as an act of 'assignment' (of someone to carry out a task), although that English expression does not convey all its meanings. Almost all Gombojab's journeys, both in-country and international, were missions assigned to him by one authoritative institution or another. The concept of the *komandirovka* was weighty and omnipresent, for it referred to an essential administrative technology: the delegation of a particular task in some distant place to a particular person on behalf of a state body. Such a journey had to be undertaken within given dates, was paid for by the sending organization, and its fulfilment was 'overseen' by, and in an overarching sense was the responsibility of, the official signing the order. In the 1920s, the 'imperial' aspect of the *komandirovka* was that the receiving organizations, especially if lower in status, were not necessarily informed of the arrival of the travellers; in fact, an indeterminate range of 'all civil and military persons' were 'invited' to give every possible assistance to the traveller in accomplishing the assignment.[14] A provincial body could write to a higher body to request that instructors/specialists be commanded to them. It was also possible for an employee to request an assignment. But such pleas might or might not be granted. One of the few surviving documents written by Gombojab was one such request to the heads of the Scientific Committee in Ulaanbaatar, begging to be sent to Leningrad to continue his studies.[15] This was turned down; he was sent to Ulan-Ude in Buryatia instead. In principle, the individual(s) named had no part to play in the drawing up of the order.[16] If the person concerned was a party member, Leninist discipline made the assignment obligatory.

There is a difference between the connotations of the Russian term and its Mongolian translation. The Russian, which derives from French *commander* or German *kommandieren*, retains a sense of the compulsory, just as the Russian word *komanda* refers to military and other obligatory commands. Even today, model samples of a *komandirovka* document usually begin in capital letters with the word 'ORDER' ('*PRIKAZ*'). The semantic background of the Mongolian translation for 'sending on assignment', *tomilon yavuul-*, lacks the same political-military edge, and links rather to other words with the root *tomi-*, referring to ideas of defining or formulating (a task). Be that as it may, with the advent of inter-governmental agreements between the Soviet Union and Mongolia from the mid-1920s, as well as the activities of political parties and the Comintern, all of which could authorize such official journeys, it became difficult to travel without the legitimating documentation. Inside Mongolia certain kinds of non-formalized travel were well understood, such as the seasonal movements of herders, traders going to marketplaces, or pilgrims attending holy sites; but otherwise, travellers on their own account were likely to be arrested as suspiciously unexplained, as possible spies, thieves or bandits. It is interesting that in the uncertain and dangerous environment of 1926, when Gombojab was sent to China to collect manuscripts for the Scientific Committee, the authorities explained that it was necessary for his travel documents to 'double' the guarantees of his authorization; this was done by using both the old Qing-era method of the seal (*tamga*) as well as the hand-signature of the secretary of the Committee, Jamtsarano. Gombojab and his colleague Bat-Ochir were allotted 18,000 Mexican dollars from the Mongolian commercial bank for the ninety-day trip. They overspent because they hired an expensive motorcar for the return journey from Hailar; they had to face a difficult accounting confrontation on their arrival home (Khishigt 2017: 26–27).

Of course, some people had to, or wanted to, travel without a *komandirovka*. But in an era when it was illegal for a Soviet citizen to cross the border without permission, such a journey was possible only for locals who could do so undercover. As an example of the system and its loopholes, let me quote from Poppe's memoirs describing a journey he took in 1926 on the reverse route from Gombojab's mentioned at the beginning of this chapter.

> I was officially notified by the chairman of the Mongolian Commission of the Academy of Sciences [in Leningrad] that I would be sent to the Mongolian People's Republic to conduct research. This was a happy event. I had been very anxious to travel to Mongolia ever since that Commission had been established ... In May 1926, Vladimirtsov, Alekseev and I went by train via Moscow to Verkheneudinsk (now Ulan-Ude), the capital of the Buryat Autonomous Republic in Eastern Siberia. There we spent a few days and were joined by our Buryat student Balji Bambeev. Saddles had to be purchased because in Mongolia one could only get Mongolian saddles which were rather uncomfortable. After buying a few saddles, we took a riverboat up the Selenga River towards the Mongolian border. After 36 hours we arrived at Ust'-Kyakhta and from there we went by horse-drawn coach to Troitskosavsk, a rather old and large town. Bambeev temporarily left us there, for he had reason to cross the border illegally. During the civil war he, like many Buryats, had fought as a Cossack officer on the anti-Communist side. For this reason, Bambeev could not obtain a Soviet travel passport and an exit visa. When on the following day the three of us had crossed at the checkpoint and moved into the Mongolian border town Altan Bulag, Bambeev was already there waiting for us. He had managed to slip across the border undetected, only about 300 or 400 metres from the checkpoint. If he had been detected the punishment would have been severe because he carried a pistol. (Poppe 1983: 85–86)

Note that the members of this small research group had different status. There were the three Russian scholars from the metropolis and the Buryat student. It is probably fair to say that *komandirovka* missions, which usually travelled as groups, were always differentiated among themselves. In any Soviet delegation, one was chosen to be the *starosta* ('senior', 'leader'). In the group of Mongolian students with which this chapter began, Gombojab was that leader (Mo. *darga*), while the mission overall was probably in the charge of the mysterious Petrov (see note 2).

Mediating Mentors and Their Circles

In drawing attention to the *komandirovka* I do not intend to convey an impression of lack of purpose or capacity to affect the circumstances – briefly 'agency' – of those travelling. Their agency can be understood as both official and personal. First, the travellers in most cases probably shared the goal of the assignment and can be understood as the bearers of institutional agency. Even if they were personally doubtful or were acting under false pretences, the *komandirovka* itself gave them a certain power to act, to proceed, to expect respectful treatment and certain dues *en route* and at the destination. But along with that officially given efficacy, the person on such an assignment took with him/herself something different, the wider purview of their own political aims and convictions. For the young Gombojab these were formed in the orbit of dominant, inspiring and independent-minded mentors, notably the Darba Bandid, the Buryat nationalist Jamtsarano, the meticulous Parisian orientalist Pelliot, and the scholarly and increasingly anti-communist Poppe. Each of these men provided him with separate networks of support, warmth and comradeship. Importantly, Gombojab was evidently an appreciated and agentive actor in these networks, as this chapter will show.

Vera Tolz (2015) has written illuminatingly on the different and even opposed viewpoints that had to be 'reconciled' by transcultural actors such as Jamtsarano. She terms these 'imperial cosmopolitanism' and 'national particularism', the former perspective being involved in Jamtsarano's representative role and intelligence activity on behalf of both the Tsarist and the Soviet governments and the latter in his ardent devotion to the Mongolian national cause and his scholarship on Mongolian and Buryat culture and Buddhism. He achieved a certain reconciliation during years 1906–late 1920s. This was when Jamtsarano was able, besides his scholarly work, to set up a modern school system in Mongolia, establish the first newspapers in the country, become a Comintern agent and founding father of the Mongolian Revolutionary People's Party, establish the Scientific Committee, and take high positions in the Mongolian government. Railing against the colonialist 'expeditions' that hoovered up artefacts, specimens and ancient documents and took them back to the Russian capital or sold them abroad (Shearer 2019), Jamtsarano insisted that all such valuable items should be kept in Mongolia. Now that Ulaanbaatar was an independent capital, he held that its new institutions were themselves justified in gathering such items from Mongol sources inside China, a task he assigned to Gombojab. Tolz (2015) argues convincingly for Jamtsarano's powerful agency also in the Russian metropolis. He was able to convince the leading scholars in Leningrad of his vision of the intrinsic value of the Mongolian culture and the need to preserve the national autonomy of the Buryat-Mongolians living in the Soviet Union. For perhaps the first time, an indigenous person was able to influence the conception of a subject population held by some among the former colonial masters. However, these professors themselves soon lost influence. In Mongolia, Jamtsarano's 'reconciliation' fell apart after 1928 when he was accused of being a 'right deviationist' and propagandist of Buddhism. He was demoted, and eventually expelled from Mongolia to Leningrad (Tolz 2015: 729; see also Rupen 1964: 183–224).

For Gombojab the diverse cultural worlds to be accommodated were even more extreme, as mentioned earlier. They spanned from the Mongol aristocratic and Buddhist environment of his childhood and his tuition under Darba Bandid Lama, via the Russo-Buryat-Soviet tutelage of Jamtsarano and Poppe, to the completely European academic world of Pelliot. I conceptualize each of these four mentor figures as nodes in separate networks of intellectual and personal influence, which only in some instances overlapped with one another. The substance of the relationships in each of these networks differed and changed over time, but all were *sui generis*, individual, comradely, sometimes competitive, and even intimate. Essentially, these were relations that had their own ways of being alongside, and to some extent within, the party and state structures. At times in the early 1920s these networks were able to perform as *drivers* for institutional mechanisms like the *komandirovka*, such as when 'uncle Tseveen' (Jamtsarano) signed the documents that propelled Gombojab on his travels. But even when, as was later the case, these people and their coteries failed and had to submit to governmental swings in policy, they remained a source of help and moral support for Gombojab. It would thus be mistaken to attempt an analysis of him simply as an individual; it was because he was entwined in relationships both institutional and personal that he was able to wind his transcultural path through the increasingly grid-like structures that developed with Stalinism.

Ideational Threshold: From Noble Disciple to Student Leader

In order to be able to interpret the clues to Gombojab's changing attitudes, it is necessary first to outline the politico-intellectual background. The aristocratic-cum-Buddhist world in which Gombojab grew up was not as rigid as its fantastically elaborate and expensive rituals appear to suggest. Even this remote Mongolian district was not a monotone isolate but already a place of cultural mobility in the Greenblatt sense. Near his father's encampment was the Rashaant Khüree,[17] the monastery of the Darba Bandid, a distinctive and important figure in the turbulent religious politics of the early twentieth century. Matthew King (2019b) has argued convincingly for the cosmopolitan character of the 'Buddhist commonwealth' that criss-crossed the boundaries of the late Qing and Tsarist empires. Although ordinary monks were forbidden to travel from their monasteries without explicit permission for a given number of days' leave (Sobkovyak 2020), high-ranking polyglot scholar-lamas were masters of both physical and cultural mobility (Humphrey and Ujeed 2013: 118). Based in monastic colleges (*datsang*) of the vast Inner Asian Buddhist ecumene, they visited one another's monasteries often at great distances. Their writings elaborated not only cosmologies but also more practical geographies of Asia and beyond. These masters had long been using logical debating contestations to query received truths and confront them with new, externally demonstrated facts about the world.

Agvaanchoijirdondüb (1870–1928), Gombojab's teacher, was the 17th incarnation of the Darba Bandid. He was an example of the transcultural in his very essence, since it was held that in his previous incarnations he had lived in India, Nepal and Tibet as well as Mongolia. Along with his studies of the spiritual continuity of his lineage, in his present life as a lama of the reformed Gelug tradition, the 17th Darba Bandid became aware of the need for this-worldly reversal of degradation. He was concerned about the imperial political structures that he felt had caused monastic and societal decay. When the 13th Dalai Lama fled from the British invasion of Tibet to Urga in 1904, Darba Bandid was among the high-ranking lamas who became his constant companions and debating partners (King 2019a: 56). The pitting of Russian against British imperialism ('the great game') must have been central to their discussions. And then, in 1921–22, Darba's home, Rashaant monastery, saw desperate battles between White and Red troops spilling over from the civil war in Russia (Baabar 1999: 213). In Niislel Khüree, a city criss-crossed by envoys, traders, missionaries and travellers from across Asia and Europe, there was a ferment of intellectual debate among the Mongolian clerical and lay elites.

By the 1910s–20s, Buddhist leaders were aware of both the anti-religious policies of the socialists and the ineluctable power of the revolutionary movement. The progressive among them, contesting the counter-discourse of conservative Buddhist thinkers (King 2019a), became convinced that the religion could be saved if it was cleansed of worldly concerns, worship of deities, ritual extravagance and the retinues of lazy, hanger-on lamas and returned to its original state of purity as a moral philosophy. In its original godless form, Buddhism would be compatible with atheist communism and furthermore it could ascribe to the same social reforms. Darba Bandid was one of the leading lamas to adopt this position. The following words are ascribed to him: 'Mongolia can no longer adhere to the old teachings. We must go by the example of other countries of the whole world. In this way we should educate boys and girls in learning' (Tuyaa 2014). When the new Scientific Committee was founded in 1921, Jamtsarano made a special visit to Rashaant monastery to invite the Darba lama to join in its work, and it was at his request that the Darba Bandid was to write a moral treatise for post-revolutionary life. This was welcomed by the government and published in 1923 as 'Pure Principles of Conduct for the People' (Tuyaa 2014). Darba wrote that the selfish nobles and lamas of the Autonomous Era (1911–21) had not cared about the sufferings and poverty of ordinary people. The new socialist policy was 'like a vision of rainfall coming to fishes beached on the jagged earth of a dried-up lake' (Myagmarsambuu 2017: 76; Bawden 1968: 270–71). In 1923, the Darba Bandid was so highly regarded that his name was suggested for prime minister when the incumbent died (Myagmarsambuu 2017: 77).[18] Under the tutelage of this compelling lama, the boy Gombojab became his 'intimate disciple' (Tuyaa 2014). He thus joined an unofficial Buddhist network of personal relationships that was progressive, transnational and agentive. It was Darba who advised Gombojab to leave the countryside and embark on a new life.

Meanwhile, there was a purely political push. In 1921, the new People's Government needed to extend its rule into the countryside and explain its policies to the herders. A scribe called Dorjpalam was sent for this purpose to the main 'urban' site of northwest Mongolia, the vast and powerful Zayayn Gegeen monastery. Here, Darba had taken over as managing Khambo Lama, as the resident reincarnation was absent or incapacitated. Dorjpalam arranged many audiences with Darba and his assistant lama Batsuur, explaining that the party and government were supporting democracy and secular education, and notably also, despite the ominous news from Russia, religion. Shortly a party cell was founded in the monastery with Batsuur Lama and Darba Bandid among the members. The opening ceremony was a religious service with prayers for the success of the party's work. A ritual mandala was constructed, to which local lords and officials bowed and made offerings of money and grains. Soon Lama Batsuur was chosen to be both leader of the party committee and the representative of the People's Government in the whole province (*aimag*) (Tamir and Aira 2016: 27). A party cell was established in nearby Rashaant in 1922 and the young duke Gombojab, aged seventeen according to party records, became a member. These were transitional years in his life; by the following year, 1923, a full transformation of his social personhood had taken place.

However, we have no evidence of what he thought, said or wrote at this period. This chapter therefore turns to the signs and traces of the 'mute meanings' referred to earlier. I will focus in turn on the presentation of self, first through the materials of social appearance (clothing, hairstyles, grooming etc.), second through naming, and third through self-reflexive photography.

Material Evidence: Attachment and Illusive Appearance

Figure 6.2. Tuvaansüren. Courtesy of the descendants of Mergen Güng Gombojab.

Before Gombojab set off for the capital, local records from late 1922 indicate that he headed a traditional herding household consisting of himself aged seventeen, his wife Tuvaansüren aged seventeen, a younger brother Wanchinbazar aged fifteen who was a training as a lama, and four still younger brothers. Not rich, they had sixty-three horses, twenty-two cows and 337 sheep and goats (Erdenbat 2017: 204). The move to the city in 1923 and to Leningrad in 1924 saw an extraordinary transformation in the persona they presented. This can perhaps best be seen by comparing photographs of Tuvaansüren before the journey, then in the capital, and then during her brief stay in Leningrad. In 1921–22, the shy-looking aristocratic girl was encased in embroidered silks, precious stones and silver jewellery, her long hair fashioned into the wide curved 'horns' of the Khalkha Mongol style for married women (Bold 2017: 236). A year or so later, as young moderns in the capital, both she and Gombojab had cut their hair short and were wearing plain unisex belted gowns (though Tuvaansüren could not resist a jaunty hat).

By 1924–25, she had become the seemingly confident, beautiful, short-haired, woman again wearing the plain Mongolian gown that signalled revolution seen in Figure 6.4. But did this represent an inner transformation? In Tuvaansüren's case, actually not. According to her present-day descendants, she wept every day in Leningrad. She took her sable furs and jewellery with her

Мэргэн гүн Гомбожав, эхнэр Туваансүрэн нар

Figure 6.3. Gombojab and Tuvaansüren, Niislel Hüree, c. 1923. Courtesy of the descendants of Mergen Güng Gombojab.

Figure 6.4. Tuvaansüren in Leningrad, 1924/25. Courtesy of the descendants of Mergen Güng Gombojab.

to Russia, though she lost almost all of them when she was tricked by fellow students into handing them over one by one to pay for promised train tickets back to Mongolia. She was unable to study. It was Gombojab who rejected her and their children, saying that if she wanted to remain dim and uncultured (*kharankhui büdüüleg*) she could do so, but he did not want to be with her in that case.[19]

The Soviet photograph of Tuvaansüren is misleading in one sense, but it is worth pursuing the matter of clothing further, for it was not a primarily aesthetic nor a personal matter. Rather, it consisted of elements that demonstrated the social meaning and even the purpose of the person so dressed. This was true of both the 'traditional' Khalkha dress worn by Tuvaansüren and her Soviet guise. The former should not be seen as timelessly archaic; in fact, it was a contemporary fashion, differing from those of other regions and other periods, bringing together culturally diverse Mongol, Chinese, Manchu, Tibetan, Daoist and Buddhist elements to form a particular, instantly recognizable, style of the time. In the countryside it would not have been a choice to wear such a costume. Rather, as Atwood (1996: 106) writes, Mongolian dress represented 'a virtually iconic ideal of womanhood, largely abstracted from personal beauty or individual fashion sense'. It was the visual face of the presentation of self as defined by social position, above all ethnic group and class. For a woman *not* to wear her jewellery would be inauspicious, indecorous and disrespectful. The correct clothing was a necessary equipment, without which one could not function socially as a woman (Atwood 1996: 107). In the cosmopolitan capital the plain unisex belted gown signalled support for the revolution, but throughout the 1920s women of even quite ordinary families still wore their hair glued into the great Khalkha-style horns seen in Figure 6.2. The issue here concerns emotional attachment. Tuvaansüren continued to yearn for her former status and cling to its material signs. For this, she was rejected by her husband and attacked on her return to Mongolia.[20]

Signalling an Intentional Personhood

Gombojab, by contrast, seems to have used clothing in a different way, not just as a face adapted to the socio-political world but also as an intentional choice indicating his personal take on his surroundings. On arrival in the capital in 1923 he abandoned the brocaded silks, embroidered boots, the long hair plaited into a queue, and the stylish hat denoting noble status of his early youth. The Scientific Committee where he took up work as student-assistant in 1924 was one of the key sites of cultural conversion in Mongolia. A place of hybrid transition, it was housed in a former prince's palace, a wooden Chinese-style building with upturned eaves and latticed windows, along with two Russian-style buildings and a yurt-like structure. Its book collection consisted mainly of sutras and works in Chinese (Ma 1949: 123–24). Gombojab's decision to cut his hair and don the plain Mongol robe was adapted to the new socialist dress code, as can been seen from a 1922 photograph of workers wearing such robes and Russian flat caps sorting out books at the Committee (Batsaikhan 2011: 190). Any such choice was an acute political marker. In 1922–23, the Revolutionary Youth League (RYL), which was closely aligned with Comintern and far more radical than the party, had already embarked on what the Chinese agent Ma[21] calls a class-based 'reign of terror', sentencing certain lords and noble-origin lamas to death (Ma 1949: 113). However, during this period, national Mongol interest, rather than class, was still the key; even the RYL's main stated aim was Mongolian independence, and it disavowed explicit Soviet-style communism (Ma 1949: 114). Jamtsarano was determined to uphold and preserve Mongol culture. The country did not have a national library or museum and one of Gombojab's main tasks in 1924 was to assist in gathering precious books and objects with which to set up such institutions.

Once he arrived in Leningrad a year later, however, Gombojab abandoned all signs of Mongolness and adopted fully European clothing. This was not 'socialist worker' or shabby 'student' garb but the smart suit, with white shirt and tie – even an elegant moustache – that placed him in the educated Soviet upper echelons with which he (unlike his wife Tuvaansüren) identified in this period. There is some evidence that this was his personal choice, for he separated himself from the other Mongol students. Most of the Mongolian students in Leningrad were housed in a dormitory attached to the Buddhist temple in Leningrad, which had been constructed in 1913–15 at the insistence of Agvan Dorzhiev, the Buryat lama who became the representative in Russia of the 13th Dalai Lama. This accommodation aimed to preserve something of a Mongol atmosphere, to support the students and shield them from 'culture shock'. As a result, they remained detached from the city's life, similarly to the micro-enclaves of ethnic populations that occurred in Paris which was such a magnet for world revolutionary activists in this period (Goebel 2015: 41–42) and to certain isolated and discriminated ethnic cohorts in 'the Red Capital' Moscow (Fowler 2007: 71–73). But Gombojab's situation was different. He went to live with Nicholas Poppe, in the home of a worldly intellectual.[22] He taught Poppe Mongolian, while Poppe taught him Russian (Poppe 1983: 89). This exchange arrangement was almost certainly put in place by the coterie of Buddhist intellectuals and scholars accreted around Jamtsarano. Gombojab remained the leader of the students, but he was now drawn into the arcane world of Altaian linguistics, ancient Mongolian chronicles and Buddhist philosophy that fascinated his mentors.

After two years in Leningrad, Gombojab was selected to take part in the Mongolian educational venture in Western Europe.[23] Some thirty-five teenage children were sent to Germany to study subjects ranging from tanning and textiles to geodesy and middle-school general education. Five of the latter were sent onwards to the lycée Michelet in Paris (Rupen 1964: 207; Wolff 1946). Gombojab's assignment was both to study linguistics under Paul Pelliot and to take care of the boys at the lycée. He travelled via Germany on a separate *komandirovka* from the Scientific Committee in the company of Jamtsarano's wife, Badmajab (her presence certainly another successful coup by the coterie). Serge Wolff, mentor of the German contingent, wrote:

> These two arrived at the same time and were particularly intelligent and interesting people. Gombojab must have been in his twenties; Mrs. Badmajab was older. He was the son of a Mongolian prince, and one could feel a certain dignity in his manner. Whether or not it had anything to do with his aristocratic background, he impressed me by his bearing, intelligence, and charm. His companion was also no ordinary person. Both came to study language and, I believe, philology; but unfortunately, they soon moved to Paris to begin their studies. (Wolff 1970: 75)

Gombojab wore an elegant Holmberg hat with a wide ribbon for his visit to Germany. By this time, he engaged easily with foreigners, unlike the reticent Mongol students. He spoke to Wolff interestingly about his homeland and showed him photographs of Mongolia (Wolff 1946: 84). He may have taken these pictures himself, as he was an enthusiastic photographer, and here we may recall Wolff's comment:

Figure 6.5. Snapshot taken in the 1920s of Gombojab, Badmajab and Serge Wolff in Berlin (Bold 2017: 234). Courtesy of the descendants of Mergen Güng Gombojab.

> Whenever a Mongol of some standing arrived in Berlin a leather briefcase had first to be bought; secondly, a gramophone; and, finally, fulfilling the highest ambition, a camera. (Wolff 1946: 83)

During his two years in France, Gombojab 's academic abilities greatly impressed Pelliot.[24] Meanwhile, his 'cultural mobility' seems to have taken on a new lease of freedom. One summer, he simply refused to be bound by the task of caring for the Mongol schoolboys in Paris, borrowed money, and set off for 'French villages', ostensibly to better his language, but in fact for a holiday in transnational, mixed company.

Badmajab similarly took the chance to experiment. In one photograph she poses dressed in a man's suit with shirt, tie and Holmberg hat. Gombojab's embrace of Europe included a visit to England, officially for medical treatment, but more likely as an opportunity to explore, meet people and find out about another way of life (Purevzhav 2016: 158). His openness can be compared with the more inward and homeland-focused stance of Natsagdorj, another older

Figure 6.6. Gombojab with friends in France, 1927. Courtesy of the descendants of Mergen Güng Gombojab.

student of noble origin among the contingent in in Germany. Natsagdorj was later to become Mongolia's great national poet, but in Germany he was a reluctant student who did not learn the language well and went home before the allotted time (Wolff 1970: 85). He, unlike Gombojab, wrote an account of his journey, titled 'Notes on the Trip to Berlin'. This, written in verse, uses traditional poetic forms to describe an itinerary of landscapes and places, but it mentions almost no non-Mongol human being (Marzluf 2021: 54).

Photography and Self-Depiction

Gombojab's interest and ability in photography has already been mentioned, and there is also evidence that he took up its possibilities for self-conscious self-portrayal. The boys in Paris seem to have been largely neglected by him, but in a letter home one of them commented that he had taken them out to buy a camera and then spent time while they all photographed themselves (Tamir and Aira 2016: 67).

A year after the Paris sojourn had ended in the disappointment of the enforced return to Mongolia followed by the 'exile' *komandirovka* to grim socialist Buryatia, Gombojab was taken on ethnographic fieldwork to Buryat

Figure 6.7. Gombojab in Buryatia, 1930. Courtesy of the descendants of Mergen Güng Gombojab.

villages as assistant to Poppe. He was photographed in a moodily romantic pose wearing a by no means everyday Buryat gown and nonchalantly tilted fox-fur hat. On inspection, this image looks like a studio photograph. In field photos of such expeditions Gombojab usually wore his 'I am an academic' urban suit even in the steppes and he never returned to live a Mongol herding life. We can deduce that having a photograph taken in Buryat national dress was a performance, an exercise in fleeting self-representation.

In all the photographs known to me, there is something self-assured and stylish about Gombojab's demeanour. Perhaps this posture was due to consciousness of his noble birth, which neither he nor the people around him ever forgot; perhaps it was a habitus, persisting through all the changes, originating from the dash and bravura proper to the young male aristocrats of his early youth.

The Name as a Sign

The domestic legend among Gombojab's descendants through his first wife Tuvaansüren is that he was a Mongol nationalist.[25] The family suggestion is that this emotional attachment came to eclipse the pro-Soviet stage of his transcultural odyssey, linking him to his Mongolian identity wherever (Paris, Ulaanbaatar, Ulan-Ude, Leningrad) he was stationed. I propose to investigate this question through examination of one of the most crucial of signs: how Gombojab named himself. The name in Mongolia has particular significance, first because it has meaning, usually designating some desirable quality or moral virtue, and secondly because the individual given such a name is socially expected to exemplify, or at the very least attempt to live up to, this quality (Humphrey 2006). Each child was given a single name, usually prefixed for social recognition by the father's name. Gombojab is a Buddhist name of Tibetan origin meaning 'refuge/defender of the faith'. There is no evidence that Gombojab strove to take refuge in religion, but in Soviet and European environments it was essential to have at least two names, and the surname he chose, Mergen ('wise person'), was a matter over which he had control.

The flipping of names/identities was true of all the transcultural Mongols and Buryats moving between countries in this period. Returning to life on *komandirovka* – and this was almost all of Gombojab's adult life – existential questions always hung over the mandated travellers since they journeyed as 'delegates' (or in some other official capacity), not as themselves. The *komandirovka* was regularly used by government agencies to send people under assumed names, especially if they were engaged in spying. Tseveen, whose surname (father's name) was Jamtsarano, for example, was primarily a scholar and activist, not a professional spy, but he also engaged in intelligence work under the name Semen Begzeev, as numerous *komandirovai* documents issued to him in that name testify (Ulimzhiev and Tsetsegma 1999; Tolz 2015: 738). It would be wrong to assume the conventional idea of a radical dichotomy between 'public' and 'private' identities, however, since it is apparent that our subjects had a hand in crafting their official name-persona. Jamtsarano must have chosen the strangely un-Russian sounding name Begzeev himself. Only he among the Comintern officials is likely to have known that his father's name, Jamsaran, is the Mongolian name for the Buddhist deity called in Tibetan Begtse.[26] Jamsaran/Begtse is a fierce god of war, depicted with bloodshot eyes, fangs and a sword. Was Jamtsarano smiling when he invented this Comintern alias for himself?

After Gombojab was dragged back from France into the Soviet environment, other episodes suggest the non-linear and personally fraught nature of using names to signal loyalties. This can be seen in the case of Gombojab's second wife, a linguist like himself. She was a western Buryat called Aggripina Nikolaevna Borzhonova, but when she was sent on *komandirovka* to Mongolia in 1928 she had rejected this Russianized identity, making a 'contrarian' cultural shift in the Soviet imperial context. She changed her name unofficially to Oyun-Bilig Borsonii (roughly 'Endowed with Intelligence, daughter of Borson'). This swing seems to have been transformation enough in her case. According to family memories, after the couple were sent to Leningrad, around 1935, Gombojab, probably sensing danger, as academics were already being arrested, tried to persuade Oyun-Bilig to emigrate to France. But she by now had two young children and was settled in the city. She refused to leave.[27]

Gombojab's own choice of 'Mergen' as his surname for use in Russia, rejecting the Mongol custom of using the father's given name – in his case Mönhochir – can be understood in the context of the political freedom to which he had been exposed in France.[28] Back in Leningrad in the 1930s he was to shock the members of a seminar, according to memories handed down about one of his fellow research students. This student was Namsraijab, a beautiful Buryat girl who had gone to Moscow in the late 1920s full of hope. She told her daughter: 'It was the end of NEP.[29] At the time, we lived "by Trotsky", Stalin hadn't yet appeared, and Trotsky held the minds of the youth. We often saw him on the square. In those days everything was simple, there were no guards'. This joyful period gave way to a time of anxiety and hunger. Namsraijab continued: 'We were terribly frightened of being bourgeois. There were horrific punishments for being bourgeois. We were taught, don't try to dress well, don't save money, don't do anything, just work hard and be loyal. Modesty in everything. God save you if you wore something "not right", something that might draw attention. That's how I was brought up in an arche-communist family'. In 1936 Namsraijab enrolled in a special postgraduate course for Mongols in Leningrad. She recalled: 'There were only four students, one of whom was Mergen Güng Gombojab. We were being schooled in Marxism-Leninism. Gombojab asked, "Can I go out into the street and shout 'Down with Soviet power'? Well, that's natural, isn't it? In Paris I could. But here, would that be possible or not?" The other students were terrified at these questions and kicked him under the table to keep quiet. The teacher was also appalled and did not know what to reply. When the repressions happened in 1937, the inquisitive Gombojab was arrested and sent to Siberia.'[30]

We cannot know the meaning of Gombojab's reckless questions at the seminar (was this dare-devil provocation, naivety, or real political indignation?). But one thing seems clear: Gombojab could now see 'the Soviet culture' from outside. Elements of it, such as the traditions of linguistic scholarship, had become part of him; but as he journeyed further, newly accreted experiences in Paris had the effect of reframing the remainder, casting it into the shadows of repression. After this, some kinds of reverse mobility were no longer possible for him. The name he chose, 'Mergen' (wisdom), is the sign by which we can deduce the attitude he took to the twists of his fate.

Conclusion

This chapter has suggested that 'transcultural mobility' took distinctive forms in the early socialist ecumene. Neither the 'subaltern' literature nor that concerning 'the colonial subject' of European imperialism are adequate guides to a situation in which revolutionary governments and Comintern were, for all their top-down ruthlessness, trying to elevate as quasi-equals peoples such as the Mongols and Buryats. The descriptive trope of 'flows' of recruits and migrants from the former colonial peripheries to the Red Capital is correct as a broad generalization, but it does not do justice to the actuality of sudden jumps, compulsion, hesitation, disguise and backtracking among the people involved. The image of 'cross-cultural mediators' is similarly under-informative. Gombojab could be considered one such mediator between 'Mongolia' and 'Russia.' But looking more closely, how much sense does that idea make when each of the two cultural entities was in a ferment of change and when the mediators were on state-ordered commissions to accomplish pre-set tasks on behalf of their own country? To approach this situation, I have argued that it is essential to understand the operation of the *komandirovka* system that was so integral to socialist institutional mobility. In that system, individuals perforce acted not on their own account but as envoys. Willingly or not, they were obliged to fulfil assignments not of their choosing. When the entire political discourse was ringing with the word 'task' (*zadacha*), both national and individual,[31] perhaps an appropriate new term for such people, and deserving of further research, is 'the entasked.' Sent to some destination, their 'transculturality' might in some cases simply not happen, as with poor Tuvaansüren sobbing over her jewels in Moscow, or it could be partially refused, as in the example of the poet Natsagdorj for whom Red Moscow was one thing but capitalist Germany was a step too far. In contrast with them, Gombojab certainly seems to have been a person who embraced the multiple identities of transcultural existence. But the question is: how can we know this?

The brutal unidirectional political environment had the effect of muting or smudging the spontaneous expression of thoughts by almost everyone. Until the Stalinist repression silenced him too, Jamtsarano was an extraordinary exception, since his high position in Mongolia allowed him to be outspoken, and his publications, notebooks and correspondence have survived. Far more people were like Gombojab. I have attempted to do justice to him through an ethnographic look at mundane *practices*, which offer a closer understanding than an analysis in terms of categories such as 'post-imperialism' or 'nationalism' and is less prone to *parti pris* analysis of people whose own positionality was so malleable. For this kind of subject, for someone like Gombojab who was far from alone in being largely silenced, who kept no diary and wrote no memoir, appearances become very significant. I am only half-joking when I say that perhaps the hats they wore are more informative than what these people are alleged to have said or thought. And even if we knew absolutely for sure that Gombojab made that outburst at the seminar in Leningrad, that would also be a momentary sign, one among so many others.

Before his suffering and tragic death in the Gulag system, there was one lighter incident in the last years of Gombojab's life which is worth noting for the irony we can retrospectively see in it. He took a bit-part as an actor in the first feature film to be made in Mongolian (Saruulbuyan 2017). This was 'A Mongol Son' (*Mongol Khüü*, 1936[32]) jointly directed by Ilya Trauberg and T. Natsagdorj. It tells the story of a rough herder boy who is tricked into believing in the glamour of a foreign world (China), is determined to go there and manages to evade the border controls during a tempestuous sandstorm, only to be disillusioned when he discovers the degenerate brutality of Chinese warlords, cheating hucksters and Japanese imperialists on the other side. Parts of the film were shot in Leningrad. Gombojab was asked to provide ethnographic advice concerning the authenticity of the scenes and the language. How bitterly ironic, though, that the role he played was the Mongolian border-guard, whose job it was to prevent the Mongol Son from going off to seek adventure in a foreign land.

Acknowledgements

I am very grateful to several people without whose assistance I could hardly have written this chapter: first Ayur Zhanaev, an indispensable aid, and Lama Dobdon Makseev, Sayana Namsaraeva, Tsonggol Natsagdorj, Tuyaa Shagdar, David Sneath, and Dolgorsürengiin Sükhee. My sincere thanks to the descendants of Gombojab for permission to use photographs in their possession.

Caroline Humphrey (University of Cambridge) is an anthropologist who has worked in Russia, Mongolia, China (Inner Mongolia and Heilongjiang), India, Nepal and Ukraine. She has researched a wide range of themes including

Soviet and post-Soviet provincial economy and society; Buryat and Daur shamanism; trade and barter in Nepal; environment and the pastoral economy in Mongolia; the history and contemporary situation of Buddhism in Inner Mongolia; and urban transformations in post-socialist cities (Buryatia, Uzbekistan, Ukraine). She has written on inequality and exclusion; theories of ritualization; the politics of memory; naming practices; ethics and conceptions of freedom. Recently she has completed an international research project on socio-economic interactions on the Russia–Mongolia–China border. Recent publications include: *A Monastery in Time: The Making of Mongolian Buddhism* (Chicago, 2013); *Trust and Mistrust in the Economies of the China-Russia Borderlands* (Amsterdam University Press, 2018); and *On the Edge: Life along the Russia-China Border* (Harvard University Press, 2021, with Franck Billé).

Notes

1. In contemporary Cyrillic script the name is transliterated Gombozhav, but I retain Gombojab as a transliteration of the Mongol script that he himself used. For consistency I do the same for other names of people of his generation.
2. The man who helped see the group through the border may possibly have been Feodor F. Raskol'nikov, known by the alias 'Petrov', who took over from Shumyatskii as head of the Comintern Far Eastern section in 1922. He was in charge of the Mongolian Revolutionary Youth League of which Gombojab was a member (Dashdavaa and Kozlov 1996; Fowler 2007: 68).
3. Batdorzh (2017: 141) quoting the oral account of Namnandorj, who was one of these students.
4. Gombojab was accused of spying on behalf of a counter-revolutionary nationalist group headed by the Buryat Tseveen Jamtsarano (Zhamtsarano) and backed by Japan. The interrogation reports of Jamtsarano and Gombojab are discussed in Khishigt, Myagmarsambuu and Dashnyam (2016: 56–69). See also Tamir and Aira (2016: 127–44).
5. Comaroff and Comaroff (1992: 35–36), quoted in Donham's discussion (2001: 139) of the relation between history and anthropology.
6. I refer here to usages, as in Tolz (2015), of 'transcultural' as more or less synonymous with 'cross-cultural' or 'inter-cultural', rather than connoting the creation of an independent new 'transcultural' subject. See discussion in Marotta 2014: 90–95.
7. This government was led by the Mongolian People's (later Revolutionary) Party and had needed Soviet help to wrest power from a Chinese incursion aiming to re-establish colonial control. However, its titular head was still the Buddhist reincarnation, the Jebtsundamba Hutugtu, and many of the ministers were lamas and (former) nobles. The Hutugtu died in 1924 and was not replaced by a new reincarnation. The Mongolian government was then dominated by incomer Buryats of moderate and all-Mongolian nationalist bent. These leaders were only removed at the end of the 1920s following the 'left turn' under Stalin in the USSR.
8. The word *mergen* formerly meant both 'archer' and 'wise'. A family legend, apparently untrue, holds that the title was given to Gombojab's distant ancestor because he was a skilled warrior archer who had saved the Qing ruler from attacking enemies (personal communication, Tuyaa Shagdar).
9. Gombojab's birthplace is now called Rashaant Sum in Khöbsgöl Aimak.

10. I use this term because it has become established in the literature about Mongolia. It is not an exact translation, however, of the Mongol *nom bichgiin khüreeleng*, literally 'scripture and writing circle'.
11. The word 'exile' is used because Jamtsarano had become a Mongolian citizen and was being expelled from his adopted country.
12. Jamtsarano died in 1942 in the Sol'-Eletskii prison camp.
13. These were attestations from the legal authorities that the person was not under legal investigation, from the financial organs that they had paid their taxes, from the police that there was no objection to them leaving the country, and two further documents concerning the financial status of the destination organization and the relation of the citizen to secret inter-state correspondence (Zhabaeva 2016: 227).
14. This can be seen from the numerous *komandirovka* documents issued to Jamtsarano in the early 1920s (Ulymzhiev and Tsetsegma 1999: 152–64).
15. Although the letter is dated April 1928, a time when Gombojab was still in Paris, it only makes sense for the request to have been made after his recall to Mongolia and Jamtsarano's expulsion to Leningrad. Handwritten in neat Mongolian script, it says that he wishes to go to Leningrad because 'uncle Tseveen' (Jamtsarano) is there and together they could produce valuable scholarly work (Saruulbuyan 2017: 198).
16. Contemporary *komandirovka* documents sometimes note in small type that the named sendee has been informed about the arrangement and sometimes include space for this person's signature, but that was not the case in the early Soviet era. See *komandirovka* attestations in Russian and Mongolian issued to Zhamtsarano when he was travelling under the name Begzeev (Ulymzhiev and Tsetsegma 1999: 152–64).
17. This was a large monastery with over 1,000 lamas and the main built structure in the area.
18. Being the incarnation of a deity, Darba Bandid was held by Mongols to have powers to read minds and foresee the future.
19. Sükhee Dolgorsüren, personal communication. When she returned to Mongolia, Tuvaansüren was destitute and she was forced to abandon her then youngest child, named Mart, under a prayer-wheel at Gandan monastery. He was rescued and adopted by a party official. Gombojab's other children were handed over, as was often the custom among nobles, to be cared for by foster parents, in one case by an ordinary serving herder family. Tuvaansüren rapidly remarried Eldev-Ochir, an influential party man.
20. In 1926 Tuvaansüren was accused at a meeting of the Youth Revolutionary League of being an unredeemable 'feudal'. The accuser asked the League to expel her and to tell Eldev-Ochir to divorce her. He however defended her (Tuyaa 2014). But that marriage too fell apart and Tuvaansüren married a third time and had three further children. She lived under a cloud as a former *taiji* (noble) and ended her days as a housewife living in a plain *ger* (felt tent). She never figured among the fashionable 'city girls' (*hüree hüükhnüüd*) who had sophisticated attributes such as playing the piano or having travelled abroad. Sükhee, personal communication.
21. Ma Ho-t'ien was a political agent sent to Mongolia by the Guomindang government to investigate the new regime. His account of his journey in 1926–27 provides a detailed description of what he saw and is one of few external first-hand accounts of the situation in the country.
22. Poppe was a Russian of German descent. His early childhood was spent in China, he received an excellent and broad education in St Petersburg under German teachers, and the family spent their summers in Finland. Here he discovered strong resistance against Russian domination (Poppe 1983: 23–27).
23. The aim of the venture was not to bypass Soviet Russia, to which many more students were sent, but to acquire specialist training and to equip Mongolia with essential technology for modernity, such as a typeface for the Mongol script and tools for cartography.

24. As part of his mission to Paris, Gombojab had been entrusted by the Scientific Committee with a rare manuscript of the Mongolian chronicle *Altan Tobchi* to take to Pelliot as a gift to aid in the professor's transliteration of the *Secret History of the Mongols*. Evidently Gombojab rapidly made a favourable impression. Pelliot's main interest was the methodology of historical philology and comparative linguistics, and the new student assisted the professor in his work with Mongol texts (Purevzhav 2016: 162). Pelliot did not know the living language and worked with dictionaries, grammars and bilingual texts (Atwood 2013: 438). After Gombojab's sudden departure, Pelliot wrote two letters to Mongolia requesting his return, extolling his talents, the great improvement of his French, and the prospects for his Chinese and Turkish. 'We could write a general history of the Mongolian written language if he could stay for a further three or four years near me. Send him back!' Pelliot urged (Purevzhav 2016: 158–59).
25. Sükhee, personal communication. Some of the family speak of Gombojab as foolish to have been deceived by the glowing promises of Soviet socialism, for which he paid with his life.
26. I am very grateful to Ayur Zhanaev for elucidating for me the rationale behind the 'Begzeev' alias.
27. Personal communication, Dolgorsürengiin Sükhee.
28. Having lived in Paris for over two years, staying in hotels and with families, Gombojab must have known about the boiling street protests by Chinese, Peruvians, North Africans, Vietnamese and others in the city (Goebel 2015: 49–52, 122–27). He would have seen with his own eyes that personal and civic liberties were incomparably greater in Paris than they were in the Soviet Union.
29. NEP, the New Economic Policy (1921–28), when Lenin relaxed extreme communist measures and allowed commerce and entertainment to flourish.
30. All quotations in this paragraph are from Andrei Yan (2017).
31. For example: 'Before us', proclaimed M.M. Sakh'yanova, 'before the group of Buryat-communists (Bolsheviks), stands a task of great importance, the task of struggling not only for the power of the Soviets but also for that of the 3rd International [Comintern], for the victory of the worker is only possible on a world scale, not limited to a national framework'. Quoted in Varnavskii 2003: 153.
32. This film, with its joyous and defiant depiction of Mongol life in the 1930s, fell victim to Soviet anxieties concerning the legacy of Chinggis Khan and was shelved for many years (Saruulbuyan 2017: 193).

References

Atwood, Christopher. 1996. 'Review Article: *Mongol Jewelry* by Martha Boyer', *Mongolian Studies* 19: 101–9.

Atwood, Christopher. 2013. 'Paul Pelliot and Mongolian Studies'. Department of East Asian Languages and Civilizations 36: 433–49. https://repository.upenn.edu/ealc/36.

Baabar (Bat-Erdene Batbayar). 1999. *Twentieth Century Mongolia*. Cambridge: White Horse Press.

Batbold, N. 2017. 'Mergen günii khoshuuny süülchin zasag noyon M. Gombozhavt kholbogdokh tusgai arkhivyn barimtuud', in N. Khishigt (ed.), *Mergen Gombozhav; Am'dral, Öv*. Ulaanbaatar: Mongolian Academy of Sciences, pp. 211–17.

Batdorzh, Ch. 2017. 'Mergen-gun Gombozhav Leningradyg ankh udaa zor'son n'', in N. Khishigt (ed.), *Mergen Gombozhav; Am'dral, Öv*. Ulaanbaatar: Mongolian Academy of Sciences, pp. 141–45.

Batsaikhan, O. (ed.). 2011. *Mongolchuud. XX zuuny ekhend*. Ulaanbaatar: Monsudar.

Bawden, Charles. 1968. *The Modern History of Mongolia*. London: Weidenfeld and Nicholson.

Bayly, Susan. 2004. 'Vietnamese Intellectuals in Revolutionary and Postcolonial Times', *Critique of Anthropology* 24(3): 320–44.

______. 2007. *Asian Voices in a Post-Colonial Age: Vietnam, India and Beyond*. Cambridge: Cambridge University Press.

______. 2009. 'Vietnamese Narratives of Tradition, Exchange and Friendship in the Worlds of the Global Socialist Ecumene', in Harry G. West and Parvathi Raman (eds), *Enduring Socialism*. Oxford: Berghahn Books, pp. 125–48.

Bold, Ch. 2017. 'Mergen Gün Gombozhav: Tüükhen zurguud', in N. Khishigt (ed.), *Mergen Gombozhav; Am'dral, Öv*. Ulaanbaatar: Mongolian Academy of Sciences, pp. 232–38.

Comaroff, John, and Jean Comaroff. 1992. *Ethnography and the Historical Imagination*. Boulder, CO: Westview Press.

Compton-Burnett, Ivy. 1947. *Manservant and Maidservant*. London: Victor Gollancz.

Dashdavaa, Ch., and V.P. Kozlov (eds). 1996. *Komintern ba Mongol: Barimtyn Emkhetgel*. Ulaanbaatar: MUAKHEG and ROSARKHIV.

Donham, Donald. 2001. 'Thinking Temporally or Modernizing Anthropology', *American Anthropologist* 103(1): 134–49.

Erdenbat, Sh. 2017. 'Mergen Gün Gombozhavyn anket, bürtgeliin tukhai tovch ögüülekhüi', in N. Khishigt (ed.), *Mergen Gombozhav; Am'dral, Öv*. Ulaanbaatar: Mongolian Academy of Sciences, pp. 204–10.

Fowler, Josephine. 2007. *Japanese and Chinese Immigrant Activists: Organizing in American and International Communist Movements, 1919–1933*. New Brunswick, NJ: Rutgers University Press.

Goebel, Michael. 2015. *Anti-Imperial Metropolis: Interwar Paris and the Seeds of Third World Nationalism*. Cambridge: Cambridge University Press.

Greenblatt, Stephen. 2010. *Cultural Mobility: A Manifesto*. Cambridge: Cambridge University Press.

Humphrey, Caroline. 2006. 'On Being Named and Not Named: Authority, Persons, and Their Names in Mongolia', in Barbara Bodenhorn and Gabriele Vom Bruck (eds), *The Anthropology of Names and Naming*. Cambridge: Cambridge University Press, pp. 157–76.

Humphrey, Caroline and Ujeed, Hürelbaatar. 2013. *A Monastery in Time: The Making of Mongolian Buddhism*. Chicago: Chicago University Press.

Khishigt, N. 2016. 'Mergen-gung Gombozhab – knyaz', uchenyi, perevodshik, obshchestvennyi deatel' (1906–40)', trans. L.G. Skorodumova and I.V. Kul'ganek, *Mongolica* 17: 6–10.

______. 2017 'Mongolyn shinzhlekh ukhaand Gombozhavyn oruulsan khuv' nemriig todruulakh n'', in N. Khishigt (ed.), *Mergen Gombozhav; Am'dral, Öv*. Ulaanbaatar: Mongolian Academy of Sciences, pp. 13–29.

Khishigt, N., G. Myagmarsambuu and G. Dashnyam. 2016. *Mergen Güng Mönkh-ochiryn Gombozhav*. Manuscript. Ulaanbaatar.

King, Matthew W. 2019a. *Ocean of Milk, Ocean of Blood: A Mongolian Monk in the Ruins of the Qing Empire*. New York: Columbia University Press.

______. 2019b. '"Unbiased Scholars" and "Superficial Intellectuals": Was There a Public Culture between Europe and Inner Asia in the Long 19th Century?' Working Paper of the HCAS Multiple Secularities – Beyond the West, Beyond Modernities. No 11. Leipzig University.

Kotkin, Stephen, and Bruce Elleman (eds). 1999. *Mongolia in the Twentieth Century: Landlocked Cosmopolitan*. New York: M.E. Sharpe.

Ma Ho-t'ien. 1949. *Chinese Agent in Mongolia*, trans. and intro. John De Francis. Baltimore, MD: The Johns Hopkins Press.

Marotta, Vince. 2014. 'The Multicultural, Intercultural and the Transcultural Subject', in Fethi Mansouri and Boulou Ebanda de B'beri (eds), *Global Perspectives on the Politics of Multiculturalism in the 21st Century*. London: Routledge, pp. 90–102.

Marzluf, Phillip P. 2021. 'D. Natsagdorj, Mongolian Travel Writing, and Ideas about National Identity', in Simon Wickhamsmith and Phillip Marzluf (eds), *Socialist and Post-Socialist Mongolia: Nation, Identity, and Culture*. London: Routledge, pp. 43–58.

Myagmarsambuu, G. 2017. 'Mergen günii khoshuuny mergediin tukhai barimtaas', in N. Khishigt (ed.), *Mergen Gombozhav; Am'dral, Öv*, Ulaanbaatar: Mongolian Academy of Sciences, pp. 72–78.

Poppe, Nicholas. 1983. *Reminiscences*, ed. Henry G. Schwarz. Bellingham: Western Washington University Press.

Purevzhav, E. 2016. 'Mongol sudlald Mönkh-Ochiryn Gombozhavyn oruulsan khuv' nemer', in N. Khishigt (ed.), *Mergen Gombozhav; Am'dral, Öv*. Ulaanbaatar: Mongolian Academy of Sciences, pp. 156–69.

Rupen, Robert A. 1964. *Mongols of the Twentieth Century: Part 1*. Bloomington: Indiana University Publications.

Sablin, Ivan. 2016. *Governing Post-Imperial Siberia and Mongolia, 1911–1924: Buddhism, Socialism, and Nationalism in State and Autonomy Building*. London: Routledge.

———. 2022. 'Siberia and Mongolia between the Russian Empire and the Comintern: Regionalism, Nationalism, and Imperialism in the Works of Elbek-Dorzhi Rinchino', preprint of the article to appear in *Jahrbuch für Historische Kommunismusforschung*.

Saruulbuyan, Zh. 2017. 'Mergen Gombozhav utga urlagiin zütgelten bolokh n'', in N. Khishigt (ed.), *Mergen Gombozhav; Am'dral, Öv*. Ulaanbaatar: Mongolian Academy of Sciences, pp. 186–98.

Shearer, David. 2019. 'Heroes Sung and Unsung: Explorers' Narratives of Mongolia, 1890s to the 1930s', *Asia* 73(4): 761–98.

Sobkovyak, Ekaterina. 2020. 'Mongolian Buddhist Clergy and Its Mobility: Restricted, Prohibited and Forced', *Acta Mongolica* 19(539): 53–64.

Tamir, T. and T. Aira. 2016. *Mergen Gün Gombozhav (namtar, marimt, ekh survalzh)*. Ulaanbaatar: Mönkhiin üseg.

Tolz, Vera. 2008. 'European, National and Anti-Imperial: The Formation of Academic Oriental Studies in Late Tsarist and Early Soviet Russia', *Kritika* 9(1): 53–81.

———. 2009. 'Imperial Scholars and Imperial Nationalisms in Late Imperial and Early Soviet Russia', *Kritika* 10(2): 261–90.

———. 2015. 'Reconciling Ethnic Nationalism and Imperial Cosmopolitanism: The Lifeworlds of Tsyben Zhamtsarano (1880–1942)', *Asia* 69(3): 723–46.

Tuyaa, Sanzhdorzhiin. 2014. 'Mergen Gung Gombozhav', *Sonin* website. https://www.sonin.mn/news/peconomy/29432 (accessed February 2022).

Ulymzhiev, D.B. and Zh. Tsetsegma. 1999. *Tsyben Zhamtsarano: Nauchnaya, prosvetitel'skaya i obshchestvenno-politicheskaya deyatel'nost' v Mongolii (1911–1931 gg.)*. Ulan-Ude: Izdatel'stvo Buryatskogo Universiteta.

Urbansky, Soeren. 2020. *Beyond the Steppe Frontier: A History of the Sino-Russian Frontier*. Princeton: Princeton University Press.

Varnavskii, Pavel. 2003 'Granitsy buryatskoi natsii', *Ab Imperio* 2003(1): 149–76.

Wolff, Serge. 1946 'Mongol Delegations in Western Europe, 1926–29', *Journal of the Royal Central Asian Society* 33(1): 75–93.

Wolff, Serge M. 1970. 'Mongolian Educational Venture in Western Europe (1926–29)', *The Mongolian Society Bulletin* 9(2): 40–100.
Yan, Andrei. 2017. 'Buryatskaya lyubov' L'va Gumileva'. https://www.infpol.ru/99454-buryatskaya-lyubov-lva-gumileva/ (accessed February 2022).
Zhabaeva, L.B. 2016. 'O komandirovke aspirantki Irkutskogo gosuniversiteta A.N. Borzhonovoi v Mongoliyu (1928 g.)', in N. Khishigt (ed.), *Mergen Gombozhav; Am'dral, Öv*. Ulaanbaatar: Mongolian Academy of Sciences, pp. 225–32.

7

Intellectual Exchange with Hands

Materiality and Cosmology in Manual Sharing Practices of an Asian Sacred Drum

Sukanya Sarbadhikary

Hands: The Exchange Problem

If money is the elementary unit of exchange in the market's imagination, then an even more basic, if not primordial conceptual unit of all exchange is the pair of human hands. This chapter re-examines the notion of exchange itself, by demonstrating ways in which hands become simultaneously material and intellectual agents, exchanging not only objects but also ideas. Distinctive developments in Western and precolonial Indian philosophical thought, together with anthropological theory, show that hands are peculiar organs with motor (action), sensory (feeling) and cognitive (thought) functions. Hands operate equally as sensory and cerebral representatives: in being both physiological conduits of stimuli response, and giving material life to cultural and intellectual intent through varied motor activities such as craftsmanship, ritual gestures, machinic activity, writing and so on. The precise intellectual import of hands involves both their cognitive/neurophysiological functions, and cultural/discursive agency; and both these intellectual dimensions of cognition and discourse play significant roles during exchange through hands. Thus, the anthropology of exchange (with hands) is inextricably connected with the anthropology of senses and cognition. Further, precisely due to hands' original features as being both intensely sensory-embodied and motor-intentional organs, philosophical debates relate them to immanent experiences and distinct human abstractions like the transcendental consciousness, soul and so on.

This chapter studies the functions and meanings of hands of distinct exchanging subjects: craftsmen (producers) and musicians (consumers) of the sacred percussion instrument, the *mridanga*, in eastern India, particularly West Bengal. It analyses practitioners' philosophy behind making, playing and meditating upon the instrument's sounds, all materialized through exchanging the object. The ethnographic context is particularly distinctive, because not only do hands here embody both materiality and cognitive and discursive intent in their acts of producing, exchanging and consuming the *object*, the *mridanga*, but following understandings in manual phenomenology, hands also materialize and exchange intellectual *ideas*. These ideas are specifically about hands being linked to a transcendental cosmos, as is also the very object (*mridanga*) that hands create/sound. The bodies and hands of the drum's makers, players, listeners, and even the object (*mridanga*) they make, exchange, play and hear, are essentially imagined as constituted of the same primordial cosmic substances, earth and clay; and material, sensory and ideational exchange among these parties is basically conjured as the transmission of equivalent spiritual potential. We thus have a most characteristic phenomenon of a seamless intellectual and affective exchange of the corporeal/cosmic potential of the exchanging subjects and object.

Context

I have been intensely engaged with my ethnographic context of religious percussion makers, musicians and a community of sound meditators knowledgeable in texts and practices of sacred sound for more than a decade, throughout the districts of rural Bengal. A popular devotional (*bhakti*) movement (*Bengal-Vaishnavism*) absorbed Bengal since the sixteenth century, led by the saint Chaitanya, and understood as passionate devotion to the deity couple, Radha-Krishna. Such ecstatic *bhakti* was extended to all castes, genders and sects. The movement's chief and most popular devotional expression was public, collective and ecstatic singing of *kirtan* (devotional music). The *mridanga* is *kirtan*'s indispensable drum accompaniment. This asymmetrical percussion instrument, with loud, grave and yet melodic rhythms, is hung from drummers' shoulders, and has the capacity to generate intense rhythmic emotions among large *kirtan* gatherings (Graves 2009, 2022). The *mridanga*, also known colloquially as the *khol*, is held as a most sacred object among devotees, its pulsing ecstasies believed to transport aesthete listeners to the sensuous cosmic abode of the divine couple.

Almost all *khol* makers and percussionists are strictly religious, and vegetarian, *tulsi*-necklace-wearing *Vaishnavas*. However, despite *Vaishnavism*'s (and *kirtan*'s) overtly expressed caste-indiscriminate devotion, caste relations have had an ambivalent presence among devotees. Thus, on one hand, Chaitanya's movement was vehemently anti-caste, and the saint especially considered sacred sound (of chants, and the *mridanga*) as an equalizer among people. On the other hand, caste remained a persistent lived experience since precolonial times (see Bayly 1999: 1–3), with 'upper'-caste *mridanga* players, for instance, never touching leather, the 'defiling' yet indispensable raw material used in the drum's construction and reserved unequivocally for 'untouchable' *mridanga* makers. Bengal's devotional/sonic philosophy indeed produces a distinctive contingency in caste relations: while being caste-differentiated in production and consumption, the drum's body and sound also potentially unite these exchanging populations. Further, *Vaishnava* philosophy infuses the instrument with yogic connotations, its instrumentalists being practitioners of meditative acoustics, such that the subjects (producers-consumers) and object (*mridanga*) of exchange are eventually drawn into relations of esoteric equivalence of their manual corporeal substance, as we shall see. Thus, bodies which are hierarchically differentiated before the process of exchange are rendered transmissible and equal – both between themselves and with the object exchanged – through specific intellectual understandings of exchange in this context.

The percussion instrument, the *mridanga*, and the hand-worlds it implicates are associated with long traditions of spiritual aesthetics. In distinctive philosophical constructions, practitioners conceptualize the human body, hands and *mridanga* as equivalent sacred reflections of a transcendental origin. This divine origin is believed to be constituted of primeval earth and sound; and the body, hands and drum too are essentially made of the same substances, it is imagined. All these vessels, therefore, when cultivated, are able to apprehend the same transcendence through their vibrations. In human hands crafting the drum, the maker's body-self (made by divine hands) viscerally extends its own earth-sound cosmic potential, externalizing through motor activity the inner sensory world of spiritual origin. The *mridanga* is then exchanged for money in the market economy. Such exchange, however, is not considered as empty of symbolic meaning, but rather as transferring/sharing spiritual potential between the exchanging agents and the object exchanged. Thus again, subsequently, in playing the instrument, the sounds shivering on the musician's hands travel in turn from the object, through the musician's inner body, to the interior causal buzz of creation. Sounds and meaning are thus exchanged seamlessly among the maker to object to player. Hands thus exchange not only the object, but also intellectual discourses which connect the external world of creation to the inner life of mediative realization.

I have learnt about the rich plethora of craftsmen's and percussionists' origin myths, oral poems, songs, construction and playing techniques, and the instrument's esoteric aurality from *kirtan*-gurus, *mridanga* makers and percussionists. There are strong cultural practices associated with the mirroring of the maker's/player's spiritual body and their instrument, through hands. These intellectual discourses are practised during *kirtan* sessions: singers pause to explain esoteric songs, and provide audiences with philosophical clarifications. Makers, players, meditators and ordinary listeners, although of different castes and orientation levels, thus internalize the same intellectual culture. The Indian philosophical concepts I discuss in this chapter, therefore, are conceptually apprehended and manually embodied by these communities through orally transmitted and practised hand-traditions.

My ethnography includes details of *mridanga* making, playing and sound meditation – all essentially mediated by hands – and readings of vernacular texts, which people internalize through vibrant oral traditions. Exchange is rendered a complex intellectual and ontological phenomenon through these descriptions: as a continuous flow between the body-mind while making, playing and listening to the drum, and as a sharing of material skin and thought among the exchanging subjects and object. Such simultaneously affective and intellectual exchange richly complicates ideas of pure economic exchange, as well as divisions in sensory and cognitive exchange, and also traditional hierarchized caste exchange where thought is reserved for upper castes and immersed corporeal activity for untouchables.

People's narratives, my own listening experiences and texts together animate the ethnography. As Bayly (1999: 12) suggests, ethnographic analyses of caste (and other everyday phenomenological experiences) have much to gain through close readings of normative cultural texts. Taken together, the material exchange of the drum between the maker and player, the exchange of ideas about the drum's philosophical significance, and the sensory exchange of the drum's skin and sounds between the craftsman, instrumentalist and listener render the exchanging bodies and even the object exchanged as equivalent cultural agents: a distinctive philosophy or intellectual exchange enabled by hands.

Contributions to Understandings of Intellectual Exchange

This chapter seeks to extend the idea of exchange itself, by arguing that its immediate (and prototypical) prerequisite, the pair of embodied hands, also conducts abstract cognitive and cultural concerns, such that material and intellectual exchange are not separable concepts. Hands, as bodily matter, always also work as agents of the mind, and manual work is thus laden with strong intellectual faculties in two senses: as cognitive mechanisms, and as discursive representatives. Hands carry cultural messages through cognitive intent, and viscerally communicate them through their manual labour and objects produced, to other social bodies. Simply, therefore, exchange (with hands) becomes both an embodied and intellectual exercise. Further, while any hand-crafted object exchanged in the market carries both material and discursive meanings, hands' simultaneous intellectual and sensory charge becomes even more immediately palpable in the case of the *mridanga*'s exchange. This is because the hand-made *mridanga* is also subsequently hand-played by the instrumentalist. The entire corpus of spiritual discourses about the drum, and cognitive workings of body-minds, are thus literally sensitively passed on and shared between the hands of the maker and player.

Thus, while intellectual exchange is generally strictly imagined as dialogues of ideas and speech, and hands imagined as conduits of material work, phenomenologically understood, hands may embody sensory/material affects and discursive/cognitive dimensions together. They thus become the most affective instances of intellectual exchange. Intellectual exchange is treated in this chapter as an always already embodied phenomenon, brought to life particularly through the sensitive experience of hands. In exchanging the drum, people also exchange intellectual ideas surrounding it, and these ideas themselves are sensory, and are enacted as crafting, sounding and transmitting by hypersensitive hands. Finally, since the discourses are materialized by charged affective and cognitive hands, they become intensely entrenched in corporeal memory, persisting therefore as strong religious traditions for over five centuries. I argue that hands' cultural roles as agents of intellectual exchange are particularly enabled by their peculiar phenomenology as simultaneously sensory and cognitive. When cultural discourses find life through hands, their intellectual exchanges embed in the material body and become more permanent.

Intellectual exchange through hands transforms aesthetic and ethical worlds, and this is evident in the primary ethnographic problem here. Traditionally, there are deft craftsmen in Bengal who manually work with clay and leather to produce drums for devotional music, and specialist drummers who buy the objects from them. However, this simplistic market exchange is located within intellectual understandings shared among the hands, bodies and minds of the drum maker, player and listener. Simply, spiritually cultivated hands are philosophically understood as also made of (cosmic) clay and sound, like the human body and the *mridanga* drum. Thus, makers believe that they manually produce or externalize their own spiritual-aesthetic embodied capacity in the form of drums, and hand them over to players, who again, through particular hand-techniques, sound the drum, interiorize its acoustic potential, conflating the drum's clay-sound body with their own, and thus realize the instrument as their embodied mirror. Techniques of making, playing, touching and sounding the drum thus enable the exchange not only of the object (and its sounds), but also of embodied ideas which draw the exchanging parties and even the object exchanged into a peculiar relation of perfect equivalence. The maker-instrument-player become seamless surrogates, sharing the vibrations of skin/sound through their hands. This is significant because makers belong to 'untouchable' castes, players to higher ones; and while the upper-caste players would never physically touch 'defiling' construction substances like leather with which makers work, when it comes to the devotional drumming universe as such, makers' and players' hands tie them as correspondent agents in the exchange of the thought and sensations of a cosmology.

This very specific emic Asian philosophy of exchange has resonances across centuries-old community practices, cosmological systems and even modern scientific discussions by the first Asian Nobel Laureate in Science, C.V. Raman: all ideas centrally concerning hands, the essential organs of human exchange. Further, these ideas about hands also enable etic comparisons with Western philosophical constructions. Thus, the particular kinds of sensory/intellectual exchanges discussed in this chapter are between the hands of the drum maker and player, between the player and listener, and between Western and Asian systems of manual philosophy. In this specific ethnographic context, the pair of exchanging hands are conceptualized as sites of both initial caste differentiation and eventual corporeal levelling based on a system of religious metaphysics. The *mridanga*'s social exchange 'contingencies' (Widlok 2017: xx), such as ostensibly hierarchical caste-mediations of instrumental relations, are thus situated within highly nuanced moral sensory cultures positing equal spiritual transmissibility among the bodies of the *mridanga*'s makers, players, listeners and the *mridanga* itself. Such radical thinking in the philosophy of exchange is enabled by hands' own phenomenology as a leveller between affect-intellect, self-other, and immanence-transcendence. In this case, therefore, the philosophical spirit of an ideal exchange is finally embodied, such that the people/categories which transfer the object/meaning between them (such as the maker-player, player-listener, body-mind and so on) are rendered absolute equivalents, since their social and epistemological differences are immaculately dissolved. In other words, through understandings of the eventual bodily substitutability among the exchanging subjects, exchange becomes a revolutionary equalizing ideal; and in the further corporeal equivalence of the subjects and the object, exchange dissolves even the material dimensions of the self-other divide.

Pure instrumentality has been questioned in the anthropology of exchange. Appadurai (1986: 3), following Simmel, defines economic exchange essentially as a person sacrificing some object towards the desire of another. Drum exchange, in our context, is not purely economic at all, since the object becomes a shared leveller of affect for both parties, and there is ultimately no experience 'at the cost of' another. The generally diverse contexts of production (with technical knowledge) and consumption (with ideological motivations) (ibid.: 41) are not sustained here, with understandings of a spiritual corporeality tying the hands of producers, consumers and the object's skin: all essentially imagined as made of the same cosmic substances.

Bayly (2009) shows that international relations in the socialist ecumene surpass profit or interest-driven exchange to include relational hierarchies as well as beneficent affect and friendship. Kapferer (1976: 7) also argued that exchange can be non-transactional. Further, 'sharing of ideas' and symbolic modes among relational groups may not result from, but indeed define what exchange entails. Such non-transactional reciprocity of ideas is also embodied in the drum's acoustic universe, and Widlok's (2017) notion of 'sharing' becomes apposite for us, to argue that intellectual and affective sharing may even *inform* market exchange. Widlok argues that cultural personhoods, especially in non-Western worlds, may embody exchange experiences as immediate sharing, including pre-reflexive inter-corporeal bodily co-presence. Further, the materiality of shared objects engenders particular forms of social relatedness, and the exchanging agents and objects then form a 'community of practice' (2017: xvii, xx, 72–77). The maker-player-listener-drum are also similar exchanging corporeal agents of longstanding affective communities, whose 'sharing' of their sounding hands/skins both surpass and define market exchange.

Exchange is also organically enabled by the materiality of the object exchanged, and through such exchange itself the object becomes meaningful (Appadurai 1986: 56). The particular ideological politics in our case renders the maker-player-object as direct philosophical homologues, and the 'objectification of persons' and 'personification of objects' thus do not remain separable ideas (ibid.: 12, 57). As the drum 'moves though different hands', it acquires a specific 'cultural biography' (ibid.: 34) of exchange, which dissolves caste and other differentiations. The fluid sharings, corporeal transformations and skin-sound transactions of makers'-players' hands and drum come closest to Marriott's ethnosociological view about Hindu personhoods as dividual and unbounded, with essential substances (skin and sound) exchanged through interpersonal and inter-intellectual contacts. Further, such biomoral orderings dissolving distinctions between subject-object, morality-materiality, mind-sensation and self-other, define the meanings of market exchange strategies in the Hindu world (1976, 1989: 2–17).

Marriott thus proposes the need for ethnosociologies of Hindu 'monist' thought, and this chapter makes an attempt in that direction. Further, the essential organs of exchange, human hands, although immediately embodied, are also analysed as intellectual actors: indispensable conduits of cognitive circuits and discursive imaginations. I show throughout that hands melt boundaries of the body-mind, habit-intention, sensorimotor functions, and self-oriented inner worlds and other-directed outer ones, extending Marriott's notions of simultaneous corporeal and moral-intellectual exchange.

In doing this, the chapter ties the anthropology of exchange with the anthropology of senses/cognition. The market exchange that follows between the craftsman who makes the *mridanga* and the drum's specialist musician implicates deeper senses of intellectual exchange – as ontological sharing – among their sonically tuned selves. Contemporary anthropology has shown that individual senses work through intersensory/synesthetic and cognitive associations (Classen 1997; Gell 1995; Marchand 2010; Scheper-Hughes and Lock 1987). Anthropological debates have also established that senses operate in culturally mediated contexts (Howes 2005). The peculiar phenomenology of hands extends these two understandings. While the entire skin-surface is the sense organ of touch, only hands reach out to the external world. It is the only sensorimotor organ: as sensory organ of tactility it receives external stimuli, and as motor organ of kinesthesis it goes outward from the body. It is the only sense, therefore, which can act upon purposive intention, including cognitive thought and cultural motivations. In this, hands' critical activity is craftsmanship, mediating/exchanging between the body (self) and world (other), habitus and intellect. In addition to physical capacities of touch and moulding, in craftsmanship, kinesthesis involves intellectual faculties of memory, intuition, calculation and anticipation. Thus hands, as synesthetic sensorimotor organs, are also intellectual conduits, and make/externalize objects we can sense, cognize and intellectually make sense of within a discursive culture, in addition to exchanging them in the market. Thus, hands become analytical subjects of exchange (both sensory/material and cognitive/intellectual), representing particular cultural imaginations.

In this chapter I provide an anthropological analysis of hands, the exchanging organs, for the first time, within a vernacular philosophical context, through (manual) theories of senses and embodiment alternative to dominant Western ones. It is critical to engage with 'indigenous theories of perception' (Howes 2005: 6), which hold radical potential in complicating dominant anthropological understandings. Thus, while in the first issue of *American Anthropologist* Frank Baker (1888) analysed the ubiquitous human and sacred role of hands as savagely fetishist, my chapter rather unravels the strong intellectual foundations of such apparently 'savage' manual constructions. The primordial means of exchange, hands, are posited here as intensely sensory as well as deeply intellectual; exchange itself imagined as material, fully embodied, as well as densely philosophical.

Acting-Feeling-Thinking Hands

Hands' phenomenology serves both material and intellectual functions. This is evident in discursive constructions about hands and their exchange potential in Bengal's sacred percussion context.

The archetypal narrative about the first *mridanga*, imagined to accompany deity Shiva's cosmic dance, is provided in the third-century BC classical Sanskrit magnum opus of Indian aesthetics, *Natyashastra* (33.4–12). A sage is bathing in a pond, when sudden rains begin. The lashing small and big raindrops pouring on different levels, textures and sizes of lotus leaves populating the water-body produce three kinds of sounds, of high, medium and low pitches. The meditating sage is captured by the vibrating variation, and envisions reproducing those tonal pitches with hands. He rushes to his ashrama, and describes the sounds to the lord of cosmic construction, Vishwakarma, who manually crafts a clay percussion instrument, its edges plaited with three differentially stretched leather surfaces, replicating the natural tonal rhythms (Bandopadhyay 1995: 164–65; Beck 2013; Pande 1996: 285–92, 301). In this narrative, aquatic sounds are viscerally soaked in with cognitive imprints in aural-imaginative memory, to finally externally replicate the toned rhythms through tactile manoeuvring.

Bare hands, which feel from the wrists through the palms to the fingertips, 'grasp' sensory images, remember or 'hold' them mentally, 'grope' for abstracted sensory concepts, develop 'grip' over intricate manual knowledge, and construct a fine drum, to finally 'hand over' – or exchange in lieu of money – the constructed percussion instrument to expert musicians, who 'strike' its different parts, producing an inimitable range of sonic affects. Such an array of nuanced manual verbs demonstrate that hands simultaneously do, feel and think; they are imbued with both sensory and intellectual potential.

Hands are thus both casts (of mind/concept) and matter (of body/percept). As the human body's most flexible motor part, they simultaneously constitute and embody the form and content of processes ranging from the most abstract to the concrete: perception, intuition and memory, to carving, striking and sensory awakening. Further, in this case, hand-as-matter does not fill some other cast, but the hand itself; and some other matter (instrument) does not fill the hand-as-cast, since the hand itself *is* the instrument with which to make the drum. When hands craft the *mridanga* and exchange it in the market, they impart and communicate both materiality and discursive meanings through it; they directly transmit their affective and intellectual energy to the hands of the receiver-musician. The exchanging parties thus share the constructed instrument, the *mridanga*, as well as its creation vessel – the total sensory, cognitive and discursive hand-instrument.

Mridanga artisans' and artists' hand histories fascinated the first Asian Nobel Laureate in Science, C.V. Raman.[1] According to Raman (1920, 1922, 1935), *mrdangam* makers rival expert acoustic-physicists, since in his time it was the only percussion instrument to produce harmonic melodies. The *mridanga*'s sonic meditators expressed the same phenomenon to me in their own idiom, by emphasizing that it is a divine construction, whose tuned rhythms, set only once during construction, can thus accompany any vocal pitch.

Hands thus are crafters of the myth and science of sound vibrations, the most valued sense in Hindu civilizational sensoria, whose cosmology asserts that acoustic energy created first life. *Bengal-Vaishnavism* borrows this epistemological premise to specifically argue that sacred sound reverberates in human bodies, and these bodies realize their transcendental potential especially when listening to *kirtan* and meditating on the *mridanga*'s sounds, as the *mridanga* is the exact cosmic homologue of the cultivated devotional body. *Mridanga* making is thus like making life, and exchanging it, like transferring hands' life-energy along with the instrument. The apparently disparate life-worlds of philosophical and scientific 'high concept', manual practice and intuitive experience, the spectrum of 'ancient texts to everyday moments of lived religion' (Mann 2014: 271), are thus tied to a deep-seated cultural habitus, where practised traditions and lexical worlds form embodied fittings hinging on the primary exchanging agents, hands. Hands as 'thing-concepts' (Holbraad 2007 cited in Chua and Salmond 2012: 110) transcend dichotomies of matter-discourse, sensation-intellect.

Marchand (2012: 263) argues that hands, despite defining essential embodied humanness and intentionality, have largely been overlooked in anthropology. I critically address this absence, and also argue that hands may even be analysed through etic exchanges of Western and Indian philosophical-anthropological perspectives (see Kleinman et al. 2014). I find two vernacular categories significant for my hand phenomenology. They are: *karan* (variously translated as sense organ, tool, instrument of knowledge, action),[2] and *indriya* (sensory energy). The ethnophilosophical category, *karan*, translatable as 'sense instrument', in tandem with the anthropology of senses, poses unique complexities mediating between: sense organ-motor organ, thought-action, subject-object, and experience-exchange. As the simultaneous tool of creation and the organ of exchange, hands dissolve boundaries between the giver (maker) and receiver (player), and also between the intellectual, feeling and acting human subject and the material object (*mridanga*).

In the context of the *mridanga*, hands are linked by practitioners to a causal source/origin. Indian philosophy posits sound-energy as the first creative force, constituting also the core of human spiritual anatomy. Practitioners also describe God as a potter, and the human body as essentially crafted of primordial earth. *Mridanga* [*mrit* (mud) + *anga* (body)] thus represents the 'first' instrumental life: made of earth and reflecting cosmic sound. Craftsmen and musicians further argue that the human body and the *mridanga* are thus mirror reflections. While carving, experiencing and exchanging the sound/touch of *mridanga*, hands thus mediate cause-effect in a distinctive way: the making hands extend outward to reproduce a spiritual mirror of the body, the object, the *mridanga*; exchange it with the musician; who conversely realizes the external object as his own transcendental potential, through playing it. A significant debate in Indian philosophy states that the effect (*karya*) always pre-exists in the cause (*kaaran*), and the instrument of construction/knowledge/experience (*karan*) thus both creates the effect and realizes the cause (Nicholson 2010: 57, 101). Similarly, in cosmic sound flowing among the hands of the maker and player, and in the object, transcendental cause (*kaaran*) makes itself known in the effect (*karya*), all through manual sensations. *Mridanga* hands therefore mediate immanence-transcendence: hands, as instruments made of cosmic earth/sound, craft the object of material earth/sound, the vessel's vibrations then realized on playing hands as constituting the transcendental cause of all existence again as universal earth/sound.

Exchange is thus rendered a radical ideal in this context, since the subjects exchanging and the object exchanged are essentially understood as equivalents. This discourse is founded upon the phenomenology of the exchanging agents, hands, as mediating between mind and matter, cognition and senses, thought and action. Hands enable the most sensitive intellectual exchange among the maker, musician and matter of sound experience, by alerting them – while making, playing and vibrating as skin – to discourses which intrinsically associate them, and posit their equivalence.

Original Hands

In this section, I discuss the specific intellectual ideas informing the *mridanga*'s exchange practices. The body-analogical notion of the *mridanga* as mirroring a cultivated human body comes alive through understandings of the originary nature of clay, the eternal sonic buzz, craftsmen's caste genealogies, and mythical beliefs about deities. The human body, percussionists say, is also a *mrit* + *anga* (*mridanga*), a clay vessel which eventually dissolves into earth. Therefore, the *mridanga* is also known as *khol*, literally meaning the body/shell. The body making/playing the *mridanga* is thus perfectly exchangeable with the object's corpus.

In Indian epistemology, earth is of two kinds: indestructible (atom-like, and with causal potential), and destructible (of the nature of effect). The latter includes the bodily organism (and hands), the smell-related sense organ and material objects (Bhattacharya 2015: 42). In the *Chandogya Upanishad* (6.1.4), a major Hindu meditation text, the father of Svetaketu (the archetypal knowledge seeker) tells him that all clay objects are transformations of one essential reality: original clay; and perfect knowledge about any object (here, the *mridanga*) leads to the cosmic origin (Lokeswarananda 1998). This episode is considered the 'locus classicus' of the thesis that all effect pre-exists in the cause (Nicholson 2010: 57), and God himself is posited as the first potter, crafting the perfect human body with his hands (ibid.: 101). This divine body in turn has the ability to apprehend its own originary clay-nature through meditation on any other clay object. Similarly, the *mridanga* practitioner can realize spiritual transcendence by immersing himself in constructing a clay drum.

Further, matter (clay) and consciousness are conjoined in Indian causation. Just as a lump of passive clay requires a potter's intelligent intervention, a superintending intellectual consciousness is also imagined to enable material life. Such consciousness is conceptualized as the male principle (*purusha*), and matter as the feminine principle (*prakriti*) (Gosling 2012: 577–78, 584). Like in understandings of original clay, notions of the united form of consciousness (male) and matter (female) are evident also in theorizations of cosmic sound. Following a sophisticated tradition of sonic theology (Beck 1995), *mridanga* musicians often sang esoteric songs, and explained what they call *dehatattva* (body theory): that the cosmic male (consciousness) and female (matter) principles, represented also by the tantric deities Shiva and Parvati, united in a sexual embrace, and that vibration resulted in the originary acoustic buzz, sensed within the cultivated human body's space as the uncaused, unstruck first sound (*anahata-naad*). *Vaishnava* practitioners also learn breathing/meditative techniques from gurus, which enable such primordial auditory vibrations to rise through an 'esoteric physiology' (Beck 1995: 97) of nerves and energy centres, including through their buzzing, rippling hands, towards the cranium.

Mridanga gurus also cited innumerable poems, received through a rich oral tradition, to explain this acoustemology (Feld 1996). They stressed that these sonic-conceptual realizations flow through their hands when they craft/play their drums. They say that the drum's left side is feminine, its right side male, and the two when struck in erotic friction sound a loving melodic rhythm. This is directly associated with the spiritually cultivated human body as constituted of male-female energies (in upper and lower bodies respectively), whose united hum resounds through its corporeal centres as the first uncaused cosmic sound. Further, instrumentalists state that just like the drum-as-body, the body-as-drum also beats original truth. Thus, trained musicians linguistically represent the *mridanga*'s mathematical beats as phonetic combinations (*bols*), and in their imagery of 'inner senses' (Csordas 1994: 89) the human body too is divided into six circular energy centres, with hidden sounds, which reverberate the same phonetics when the practitioner strikes the drum. Both the player and listener are then able to hear the same drum-*bols* inside themselves, as well as in the percussion being played outside. The player-listener-meditator, through yogic breath techniques, then claims to realize the *mridanga* within: the earth-sound body and earth-sound instrument becoming homologues. The musician's hands thus fuse the effect and cause – instrument and body – in the original buzz (Sarbadhikary 2015: 205–13).

Thus, all participants of the *mridanga*'s lifeworld, despite differences of caste for instance, internalize the same discursive understandings about the identity of their bodies and instrument. These bodies share the spiritual elements of clay-sound vibrations, and hands cause a seamless exchange among the instrument's maker, player, listener and drum. This exchange is intensely sensory, and through such visceral materiality the intellectual exchange about essential equivalence among the drum sounders is constantly regenerated.

The right and left hands have been interpreted in Western anthropology as representing 'organically asymmetrical' moral polarities: of the good and bad, sacred and profane (Hertz 2013). Mines (1982) suggested that this hierarchy is also present in Indian life. I argue, however, that such hand pre-eminence is not universal. In Indian metaphysics, the right hand represents male energy, the left female energy (Chakrabarty 2020: 59–62), and the two together – equal in moral-aesthetic significance – in crafting and striking the *mridanga* unwrap the ontology of cosmic sound, and a radically alternative intellectual ideal of exchange among otherwise differentiated/marked bodies and objects.

These conceptual deployments are also active in communities' myths and caste genealogies. The story of a popular poem among percussionists, titled *Sri Badyar Bani* (The Drum's Syllables), repeated to me in several villages, goes as follows. Once Parvati asked Shiva to explain passion. Unable to explain the true meaning to her in any other way, Shiva united with her. The *mridanga* then vibrated for the first time, and the couple danced to its rhythms. The *mridanga* was thus born literally as the material embodiment of divine male-female sexual union. Practitioners further explained that from Shiva (the right hand), the *mridanga* borrowed its rhythms, and from Parvati (the left hand), its sensuous melody, thereby becoming the embodied exchange of toned rhythm and consciousness-matter. In the musician's right and left hands deftly striking the instrument together, the body and drum buzz with primordial cosmic sounds.

Two castes craft Bengal's *mridanga* with their bare hands: *kumbhokaars* (potters), with the Pal surname, make the earthen body, and *muchis/chamars* (leatherworkers), the Das-s, attach the leather strings. *Kumbhokaars* claim to be the first people on earth, reminding us of clay's originality. *Muchis* have a complex genealogical narrative. In a remote drummers' village in Bengal's Murshidabad district, a leatherworker percussionist family showed me their first caste ancestor, Muchiram Das's picture. The printed name, however, was Ravidas, a leatherworker and devotional poet-singer from medieval North India. This demonstrates caste imaginations with an extant Indian network (see Bayly 1999: 4–5), with identities based on leather hand-labour and percussion/music traditions. The family elder narrated a poem from his notebook, titled *Muchir Jonmo Ba Jontrer Utpatti* (Birth of the Leatherworker *or* Percussion), the coeval birth narrative of the caste bodies and instrument being significant.

The poem has passed orally down caste generations. According to its story, Shiva, after defeating many demons, began an ecstatic dance. But without any rhythm accompaniment, he lost his beat, and half his body. Seeing this, the deity Vishnu became tense, and sweated profusely. From the sweat of his forehead, Muchiram Das was born. Earth then offered her clay, the divine cow, Kapila, her skin, music offered her *ragas*, and Muchiram crafted the first *mridanga* to enable Shiva's perfected dance. Percussionists state further that Chaitanya had instructed that only Das-s should make *mridangas*, since other castes would acquire sins if they used their hands to flay sacred cow skin.

These caste genealogies conjure the *mridanga*'s synesthetic lifeworld through hands. Sweat (from which Muchiram was born) represents smell, associated in Indian epistemology with earth; smell and touch are related through the skin; and the leatherworker's hand-touch and eye coordination, *darshan* (sight) and *sparshan* (touch) – phenomenological homologues in apprehending material form (Chakrabarty 2020: 56) – produce the *mridanga*'s cosmic sound. Further, while players belong to higher castes and never touch the raw substances, while exchanging the constructed instrument, along with the object, the maker transfers or 'hands over' the full-bodied sensory energy of his cultivated hands to the player, and the instrumentalist's hands then share the pulsating ontology – equating their clay-sound bodies – with the instrument and its makers.

The apparent caste paradox in the drum's material exchange between producer and consumer is thus liquidated by the intellectual exchange of a corporeal philosophy tying the exchanging agents: the hands of all participants of the *mridanga*'s universe. The entire corpus of etymologies, genealogies, anecdotes, myths and explicit theological constructions demonstrate that the untouchable *mridanga* maker, musician, and even the drum, are synesthetic expressions of the same cosmic buzz. Hands materialize this distinctive intellectual exchange of centuries-held ideas about subject-object equivalence.

Philosophy of Hands

Hands, being agents of material and intellectual exchange among producers, consumers and the instrument in Bengal's devotional sonic universe, may be analysed through their general phenomenological capacities. From emic ethnographic conceptions about hands which enable a very distinctive understanding of exchange, this section compares etic notions (Western and Indian philosophical ideas) about the phenomenology of hands. This cross-epistemological exchange shows that these systems understand hands similarly: as both material and intellectual embodiments, and further, associated with transcendental notions of cosmic causation. These understandings in the philosophy of hands have also impacted anthropological developments.

Mridanga craftsmen manually replicate/create sounds which they hear and hold in memory, since ears and hands have particular kinds of sensory concomitance. Cochlea-like palms are synesthetic and cognitive organs, sounding, touching, smelling, seeing (through measured anticipation), and leading, through rational intuition, towards conceptual clarity about construction. Recent anthropology has also stressed the general synesthetic nature of human and artefact experience. However, these works have generated universal models (Chua and Salmond 2012: 107). Ethnographic and philosophical accounting of 'ontological difference' is imperative in understanding alternative sensorial ideologies/taxonomies (ibid.: 109).

Hands pose unique philosophical problems: as motor organs they act upon the external world, and as sensory organs they internally gather information for the mind. Then, through a synesthetic, intuitive form, these impressions constitute concepts. Thus, many concept-formation metaphors, like grasping, gripping, forming and so on, are manual, and in Bengali too, *dharan* literally means 'to hold', from which derives *dharana*, or clarified concept (Chakrabarty 2020: 52, 61). Again, the term *karan* refers to varied states: action, caste occupation, instrument/means of knowledge, the instrumental case in grammar, sense organ, body, ascetic posture, plastering or spreading with hands, and so on.[3] These meanings form an intricate hand-web in the context of the *mridanga*: particular castes use their hands in a heightened sensory fashion, manipulating material (ablative) to craft an object (accusative), with an ascetic's concentration, caressing clay and leather, to produce a range of harmonic rhythms. Hands are thus agents of both action and knowledge. They mediate between body/percept and mind/concept.

In Indian epistemology, *indriya* (sensory energy) is distinct from Western understandings of physiological sensory organs, and tied to ideas of transcendental cause (*kaaran*) and immanent effect (*karya*). *Indriya* is a condition determining *how* an organ perceives (Bhattacharya 2015: 43, 53–54). It is theorized as life's feminine mobilizer (*prakriti*), which emanates from the cosmic male causal principle (*purusha*); and takes on atomic forms, finally congealing as physical matter. The epistemological imagination is such that the first energy-emanation is sound-potential which generates the ether-atom (penetrability), which combines with matter to produce physical sound; then touch-potential combines with sound particles to generate the air-atom (mechanical pressure); followed by the water-atom (sticky attraction), and the earth-atom (consistent texture) (Dasgupta 1922: 252–54). This synesthetic energy universe which actively coheres consciousness with matter is palpable in the *mridanga*'s constructions. *Karan* or hand-instruments both produce the immanent form of the *mridanga* (*karya*/effect), and through playing it, also contemplate and realize the indestructible, transcendental cause (*kaaran*) of universal life as sonic vibration. Effect and cause are thus tied through hands. *Mridanga* makers' hands fondle moist clay to produce sophisticated sound, both clay and sound understood as primeval cosmic expressions (see also Nicholson 2010: 29–30), and *mridanga* players then sound the material clay-vessel to interiorly understand the drum's-body's spiritually equivalent exchange. The drum's makers and players thus have related ways of realizing the unity of effect-cause, immanence-transcendence, through their hands.

Intellectual discourses concerning the *mridanga* are exchanged among practitioners as both sensory transmission and cognitive communication. In this, hands' phenomenological capacities as simultaneously affective and conceptual – the latter bearing multilayered significance in giving intuitive tactile and sonic form to perceptive cues, communicating those cues between craftsmen and musicians, and infusing matter with the discursive intent of cultural ideas – play a critical role.

Hands' in-betweenness among mind-body, cognitive-sensory dimensions and transcendence-immanence is also productively analysed in Western philosophy. Just as hands reflect divine consciousness in Indian philosophy, Aristotle asserted in *De Anima* that hands are the sense of all senses, instrument of all instruments, and mirror of the soul (Shorten 1983: 1). He added: '... the soul is a form for forms, just as the hand is a tool for tools' (ibid.). Like hands as meta-tool users essentially determine matter's manipulability, all image forms congeal in the soul's apprehending abilities. Aristotle's mediation between the 'sensible' and 'thinkable' through hands (ibid.: 13) pre-empts Immanuel Kant's (1978) position on sensibility or intuition. Kant argued that touch anticipates form through hands, as senses form imprints through imagination. The abilities to form and sense together constitute rationality, according to Kant, and rationality's most embodied expression, he asserts therefore, are human hands (1978: 42, 240). The immediate medium of exchange, hands, are therefore tools of cognitive, moral and aesthetic rational life for Kant, and these simultaneous capacities fundamentally add to theorizations of exchange in our ethnographic context, as discussed above.

The philosophical thrust on hands has influenced cognitive anthropology, cognitive science of religion, phenomenology, neuropsychology, neurophysiology and so on. Overriding the nature-nurture binary, Marchand (2012: 268) thus argues that the brain, through the spinal cord and nervous system, down to fingertips, forms a single sensorimotor web. Tallis (2003) also proposes a philosophical anthropology binding biology and metaphysics, referring to humans' peculiar agentive evolution as 'handkind'. Wilson (1998) simply states therefore that 'brain is hand and hand is brain' (ibid.: 307), and argues that hands' inimitable structure of sensorimotor and cognitive abilities constitutes human intellect and self-consciousness.

Taken together, therefore, Indian and Western philosophical-anthropological ideas of the hand-mind, hand-brain, hand-body, hand-matter, hand-consciousness and so on provide significant vantage points on hands' sensory and intellectual functions. The essentially tied concerns in cosmology, anthropology and phenomenology have influenced my interpretations of the lifeworld of the *mridanga*, whose makers, players and meditative listeners understand the drum's resonance as the original cosmic buzz, while their exchange of the sacred drum's touch and sounds draws them as equivalent agents of an intellectual universe.

Producing, Consuming, Sounding Hands

Mridanga instrumental techniques involve hand-practices which draw sensory and cognitive correspondences between its makers and players. Similarly, the player's hands produce sympathetic effects in the listener's body. Ethnographic descriptions of making/playing/feeling the *mridanga* are thus simultaneous analyses of hands, and their intellectual and affective exchange of ideas which equate the substantive constitutions of the bodies of the drum's producer, player, sonic consumer, and even the object itself.

The sacred membranophone, the *mridanga*, is a conical clay drum, 23–24 inches in length and 42–45 inches in diameter, its rims and body-straps made of cow skin. The right-hand side, when struck, produces a sharp tune with loud resonance, and the bigger-mouthed left side a grave, bass, hollow thud. The *mridanga* sounds forcefully addictive, with full reverberation between rims, and a subtle echo audible within proximity. Its distinctive acoustic producing tonal sounds essentially depends on minute fine-tuning by stretching with palms its thirty-two longitudinal leather straps. Gripping them tightly, the maker pulls them with thorough, equal tension and distributed force, while also ensuring differential tightness (stretched on the right side and flappier on the left) to produce harmonic rhythms. *Mridanga* makers and players unequivocally told me that they understand the thirty-two leather weaves as thirty-two syllables of the devotional chant popularized by Chaitanya (Ha-re-Krish-na-Ha-re-Krish-na-Krish-na-Krish-na-Ha-re-Ha-re-Ha-re-Ra-ma-Ha-re-Ra-ma-Ra-ma-Ra-ma-Ha-re-Ha-re). These chants, they said, also constitute the devotional human body, once again drawing ontological correspondence between the bodies of the drum and devotees. Manual pulling of the strings is thus interpreted as realizing the instrument and meditative body as equivalent vibrations.

Instrumentalists' knowledge about craftsmanship and playing is linked with cultural understandings of aural meditation. Specialist players are not only experienced in difficult rhythm techniques, but, like makers, are mostly part of an oral sound yogic tradition equating the drum with the body's constitution. The percussion instrument, they emphasized, is not an ordinary musical instrument, but direct embodied divinity (*sakkhat bigroho*), its distinctive tonality therefore not requiring external artificial tuning. Once crafted by the experienced caste maker, the drum is said to acquire sacrality. When the drum is subsequently exchanged in the market, the maker also shares his manual sacrality with the player. Further, being part of the same religious culture, the maker and player conceptualize its metaphysics similarly. Thus, in a peculiar practice for percussion instruments, Sanskrit mantras are offered to the *mridanga* before performances.

I have keenly observed that as the player's hands variously strike, grip and tremble with fingers, thump, produce friction through rubbing with palms, and thud with the wrists on the *mridanga*'s body, it produces complicated rhythmic structures – whose precise mathematics are memorized by players – and also harmonic reverberation which impacts the listening body with a thunderous yet tuneful audition. Through my later discussions with experienced players, I understood that the right side's sharper resonance and left side's hollow echo together produce different tones with congruous relations. Such a rare tuneful timbre which together moves players' and listeners' bodily biorhythms also affects spiritual imaginations, centring the body-instrument. The *mridanga*'s sonic materiality is thus intellectually conceptualized as divinity. This material and spiritual sensibility is exchanged between the hands of the maker-player and the bodies of the player-listener.

Traditionally, the lowest and 'untouchable' castes make the instrument, while players, belonging to upper castes, are not involved in craftsmanship, the stench of leather and clay's immediate skin-touch considered defiling for their hands. Upper-caste players, however, use their hands in the most hyper-sensitized manner to sound the already-crafted instrument. The sensory mind-bodies of both makers and players are indeed trained to be equivalent in expertise, by respective gurus, through decades of intensive teaching. The production of sound thus depends on sedimented skills and exchange between their hands' tactile-auditory capacities. The untouchable maker's mind embodies an empathic manual continuity of exchange with the upper-caste player's body, as it cognitively anticipates all the toned rhythms that the player's hands shall yield, based on his initial manoeuvring of matter. As a craftsman commented about his relationship with a player, who has been a faithful procurer of his *mridanga*s for several decades, and whose fathers were also loyal associates in the instrument's market exchange, 'a pair of good hands always identify another'. So, makers' and players' exchange of material and intuitive hand-practices produces synchronous affects in a sonic universe. Their kinaesthetic viscera and synesthetic relations together 'form the auditory membrane' of conceptual exchange (Hirschkind 2006: 27; Wilson 1998: 97).

Alongside economic and ritual/symbolic exchange, makers and players are therefore part of the same philosophical culture of sacred sound, which involves exchange between them at much subtler levels too. Thus, the 'lower'-caste origin narratives and 'upper'-caste playing aesthetics conjure similar ideas about the acoustic universe. The *mridanga* thus mediates between the hand-worlds of the social economy of caste, and sonic philosophy. This offers the possibility of a fundamental reconceptualization of the phenomenon of exchange: different castes and production-consumption vocations are drawn into relations of symphonic equivalence, such that their differences are eventually dissolved through the exchange of intellectual discourses concerning their essential corporeal sameness. Such sameness is uniquely shared between the exchanging parties, as well as the object exchanged. Further, such intellectual exchange is in fact afforded by the phenomenological status of the medium of exchange, hands themselves, as simultaneously material and discursive, immanent and transcendent.

I developed a special rapport with Shyamal Das, a middle-aged, deft *mridanga* craftsman, in southern Kolkata. His *mridanga*s are highly sought after by Bengal's urban and rural buyers. I observed his meticulous crafting process sitting on many occasions in his shop. A *mridanga* maker easily works for twelve uninterrupted hours, and each work-stage depends on hereditary corporeal knowledge and skilled cognitive practice. *Mridanga* making is thus about a thorough mind-body exchange for the maker.

Suppliers provide makers with the *mridanga*'s clay mould and the cow-hide. Clay (*mati*) is considered fundamentally sacred. I studied a potters' village, Panchmura (Bankura district), where, in the Indian philosophical image of God-as-earthmaker, potters form the *mridanga*'s shell (like the human body) through dextrous play of malleable earth and playful fingers. They assess the earthy consistency, thicken it with water and fire it well to make the texture resistant: sound then remains contained, rebounding within the vessel's walls rather than escaping through porous earth texture. Craftsmen used the *pora-mati* (burnt clay) metaphor and explained that the earth-made human body – heated through spiritual discipline – mirrors processed burnt clay. Both the body and drum, when appropriately cultivated, realize the transcendental sonic buzz of cosmic male-female union within themselves. The hands that make and play the divine drum therefore realize the body-drum's equivalence.

Mridanga makers' tactile knowledge includes details about raw-skin portions, and different kinds of hand-pulls. All handwork needs to be moderate, since being made of mud, the instrument can otherwise break. Cow-stomach skin is loose and expandable, and thus excluded, as it cannot produce quality sound. For the *mridanga*'s right side, which produces a sharp tone, skin is flayed from the cow's least-stretchable shoulder region; for the left-side hollower mouth, softer calf-skin is chosen. The skin's rough edges are scraped with a knife, then all leather is soaked in water, cleaned, squeezed to drain the water, dried, pencil marks are made on it with specific measurements, and it is cut in perfect circles to fit the circumference. Smashed clay moistly clotted with a glue made of rice-paste is then plastered on the two sides' middle portion symmetrically in concentric circles. Eventually, the skin for the two sides is well processed and acquires paper-like manoeuvrability: soft, swift, smooth, and supple to the touch. Circular pieces of leather are then spirally cut to produce thirty-two long strips, vertically tied to horizontal spherical leather fittings on the two ends. The strings are finger-woven with equal adjacent tension across the circumferences, but differential tightness on the right and left sides. This synchronicity is trying, and involves skilful balancing: feet push the *mridanga*, and hands simultaneously pull the strings. The entire range of craftsmen's manual processes – flaying, assessing flaccidity, scraping, soaking, cleaning, squeezing, drawing, cutting, smashing, clotting, plastering, tying, tautening and scaling – indicate the intense embroilment of sensory hands with intellectual processes of measurement, memory and anticipation.

These work-stages require powerful concentration, sensory nimbleness and immaculate coordination of mind-hands-eyes-feet, through what Shyamal proudly calls *andaaj* (intuition). Craftsmen's continuous repetition is unfailing, in both cognitive alertness and bodily attention. Similarly, Marchand (2012: 264–66), in describing bimanual coordination, speaks of a 'Zen'-like meditative present-focus balancing mental and sensory practices. Most craftsmen, however, never explained *mridanga*'s construction conceptually, but only offered concrete details. This is not because they are steeped in unthinking materiality, but as Shyamal said, 'These matters are ... part of our intuition'. Millroy (1991: 5, 20) similarly argued, while working with geometric concepts in a carpentry workshop, that craftsmen's 'frozen' intellectual mathematics are hidden in *concrete problematics*. Thus, conceptual truths are engraved within material hand-experiences, an intellectual-sensory exchange sedimented as manual habitus.

The details of the maker's construction process enable us to conceptualize how the player's hands produce the drum's divine sounds. This is because, through generations, the maker's (producer's) and player's (consumer's) hands have learnt how to exchange affects, and respond to each other's vocations. Their sharing of the drum's material ontology is the particular form of intellectual exchange here, made sense of by all participants concerned through discourses of a common religious culture.

Mridanga learning is complex, and through experienced hands its originality comes to life. C.V. Raman was caught by how *mrdangam* craftsmen's hands design percussion harmonic beats, and players' hands manifest them: acoustic science ingrained in manual exchanges.[4] *Mridanga* beats are mathematically intense, with long intervals and arithmetic formulations of pace and tempo. Thus, alongside the concentrated use of all fingers, including the thumb (rare in other percussion instruments), extensive mental calculations are extant. Exactly like makers, *mridanga* players also display nuanced exchanges of hand-techniques and cognitive assessments. Musicians explained that craftsmen construct three leather parts on the *mridanga*'s surfaces, depending upon how much they pull, tauten, rub, tighten or plaster them: a central volatile portion creating undulating soundwaves, a black rice-paste-thickened middle portion flattening the waves, and a hard rim of thick consistency. They explained further that although the *mridanga* has a sharp resonance, its tune, if extremely high, would crack the sound's tonality. The instrument's harmonics thus go up to a certain octave, then become indistinct and fade with a nasal tapering when the edges are played.

Mridanga makers demonstrate a mathematically concrete science of this harmony production, achieved by congruously joining/superposing/condensing with their hands the different leather straps (see also Raman 1922: 476; 1935: 457). Similarly, *mridanga* players demonstrated how the drum's tonal experience is produced through their manoeuvrable techniques of placing, striking and releasing fingers on the black, white middle and white edge portions. The central portion produces maximum tonality with finger, palm and wrist placements/movements, the black portion produces a suppressing sound, and the rim a sharp, nasal tone (Raman 1922: 477). Once again, explained through the science of acoustic production, the drum's efficacy is the result of intellectual and affective manual sharing between the maker and player.

This hand sharing and intellectual exchange about its discursive meaning also transfers to the listener's body. The mathematical loud thuds and tuned feel invariably make the people of *kirtan* collectives clap their hands and sway their bodies. With loud strikes, I always felt the bumpy rhythm beat in the lower abdomen, chest, ears and spine, while the tuneful echoes ring in the eardrums, and the climax reached when a rhythm cycle ends to merge with the higher *mridanga* nasal tones felt at the back of the head as a fading buzz. My head would reel in an ecstatic aftertaste of the intense hollow sounds rumbling inside the body, and the ringing ears would fuse and rest in a cranial humming nasal sensation. I also felt goosebumps and a spinal shudder at this point, and these affects finally culminated in my hands becoming numb. Thus, while the maker's and player's hands are already tied in constructing and sounding harmonic *mridanga* rhythms ending with a distinct nasality, listening intently to the drum while also observing the player's skilful hands makes the listener also literally feel/imprint the player's hands: drumming vicariously and realizing the drum within. The transcendental causal buzz which percussionist meditators explained as being the uniting principle of the body and *mridanga*, then cause the listener's spine to also sense the nasal ring of cosmic sound, ending in the spine's bio-channel: the hands and fingertips.

Thus, hands construct a harmonic percussion instrument, hands manifest resonance in rhythm, and hands intuit the cosmic first hum of existence. Practitioners' sonic meditation practices draw further aesthetic similitudes between the *mridanga*'s body and devotee's body-*mridanga*. With religious cultivation, both vessels, they emphasized, experience the universal nasal drone (*naad*). The profound sensory exchange among the hands of the drum maker, player and listener thus materializes within their intellectual exchange of ideas correlating their spiritually cultivated bodies, hands and acoustic universe with the perfectly crafted and sounded *mridanga*. So, craftsmen enable the *mridanga* to sound differently with varied strikes, and musicians believe that these sounds correspond to the *mridanga*'s secret alphabet combinations (*bols*) held in its various parts. These hums, while played by *mridanga* instrumentalists, are also exactly replicated through oral mimicking. I have closely observed percussionists' hand-sound mechanics. During any *kirtan* performance, at first the *mridanga* player only accompanies, his hands moving in cadences set by the singer. After some time, the singer literally gives him a free hand, when, musicians explained, rhythming becomes a directly spiritual act: their immanent hands then realize and unite with the transcendental body-instrument. Their meditative posture is then evident: they stand up with the *mridanga* hanging from their shoulders, shut their eyes tight, escalating and relaxing beats at will, jump high with intense rhythms, sometimes shouting the corresponding *bols*, at times stopping the drumming completely, orally narrating animated *bols*, and then returning to play them with their hands, since their hand-mouths echo the same inner vibration (*naad*), and eventually reach a trance-like climactic state. While

I cannot play the *mridanga*, my listening hands exchanged the same sensations with the player, as his do with the maker's.

The player's trance is palpable in the arrested or frozen position of the head and spine, and his transfixed eyes. Unlike other beats in which the two hands move variously, at this point the hands shake on the exact axis along central positions of the left and right sides with the same intensity, caught in a dazed stirring stillness. The nasal climactic sound produced at this point is known as the AUMMMMM... (or *guruguruguruguru...*) sound, which practitioners asserted embodies for the player's-listener's-meditator's inner body the original transcendental hum representing cosmic male-female union. The maker's manual construction thus transfers the *mridanga*'s entire sacred potential, including the nasal AUM hum, to the player's hand-capacities, and his playing, in turn, shares it with the listener's body and hands. Participants of the *mridanga* universe exchange not only the material object, but also its sensory and intellectual potential in entirety.

Percussionist meditators specifically explained how they experience the simultaneous transcendence of the body and drum. Harekrishna Haldar grew up in Navadvip, Chaitanya's birthplace, the most important centre of *kirtan* and *mridanga* worship. He clarified sound metaphysics well, as he regularly explains the philosophies during *kirtan* performances. He said: 'Both our body and *mridanga* are produced through vibrations of Radha-Krishna's sexual union, felt as the AUM (alternately *guruguruguruguru...*) buzz. This pleasurable hum is experienced at the hands' contact point of the body-instrument ... and hands attain *siddhi* (spiritual perfection) ... AUM also transforms to different yogic sounds in the body's *chakras* (energy-centres, arranged along the spine and corresponding to the anus, genitalia, navel, chest, throat and head), and fades with the nasal "M" sound in the forehead region'. Similarly, the *mridanga* too is imagined by percussionists as divided into vertical energy centres just like the body, its sounds also merging in the drum's rim as a nasal drone. This rim-sound is alphabetically represented through nasal *bols*, like *jha*, *jhni*, *jhini* and so on.

The sacred drum's metaphysics thus hinges on obsessively shivering hands, the immediate medium of participants' sensory and intellectual exchange. Gourchandra Pal, Navadvip's (and Bengal's) senior percussionist and sound meditator, summarized the final stages of the drum experience: 'Our bodies and instrument are manifestations of AUM ... when playing the *mridanga*'s two sides for a long time, our breathing almost stops ... and hands become numb and sensitive. The hands and entire body shake with a buzz (AUMMMM... sound). This tremoring embodies cosmic vibration, and is called *murchon* or *maton* (fainting/ecstasy)'. Gurus instruct players not to stop striking the *mridanga* then, despite the fatigued, lazy hand sensation, since the nasal hand-tingling, rather than being understood as neuropathy, is relished as divine grace.

In the intellectual world of the *mridanga* shared among its maker, player and listener, the body/hands and instrument are thus perfect homologues. The harmonic percussion instrument is modelled after the yogic body, and the body cultivated as a tuneful percussion instrument. This body itself is an exchangeable corpus among the producers, consumers and the instrument itself.

In sum, then, the market exchange of the *mridanga* is situated within much larger discursive contexts of affective and intellectual sharing of sacred sound practices among the makers and players of the sacred drum. Despite caste differences among them, they have intuitive senses about each other's manual experiences. There are also precise sensory and cognitive exchanges in the production and consumption practices of the instrument's sound. Further, there are similar sensory exchanges between the player's and listener's bodies and hands. Material market exchange is thus propelled and continued due to the ingrained memory of sensory exchanges sedimented over generations among *mridanga* makers, players and aesthetes. Such material and intense affective exchanges are made sense of, materialized and actualized through intellectual exchanges of religious ideas merging bodies, hands and percussion.

Conclusion: Rethinking Exchange with Hands

An ethnographic and analytical focus on hands – the most immediate and primordial agent of exchange – helps to radically reimagine the question of exchange, since it effectively dissolves boundaries of material, sensory and intellectual sharing. As sensorimotor organs, hands both sense intensely and work with motor intent. Such motor intent implicates both cognitive skill and discursive imaginations. Thus, hands are able to simultaneously engender material exchange in the market, and both sensory and intellectual exchanges among the exchanging agents.

This chapter has demonstrated that the material exchange of the religious percussion instrument, the *mridanga*, in Bengal's markets has a long history, which derives its rationale and impetus from deeply held discursive ideas about nuanced sensory exchanges which take place between the hands of the producers and consumers of the *mridanga*, as well as the drum itself. The *mridanga*'s material and symbolic exchange thus materializes within cultures of an intellectual exchange about hands. Further, intellectual exchange also occurs through and between hands themselves, since hands' affective and cognitive-discursive properties are analysed as organically coeval. The intellectual exchange among the *mridanga*'s participants essentially understands the (differential caste) hands and bodies of 'untouchable' makers, specialized musicians and meditative listeners as ontologically equivalent with each other and even the object exchanged (*mridanga*), since all participants of the exchange process are conceptualized as spiritually cultivated representations of divine sound. Further, such simultaneous affective and intellectual exchange is enabled by the phenomenology of hands themselves, which are transgressing mediums between matter-consciousness, body-mind, sensory-motor skills, action-thought, person-object, self-other, and immanence-transcendence.

Following routes of an ethnophilosophical ethnography, and bringing together discussions in anthropology, (Western and) Indian philosophy, and lived narratives of makers, players and meditators of the *mridanga*, this chapter has analysed craftsmen's and instrumentalists' hands as producers and consumers of an auditory cosmos, experienced equally within the musical instrument and physical body. It has described imaginations about hands as experiencing, understanding, creating and eventually dissolving in a buzzing cosmic origin of sound. In hands making the *mridanga*, the craftsman's body externalizes its own sonic/spiritual potential. Then, as the maker sells/hands over the *mridanga* to the player, he not only exchanges the object, but more significantly shares the instrument's, and thereby his own, corporeal spirituality with the player. Their hand-skins then unite as equivalent reflections of sacred sound, and also the drum. Subsequently, in hands playing the *mridanga*, the player's body internally merges with the instrument sounds. The body-instrument's echoes finally fade in a cosmic ether-buzz, whose nasal tones are sensed on literally tingling hands. Finally, these sensations are exchanged between the player's and listeners' bodies. We thus have a situation of continuous and contiguous affective and intellectual exchanges: for all participants of exchange, between their sensory and cognitive dispositions, between the hands of the maker and player, and the bodies of the player and listener. Affective exchanges of sound are made possible through intellectual exchanges, and these together engender the meaning of the *mridanga*'s market exchange.

Ideas of both instrument and exchange have thus been recast: the object or musical instrument, the person's senses (as instruments of knowledge) and hands (as instruments of production, drum playing, as well as exchange) have been established as equivalent agents in a discursive tradition. Such rare experiences of affective equivalence among exchanging persons and objects are understood and propagated through active intellectual exchanges among the people, transmitted over generations, and directly shared through practised cultivations of hands and drum skins.

This chapter's contributions, therefore, are to conceptualize exchange as simultaneously material, sensory and intellectual. All exchange occurs in discursive contexts, and hands, as primary agents of exchange, phenomenologically mediate as sensory organs of cognitive blueprints and motor organs of discursive intent, these dimensions of cognition and discourse making hands critical agents of intellectual exchange. Hands are thus most immediate mediums of discourse and affect sharing. Second, our ethnographic context enables a radical ideal of exchange, wherein differences and hierarchies of the participants of exchange, and the object exchanged, are ultimately undone. Third, it is precisely in the materialization of such a philosophy of exchange with human hands that the intellectual exchange of Bengal's devotional and musical discourse finds revitalized life over centuries.

The powerful Hindu goddess, Kali, wears a waistband of severed human hands, this 'fetish' (Baker 1888) signifying devotees sacrificing their hands, the instruments of knowledge, karmic actions and exchange – what Indian (and

Western) philosophical traditions identify as markers of human supremacy, rationality and feeling – to the dark deity of transcendence. Exchange then does not remain only a matter of the transfer of objects and thoughts, but becomes also the radical potential of undoing immanent differences through material, sensory and intellectual sharing.

Sukanya Sarbadhikary works at the interface of the anthropology of religion, anthropology of embodiment, religious studies and philosophy. She tries to locate the body, materials, senses, intuition, experience, imagination and sacrality in the interstices of everyday lives and strong philosophical traditions. Her first work was an intensive ethnography among different kinds of Bengal-Vaishnavas, focusing on diverse experiences of religious place and sensory apprehensions of divine affect. Her book, *The Place of Devotion: Siting and Experiencing Divinity in Bengal-Vaishnavism* (University of California Press), was published in 2015. She is also passionately interested in aesthetics and sound, and their relations with sacred embodiment. She is currently working on a range of devotional instruments, communities involved in their making, playing, listening, meditating, and associated traditions of sonic metaphysics in Bengal.

Notes

1. His theorizations were based on the Carnatic drum, the *mrdangam*, strongly resembling the *mridanga* in its construction and functioning.
2. For details on the discursive uses of the term *karan* in Hindusim, see https://www.wisdomlib.org/definition/karana.
3. For explanations of these various meanings of the term, see https://www.wisdomlib.org/definition/karana.
4. Raman's sound-physics bears distinct parallels with practitioners' narratives (Raman 1920: 500; 1922: 475–77; 1935: 455–58, 460; see also Tarlekar 1991: 165–70).

References

Appadurai, Arjun. 1986. 'Introduction: Commodities and the Politics of Value', in Arjun Appadurai (ed.), *The Social Life of Things: Commodities in Cultural Perspective.* Cambridge: Cambridge University Press, pp. 3–63.

Baker, Frank. 1888. 'Anthropological Notes on the Human Hand', *American Anthropologist* 1(1): 51–76.

Bandopadhyay, Sureshchandra (ed.). 1995. *Bharata Natyashastra.* Calcutta: Nabapatra Prakashan.

Bayly, Susan. 1999. *Caste, Society, and Politics in India from the Eighteenth Century to the Modern Age.* Cambridge: Cambridge University Press.

———. 2009. 'Vietnamese Narratives of Tradition, Exchange and Friendship in the Worlds of the Global Socialist Ecumena', in Harry G. West and Parvathi Raman (eds), *Enduring Socialism: Explorations of Revolution and Transformation, Restoration and Continuation.* New York: Berghahn Books, pp. 125–47.

Beck, Guy L. 1995. *Sonic Theology: Hinduism and Sacred Sound*. Delhi: Motilal Banarsidass.

_____. 2013. 'Divine Musical Instruments', in Knut A. Jacobsen (ed.), *Brill's Encyclopedia of Hinduism* (Vol. V). Leiden: Brill Academic Publishers, pp. 36–44.

Bergson, Henri. 1991. *Matter and Memory*, trans. N.M. Paul and W. Scott Palmer. New York: Zone Books.

Bhattacharya, Gopinath. 2015. *Tarkasamgraha-Dipika on Tarkasamgraha by Annambhatta* [Commentary on Annambhatta's Tarkasamgraha]. Kolkata: Progressive Publishers.

Chakrabarty, Arindam. 2020. *E Tonu Bhoriya: Darshan Apadmastak* [Philosophy of the Body]. Kolkata: Anushtup.

Chua, Liana, and Amiria Salmond. 2012. 'Artefacts in Anthropology', in Richard Fardon et al. (eds), *The Sage Handbook of Social Anthropology* (Vol. 2). London: Sage, pp. 101–14.

Classen, Constance. 1997. 'Foundations for an Anthropology of the Senses', *International Social Science Journal* 49 (153): 401–12.

Csordas, Thomas J. 1994. *The Sacred Self: A Cultural Phenomenology of Charismatic Healing*. Berkeley: University of California Press.

Dasgupta, Surendranath. 1922. *A History of Indian Philosophy*. Cambridge: Cambridge University Press.

Feld, Steven. 1996. 'Waterfalls of Song: An Acoustemology of Place Resounding in Bosavi, Papua New Guinea', in Steven Feld and Keith H. Basso (eds), *Senses of Place*. Santa Fe: School of American Research Press, pp. 91–135.

Gell, Alfred. 1995. 'The Language of the Forest: Landscape and Phenomenological Iconism in Umeda', in Eric Hirsch and Michael O'Hanlon (eds), *The Anthropology of Landscape: Perspectives on Place and Space*. Oxford: Clarendon Press, pp. 232–54.

Gosling, David L. 2012. 'Science and the Hindu Tradition: Compatibility or Conflict?', *Zygon* 47(3): 575–88.

Graves, Eben. 2009. 'Chaitanya Vaishnava Perspectives on the Bengali Khol', *Journal of Vaisnava Studies* 17(2): 103–26.

_____. 2022. *The Politics of Musical Time: Expanding Songs and Shrinking Markets in Bengali Devotional Performance*. Bloomington: Indiana University Press.

Hertz, Robert. 2013. 'The Pre-Eminence of the Right Hand', *Journal of Ethnographic Theory* 3(2): 335–57.

Hirschkind, Charles. 2006. *The Ethical Soundscape: Cassette Sermons and Islamic Counterpublics*. New York: Columbia University Press.

Howes, David (ed.). 2005. *Empire of the Senses: The Sensual Culture Reader*. Oxford: Berg.

Kant, Immanuel. 1978. *Anthropology from a Pragmatic Point of View*, trans. Victor Lyle Dowdell. Illinois: Southern Illinois University Press.

Kapferer, Bruce (ed.). 1976. *Transaction and Meaning: Directions in the Anthropology of Exchange and Symbolic Behaviour*. Philadelphia, PA: Institute for the Study of Human Issues.

Kleinman, Arthur, Veena Das, Bhrigupati Singh and Michael Jackson (eds). 2014. *The Ground Between: Anthropologists Engage Philosophy*. Durham, NC: Duke University Press.

Krishna, T.M. 2020. *Sebastian and Sons: A Brief History of Mrdangam*. Chennai: Context.

Lokeswarananda, Swami. 1998. *Chandogya Upanisad*. Retrieved 19 October 2020 from https://www.wisdomlib.org/hinduism/book/chandogya-upanishad-english/d/doc239255.html.

Mann, Richard D. 2014. 'Material Culture and the Study of Hinduism and Buddhism', *Religion Compass* 8(8): 264–73.
Marchand, Trevor H.J. 2010. 'Making Knowledge: Explorations of the Indissoluble Relation between Minds, Bodies, and Environment', *Journal of the Royal Anthropological Institute* 16(1): 1–21.
———. 2012. 'Knowledge in Hand: Explorations of Brain, Hand and Tool', in Richard Fardon et al. (eds), *The Sage Handbook of Social Anthropology* (Vol. 2). London: Sage, pp. 261–72.
Marriott, McKim. 1976. 'Hindu Transactions: Diversity without Dualism', in Bruce Kapferer (ed.), *Transaction and Meaning: Directions in the Anthropology of Exchange and Symbolic Behaviour.* Philadelphia: Institute for the Study of Human Issues, pp. 109–42.
Marriott, McKim. 1989. 'Constructing an Indian Ethnosociology', *Contributions to Indian Sociology* 23(1): 1–39.
Millroy, Wendy L. 1991. 'An Ethnographic Study of the Mathematical Ideas of a Group of Carpenters', *Learning and Individual Differences* 3(1): 1–25.
Mines, Mattison. 1982. 'Models of Caste and the Left-Hand Division in South India', *American Ethnologist* 9(3): 467–84.
Nicholson, Andrew J. 2010. *Unifying Hinduism: Philosophy and Identity in Indian Intellectual History.* New York: Columbia University Press.
Pande, Anupa. 1996. *A Historical and Cultural Study of the Natyasastra of Bharata.* Jodhpur: Kusumanjali Prakashan.
Raman, C.V. 1920. 'Musical Drums with Harmonic Overtones', *Nature* 104(2620): 500.
———. 1921. 'On Some Indian Stringed Instruments', *Proceedings of the Indian Association for the Cultivation of Science 7: 29–33.*
———. 1922. 'The Acoustical Knowledge of the Ancient Hindus', *Asutosh Mookerjee Silver Jubilee* 2(179–85): 473–78.
———. 1935. 'The Indian Musical Drums', *Proceedings of the Indian Academy of Sciences, Section A* 1(3): 455–67.
Sarbadhikary, Sukanya. 2015. *The Place of Devotion: Siting and Experiencing Divinity in Bengal-Vaishnavism.* Oakland: The University of California Press.
Scheper-Hughes, Nancy, and Margaret Lock. 1987. 'The Mindful Body: A Prolegomenon to Future Work in Medical Anthropology', *Medical Anthropology Quarterly* 1(1): 6–41.
Shorten, Sarah J. 1983. 'Towards an Understanding of De Anima 432a 1: Aristotle's Analogy between the Soul and the Hand', *The Society for Ancient Greek Philosophy Newsletter* 1: 1–18.
Tallis, Raymond. 2003. *The Hand: A Philosophical Inquiry into Human Being.* Edinburgh: Edinburgh University Press.
Tarlekar, Ganesh H. 1991. *Studies in the Natyashastra: With Special Reference to the Sanskrit Drama in Performance.* 2nd edn. Delhi: Motilal Banarsidass.
Widlok, Thomas. 2017. *Anthropology and the Economy of Sharing.* London: Routledge.
Wilson, Frank R. 1998. *The Hand.* New York: Vintage Books.

8

Cooking the 'Imperialist West'

The Exchange of Non-Marxist Non-Evolutionist Ideas in Vietnamese Institutionalized Anthropology in the Pre-Renovation High-Socialist Period

Lam Minh Chau

Introduction

Intellectual exchange has on numerous occasions taken the form of a 'clash of civilizations' (Huntington 1996). But as anthropologist Susan Bayly repeatedly shows throughout her scholarly endeavours, particularly through her works on past and contemporary Vietnam, intellectual exchange is also 'a bridging of worlds' (Bayly, this volume). Inspired by her accounts of post-colonial Vietnamese intellectuals as active moral agents capable of traversing and connecting knowledge systems supposed to be mutually antagonistic (Bayly 2004, 2007), this chapter seeks to add insight to an enduring, and still vibrant, line of enquiry in anthropology about intellectual life in both revolutionary socialist and post-/late-socialist contexts (Gellner 1977; Humphrey 1984; Tishkov 1992). My focus is on a striking theme in the recollections of many Vietnamese anthropologists about an important chapter of their scholarly life in the 1970s and 1980s pre-Renovation high-socialist period, and a theme that is powerfully conveyed in their published works as well as non-public letters they exchanged with one another in this period.[1] At the time, my interlocutors were employed in public research institutes and universities in northern Vietnam. Yet the narratives and written works by those 'state' anthropologists showed that they actively engaged in the exchange and dissemination of ideas and theoretical views widely associated with 'Western' non-Marxist, non-evolutionist anthropological perspectives, particularly those associated with cultural relativism and structuralism.

The literature on pre-Renovation Vietnamese anthropology (Nguyễn Văn Tiệp 2011; Truong 2014; Nguyễn Duy Thiệu 2016) has described the institutionalized discipline of anthropology practised in state research institutions and universities in northern Vietnam in the 1970s and 1980s as a highly restricted 'sphere of intellectual exchange'. My use of the term 'sphere' is inspired by, yet not fully identical to, Bohannan and Bohannan's influential use of the concept (1968), which refers to a system of exchange in which objects are classified according to different spheres of values, and restrictions exist to prevent the exchange of objects in one sphere with those in another. Instead, I use the term 'sphere' to describe a network of exchange regulated by specific rules regarding what can be circulated within the network. Examples of such spheres include Frances Pine's account of a norm in the Polish highlands that exchanges within the house economy and village community should be made in the form of gifts, not direct monetary payment (2002: 85); or Heonik Kwon's study of a rule in Vietnamese traditional ritual economy that one should offer gods and ancestors votive money in the forms of gold and silver bars, not brass coins, which should be offered only to wandering ghosts (2007: 83).

In the international literature on pre-Renovation Vietnamese anthropology, state anthropologists have widely been described as being confined to an officially sanctioned Soviet version of Marxist evolutionism as the single theoretical framework for scholarly discussion (Luong 2006: 374). The reason for such confinement was either because they were oblivious to, or unable to access, non-Marxist, non-evolutionist theories, or because for them such ideas were too bourgeois, imperialist and reactionary to be legitimate objects of intellectual exchange, the circulation of which would contaminate the institutionalized discipline of anthropology as a site to facilitate the transformation of the country's ethnic minority citizens in line with Marxist ideals of social evolution (Evans 2005: 43–46; Nguyen Van Chinh 2019: 91).

This chapter presents a different account of the so-called 'state' anthropologists. By exploring the recollections of their scholarly life in the pre-Renovation period, together with examining their published works and non-public written communications they had with one another during this particular chapter of Vietnamese anthropology, I draw attention to active exchanges of Western theories within the institutionalized discipline of anthropology in northern Vietnam. By so doing, I first lend weight to scholars such as Bayly (2004, 2007) and Truong (2014), who convincingly demonstrate that even under high-socialism, intellectual life in Vietnam was far from being cut off from the 'Imperialist West' (Evans 2005: 46). Instead, Vietnamese scholars and anthropologists were able to live a life of remarkable connectivity, in which they were linked to 'Western' anthropological knowledge in diverse and creative ways.

As I will show, the anthropologists I knew amassed Western knowledge from a wide array of sources. They included translations of Western works in French by senior scholars who had been influenced by French scholarly traditions in the pre-Revolution era (before 1945) (Kleinen 2005), as well as used books and scholarly texts available at street vendors in Vietnam's capital Hanoi after the collapse of the US-backed regime in the south and since the country was reunified under the leadership of the Communist Party of Vietnam in 1975 (Bayly 2004: 332). Another crucial source was verbal communications with senior anthropologists richly endowed with cosmopolitan knowledge, thanks to their training in Western countries before the 1945 Revolution, their fluency in French by virtue of family background, or experiences as experts (*chuyên gia*) in former French-ruled colonies (Bayly 2004, 2009).

Yet if access to Western theories was one thing, treating them as objects of exchange to be circulated within the 'state' sphere was quite another. Thus, the second goal of this chapter is to understand the sense those anthropologists made of Western theories, in the face of the remarkable pressure on them to defend state anthropology as a sphere to uphold Marxist ideals of social evolution and to promote those ideals among the country's ethnic minorities.

In the limited literature on the encounter between Vietnamese anthropologists and Western theories in this period, the search for and exchanges of Western ideas were driven by both their dissatisfaction with Marxism-Leninism as the only theory officially available to them in their training and later scholarly endeavours, and by a determination to break away from an imprisoning sphere of intellectual exchange, the purpose of which – that is, the facilitation of a Marxist frame of social evolution among ethnic minority groups – was considered cold and instrumental (e.g. Truong 2014).

While my informants did convey a sense of dissatisfaction with the fact that only Marxism-Leninism was accepted as the medium of scholarly exchange in the 'state' sphere, they did not describe the Western ideas they learned and shared as challenging the goal of state anthropology to promote social evolution. Instead, for them, Western ideas offer both exciting knowledge and novel means to sustain the vitality of institutionalized state anthropology, by providing new insights into effective paths for promoting social evolution among ethnic minorities, in ways Soviet-style Marxist theories had insufficiently addressed. Thus, their exchanges of those ideas were definitely not intended to be a disruption of the 'state' sphere. By breaching the sphere's boundaries, they contribute to reinforcing it.

I therefore coin the phrase 'cooking the "Imperialist West"'. This phrase is inspired by Carsten's work on Malaysian women, who spent the money their husbands earned when working outside the home on the food they cooked and shared among family members, thereby converting money from a symbol of commercialized and individualized labour into an embodiment of the spirits of collectivism, mutual sharing and non-calculation that could be safely exchanged within the home sphere as moral objects (Carsten 1989: 132). In a similar vein, the Vietnamese 'state' anthropologists, through their own distinctive interpretation of Western theories, 'cooked' those ideas into novel forms suitable to be circulated within the institutionalized anthropology.

Inside the State Sphere

Most of the anthropologists I worked with originate from the countryside, having passed a highly competitive entrance exam to become students in the Faculty of History of Hanoi University. Until the late 1970s, it was the only tertiary education institution in northern Vietnam where anthropology was taught, under the name *Dân tộc học* (ethnology/ethnography).[2] Upon graduation, most have been employed in public universities and research institutions, notably Hanoi University and the Committee for Social Sciences (now Vietnam Academy of Social Sciences). It is precisely thanks to such specific academic training and affiliations that my interlocutors are among the few who still retain vivid memories of the official space for anthropological exchange and practices in the pre-Renovation period.

Typical of Vietnamese anthropologists who became university undergraduates in the early 1970s, Prof. Ba did not choose anthropology as his major at first. Now in his late sixties, he recalled that he originally applied to the Faculty of Literature, then one of only two faculties of social sciences at Hanoi University. Yet back then the subject they would study was not chosen by students themselves, but instead administrative decisions were made by university managers. Prof. Ba was assigned to the Faculty of History, an unexpected turn that began his bond with anthropology for the next forty years. Upon graduation, he became a lecturer in ethnology at Hanoi University, where he worked until retirement.

In Prof. Ba's days as a university student, anthropology, under the name of ethnology, was offered not as an independent undergraduate programme, but only as part of the programme in History. This teaching model was influenced by the way anthropology was taught in the Soviet Union. In the 1960s, senior Soviet anthropologists were sent to northern Vietnam to help prepare textbooks and teaching curricula. Prof. Ba told me when I accompanied him on a visit to his alma mater:

> In the first three years of our undergraduate programme, students only had a sixty-hour 'Introduction to Ethnology' course [*Cơ sở dân tộc học*]. Not until the end of the third year did we get to choose ethnology as the major to commit to during the final year.

Undergraduate students had merely two textbooks for official learning materials in ethnology. The first was a translation of a Russian textbook, *Introduction to Ethnology*, by E.P. Buxughin, a Soviet ethnologist invited to Hanoi University to lecture and help coordinate the teaching of the new discipline in the early 1960s. In the early 1970s, another textbook of the same title, *Cơ sở dân tộc học* (*Introduction to Ethnology*), was written in Vietnamese. The author, Phan Hữu Dật, was among the first Vietnamese to obtain the Kandidate Nauk degree (Candidate of Science) in ethnology from the Soviet Union. The textbooks were later supplemented by articles published in newly established journals, notably the *Journal of Ethnology* (*Tạp chí Dân tộc học*) launched in 1974. However, until the 1980s, what those textbooks and articles offered were either descriptive accounts by Vietnamese ethnologists without theoretical framing, or translations of selected works by Soviet scholars such as Bromlei and Tokarev that embraced strictly evolutionist and Marxist perspectives (Bromlei 1974; Tokarev 1976).

For those who studied ethnology and later became professional anthropologists in state research institutions in the 1970s and 1980s, social evolutionism was the only accepted theory and Marxism-Leninism was considered the only 'scientific method' (*phương pháp khoa học*) (Nguyễn Văn Tiệp 2011). Prof. Ba recalled vividly what he and his peers were taught in their first year at university, on a course regarded as foundational to all students in the faculty: *Phương pháp luận sử học* (Methodologies of Historical Studies). This course was meant to equip students and future researchers with knowledge of Marxism-Leninism, regarded as the single proper worldview and theoretical approach, to be embraced at all times in their learning and work. Prof. Ba recalled:

> We learned about the thoughts of Marx, Engels, Lenin and Stalin about history. Basically, we were taught that the history of mankind was a development through five socio-economic forms, from lower to higher, each was characterized by a particular force of production and a relation of production. This applied to all human societies. The task of ethnology, a subfield of historical science that focused on the history of ethnic groups, was to explore how an ethnic group had developed through time, to which socio-economic form that ethnic group currently belonged, and most importantly, how to guide that ethnic group to advance to higher forms of social evolution, which basically meant a classification of their cultural practices into progressive ones, to be promoted, and backward ones, to be eradicated. (See also Buxughin 1961: 57)

The dominance of the Marxist evolutionist framework in pre-Renovation state anthropology not only defined the ultimate goal of anthropology as the promotion of social evolution among ethnic minorities, but also regulated what should be considered proper, scientific methods to achieve that goal. Prof. Le, another undergraduate student in the faculty in the 1970s, who later became a senior fellow at the Vietnam Academy of Social Sciences, recalled:

> During our university training and later our work in state research projects, the topics of studies were very limited: ethnic history, material culture, cultivation techniques, land ownership, class differentiation and social organizations. Back then the main goal of state research projects was to identify cultural practices of ethnic groups and determine the position of a given ethnic group in the development ladder, so as to devise policies to help them develop in accordance with Marxist-Leninist theory of social evolution. Therefore, we had to focus on aspects of their cultures that could indicate where they were, in what ways they were lagging behind, what practices to promote and what to eradicate. Of course topics of particular concerns were the force of production, i.e. whether they were wet-rice or slash-and-burn cultivators; and relations of production, i.e. types of land ownership and the degree of class differentiation.

Prof. Le's experience was far from unusual. All the anthropologists I worked with recalled that in state-funded studies in which they participated before Renovation, aspects of ethnic lives that did not indicate the level of social evolution of ethnic groups, such as decoration motifs, funeral songs, symbols and local knowledge, were rarely the focus of attention. They were considered trivial topics (*vụn vặt*), to be ignored so as to focus on important topics such as forces of production and relations of production (Nguyễn Huệ Chi 2005).

Prof. Ba recalled a similar experience as he participated in the only fieldwork trip during his undergraduate study: a one-month fieldwork study organized by the Faculty of History. It was an annual course of intensive training, arranged for all second-year students, in which about 100 students were sent to live in a far-away community, often in rural and ethnic minority regions.

While intended to familiarize students with how to conduct ethnographic research, those fieldwork trips were frequently expected by higher authorities to carry political agendas. Prof. Ba recalled the official goal of his fieldwork training in 1974: to learn about scientific socialism (*chủ nghĩa xã hội khoa học*). The trip was launched soon after the promulgation of a major resolution of the Communist Party on three revolutions (*Ba cuộc cách mạng*). For the faculty leaders at the time, the fieldwork trip was an opportunity to educate students on the first and most important revolution, in relations of production. Prof. Ba's cohort thus was sent to a village regarded as a role model in implementing the cooperativization movement in agriculture (*phong trào hợp tác hóa nông nghiệp*), the cornerstone of the revolution in relations of production in the countryside (Standing Committee of the National Assembly 1969). What was supposed to be a period of intensive fieldwork training had been redesigned as a time to inculcate political agendas. As Prof. Ba recalled:

> At days we helped villagers with farm work on cooperative fields. At nights we attended meetings of the local cooperative, listening to reports, directives, and resolutions. Throughout the trip, we received no fieldwork training. Instead, we were asked to participate in local life as deeply as possible, to understand how the revolution in relations of production was taking root in the countryside.

The influence of Marxism set substantial limits not only on the topics Vietnamese state anthropologists should study, but also on how to make sense of what they found. For example, a key task of Soviet-style Marxist anthropology was to classify cultural practices of a given ethnic group into progressive ones (*tiến bộ*) and backward ones (*lạc hậu*). The former should be promoted because they would facilitate the transition of an ethnic group to higher levels of evolution. The latter should be eradicated because they would obstruct the transition (Buxughin 1973: 57). However, the identification of 'progressive' and 'backward' practices was based on a universal set of standards, which did not always do justice to the sophistication and local embeddedness of cultural forms and institutions under study (Keyes 2002; Phạm Như Cương 1989: 9-17; Evans 2005). As Prof. Ba explained:

> Back then it was simple. Handicraft items produced by artisanal, locally specific methods were always inferior to those produced by industrial production. A hand-made piece of cloth was always inferior to a piece made by machine in a factory. Local knowledge should be replaced with scientific knowledge. A lavish funeral was definitely a backward, wasteful custom of superstition, to be eradicated without question.[3]

The dominance of Marxism and evolutionism meant that non-Marxist, non-evolutionist theories were widely criticized in state anthropology: as Western, idealistic (*duy tâm*), subjective (*chủ quan*), reactionary (*phản động*), and as tools of oppression wielded by the ruling class, colonial rulers and imperialists (Phan Hữu Dật 1973: 1). Prof. Le recalled that Bronislaw Malinowski was mentioned in a methodology lecture as an object of criticism: someone with a 'reactionary' perspective, who 'dedicated his entire life serving British and American imperialists'. Malinowski was particularly criticized because he held that non-Western societies were in a state of equilibrium that 'should not be touched'. In the view of Soviet-style Marxist anthropology, this approach was driven by the 'Imperialist' mindset of Western colonial rulers, who sought to dominate non-Western peoples without the will to help them develop (Buxughin 1961: 47). Marxist anthropology, by contrast, had as its ultimate aim the facilitation of the transition of all ethnic groups and nations to higher stages of social evolution.

Another example of the official hostility towards non-Marxist, non-evolutionist theories was illustrated in the case of the renowned Vietnamese anthropologist, Nguyen Tu Chi (1925–95). Born to a family of intellectuals in the revolutionary tradition, Tu Chi was fluent in French, and worked in Guinea between 1961 and 1963 as one of many experts (*chuyên gia*) the Democratic Republic of Vietnam (DRV) sent to African states as both tokens of selfless friendship and a means of earning much-needed remittances for the country (Bayly 2009). Widely acknowledged as one of the most well-known Vietnamese anthropologists of the twentieth century (Truong 2014), Tu Chi was particularly famous for his pioneering works that employ Lévi-Strauss's structuralism to examine the social structure and cosmologies of the Viet and Muong ethnic groups in northern Vietnam (Trần Từ 1978, 1984).

Yet although Tu Chi was much respected by students and young anthropologists of Prof. Ba's generation, he was officially viewed in the 1970s and 1980s as a problematic figure, and his efforts to disseminate structuralism to younger colleagues were often met with vilification. In a tribute article to Tu Chi, his cousin Hue Chi recalled a dramatic event in 1972, when Tu Chi was an academic staff member at the Institute of Ethnology, Committee for Social Sciences. He was invited to present a talk on a Western theory of his choice for the institute's staff. His talk on Lévi-Strauss's structuralism was enthusiastically received, causing him to extend the talk that was scheduled for one day to three days. Yet on the last day, a committee senior official was informed of the talk and became enraged. For him it was an act of 'propagating capitalist scholarship while the country was fighting the American' (Nguyễn Huệ Chi 2005). The talk was immediately stopped, the institute's leaders had to submit a 'self-criticism' report (*báo cáo*) to account for the event, and Tu Chi eventually left the institute.

Tu Chi and his works remained targets of official criticisms for the rest of the pre-Renovation period. His main topics of enquiry, notably decoration motifs, women's skirts and funeral songs, were all considered 'useless' (*vô bổ*). They offered little insight into forces and relations of production of an ethnic group, which according to Soviet-style Marxist anthropology were the only topics of study that could help facilitate social evolution. Tu Chi was also criticized because he defended cultural practices of ethnic minorities officially regarded at the time as unquestionably backward, to be eradicated, instead treating them as sophisticated and valuable (Truong 2014).

Transcending Boundaries

Despite the tremendous constraints on anthropological research and practice before Renovation, the memories shared by anthropologists I worked with are far from accounts of those who passively complied with official rules regarding what could be circulated within the institutionalized discipline of anthropology as a highly regulated 'sphere of intellectual exchange'. What they convey are powerful recollections of how they actively moved beyond the boundaries of Soviet-style Marxist evolutionism to engage with other anthropological approaches.

While acknowledging the dominance of Marxist evolutionism in publicly available texts, anthropologists I know emphasized that there were opportunities to access a much wider range of anthropological theories through non-public sources, three of which deserve attention. The first were scholarly materials available in the library of the Faculty of History. Although a modest in-house library, it stored a rich collection of academic texts in French, Russian and Chinese, contributed by faculty members and academics who considered the faculty a worthy address to which to donate their valuable texts.

Many of those works were translated into Vietnamese by a group of non-teaching faculty staff. Most of them were of highly educated backgrounds. Some were mandarins under the Nguyen, Vietnam's last imperial dynasty overthrown in the 1945 Revolution. With various factors preventing them from attaining higher positions in the post-Revolution state system, particularly 'bad-class' background or affiliation with the overthrown monarchy (Malarney 2002), they joined the faculty to work exclusively as translators of academic materials.

The materials they translated were often available in the form of a single handwritten copy, as there was no typewriter. Such valuable copies were for in-house loan only, meaning that students and even faculty members had to read them inside the library's cramped space. Yet former students of the faculty told me that they devised a system to make those materials into forms that could be more widely circulated. 'We divided ourselves into groups, each was responsible for making handwritten copies of certain texts. Then we shared them with each other', explained Prof. Ba. Although the students originally planned to share the texts among themselves only, those handwritten copies became objects of exchange within a much larger network, including fellow anthropologists in other state institutions. Prof. Ba showed me a handwritten copy he made himself. It clearly had changed hands a lot, being filled with notes and comments in different colours of ink by those who had participated in this network of scholarly exchange.

Of the translated texts most widely circulated among the students, faculty members and anthropologists outside the faculty, accounting for the largest number were works by Soviet scholars, such as 'Nations, Races, and Cultures' by Cheboksarov and Cheboksarova (1985); and texts by Chinese scholars on the history and cultural customs of ethnic groups residing on the land that is now Vietnam in the past, such as 'Lĩnh ngoại đại đáp' 嶺外代答 by Chu Khứ Phi 周去非. Yet the most sought after were works by French colonial scholars written in the pre-Revolution period, two of which were particularly influential on Prof. Ba and anthropologists of his generation: *Les Paysans du Delta Tonkinois* by Pierre Gourou (1936) and *Les Muong* by Jean Cuisinier (1946).

The second source of Western non-Marxist materials much valued by my interlocutors were books on sale at various used book stores and street vendors across the capital Hanoi.[4] For most university students before the Renovation, used books were a much-preferred source of learning materials may be compared to brand-new books available in official bookshops. This was not only a matter of price. As Prof. Le recalled:

> In official libraries and bookshops, you could only find a very limited range of texts: classic works by Marx and Engels, anthologies of works by Party leaders, translation of orthodox works by Soviet scholars. Yet in used book stores and street book vendors, you could run into books printed in the pre-Revolution period, works by Western scholars, even non-Marxist works that no state publisher would accept for mass publication.

It was on a visit to a used book store in a deep alley of Hanoi that Prof. Le obtained one of the most treasured books in his family library, now located on his house's third floor: 'I was looking for some novels when I ran into a much-worn text, "*La civilisation primitive*"'. Thanks to his fluency in French, he immediately recognized what it was: Edward Tylor's infamous *Primitive Culture*. It was a book widely talked about among students in the faculty, and regarded by many of their teachers and senior anthropologists as a must-read. However, it could not be found in university libraries or public bookshops as its author was regarded as a 'colonial' scholar. 'It cost everything I had in my pocket that day', Prof. Le said warmly.

Such memories were widely recalled by anthropologists I know. All showed me much-used books they obtained from street vendors before the Renovation. In addition to works by foreign scholars, I was struck by books written by anthropologists working in the Republic of Vietnam (RVN), the American-backed regime defeated by the DRV in 1975. After the reunification in 1975, various works that had been published in the RVN were quietly brought to the north by returning northern Vietnamese military servicemen and civil servants. As shown below, although never treated as legitimate sources of knowledge by DRV officials, these works were greeted with great enthusiasm by northern anthropologists as novel sources of insight into the anthropological world.

Books of this kind were all much worn, and there were clear signs that they had been exchanged a lot. For owners of such books at the time, they were personal treasures. Prof. Ba showed me one of his most cherished texts, with a hard cover he had made himself to protect it. Yet my interlocutors were also generous sharers, rarely refusing to lend out those texts to fellow anthropologists. A former junior of Prof. Ba at Hanoi University recalled:

> One day I told brother Ba in a casual conversation, 'Have you read *Les Paysans du Delta Tonkinois*? I was dying to read it, but no one had it'. Some days later, he suddenly called me out and pulled out from his bag a handwritten copy he made himself. 'Treat it with care, and remember to return it'.

For a small group of anthropologists, there was a third source of knowledge into non-Marxist traditions that was particularly influential in their career life: the communications they had with anthropologists of earlier generations, who were well known among the younger scholars for their rich knowledge of theories and practice beyond the boundaries of Marxist Soviet anthropology.

I return to the case of Prof. Tu Chi. Despite Tu Chi's officially marginalized status before Renovation, a small group of young researchers, most of them full-time employees in state research institutions, actively sought his mentorship. A case in point is Dr Nguyen, another senior researcher at Vietnam Academy of Social Sciences. 'For young ethnologists at the time, learning from Tu Chi was an obvious choice for those who wanted something new, beyond what was available in official teaching programmes. Few other than Tu Chi could help us', he said.

While Dr Nguyen used the term 'teach', he and other unofficial students of Tu Chi never learned from him through formal classes. Tu Chi never held any official teaching position at a university. He instead transferred knowledge to younger colleagues through casual, intimate discussions they had in his house or on the streets, while they were having tea and sipping rice spirit together. 'Sometimes he came to my house. A bottle of rice spirit and a dish of roasted peanut were everything I could offer him. Yet he kept telling me his ethnographic stories from noon to midnight', recalled Prof. Ba, another of Tu Chi's informal students.

It was Tu Chi who alerted those such as Prof. Ba and Dr Nguyen to important non-Marxist texts, from Tylor's *Primitive Culture* and Frazer's *Golden Bough* (1976), to André Leroi-Gourhan's *Evolution et Techniques* (1945), and particularly Lévi-Strauss's works. Dr Nguyen noted that Tu Chi never mentioned theories directly: 'He rarely talked about theories. Most of the time he simply shared his experiences from the field, what he saw in Vietnam and Guinea. Yet we knew he was quietly mainstreaming theoretical ideas into his talks'. Prof. Ba had the same impression. He believed it was an act of caution Tu Chi took after the painful experience of his lectures on Lévi-Strauss being subject to official scrutiny.

While the discussions between Tu Chi and the young scholars have been mentioned in the literature on pre-Renovation anthropology (Truong 2014; Bùi Xuân Đính 2016), less attention has been paid to the network of exchange that those scholars created themselves. Within the highly restricted 'state' sphere, knowledge they learned from Tu Chi became exciting objects of exchange they enthusiastically shared with others. A colleague of Prof. Le recalled:

> Brother Le always came to see me after he met Tu Chi. Sometimes even at dinner time. He simply dropped by on his bicycle, and said: 'I just met old Tu [*cụ Từ*, a respectful way of addressing Tu Chi]. He said something very interesting. You must hear it. Let's go for a beer. Your treat'.

Structuralism and Relativism

Among the non-Marxist non-evolutionist theories my interlocutors acquired from unofficial sources and exchanged with one another, two are regarded as particularly influential in their theoretical views. The first is structuralism, something they learned mostly from their unofficial mentor, Tu Chi. As Dr Nguyen said:

> Tu Chi never spoke to us directly about structuralism. He rarely mentioned the name of Lévi-Strauss. Yet he conveyed structuralist ideas to us in almost everything he discussed, from the Muong's cosmology, their realms of life and death [*cõi sống và cõi chết*], and funeral songs. He was particularly passionate about symbols and their meanings, particularly decoration motifs found on Muong women's dress, the Dong Son bronze drums of the Kinh-Viet, and roofs of houses of the J'rai in the Central Highlands.

Structuralist perspectives learned from Tu Chi inspired Dr Nguyen and his colleagues in two main ways. First, it reminded them of the importance of moving beyond strictly Marxist concerns such as forces of production and relations of production, so as to explore a much wider range of ethnic cultural practices, notably rituals, symbols and meanings. Second, it was critical to shift the focus from ranking them in accordance with the Marxist frame of unilinear evolution to identifying what humankind had in common in terms of perspectives, worldviews and cosmology. Dr Nguyen stated:

> What ethnologists should pay attention to when studying weaving practices of the Muong, for example, was not only their weaving tools and techniques and how advanced or backward they were in accordance with universal standards, but also decoration motifs they used on weaving products, the meanings of these symbols, so as to identify ways of thinking shared by all ethnic groups and human beings.

The other highly influential theory is cultural relativism. Similar to structuralism, relativism was officially regarded before Renovation as 'Western' and bourgeois, as many of its core arguments were in conflict with Marxist evolutionism. Prof. Ba recalled that he first became aware of this theory in the early 1980s, yet not in the way relativism is taught to anthropology students today. He was not aware of Franz Boas, nor major texts by cultural relativists such as Margaret Mead and Ruth Benedict. Neither did he gain access to relativism systematically, as a complete theory about cultures being the products of adaptation to historical and social contexts. Instead, relativism came to him in bits and pieces, from French, Russian and Chinese texts he read and discussions with senior scholars.

I was struck by what Prof. Ba considered the text through which the idea of relativism was first introduced to him: another much-worn book by an eminent scholar in the RVN, Bình Nguyên Lộc, published in 1971. One of Prof. Ba's senior colleagues at university introduced the book to him, insisting that he read it despite the fact that it was published under the RVN regime. On the first page, the author quoted Pierre Huard, a French physician and anthropologist: 'No culture should be ashamed of itself, and no culture has the right to despise other cultures' [Aucune culture ne doit avoir honte d'elle-même, pas plus qu'elle ne saurait mépriser les autres]. Prof. Ba recalled:

> The idea surprised me. It was clearly not in line with officially approved perspectives [he meant Soviet-style Marxist theories]. Yet for me it should not be immediately rejected or criticized just because the author was a scholar from the other side [the RVN]. By contrast, it was something to treat seriously, because we knew scholars from the RVN had the opportunity to engage with a wider range of perspectives than we did.

Prof. Ba did not know the ideas he was learning were something widely taught in Western countries as 'cultural relativism', a term he only learned much later. However, he felt strongly that the new perspective offered a novel reference point to make sense of the life of the ethnic minorities he worked with, in ways that had not been satisfactorily explained by mainstream Marxist theories of unilinear evolutionism. Ever since Marxist evolutionism was first introduced to him, he had sensed it should be treated with caution. 'The more I worked with ethnic minority people, the more I realized they were far from backward, or ignorant. They were kind, hard-working, and creative. Many of their cultural practices were beautiful and sophisticated', said Prof. Ba, recalling how impressed he was by the skills his ethnic minority informants demonstrated when building stilt houses, and how they cleverly designed irrigation systems to channel water from rivers through challenging mountain terrains to rice fields. Prof. Ba thus was excited about the idea of cultures being equal.

> As soon as I was aware of the new idea, it immediately made much sense to me, given what I had experienced when working with and living amongst ethnic minorities. Clearly their cultural practices had many aspects that should be preserved and respected, because they were actually the results of their creative adaptations to the particular natural and social environments in which they lived, so as to meet their specific needs and aspirations. These practices must not be dismissed as 'backward' and something to be eradicated.

It was fascinating that for Prof. Ba there was evident similarity between the idea of cultures being equal and the idea conveyed by French colonial anthropologists, particularly Gourou. Although my interlocutors still describe Gourou as one of the '*học giả thực dân*', literally 'colonial scholars', particularly for their orientalizing perspectives in which they treated their subjects of study as retainers of 'exotic culture' (Kleinen 2005: 345), they all express remarkable respect for those 'colonial' works. 'The materials in those books were so detailed, meticulous, and comprehensive', said Prof. Ba, using the term '*toàn diện*' (comprehensive). They particularly admired those 'colonial' works for providing a broad-range view of ethnic lives and for showing respect towards local cultures, instead of treating ethnography as a discipline confined in focus, concentrating only on topics of immediate interest to Marxism and dismissing other cultural practices as backward and lowly.

> I was fascinated by what Gourou wrote: that the small-scale, low-productivity agricultural economy of peasants in Tonkin [northern Vietnam] was actually in great harmony with the particular natural and social environments of the Red River Delta where they had lived for centuries, and very much tailored to the needs of the peasants, which were simply to have enough to eat rather than to get rich.

The acquisition of novel theoretical perspectives, through works by RVN scholars or colonial anthropologists, was a prominent theme in my interlocutors' narratives. Rather than treating those bodies of knowledge with disdain and as mere subjects for criticism, their narratives convey a sense of enthusiasm for novel ideas and mutual scholarly respect for those officially classified as 'colonial', 'enemy' or 'reactionary'. There was absolutely no sense of them being confined to Soviet-style Marxist evolutionism as the only exchangeable theoretical perspectives within the 'sphere' of state anthropology, either because they were passive, lacking motivation for learning and uncritically embracing the views imposed on them without independent perceptions of their own, or because they were narrow-minded and treated works by Western, non-Marxist non-evolutionist scholars as reactionary and toxically idealistic

(Nguyen Van Chinh 2019: 92). What I document shares great similarities with Bayly's account of intellectuals in post-Revolution northern Vietnam as eager learners and active explorers of diverse knowledge systems, who were far from being confined by ideological fault-lines (2004, this volume).

Cooking Theories

While I have constantly been struck by my interlocutors' active engagement with and exchange of Western theories, what is equally striking is the way they interpreted the novel ideas they learned and shared. Of course, a central feature in their narratives was how the new theories offered novel frameworks to understand aspects of ethnic minority lives that Marxist evolutionism could not. Yet another powerfully conveyed theme was that they did not see those Western theories as undermining or in conflict with the official goal of state anthropology: to foster social evolution. The following quote was taken from a letter Prof. Ba exchanged with a junior colleague. Prof. Ba had lent the colleague a book by RVN scholar Binh Nguyen Loc to introduce relativist ideas to him. The junior, excited yet confused by the ideas, sought Prof. Ba's advice on how to make sense of relativism. Prof. Ba replied:

> Relativism is right to say that each culture is created by its own surrounding conditions. Thus no culture should be regarded as backward, nor forced to change in ways similar to others. Yet relativism does not dismiss evolutionism. It just gives us a different idea about how to facilitate social evolution. All cultures and societies will still evolve from lower to higher forms, but they will do so in their own way, in accordance with their own conditions. In this sense, relativism is actually a useful tool for ethnology. It shows us that in order to help our ethnic minority compatriots achieve a better life, we must not force them to change in the way we want. Instead, we must help them develop in the way they want.

Prof. Ba did not use such terms as 'modern' (*hiện đại*) or 'progress' (*tiến bộ*), in ways that convey a sense of universalization and arbitrary judgement of local practices by external standards. Instead, he used such terms as 'develop' (*phát triển*) and 'a better life' (*một cuộc sống tốt đẹp hơn*) in combination with remarkable phrases, 'in accordance with their own conditions' (*phù hợp với điều kiện của họ*) and 'in the way they want' (*theo nhu cầu của họ*). This was, for him, precisely how ethnology/anthropology should facilitate social change among ethnic minority people. He told me:

> On a fieldwork trip to a northwest mountain, I stayed with a host family of ethnic Muong, in a stilt house. The house was old and had seriously deteriorated. As the family was classified as a poor household, they were eligible for state funding to rebuild the house. However, when local officials proposed to build them a new house of bricks and concrete built directly on the ground, similar to those of the Kinh in the lowland, they refused. Yet it didn't mean they didn't want a better house. They

absolutely wanted a house that was more stable, with better roofing, even with electricity. But a better house in their view was still a stilt house, which was more suited to the mountain environment, where stilt houses can protect you from wild beasts, flash floods and mosquitoes. The task of ethnology then was to find ways to help them improve their stilt houses, rather than forcing them to convert to lowland-style houses.

Remarkable interpretations of relativism of this kind were widely communicated by anthropologists of Prof. Ba's generation, not only in verbal discussions or non-public exchanges of letters, but also through written works published before Renovation. It should be noted that my informants never mentioned the term 'relativism' in their published works. Given official criticisms of Western theories in pre-Renovation institutionalized state anthropology, a common solution my interlocutors employed had been to use those theories without mentioning them explicitly.

In the works of many state anthropologists of this generation, there was an argument I encountered with striking frequency: the importance of promoting traditional cultural values (*các giá trị văn hóa truyền thống*) of ethnic groups in the process of development. In classic Marxist theories, as Prof. Ba explained, industrialization was treated as the highest, most advanced form of production. Development/social evolution in the classic Marxist sense, therefore, means abolishing 'traditional', that is, pre-industrial forms of production, such as handicraft workshops and artisanal techniques, and replacing them with machines and industrial production.

A key theme in the works of those anthropologists, however, was that industrialization was not the only way to achieve social evolution. It could also be achieved through refinement/improvement of traditional, ethnically distinctive techniques, because it was those traditional techniques that were much more suited to the specific needs of each ethnic group. The following quote was taken from an article published in the mid-1980s by Dr Luong, a junior colleague of Prof. Ba, on how to develop weaving practices of ethnic minorities:

> Today developing weaving production of ethnic minorities to meet the growing need of the people has become a crucial task. To achieve this goal, it is important to promote traditional folk knowledge in weaving ..., particularly family-based, lineage-based and locally based handicraft techniques ... Even in the age of industrialization and post-industrialization, ethnic groups still retain their need for distinctive ethnic and local cultural characteristics. In this aspect, it is artisanal, handicraft production, not industrial production, that can meet such need.

Such narratives suggest that when those anthropologists communicated relativist ideas to other scholars within the state sphere and to the public, they did not seek to disseminate criticisms of the official goal of state anthropology to facilitate social evolution. For those anthropologists, Marxist approaches have proven insufficient to address that aim, and it was in Western, non-Marxist theories that they thought they had obtained the solution to address this gap. The relativist ideas they communicated through public scholarly exchanges had been converted into novel forms, much in line with the idea of social evolution: the principle of respecting other cultures was interpreted as a matter of active, sensitive and sympathetic intervention into ethnic minority lives, rather than as a matter of leaving them intact.

Structuralism was another Western theory that my interlocutors saw as an important new tool to facilitate social evolution. Dr Nguyen shared with me a written note he exchanged with a friend and fellow state anthropologist, showing his excitement about the value of structuralism in promoting social change.

> On the one hand, structuralism reminds us that human beings all think in the same way. Thus all cultures are actually created from similar thinking. Therefore, we must treat all cultures, all ethnic groups as equal. Yet on the other hand, if deep inside, human beings think in similar logics, then it means other ethnic groups can also think like us. They also have aspirations for change and a better life. They may also want what we want, do what we do. In light of structuralism, the mission of ethnology to facilitate social evolution is both correct and feasible. We can help ethnic minorities change and share our achievements with them. Structuralism, however, reminds us that to do so, we must really understand what they think deep inside. We cannot force them to become like us in every way, but only in ways we are similar.

In the same letter, Dr Nguyen recalled a fieldwork experience when he lived among a Hmong community, an ethnic group widely stereotyped in official narratives as anti-modern. 'Local officials kept complaining that their way of thinking was too "backward" [*lạc hậu*] and different from us [the Kinh majority]. For example, they could not be persuaded to change from shifting, slash-and-burn cultivation to permanent settlement and wet-rice cultivation similar to the Kinh', Dr Nguyen recalled. However, an incident made Dr Nguyen question these criticisms:

> One day the son of my host family had a serious fever. The father went to the forest to get some leaves and boiled them with water for him to drink. He also invited a sorcerer to perform a healing ritual. Yet the boy's situation did not improve. When I asked to see the boy, I recognized it was malaria. The boy would die unless he received treatment. So I immediately persuaded the family to take him to hospital. They finally agreed as the boy's condition got worse. The father and I carried the boy to a local infirmary 20 kilometres away, on my motorbike as there was none in the village. Fortunately, the dose of quinine prescribed by local medical staff effected a cure.

What struck Dr Nguyen was the tragic story of the boy's sister who was infected with the same disease, which was recalled to him by the father. In the father's words:

> She had the same disease some years earlier, but she was not that lucky and eventually succumbed to the sickness. We knew we needed more effective means of cure. But we did not have the conditions. Back then there was no infirmary, nor

> motorbike, nor medicine. All we could do when somebody got sick was to get medicinal leaves and invite a sorcerer. Had we got what we have now, my daughter would have been saved.

That moment made Dr Nguyen recall what his mentor Tu Chi had taught him. He wrote this in the letter to his colleague:

> Old Tu said while our cultures might be different, deep down we all thought in the same way. What he said definitely applied here. The Hmong I worked with did not want to become permanent settlers like us, nor did they want to practice wet-rice agriculture. But it did not mean our thoughts were entirely different. Deep down, their thinking was also one of change, towards the better for them and their children. They were also capable of understanding the value of modern technologies, of motorbikes and quinine. There were clearly areas where we could help them change for the better.

What is conveyed is a creative interpretation of structuralism: its core argument about the structures of ideas shared by all human beings is perceived in a distinctively Vietnamese way, as the similarity in aspirations for social evolution and constantly improving living standards among all ethnic groups. The view that all human beings share the same structures of ideas is seen as highly compatible with the goal of state anthropology to foster social evolution. It means that introducing one's views and practices to others is not always an arbitrary imposition of external standards that never make sense in local contexts, but something that can be accepted, provided that it is introduced cautiously and sympathetically.

There is certainly a possibility that the emphasis on social evolution in those narratives and written works was merely a cover employed to protect the anthropologists from official suspicion and criticisms. In the highly regulated sphere of institutionalized state anthropology in pre-Renovation Vietnam, questioning social evolution was a taboo that might be fatal to one's career, as the example of Tu Chi illustrates.

Yet I am reluctant to treat my interlocutors' narratives as mere cover-ups, for two reasons. First, those distinctive interpretations of Western theories, as shown earlier, were reflected not only in their published works, but also in non-public written communications they exchanged with each other. Second, even in our conversations today, Prof. Ba, Prof. Le and Dr Nguyen still convey explicit unease with the idea that ethnic groups should be left to exist in their own way. While they agree with relativism and structuralism that human beings should not be divided into civilized and backward, and no culture should force another to change according to its standards, they still hold that the most important and unique contribution of anthropology is the facilitation of social evolution from lower to higher levels. In the context of Renovation, Western theories are no longer treated as a taboo. Evolutionism has lost much of its potency in Vietnamese anthropology, and has increasingly come under attack, not only by Western scholars but also by Vietnamese anthropologists trained in

Euro-American countries (Keyes 2002; Nguyen Van Chinh 2019). Upholding social evolution, therefore, is no longer a safe political choice today, but a daring scholarly decision that makes them vulnerable to criticisms and marginalization within their own intellectual community.

Yet my interlocutors remain firmly attached to the idea of social evolution as a distinctive contribution anthropology can make, although their vision of how that goal can be achieved is far from one defined by a Soviet-style Marxist framework. As Dr Nguyen said:

> Human cultures can be different, yet we have one thing in common: no culture will stay still forever. All cultures will constantly change, for the better, because it is an aspiration shared by all human kinds. Therefore, it is important that we find way to support ethnic minorities, to help them change for the better. However, we must really understand what they think, in what ways we are really similar, so as to help them in the right way. And if they want to develop in their own way, suitable to their own conditions, we must respect their choices.

In Carsten's account of 'cooking money', when money was brought into the house, it was no longer a symbol of individualism and division that threatens the household as a 'sphere of exchange' defined by unity and kinship ideals. Instead, money was qualitatively transformed, or 'cooked', by women in ways that sustained the household. Inspired by Carsten's work, I argue that when my interlocutors brought Western non-Marxist anthropological knowledge into the sphere of institutionalized anthropology, such knowledge was transformed by their creative interpretation, from something officially chastised as a toxic product of the 'Imperialist West', into novel sources of intellectual inspiration that give the sphere fresh vitality.

Conclusions

This chapter has followed the remarkable challenges but also the striking activeness and creativity of the scholarly lives of Vietnamese anthropologists who began their professional careers in northern Vietnam in the pre-Renovation period. Combining documentation of the narratives of senior contributors to the discipline with exploration of their published works and unpublished letters they exchanged with one another, this chapter lends weight to recent scholarly efforts to challenge the widely held stereotype of pre-Renovation Vietnamese anthropology as slavishly based on a crude version of Soviet Marxist anthropology, and to argue for a recognition that Vietnamese anthropologists in the pre-Renovation period were much more diverse in theoretical perspectives than is usually assumed (Truong 2014; Nguyễn Duy Thiệu 2016; Lương Văn Hy 2016: 12).

Another view this chapter calls into question is that while pre-Renovation Vietnamese anthropology indeed featured a diverse range of anthropological approaches, Western theories were only circulated at the margins of institutionalized practice (Truong 2014). This chapter shows that there were active exchanges and communication of non-Marxist, non-evolutionist theories within state spheres, through the sharing of books and scholarly texts, the exchange of letters between state anthropologists, and the publication of written works. What I regard as even more striking is the distinctive sense my interlocutors made of Western non-Marxist theoretical frameworks that they were exchanging: as very much in sync with, rather than in opposition to, the idea of social evolution that Vietnamese state anthropology was tasked with promoting in this period.

My aim is not to dismiss accounts of Vietnamese anthropologists who upon their encounter with Western theories became disillusioned with both Marxism and the goal of state anthropology to foster social evolution (Truong 2014). I acknowledge that the view of the anthropologists I have described is not necessarily the dominant way of perceiving Western theories among Vietnamese anthropologists in the pre-Renovation period. The aim of this chapter has simply been to draw attention to the diversity of experiences among anthropologists of this generation, and the different senses they made of their adventurous, but equally exciting, encounter with the 'Imperialist West'. What I document here shares instructive similarity with Susan Bayly's pioneering works on intellectuals (*trí thức*) in post-colonial, socialist and late-socialist Vietnam as agents capable of deploying and 'bridging' a remarkable array of supposedly antagonistic knowledge realms (2004, 2007), in ways very different from what has often been depicted of intellectuals in various post-colonial and socialist Asian contexts: either treating knowledge traditions of Western origin as bourgeois and reactionary, or dismissing Soviet, Marxist perspectives as inhumane, oppressive and internally colonizing.

Lam Minh Chau is Associate Professor of Anthropology and Chair of Social and Economic Anthropology at the College of Social Sciences and Humanities, Vietnam National University, Hanoi.

Notes

1. Renovation (Đổi mới) refers to a series of market reforms officially launched in Vietnam in 1986, which entailed abolishment of the high-socialist command economy and rapid introduction of market-oriented economic policies (Beresford 2008).
2. Ethnology, or ethnography, refers to a recognized academic discipline in the Soviet Union that corresponds to social or cultural anthropology in the West. Its main concern was originally with archaic societies and later was shifted to ethnicity and more synchronic issues (Gellner 1977). In the Soviet Union ethnology was considered a subfield of history (Humphrey 1984: 311).
3. On the treatment of religious practices as 'superstitious' in Asian contexts, see Malarney (2002) and Nedostup (2009).

4. In the 1980s, as Vietnam was in an economic crisis, state authorities reluctantly turned a blind eye to small-scale grey-market trading operations of various kinds, including street vendors in major cities (Đặng Phong 2005).

References

Bayly, Susan. 2004. 'Vietnamese Intellectuals in Revolutionary and Postcolonial Times', *Critique of Anthropology* 24(3): 320–44.

———. 2007. *Asian Voices in a Postcolonial Age: Vietnam, India and Beyond.* Cambridge: Cambridge University Press.

———. 2009. 'Vietnamese Narratives of Tradition, Exchange and Friendship in the Worlds of the Global Socialist Ecumene', in Harry West and Pavarthi Raman (eds), *Enduring Socialism: Explorations of Revolution, Transformation and Restoration.* Oxford: Berghahn Books, pp. 125–47.

Bình Nguyên Lộc. 1971. *Nguồn gốc Mã Lai của dân tộc Việt Nam.* Sài Gòn: Bách Bộc.

Beresford, Melanie. 2008. 'Doi Moi in Review: The Challenges of Building Market Socialism in Vietnam', *Journal of Contemporary Asia* 38(2): 221–43.

Bohannan, Paul, and Laura Bohannan. 1968. *Tiv Economy.* Evanston, IL: Northwestern University Press.

Bromlei, Yulian Vladimirovich. 1974. 'Thử phân loại các loại hình tộc người (An attempt at classifying ethnic communities)', *Tạp chí Dân tộc học* 1(1974): 98–122.

Bùi Xuân Đính. 2016. 'Từ Chi và nghiên cứu về làng xã – những điều ông dạy học trò', in Nguyễn Văn Sửu, Nguyễn Văn Huy, Lâm Bá Nam and Vương Xuân Tình (eds), *Nhân học ở Việt Nam: Một số vấn đề lịch sử, nghiên cứu và đào tạo* [Anthropology in Vietnam: History, Research and Teaching]. Hà Nội: Knowledge, pp. 143–54.

Buxughin, E.P. 1961. *Dân tộc học đại cương [An introduction to ethnology],* Vietnamese translation by Đặng Công Lý and Lê Thế Thép. Hanoi: Education Press.

Carsten, Janet. 1989. 'Cooking Money: Gender and the Symbolic Transformation of Means of Exchange in a Malay Fishing Community', in Jonathan Parry and Maurice Bloch (eds), *Money and the Morality of Exchange.* Cambridge: Cambridge University Press, pp. 117–41.

Cheboksarov, N.N., and I.A. Cheboksarova. 1985. *Narody, rasy, kul'tury* [Nations, Races, Cultures]. Moscow: Nauka.

Chu Khứ Phi. *Lĩnh ngoại đại đáp [Vietnamese translation].* Library of Faculty of History, College of Social Sciences and Humanities, Hanoi.

Cuisinier, Jeanne. 1946. *Les Muong: geographie humaine et sociologie.* Paris: Institut d'ethnologi.

Đặng Phong. 2005. *Lịch sử kinh tế Việt Nam 1945–2000 (tập 2).* Hà Nội: Khoa học Xã hội.

Evans, Grant. 1985. 'Vietnamese Communist Anthropology', *Canberra Anthropology* 8(1–2): 116–47.

Evans, Grant. 2005. 'Indigenous and Indigenized Anthropology in Asia', in Jan Van Bremen, Eyal Ben-Ari, Syed Farid Alatas (eds), *Asian Anthropology.* London: Routledge, pp. 44–54.

Frazer, James. 1976. *The Golden Bough.* London: Macmillan.

Gellner, Ernest. 1977. 'Ethnicity and Anthropology in the Soviet Union', *European Journal of Sociology* 18(2): 201–20.

Gourou, Pierre. 1936. *Les Paysans du Delta Tonkinois.* Paris: Les Editions d'Art et d'Histoire.

Humphrey, Caroline. 1984. 'Some Recent Developments in Ethnography in the USSR', *Man* 19(2): 310–20.
Huntington, Samuel. 1996. *The Clash of Civilizations and the Remaking of World Order*. New York: Simon and Schuster.
Keyes, Charles. 2002. 'Presidential Address: "The Peoples of Asia" – Science and Politics in the Classification of Ethnic Groups in Thailand, China, and Vietnam', *Journal of Asian Studies* 61(4): 1163–203.
Kleinen, John. 2005. 'Tropicality and Topicality: Pierre Gourou and the Genealogy of French Colonial Scholarship on Rural Vietnam', *Singapore Journal of Tropical Geography* 26(3): 339–58.
Kwon, Heonik. 2007. 'The Dollarization of Vietnamese Ghost Money', *Journal of the Royal Anthropological Institute* 13: 73–90.
Leroi-Gourhan, André. 1945. *Evolution et Techniques*. Paris: Éditions Albin Michel.
Luong, Hy Van. 2006. 'Structure, Practice, and History: Contemporary Anthropological Research on Vietnam', *Journal of Vietnamese Studies* 1(1–2): 371–409.
Lương Văn Hy. 2001. 'Lời giới thiệu', in Emily Schultz and Robert Lavenda (eds), *Nhân học: Một quan điểm về tình trạng nhân sinh* [Anthropology: A Perspective on the Human Condition]. Hà Nội: Chính trị Quốc gia, pp. 7–8.
______. 2016. 'Nhân học: Lịch sử, nghiên cứu về Việt Nam, và đào tạo', in Nguyễn Văn Sửu, Nguyễn Văn Huy, Lâm Bá Nam and Vương Xuân Tình (eds), *Nhân học ở Việt Nam: Một số vấn đề lịch sử, nghiên cứu và đào tạo* [Anthropology in Vietnam: History, Research and Teaching]. Hà Nội: Knowledge, pp. 11–36.
Malarney, Shaun. 2002. *Culture, Ritual and Revolution in Vietnam*. Honolulu: University of Hawai'i Press.
Marr, David. 1978. 'The State of the Social Sciences in Vietnam', *Bulletin of Concerned Asian Scholars* 10(4): 70–77.
Nedostup, Rebecca. 2009. *Superstitious Regimes: Religion and the Politics of Chinese Modernity*. Cambridge, MA: Harvard University Asia Center.
Nguyễn Duy Thiệu. 2016. 'Từ Chi với trường phái dân tộc học đề cao nghiên cứu thực địa', in Nguyễn Văn Sửu, Nguyễn Văn Huy, Lâm Bá Nam and Vương Xuân Tình (eds), *Nhân học ở Việt Nam: Một số vấn đề lịch sử, nghiên cứu và đào tạo* [Anthropology in Vietnam: History, Research and Teaching]. Hà Nội: Knowledge, pp. 155–72.
Nguyễn Huệ Chi. 2005. 'Từ Chi – Anh tôi', *Tạp chí Văn hoá Nghệ thuật* 8(2005). http://www.talawas.org/talaDB/showFile.php?res=5129&rb=0306.
Nguyen Van Chinh. 2019. 'Vietnamese Anthropology at the Crossroads of Change', in Eric Thompson and Vineeta Sinha (eds), *Southeast Asian Anthropologies*, Singapore: NUS Press, pp. 83–110.
Nguyễn Văn Tiệp. 2011. 'Từ thực tiễn đào tạo và nghiên cứu dân tộc học/nhân học Việt Nam, góp thêm ý kiến về việc xây dựng và phát triển Nhân học hiện nay', *Tạp chí phát triển Khoa học và Công nghệ* 14(3): 5–18.
Phan Hữu Dật. 1973. *Cơ sở dân tộc học*. Hà Nội: Đại học và Trung học chuyên nghiệp.
Phạm Như Cương. 1989. 'Xác lập những định hướng xã hội cho sự phát triển của Tây Nguyên', in Ủy ban Khoa học Xã hội Việt Nam, *Tây Nguyên trên đường phát triển*. Hà Nội: Khoa học Xã hội, pp. 9–17.
Pine, Frances. 2002. 'Dealing with Money: Zlotys, Dollars and Other Currencies in the Polish Highlands', in Ruth Mandel and Caroline Humphrey (eds), *Markets and Moralities: Ethnographies of Postsocialism*. Oxford: Berg, pp. 77–97.
Standing Committee of the National Assembly. 1969. *Điều lệ tóm tắt của hợp tác xã sản xuất nông nghiệp*. Hà Nội.

Tishkov, Valery. 1992. 'The Crisis in Soviet Ethnography', *Current Anthropology* 33(4): 371–94.
Tokarev, Sergey Aleksandrovich. 1976. 'Góp phần nghiên cứu phương pháp khảo sát dân tộc học về văn hóa vật chất', *Tạp chí Dân tộc học* 2: 114–25.
Trần Từ. 1978. *Hoa văn Mường*. Hanoi: Văn hóa dân tộc.
______. 1984. *Cơ cấu tổ chức của làng Việt cổ truyền ở Bắc Bộ*. Hà Nội: Khoa học Xã hội.
Truong Huyen Chi. 2014. 'The Margin Contextualized: Nguyễn Từ Chi (1925–1995) and an Alternative Ethnography in the Socialist Vietnam', *Moussons* 24, doi:10.4000/moussons.3116. http://journals.openedition.org/moussons/3116.
Tylor, Edward. 1871. *Primitive Culture*. London: John Murray.

9

The Ideal of Intellectual Exchange
Study Abroad, Affect and the Ambivalences of Citizenship in Post-Suharto Indonesia

Nicholas J. Long

Writing for a volume on 'intellectual exchange' compiled in honour of Susan Bayly, my mind immediately turns to a series of fieldwork conversations that emerged from my collaboration with Susan on our ESRC-funded project, 'The Social Life of Achievement and Competitiveness in Indonesia and Vietnam'. This project had involved no small amount of intellectual exchange between the two of us as we compared how the struggle to become competitive participants in a global knowledge economy had led distinctive concepts of 'achievement' to emerge in our respective fieldsites. Susan had shared with me details of Vietnam's Human Capacity Research Centre, an institution that provides psychic, geomantic and paranormal services while also seeking to 'scientise the Centre's provision of psychic ... expertise by setting credible attainment markers ... comparable to those of the nation's other classes of doers and attainers' (Bayly 2013: 175). I often discussed this nugget of comparative ethnography with the people I spoke to during fieldwork in Indonesia's Riau Islands Province. This could itself be understood as an act of intellectual exchange – sharing the findings of another scholar in order to broaden my interlocutors' awareness – although I was also interested to gauge their reactions. Some were dismissive. 'Sounds like the Vietnamese have been watching too much Harry Potter!' laughed one government official. Yet for others, the vignette awakened their own yearnings for intellectual exchange – defined here broadly, following Carter and Spirling (2008: 375), as 'the transfer of knowledge, ideas, and techniques'. 'Can you get a Bachelor's Degree in Supernatural Skills if you study at that institution in Vietnam?' wondered Padmana, a softly-spoken paranormal practitioner in his early twenties.[1] 'I want one.'

Though Padmana may have been disappointed to learn that the Human Capacity Research Centre was no Hogwarts of Hanoi, his remarks raise several issues of direct relevance to an anthropology of intellectual exchange. One, for instance, concerns how we define the boundaries of 'the intellectual': do occult knowledge and supernatural abilities fall outside this domain, or can the divisions between such traditions of knowledge and those of the secular sciences be 'bridged', as Bayly intimates in her contributions to this volume?

However, what was most striking to me about my conversation with Padmana was his fierce, immediate and viscerally palpable yearning – despite the many opportunities he had to undertake apprenticeships with paranormal practitioners across Indonesia – to gain a formal qualification in his craft from an overseas institution. In that, he resembled many of his contemporaries, who also dreamed that they, or their children, would one day get to study abroad. In this chapter I draw on over thirty-six months of fieldwork to ask why and to what effect the aspiration to partake in formalized intellectual exchange overseas has become instantiated across Indonesia. Theoretically, I use this material to outline what an anthropology of intellectual exchange might have to gain by approaching intellectual exchange not as a practice, but as an object of desire and contemplation – as an ideal.

Envisioning Intellectual Exchange

What kind of analytic object should 'intellectual exchange' be for an anthropologist? One possibility is to consider it as a practice. Indeed, many scholars writing of intellectual exchange do so in a resolutely empiricist manner, tracing the means by which knowledge develops and ideas spread as a result of particular, situated encounters. Their work offers valuable insights into the genesis of intellectual traditions. Moreover, by revealing how collective processes of dialogue and collaboration are integral to the generation and circulation of ideas, such studies displace commonplace narratives of 'individual brilliance' or the 'hegemonic imposition' of epistemological frameworks in favour of more subtle and equitable attributions of responsibility for intellectual developments (see e.g. Lewis 2004; Merkel 2017). Paradoxically, however, while this literature has made important contributions by insisting upon the centrality of exchange to intellectual history, there has been, as Merkel (2021) notes, a tendency to leave intellectual exchange itself undertheorized. A second important strand of scholarship on the practice of intellectual exchange thus comes from philosophical anthropologists and participant observers of intellectual settings who examine how factors ranging from linguistic conventions to institutional hierarchies can either facilitate or impede the articulation and circulation of ideas and knowledge (e.g. Davern and Eitzen 1995; Ermarth 1993; Garnett 2006). This body of work often carries a normative thrust, identifying limitations in current practice and inviting readers to envision arrangements through which intellectual exchange might be conducted otherwise.

Anthropologists of intellectual exchange can engage with such normative interventions in several ways. These are conversations that are deeply relevant to our profession and which demand our participation: important questions are raised regarding our own intellectual exchange practices, and whether and how the discipline might benefit from various kinds of institutional reform (see e.g. Diallo and Friborg 2021; Lee 2021). Yet alongside inviting new ways of envisaging intellectual futures, such normatively oriented conversations also reveal something important about intellectual exchange as an ethnographic phenomenon. They remind us that the experience of intellectual exchange is mediated by its proximity to or divergence from particular *ideals* of how intellectual exchange could or should be practised – in ways that may prove consequential not only for the trajectory of the exchange, but for various aspects of the participants' subjectivities, not least their propensity to participate in future exchanges. With this observation – which holds true regardless of one's normative stance on the ideals in question – I hope to nudge the anthropological study of intellectual exchange beyond both the historical and normative tendencies that predominate in the existing literature (important though these both are), to instead explore how the affective dynamics surrounding ideals of intellectual exchange can prove constitutive of subjectivity.

In making this argument, I build on three key theoretical insights from existing anthropological work on ideals. The first is that the exercise of normative reason is neither necessary nor sufficient for an ideal to take hold. Instead, ideals are reflective of what Moore (2011: 15–18) terms 'the ethical imagination'. This helpfully expansive concept refers to 'the form and means ... by which individuals imagine relationships to themselves and to others', bringing conscious thought and social imaginaries into the same analytical frame as embodiment, affect and fantasy to understand how hopes, desires and (dis)satisfactions are forged. The second insight is that the experience of disjunctions between ideals and reality can spur a wide range of social behaviours and forms of cultural production. If, in some cases, ideals are subjected to scrutiny and debate, even coming to be displaced (Mayblin 2012; Stewart 1996), in others, great effort is spent on mediating such disconnects (Miller 2001). In others still, the difficulty of realizing an ideal may entrench its idealization (Trawick 1990) while suffusing everyday life with emotionally contagious feelings of ambivalence, melancholy and dissatisfaction (Gammeltoft 2018). Which of these outcomes will occur in any given case is far from assured, but is shaped in part by the hold an ideal has over us – which is precisely why it is so important to understand ideals through a rubric such as the ethical imagination, in which affect, fantasy and attachment carry as much weight as deliberative reason. The final insight is that the culturally generative force of ideals can be evident even when they relate to lives other than one's own. By reflecting on and discussing the experiences of friends, celebrities, fictional characters, or even abstracted social types, ideals can be both reworked and upheld, yardsticks for measuring what is typical and unusual are forged, and a wider, emotionally shaded sense of how the world operates is established (Mayblin 2012; Miller 2001; Stewart 1996). This point is especially important within the context of this volume because it underscores that intellectual exchange is not just a matter of relevance and interest to the people undertaking intellectual pursuits. Rather, it can be of salience to much broader publics – especially in the context of a self-proclaimed global knowledge economy, in which education, innovation and human resource quality can all be seen as essential for a prosperous national future. This, as I now show, is very much the case in Indonesia – where the possibility of undertaking specific forms of intellectual exchange (most notably formal study overseas) has become not just a personal ambition for the academically inclined but a widespread public concern.

Transnational Intellectual Exchange: The History of an Indonesian Aspiration

During the colonial period, the numbers of Indonesians pursuing, or even contemplating, study abroad was minimal. Southeast Asia had of course long been integrated into a 'broader Islamic ecumene' (Hefner 2009: 14), with small numbers of Muslims travelling to study in the Middle East; such opportunities increased in number following the opening of the Suez Canal and the legalization of the *hajj* (Dhofier 1992: 21). Moreover, as both Dutch- and Chinese-medium schools became established in the Netherlands East Indies, some Indonesians began to pursue further education abroad: sometimes in China; sometimes in Europe (Stutje 2013; Theo 2018: 51). Nevertheless, all these opportunities were available only to a wealthy few: aristocrats, urban elites and higher commercial classes. The vast majority of Indonesians had no access to formal schooling during this time, let alone higher education (van der Kroef 1957).

After independence, developing the country's education system became an urgent policy priority. Simultaneously, scholarships were becoming increasingly significant as expressions of aid, solidarity and diplomacy during an era of decolonization and Cold War tensions (Tournès and Scott-Smith 2018). Opportunities proliferated for Indonesians to study abroad. As Dragojlovic (2010: 59) notes, 'Indonesia, under the active leadership of President Sukarno had taken a major diplomatic role in the affairs of the Third World' while simultaneously 'balanc[ing] its foreign policy in relation to the USSR, China and USA. This foreign policy facilitated a rich transnational exchange across the countries of the Eastern bloc, the USA and the Non-aligned Movement'. Following the anti-communist violence of 1965–66 and the associated rise to power of President Suharto, however, diplomatic ties with the Eastern and Soviet Blocs were frozen. Many Indonesians studying in socialist states became political exiles.

An interest in transnational education nevertheless persisted. A key anxiety for Suharto's 'New Order' regime – authoritarian, developmentalist and strongly influenced by modernization theory – was that the Indonesian population lacked the skills, knowledge and 'development-mindedness' necessary for prosperity (see MacDougall 1976). Such concerns persist to this day, and are currently expressed through the idiom of 'human resource quality' (*kualitas sumber daya manusia*), reflecting the extent to which 'policy-making in Indonesia is heavily influenced by the theory of human capital investment introduced by Becker' (Indrawati and Kuncoro 2021: 33). Indeed, Becker's ideas (1964), which posit training, work experience and education as foundational to both personal and national development and prosperity, are widely subscribed to by Indonesian citizens, who frequently emphasize education's emancipatory potential (see, e.g., Newberry 2017; Schut 2019), even as they sometimes lament their education system's present shortcomings. Despite high rates of educational participation, Indonesian school and university graduates have less competitive skillsets than their international counterparts; reasons include knowledge deficits among educators, outdated facilities, and a lack of research infrastructure in Indonesian universities (Indrawati and Kuncoro 2021: 32–44). Pending domestic reforms, then, much hope is attached to the prospect of an education overseas – particularly at tertiary level, when the knowledge and skills being taught are most advanced and specialized (Welch 2007).

Most Indonesians whom I met during fieldwork dreamed of pursuing international study in a Western nation or in capitalist Asia (e.g. Singapore, Malaysia, Japan or South Korea), an imaginary that seems to preserve the (geo)political outlooks cultivated under the New Order. Where students actually end up studying, however, reflects the availability of financial support. While the US has tempered its provision of scholarships following the end of the Cold War, other states, including Japan, India, Turkey, Singapore and China, have begun to identify higher education bursaries as a key arena for international cooperation and diplomacy (King 2011; Tournès and Scott-Smith 2018: 17–19). Amidst these developments, and increasing pressures to self-fund a transnational education where possible, Guggenheim (2012: 149) estimates around forty-five thousand Indonesians are studying abroad at any given moment in time.

In a recent article, Gellert (2015: 386–88) critiques contemporary Indonesian educational attitudes as unduly oriented towards securing membership in a community of 'global, English-speaking, placeless professionals and consumers' – a point he sees exemplified in, for example, a teacher's hope that a high-potential student might one day contact him to say (in English), '*Sir, I have received a scholarship to America*'. Gellert is certainly correct to observe that such cosmopolitan opportunities are disproportionately available to an already 'privileged and transnationalised segment of the population' (2015: 389) and that other realizations of 'potential' should be celebrated and encouraged. Yet one should not overstate the extent to which membership of a transnationalized community is integral, rather than incidental, to aspirations of study overseas. Al Qurtuby (2020: 47–48), for instance, argues that Indonesian Muslims' desire for international education should be understood with reference to the longstanding Islamic concept of *rihla* (travel embarked upon in search of knowledge, whether religious or secular). Endorsed in the Qur'an and Hadiths, *rihla* not only offers Muslims the promise of wisdom but also of receiving God's rewards and being assured entry into Paradise after death (2020: 48). Moreover, for many Indonesians, citizens and policy makers alike, the appeal of international study has long been that it allows students to bring the skills and knowledge they acquire overseas *back to Indonesia* so these new talents can be put into practice to improve the national situation. Some research participants noted that returning to Indonesia was an explicit condition of receiving a scholarship – although Indonesians who have studied abroad frequently cite their 'frustration' at being unable to use internationally-acquired skills and knowledge (whether because of inadequate facilities or entrenched attitudes among colleagues) as a principal downside of the experience (Cannon 2000; Keats 1969). Such findings significantly complicate the claim, latent in Gellert's critique of Indonesian education, but stated more baldly by several other prominent Southeast Asianists, that foreign education is best understood as one of the 'status or positional goods' most urgently sought by Asia's emerging middle classes (Chua 2000: xi) and that Indonesians value education more as a 'symbol of modernity', or for the title it conveys, than for the knowledge transfer it entails (Gerke 2000: 148). While international education undoubtedly offers personal benefits to one's status, it is important to recognize that these frequently sit alongside, and to some extent derive from, the meritorious implications of becoming a conduit of intellectual exchange.

Equally, 'people who study overseas' are widely considered to be important national assets. There are of course cases in which overseas graduates are viewed ambivalently upon their return and accused of arrogance or of having forgotten their roots. Yet even in these cases there is typically a grudging respect, linked to both the skills and knowledge they have acquired and a sense that they must be people of exceptional potential to have been accepted by an overseas institution. Margareta Astaman, an Indonesian writer who studied in Singapore, summarizes the prevailing attitude – which she too had internalized – as she describes her departure from Indonesia:

> Imagine an early morning flight full of the cleverest kids from across Indonesia. Our heads are held high, full of hopes and self-belief. The people accompanying us have proud smiles on their lips.
>
> *We are the chosen ones.* The champions above all the other school champions .... Our talent has already attracted the attention of the Singaporean government. We are not like domestic workers or manual labourers, who hold the status of *Foreign Worker.* We have been invited as *Foreign Talent.* (Astaman 2010: 12–13)

To summarize, in contemporary Indonesia, issues such as the destinies of high-achieving, high-potential citizens and the circuitries of intellectual exchange are not just matters of individual aspiration but of broader public and political concern. The corollary of this is that public understandings of how such nationally significant intellectual exchange is occurring can prove highly consequential for Riau Islanders' (and other Indonesians') sense of their place in the world, the futures they consider possible, and their relationship to the state. In the following sections, I develop this line of argument by turning to two discursive flashpoints that featured prominently during my fieldwork: the question of access to the possibility of intellectual exchange via overseas study, and the question of how Indonesians studying overseas are treated – an issue which became especially heated following the mysterious death of an Indonesian student on a Singaporean campus in 2009. The analysis reveals that although travelling overseas for intellectual exchange may be experienced in various ways by individual Indonesians (the fulfilment of one's national duty; an ordeal; an exciting escape from a nation in which one feels limited or excluded), the broader ideal of intellectual exchange serves as a touchstone for public feelings of disappointment in the Indonesian government and despair for the nation's future. Such feelings warrant analytic attention for several reasons. In the most extreme cases they may turn Indonesians away from the political ideal of the democratic nation-state and towards radically alternative forms of government, such as Islamic theocracy or a return to authoritarianism (Long 2016). Yet even absent such impact upon political horizons, they can imbue everyday life with a tangible sense of despondency and unfairness – what Throop (2014) might label a 'moral mood' – thereby proving highly consequential for what it is to live in Indonesia today.

Accessing Intellectual Exchange

> *I have to get that scholarship. There is no other option, I have to get it!* Those were the words that rang in my heart every time I stood in front of the mirror. That scholarship was a ticket out of a life I couldn't be proud of. (Hirata 2005: 272)

These words are spoken by Ikal, the narrator of Andrea Hirata's novel *Laskar Pelangi* ('The Rainbow Troops') shortly before the story's end. The book follows the fate of ten disadvantaged students attending a ramshackle school on the island of Belitung who nevertheless have a passion for education and learning. Having graduated, and after twelve unfulfilling years spent as a postal worker, Ikal sees an advert for a scholarship in the European Union. He enrols in an undergraduate degree, studies obsessively at the Indonesian Institute of Sciences, and, thanks to an outstanding research proposal on transfer pricing models for the telecommunications industry, is able to 'repay [his] moral debt' to his teachers and classmates by securing the funding. This denouement is bittersweet, however, as Lintang – the most talented of the pupils – must abandon his schooling following his father's death and ends the story working on a sand barge.

Laskar Pelangi became Indonesia's bestselling novel of all time: an outcome that simultaneously reflects its charming, memorable characters and its trenchant critique of inequality. This latter concern is expressed most vividly in the fate of Lintang, but is also evident in Ikal's own struggle to secure an opportunity to study abroad, doing so against the odds, and only as a result of truly prodigious efforts. Indeed, given the importance of scholarships to the fulfilment of personal destinies and societal obligations – for very few Indonesians could afford to study overseas without them – the question of their availability and distribution featured keenly in my interlocutors' minds. One of the requests that I most frequently received during fieldwork was to advise on how to secure a scholarship to study in the United Kingdom.

An unusual version of such a request came in 2013, when Pak Rafiq, an official in the Riau Islands Department of Education, summoned me urgently to his office. He and his colleagues were brainstorming plans for enabling students from the Riau Islands to study overseas and were eager for my input. Every year, Rafiq explained, the provincial government planned to award their top ten high school graduates full scholarships to study overseas in one of five areas: economics, engineering, marine sciences, tourism, and religious studies. The selection of these fields was interesting in itself, revealing much about how the provincial government envisaged the areas in which high-quality human resources were required. Economics and engineering were necessary given the province's recent reliance on export-oriented manufacturing. Marine sciences and tourism had been identified as two particular growth areas for the Riau Islands province, the surface area of which was 96% water, and which boasted numerous beaches and heritage sites that were felt to have hitherto unrealized touristic potential. Meanwhile, the scholarships for religious studies reflected a growing conviction across Indonesia that religious piety was a principal line of defence against the evils of corruption (Rudnyckyj 2010).

The 'religious studies' being supported appeared to be exclusively Islamic; Rafiq and his colleagues had already decided that scholarships in this field should be taken up in Egypt. Their choice departs interestingly from the late twentieth-century view that Indonesians should pursue their interest in Islam at Western universities so as 'to integrate national and Islamic intellectualisms' (Dhofier 1992: 26). However, it can be seen as reflecting both an illustrious history of Indonesian Muslims travelling to Egypt to further their knowledge of Islam (including Indonesia's former president Abdurrahman Wahid) and the more recent enthusiasm among Indonesians for travelling to the Middle East so as to become active participants in global Islamic discourse (Laffan 2004: 20–21). The office had also settled on Germany as the location for engineering – a selection that appeared to have been inspired by the auspicious biography of New Order technocrat and post-Suharto president B.J. Habibie. Habibie, who held a doctorate in aerospace engineering from RWTH Aachen University, was respected for this achievement across Indonesia but was an especially revered figure in the Riau Islands owing to his role in making the island of Batam an area of special economic development (Nur 2000). However, the question of where scholarships for the other three disciplines would be held remained undecided.

My summons had been inspired by the idea that, as a faculty member at the London School of Economics and Political Science, I might be able to broker a scholarship for Riau Islands students to study economics in London every year. Such hopes were quickly scotched when I revealed that the Indonesian high school leaving certificate is not recognized as sufficiently rigorous for admission to the LSE, but Rafiq did a good job of hiding his disappointment at this news. His department was, he explained, planning a reconnaissance trip to Europe in the near future to see what was available and whether they could broker any Memoranda of Understanding (MoUs). My input would still be helpful for working out where to target.

A key priority was to identify where would be best for tourism studies. Rafiq's own inclination was that Austria would be good, and Switzerland even more so, but his junior colleague Iskandar had doubts. These only intensified when I mentioned that, to my knowledge, much of the tourism in Austria and Switzerland revolved around skiing. 'We should be sending them to Australia,' Iskandar insisted, 'the attractions are more like the ones we have in Indonesia.' Rafiq, however, had been thinking that Australia would be a better fit for marine sciences. The department had originally hoped to send the marine tranche of students to Japan, partly because Iskandar had identified a scholarship scheme in which students received contributions towards their living costs, but also because Japan was renowned as a powerful fishing nation. To their dismay, however, they had struggled to find any marine sciences programmes in Japan that focused on the fisheries sector. Perhaps, Rafiq reflected, Japan could be a good option for economics....

Several aspects of this ethnographic vignette stand out as being of interest. Firstly, we see how the planning and aspirational labour taking place within this government office are shaped by particular normative visions of intellectual exchange. Even under the status quo, the majority of the Riau Islands' top ten students would likely go on to further study or training. What Rafiq, Iskandar and their colleagues are attempting to do is insert the students into particular circuits of exchange, envisaged as generating maximal value for the students – and for the province – upon their anticipated return to Indonesia. We can see clearly how the governmental vision for intellectual exchange is driven by a specific ethical imagination, underpinned by market logics and religious nationalism, rather than, say, a commitment to supporting individual vocations or aptitudes: there is little scope in this scheme for a gifted Riau Islands biochemist to discover a cure for cancer, let alone for a budding historian, literature scholar or anthropologist to hone their craft. Moreover, absent an existing institutional framework in the Riau Islands that could facilitate such travels, the vignette points to an incipient ethical imagination of how a circuitry of intellectual exchange could and should be established. Governmental ideals are informed by the exercise of deliberative reason (as in Iskandar's discovery of generous maintenance support in Japan), but also more affective, unconscious or instinctive elements, from the aura of familiar prestige that comes from following in the footsteps of presidents to the sense that places such as Switzerland and Austria *must* be good places to study tourism – either because of their impressive reputation as tourist destinations or, as more cynical research participants were inclined to suggest, because of the education officials' own desires to visit them and ski through snowy vistas under the pretext of establishing an MoU. Equally striking was how volatile prospective destinations could be – their prioritization contingent on the vicissitudes of office interactions, and easily deflected by a suggestion from a colleague or an intervention by a visiting anthropologist. Even as intellectual exchange was unflinchingly sought out, its possible dynamics seemed highly malleable.

Despite such openness to possibility, however, almost ten years on, no scholarship arrangements for Riau Islands students have been established. The limited opportunities to study overseas have become a source of great public frustration in the Riau Islands, yet where blame should be apportioned is far from clear. In interviews with high-achieving schoolchildren, I repeatedly encountered claims of disappointment that their achievements were not better 'valued' (*dihargai*) and was often asked to advise the government that more overseas scholarships should be made available. Many research participants suspected there was ample money in departmental budgets for such opportunities but that it was being squandered on vanity projects, corrupted away, or diverted to those who had personal connections with government officials (see also Long forthcoming). Such misdeeds may sometimes be taking place, but ethnographic encounters such as the one outlined above suggested to me that education department officials were often in as deep a thrall to the prospect of overseas intellectual exchange as the students for whom they were planning, but simply unable to negotiate a suitable arrangement with universities that preferred to have greater control over their own admissions or to allocate block scholarships at the national level.

In practice, it seems unlikely that the inequities of access frustrating my interlocutors could be fully resolved without fundamental structural changes to global education markets. However, the predominant narrative that sees intellectual exchange as wholly possible if only there were better, more responsible action on the part on individual state officials proves a seductive one. Rather than positioning Indonesians as globalization's losers, it allows a sense of parity with other nations to be maintained, at least when it comes to one's most able achievers. The problem is one of how the state mediates access to financial support, rather than either cultural, structural or personal circumstances constraining the ability of Indonesia's brightest, or intractable structural obstacles that lie outside Indonesia's control. Paradoxically, then, while intellectual exchange is often held up as something that stands to equip high-potential young people with the knowledge and insights needed to render them ever-more valuable assets to the nation, the expectations and desires surrounding this ideal, the disappointments to which idealizing intellectual exchange can give rise, and the resultant clusters of narratives that are used to make sense of the situation, all contribute to feelings of disenchantment and alienation towards Indonesia and its (system of) government.

An Opportunity to Die For?

Never has study abroad been as hotly discussed across Indonesia as in the weeks and months following 2 March 2009. That was the day on which David Hartanto Widjaya,[2] an Indonesian undergraduate studying Electrical and Electronic Engineering at Singapore's Nanyang Technological University (hereafter NTU), fell four storeys to his death from a link bridge on campus while his final year project (FYP) supervisor, Prof. Chan Kap Luk, lay bleeding from stab wounds in a nearby office.

As the coroner's inquest unfurled, the Singaporean media painted a grim picture of the events leading up to that fateful morning. David, an Indonesian Buddhist of Chinese ancestry, had been 'an outstanding student who came to Singapore on an ASEAN scholarship', wrote *The New Paper*, but from the second year onwards, he had 'changed' (Chong and Yong 2009a). He no longer studied diligently throughout the year. Instead, he skipped lessons and tutorials, spending hours every day playing *World of Warcraft*, *Defence of the Ancients* and *Destiny Online*. His GPA had deteriorated to the point that his ASEAN scholarship was withdrawn. He was also struggling to make headway with his FYP, a project provisionally entitled 'Multiview Acquisition for Person Adaptive 3D Display', which involved combining input from multiple cameras and projectors to create three-dimensional holograms. 'Things had become so bad,' the paper reported, 'that [David] was scared of [Prof Chan] ... He avoided the professor and would sneak away rather than face him because he had fallen behind.' Prof. Chan had even 'scolded him' at a weekly meeting because David had failed to give any update on his work.

Then, on the morning of 2 March, David turned up unexpectedly at his supervisor's office. Prof. Chan told the inquest that David had brought along a USB stick containing his FYP work (Chong and Yong 2009b). However, the office computer did not have the software necessary to run the demonstration David had prepared, nor did Chan have time to relocate to his lab. Chan therefore asked David to give a brief oral summary of what had been done, and listened to this overview while continuing to work on some lecture slides at his computer. David's voice became shaky, and he began mumbling indiscernible words. Then Chan felt a blow to his back. He spun around and saw David wielding a knife. A struggle ensued, during which Chan took control of the weapon. David fled from the office and, according to eyewitness reports, jumped to his death. Subsequent examination of David's laptop revealed a file entitled 'Last Word', composed on 25 January 2009, in which David described how difficult he was finding life at university in Singapore, his fears that he was not strong enough to continue, and his thoughts of ending his life. Based on this evidence, and reports from forensic pathologists, the Singapore state coroner ruled David's death a suicide (Spykerman and Thomas 2009).

This version of events exhibits a narrative and ethnopsychological logic widespread in Singapore and the Malay World, namely that of the man who '[upon being] grievously offended responds with uncontrollable rage' (Lee 1981: 237), embarking upon a murderous and self-annihilating *amok* rampage.[3] *Amok* has conventionally been associated with the Malay mind, rather than the psychology of ethnically Chinese individuals such as David, although there have been reports of *amok* among Chinese who have 'lived in close proximity' with Malays in both Singapore and Indonesia (Kon 1994: 688). Yet, as Williamson (2007: 348–49) notes, the discourse of *amok* has its own pernicious poetics: in British Malaya, the 'madness' of *amok* violence served as a potent sign of the 'anti-modern'; a trope that secured 'a colonial divide between coloniser and colonised' and thus served as a source of fascination and pleasure. It is not unreasonable to suggest that the fevered Singaporean interest surrounding the David Widjaya case – while never formally labelling it as a case of *amok* – results in part from a similar frisson arising at the thought of 'mad', 'anti-modern' Indonesian violence encroaching into the hyper-rational technomodern space of a Singaporean electrical engineering faculty. Certainly, David emerges in the Singaporean narrative as the antithesis of an ideal achiever-citizen poised to flourish in the knowledge economy. Troubled, indolent, struggling or insane, his intellectual potential becomes almost the least noteworthy aspect of his story. It certainly does not seem to have characterized his time in Singapore: Prof. Chan told the inquest that he had only discovered that David was an ASEAN scholar after his death (Chong and Yong 2009b).

However, David's demise prompted a different set of accounts in Indonesia, where many citizens considered the coroner's verdict a cover-up for a more sinister truth: David had been murdered. This possibility had first been mooted by David's parents. They refused to believe that their son would take his own life, not least because the alleged emotional triggers were unconvincing. As a relatively wealthy family, they could cover the additional tuition costs arising from the withdrawal of David's scholarship, especially since he was soon to graduate. They further claimed that his FYP was already 90% complete, casting doubt on the contention that the stress of the project had tipped David over the edge. David's father also reported meeting a witness who had heard someone screaming 'they are trying to kill me' in the vicinity of Prof. Chan's office at the time David died. The family assembled an independent 'Verification Team' (*Tim Verifikasi*) composed of twelve bloggers and citizen journalists from across Indonesia, which travelled to Singapore to inspect the crime scene and speak to people on campus. The team also solicited an independent forensic analysis, which highlighted details – such as the number of wounds on David's body, and the angle at which his ankle had broken – that appeared inconsistent with the accounts given by Prof. Chan and on-campus witnesses. Suspicions were stoked further after Zhou Zheng, a project officer in NTU's School of Electrical and Electronics Engineering, was found hanged in his staff apartment on 6 March, and Hu Kunlun, a research fellow in the same school, was killed in a road traffic accident on 27 March. Many Indonesians suspected these deaths to be linked to David's.

My friend Wilson, an irrepressible Toba Batak in his forties, was convinced that David had been the victim of foul play. After the Singaporean Coroner's Court had issued its verdict, members of the Indonesian press had been invited to inspect the evidence and ask any questions they had regarding the case. Wilson, a seasoned Riau Islands journalist, had been among them. He shared the story with me and a host of other Bataks from his patrilineal group at a lively dinner following a wedding at a local church. He told us how he had seen all the evidence relating to the case and how there was only one conclusion to be reached.

The truth, Wilson explained, was that David Hartanto Widjaya was a genius who had discovered all sorts of extraordinary things, devising incredible inventions that his supervisor had never even thought of. Prof. Chan had wanted David to stay with him in Singapore to do a Ph.D. so they could develop new technologies for Singapore, but David had refused because he was determined to return to Indonesia and use his knowledge and skills there. After David had declined Prof. Chan's offer, the NTU academic realized exactly what was at stake if David were to return home. David had the brilliance and the aptitude to develop new forms of technology that would lead to Singapore losing out to Indonesia – one example being a new form of 'hand phone' in which one would make calls by speaking directly into the palm of one's hand.[4] Unable to stand the thought of Indonesia gaining access to this superior technology, Prof. Chan had initially attempted to stab David with a knife. When this proved unsuccessful, he had pushed David off the link bridge. Supposed 'eyewitnesses' were either in on the plot or had been bribed to fabricate or falsify their testimonies. The one who had refused – Hu Kunlun – had been mown down by a car.[5] Wilson explained how he had initially thought that the cover-up was orchestrated by the campus authorities in order to protect NTU's reputation. Yet the coroner's complicity in promulgating the 'suicide' verdict led him to conclude that the whole affair had been orchestrated by none other than the Singaporean government, in order to subordinate (*menggagalkan*) Indonesia. Wilson spoke fluently and compellingly; his friends listened spellbound, shaking their heads and tutting at the audacity of the crime. 'So in other words, this was political?!' asked Gordon, a high school maths teacher, with horror in his voice. 'Turns out the world of overseas education is a dangerous one….'

In Wilson's narrative, David is cast not as a troubled youngster or delinquent gaming addict whose intellectual attainments presaged a tragic fall from grace that brought shame upon his nation. Rather, he is the quintessential Indonesian achiever. This is a common feature of Indonesian narratives surrounding David's death, many of which highlight that he had travelled to Mexico to represent Indonesia in the 2005 International Mathematics Olympiad – one of the most prestigious of all academic achievements.[6] David is repeatedly referred to as a 'prodigy', a 'genius' and 'brilliant'. One vlogger even dubs him 'the Tony Stark of Indonesia' (Arum Story 2021), referencing the alter-ego of 'Iron Man' in Marvel Comics and the recent Avengers film series: a billionaire industrialist and inventor with an interest in 3D holograms and an estimated IQ of 270 (Floorwalker 2019). The implication – that someone so talented could not plausibly have surrendered his studies to the pleasures of online gaming or embarked upon an *amok* rampage – often underpins Indonesians' sense that the story emanating from Singapore is somehow 'odd' (*aneh*; *janggal*), or lacking in credibility. As a fellow Chinese Indonesian studying in Singapore told Goh (2011: 9, emphasis mine): 'We didn't expect him to kill himself – *not for a scholar, and not in Singapore*'. Most striking in Wilson's account, however, is a presumption of David's ongoing determination to participate in intellectual exchange on nationalist, Indonesian terms. He would go to Singapore to learn from experts housed in world-class facilities, thereby realizing his evident potential, *but he would then return to Indonesia*. Indeed, it was his commitment to bringing his knowledge and capabilities back home, rather than using them to further the ambitions of Singaporean academic interests, that had ultimately cost him his life.

Wilson's mention of a 'hand phone' invention is relatively idiosyncratic, but it shares with most accounts a conviction that David's death was linked to his intellect and ingenuity, and a tendency to portray him as the tragic embodiment of the predominant Indonesian public ideal of intellectual exchange, which was itself reiterated and fortified through the extensive commentary on the incident. Such interpretations rapidly displaced the suspicions of a sexual or romantic dimension to the case, which some commentators, including David's brother, had proposed in its immediate aftermath (Chan 2009; Mesakh 2009). Most commentators suspected it was David's undergraduate research into display technologies that had led him to be killed. Such advanced technology had potential for a wide range of lucrative applications – including in military operations. Taking knowledge of it back to Indonesia would have made David a threat to Singaporean economic and tactical interests. Students and staff on the NTU campus told the Indonesian Verification Team that David's research was a 'Ph.D. calibre project', lamenting that it was he – of all possible students – who had died (Anon. 2009; Riza 2009). All this led many to suspect malpractice on the part of the Singaporean state, or perhaps sinister international networks that had Singapore under their control (Suwignyo 2013). Nevertheless, in all cases, the same underlying logic was clear: intellectual exchange, for Singaporeans, was not an untrammelled effervescence of ideas that should be pursued and gloried in for their own sake, but an exchange that could only take place on strictly defined terms that served to reinforce Singaporean hegemony. As Gordon the maths teacher had observed, the world of overseas education was not neutral and benign, but rife with politics and danger – especially for those best placed to benefit from it. From this perspective, to pick and choose destinations for international study based on their imagined prestige, sophistication and quality – as many Indonesian applicants do, and as I had observed being undertaken in my visit to Rafiq's office – was at best naïve and at worst negligent. It overlooked the extractive and predatory elements of schemes that purport to develop human resources, such as scholarship schemes that oblige foreign students to work for a period of time in Singapore so as to enhance the country's productivity (Febriani 2016: 604).

Indeed, themes of negligence and care can explain why the David Widjaya case has exercised such a powerful grip on the Indonesian imagination, continuing to provoke speculation even to this day. Conspiracist suspicions no doubt partly reflect the 'generalised distrust in appearances' that characterized the first decade of Reform-era Indonesia and spawned a generation of 'citizen reporters' and 'democratic detectives' determined to expose the ways in which political and economic interests were influencing various spheres of everyday life (Gibbings 2013). Iwan Piliang, the head of the Verification Team, had dedicated his life to exactly such practice, and had been motivated to assist David's family after watching footage of the incident on *Channel News Asia* and having an immediate feeling that something about the story was *janggal*, or not quite right (Riza 2009). But if suspicious dispositions had prompted many to suspect there was more to David's story than met the eye, what sustained their interest in the case was the Indonesian government's apparently lackadaisical attitude towards securing justice for a citizen who had potentially been murdered overseas.

Besides, David was not just any citizen. In an interview with the online magazine *Perspektif Baru* (Riza 2009), Iwan Piliang revealed that he had something he wanted to tell the government: not only was Indonesian culture (*kebudayaan*) in decline, but Indonesia had become a country in which civilization (*peradaban*) itself was reaching the lowest possible depths. 'David once elevated the name of Indonesia when he represented us in the Maths Olympiad in Mexico,' Piliang explained. 'Then he was taken by Singapore and given a scholarship because of the brilliance of his mind, and conducted research that could probably have given rise to something important. We stay silent about David, who was smart but described by his campus as someone brutal, because we never think of intangible qualities like intellect as assets.' Piliang explained how he hoped that one day soon, Indonesia would begin to value 'brilliant kids' as assets equivalent to metal ores and coal – not only seeking justice for them, but also investing more heavily in the domestic higher education sector so that talented Indonesians did not have to travel overseas to study in jurisdictions where they had minimal protection.

Fassin (2021: 130) notes that the articulation of conspiracy theories enables their narrators to construct themselves as moral persons, especially vis-à-vis the nefarious entities who are supposed to have orchestrated the conspiracy. It is undoubtedly true that, in Indonesian accounts, the Singaporean state emerges as a villain *extraordinaire*. Yet an equally interesting moral positioning is occurring with respect to the Indonesian government, which is seen as abrogating its responsibility both to its citizens overseas and to all those citizens who would have benefitted from David's participation in intellectual exchange. The government's official stance was that they had offered David's family support via the Indonesian Embassy in Singapore but could not get involved in matters that were properly the jurisdiction of the Singaporean Coroner's Court

(Hermawan 2009). Yet commentators were more disparaging, responding to the situation with cynical humour. 'The people going to Singapore are an independent verification team. Why hasn't it been the Indonesian government asking to conduct an official verification in Singapore?' asked one commentator: 'Maybe they're all too busy with their election campaigns? He... he...' (SidikRizal 2009). 'I just hope that the authorities in Singapore are moved to unravel the mystery of David's death,' wrote another – 'The leaders of Indonesia? Ahhh, they're too busy campaigning and deprecating themselves in front of large crowds' (Sams 2009). Significantly, despite a change in political regime, this sense of discontent has not abated. More than ten years on, commentators are continuing to bemoan the government's limited support to the Widjaya family, and its reluctance to press for a reopening of this cold case (e.g. Arum Story 2021; Santosa 2020).[7]

The implications of such sentiments should be neither overstated nor understated. Though I encountered no cases where the David Widjaya case had, in and of itself, precipitated a change in someone's political outlook, discussion surrounding the case could heighten existing sensibilities: that Indonesia was vulnerable to the malign intentions of foreign powers upon which it was nevertheless dependent for skills and knowledge; that Indonesians embarking upon auspicious but high-risk projects of intellectual exchange could not rely on protection from the government; and that democratization, although conducted in the name of reform and of empowering the citizenry, had ushered in a political class preoccupied with self-interest and safeguarding their electoral prospects rather than public service. Such sentiments could contribute to a growing sense within Indonesia that democracy was not the 'right' political system, heightening the appeal of perceived 'strongman' political figures, and leading some to hope for a shift towards more explicitly Islamic forms of governance (see Long 2016). Even for those who remained attached to the democratic ideal, cases such as David's could compound feelings of disappointment that the new national order was not truly leading to the citizenry being cared for – either in terms of securing justice for their deaths, or in terms of safeguarding the circuitry of intellectual exchange on which Indonesia's future depended.

Meanwhile, for those contemplating study abroad – who already had to balance the moral and practical opportunities it offered with the discomforts and dangers of being far from home (Cannon 2000) – the coverage of David's case only sharpened their sense of what could be at stake in such intellectual exchange activities. Few feared they would be murdered, but the case heightened awareness that they might not be protected overseas. Was it worth the risk? Some thought not, invoking the aphorism '*Daripada hujan emas di negeri orang, lebih baik hujan batu di negeri sendiri*', which translates as 'Rather than golden rain in someone else's country, it's better to have rain of stone in your own country' and suggests one is always better off staying at home (Rani 2009). The case also led some to question whether life on campus overseas was so harsh that it could actually drive even a stellar scholarship student to suicidal *amok* violence.

One person entertaining this latter possibility was Margareta Astaman, the *chosen one* whose account of arriving in Singapore was discussed earlier, and who was herself a student at NTU. Her memoir of life in Singapore outlines how, despite the glamour and excitement of being a scholarship student, the experience proved alienating. 'Sometimes it was forgotten that talent was emplaced within a human being,' she reflects, 'we were seen only in terms of what we are able to accomplish, rather than as people. *What patented inventions can we produce? What journal can we write an article for? How can our accomplishments increase GDP?*' (Astaman 2010: 13). On top of these demanding expectations and the challenging syllabus, she was also expected to get involved in extra-curricular activities. It was too much. 'For years,' she writes, 'I have tried to tell the people around me how it makes sense that an NTU student who is bright, who is living comfortably in Singapore, and who is highly regarded could be doomed to end up on a railway line or in a psychiatric hospital' (2010: 16). Yet nobody would believe her. For Astaman, David's death offered an unexpected, and bitterly welcome, opportunity to share her experiences and to question the value of an education system that treats human beings like machines.[8] Yet, even this trenchant criticism is laced with ambivalence, as Astaman ultimately does not regret her time overseas: 'by mentioning a series of achievements believed to be only possible if she had not chosen to stay in Jakarta, she convinces us that above all the stressful culture, being a successful person at [a] young age is worth fighting for. For this, she owes Singapore' (Febriani 2016: 605). Despite everything, and despite their frustrations with the government, intellectual exchange continues to endure as an ideal for those Indonesians able to secure the opportunity and prepared to weather its risks.

Conclusion

Valuable though it can be for anthropologists to focus on the actualities of intellectual exchange as practised, this chapter has advanced a parallel case for the importance of attending to the ways in which intellectual exchange serves as an object of desire, contemplation and discussion, analysing the generative force of the ways it is idealized. I have shown how, with human development standing out as an urgent imperative, the ideal of transnational intellectual exchange has become an animating trope of both governance and citizenship in Indonesia. In its most positive version, overseas study is a priceless if demanding opportunity through which citizens can render Indonesia's skills and knowledge base on par with those of more prosperous, nations – if only their access were not hampered by a pitiful shortage of scholarships. In its most negative version, overseas study is a high-risk endeavour in which gifted Indonesians are put at the mercy of ostensibly benevolent educator-hosts who will stop at nothing to drain their brains or suppress their return in order to maintain global and intra-Asian hierarchies and inequalities. In both visions, the young achiever serving the nation needs the nation's support – and in both cases, the Indonesian government is found distinctly lacking. The divergence between citizens' ideal of intellectual exchange and what they perceive to be the reality – whether that be education officials corrupting away scholarship money or government ministers disregarding the murder of their nation's Tony Stark in order to pursue re-election – thus serves as one of many faultlines in contemporary Indonesian political subjectivity. Whether one responds by becoming a dedicated citizen reporter, gritting one's teeth and doubling down in pursuit of a scholarship, or quietly surrendering to a sense of hopelessness for the country's future, a sense of Indonesia's vulnerability in the realm of human development is keenly and consequentially felt.

On the one hand, material of this kind supports normative arguments calling for structural reforms within arenas of intellectual exchange so as to render them more accessible and inclusive. As Garnett (2006: 534) argues, intellectual development can only be possible following 'the removal of substantial unfreedoms' and the reform of 'institutional circumstances that affect a person's ability to exercise his or her academic freedoms'. Yet the ethnographic materials outlined here also complicate such arguments by revealing how one's ideals of intellectual exchange and one's understanding of the barriers to those ideals' realizations are themselves grounded in narrative logics and affectively compelling intuitions that have their own situated histories, reflective of specific national, geopolitical and perhaps personal circumstances. These may not straightforwardly correspond to what is happening in practice: Hanoi's Human Research Capacity Centre will never grant Padmana a degree in Supernatural Studies; government officials sometimes do try their best to secure scholarships for their students (albeit without success); ultimately, none of the explanations offered for the David Hartanto Widjaya case offer a watertight account of what led him to fall to his death – and so they cannot be straightforwardly or fully addressed simply via processes of institutional reform. Even as we strive to improve our own practices of intellectual exchange, such material serves as a reminder of the importance to remain reflexive about the factors and attachments informing our own ideals, anxieties and frustrations, and the process by which we identify both obstacles to our ideals' realization and possible solutions for overcoming these. Anthropologists must recognize that the effects associated with the ideal of intellectual exchange can be just as consequential as the practice of transferring of skills, knowledge and ideas. Indeed, much of the promise and value of an ethnographically grounded anthropology of intellectual exchange, of the kind called for by this volume, is that it allows such affects to be documented, and subjected to critical analysis, in their own right, to afford a broader understanding of the many ways in which intellectual exchange shapes both individual lives and the sociocultural worlds that we share.

Acknowledgements

This research was supported by ESRC grant RES-000-22-4632, and a British Academy Postdoctoral Fellowship. Research permission was granted by RISTEK, with institutional sponsorship provided by STISIPOL Raja Haji Tanjungpinang. I am grateful to Magnus Marsden and three anonymous reviewers for comments on earlier versions of the text, and to everyone in Indonesia who took part in my research.

Nicholas J. Long is an Associate Professor of Anthropology at the London School of Economics and Political Science (LSE), where he works on the anthropology of Indonesia and on responses to COVID-19 in the UK and Aotearoa New Zealand. He won the 2019 Stirling Prize for Best Published Work in Psychological Anthropology for his article 'Suggestions of Power: Searching for Efficacy in Indonesia's Hypnosis Boom'.

Notes

1. I have used pseudonyms for all the fieldwork interlocutors cited in this chapter. When discussing the works of writers, bloggers, news commentators and individuals profiled in media stories, I have retained their original names, since these are already a matter of public record.
2. Some sources spell David's surname as 'Widjaja'.
3. Several Indonesian commentators explicitly identified David's actions (as reported in the Singaporean media) as an example of *amok/amuk* (e.g. Siagian 2009; Smith 2009).
4. The term 'hand phone' is widely used in Indonesia and Singapore to refer to a cellular mobile or smartphone.
5. Wilson did not make any reference to the death of Zhou Zheng, but other accounts speculate that he was either a witness to David's murder who was killed for his silence or had been involved in the murder and hanged himself out of remorse.
6. Strikingly, no mention is typically made of David's performance in the international contest; Olympiad records show he placed 356th, with a total score of 4 out of a possible 42.
7. There are interesting parallels here with Marsden's account of Afghan traders living overseas, who commonly report feeling 'left abandoned' by the Afghan state and disadvantaged vis-à-vis merchants from countries perceived as providing more effective diplomatic and consular support. In both cases, feelings of abandonment lend a distinctive affective tenor to international mobility. Moreover, Marsden's interlocutors 'take active steps to establish alternative centres of diplomacy' (2016: 70), just as Indonesian citizens took active steps to establish an alternative verification team. Such material highlights the ongoing importance of attending to practices and perceptions of national statecraft when investigating forms of global mobility and intellectual exchange that initially seem 'global', 'cosmopolitan' and 'world-bridging' in character.
8. Other international study destinations can elicit negative reactions for different reasons. For example, Abaza (1991: 356–57) found that Indonesian students at Al-Azhar University in Cairo struggled with the memorization-based learning style, the difficulty of the Qur'anic examination, and the nonchalant attitudes of their Egyptian peers. Meanwhile, Theo (2018: 104–5) notes that Indonesian students embarking upon study abroad in China can be beset with anxieties stemming from Cold War-era stereotypes of communism, although she observes that such perceptions are often quickly overturned once in-country.

References

Abaza, Mona. 1991. 'Some Research Notes on Living Conditions and Perceptions among Indonesian Students in Cairo', *Journal of Southeast Asian Studies* 22(2): 347–60. https://doi.org/10.1017/S0022463400003921.

Al Qurtuby, Sumanto. 2020. 'Islam, Travel, and Learning: A Case Study on Indonesian Muslim Student Diasporas in Saudi Arabia', *Journeys* 21(2): 42–66. doi:10.3167/jys.2020.210203.

Anon. 2009. 'Four Key Witnesses to Testify for David', *The Jakarta Post*, 28 April. https://www.thejakartapost.com/news/2009/04/28/four-key-witnesses-testify-david.html.

Arum Story. 2021. 'Misteri Kematian David Hartanto Widjaya, Tony Stark Indonesia'. Retrieved 2 April 2021 from https://www.youtube.com/watch?v=bgOOp24t0Ac.

Astaman, Margareta. 2010. *After Orchard: Margarita's Chat*. Jakarta: Kompas.

Bayly, Susan. 2013. 'For Family, State and Nation: Achieving Cosmopolitan Modernity in Late-Socialist Vietnam', in Nicholas J. Long and Henrietta L. Moore (eds), *The Social Life of Achievement*. Oxford: Berghahn Books, pp. 158–81.

Becker, Gary S. 1964. *Human Capital: A Theoretical and Empirical Analysis, with Special Reference to Education*. New York: Columbia University Press.

Cannon, Robert. 2000. 'The Outcomes of an International Education for Indonesian Graduates: The Third Place?', *Higher Education Research & Development* 19(3): 357–79. https://doi.org/10.1080/758484349.

Carter, David, and Arthur Spirling. 2008. 'Under the Influence? Intellectual Exchange in Political Science', *PS: Political Science and Politics* 41(2): 375–78.

Chan, Crystal. 2009. 'NTU Prof Says There's No Truth to Online Accusations', *The New Paper*, 21 March. https://www.asiaone.com/News/Education/Story/A1Story20090320-129863.html.

Chong, Shin Yen, and Amanda Yong. 2009a. 'Bright Student, Dark Problems', *The New Paper*, 23 May. https://www.asiaone.com/News/Education/Story/A1Story20090522-143266.html.

———. 2009b. 'I Pushed Him Away, But He Kept Coming Back', *The New Paper*, 24 May. https://www.asiaone.com/News/Education/Story/A1Story20090522-143268.html.

Chua, Beng Huat. 2000. 'Preface', in Chua Beng Huat (ed.), *Consumption in Asia: Lifestyles and Identities*. London: Routledge, pp. xi–xiv.

Davern, Michael E., and D. Stanley Eitzen. 1995. 'Economic Sociology: An Examination of Intellectual Exchange', *American Journal of Economics and Sociology* 54(1): 79–88. https://doi.org/10.1111/j.1536-7150.1995.tb02632.x.

Dhofier, Zamakhsyari. 1992. 'The Intellectualization of Islamic Studies in Indonesia', *Indonesia Circle* 20(58): 19–31. https://doi.org/10.1080/03062849208729783.

Diallo, Oda-Kange Midtvåge, and Nico Miskow Friborg. 2021. 'Subverting the White Cis Gaze: Toward a Pedagogy of Discomfort, Accountability and Care in the Anthropology Classroom', *Teaching Anthropology* 10(4): 17–35. https://doi.org/10.22582/ta.v10i4.622.

Dragojlovic, Ana. 2010. '"Sukarno's Students": Reconfiguring Notions of Exile, Community and Remembering', *Review of Indonesian and Malaysian Affairs* 44(1): 53–81.

Ermarth, Michael. 1993. 'Intellectual History as Philosophical Anthropology: Bernard Groethuysen's Transformation of Traditional *Geistesgeschichte*', *The Journal of Modern History* 65(4): 673–705. https://doi.org/10.1086/244722.

Fassin, Didier. 2021. 'Of Plots and Men: The Heuristics of Conspiracy Theories', *Current Anthropology* 62(2): 128–37. https://doi.org/10.1086/713829.
Febriani, Rima. 2016. 'Studying and Negotiating Kiasuism: Transnational Education Experiences in Margareta Astaman's *After Orchard*', *Proceedings of International Conference on Language, Literary and Cultural Studies (ICON LATERALS)* 2016: 595–607. https://doi.10.217716/ub.icon_laterals.2016.001.1.40.
Floorwalker, Mike. 2019. 'How High Is Tony S'ark's IQ?', *Looper*, 21 August. https://www.looper.com/162925/how-high-is-tony-starks-iq/.
Gammeltoft, Tine. 2018. 'Domestic Moods: Maternal Mental Health in Northern Vietnam', *Medical Anthropology* 37(7): 582–96. https://doi.org/10.1080/01459740.2018.1444612.
Garnett, Robert F. 2006. 'Paradigms and Pluralism in Heterodox Economics', *Review of Political Economy* 18(4): 521–46. https://doi.org/10.1080/09538250600915725.
Gellert, Paul K. 2015. 'Optimism and Education: The New Ideology of Development in Indonesia', *Journal of Contemporary Asia* 45(3): 371–93. https://doi.org/10.1080/00472336.2014.978352.
Gerke, Signe. 2000. 'Global Lifestyles under Local Conditions: The New Indonesian Middle Class', in Chua Beng Huat (ed.), *Consumption in Asia: Lifestyles and Identities*. London: Routledge, pp. 135–58.
Gibbings, Sheri. 2013. 'Unseen Powers and Democratic Detectives: Street Vendors in an Indonesian City', *City and Society* 25(2): 235–59. https://doi.org/10.1111/ciso.12018.
Goh, Sunny. 2011. 'Chinese Indonesians Pursuing Higher Education in Singapore: A Grounded Theory Approach', Ed.D. dissertation. Leicester: University of Leicester.
Guggenheim, Scott. 2012. *Indonesia Rising: The Repositioning of Asia's Third Giant*. Singapore: ISEAS.
Hefner, Robert W. 2009. 'Introduction: The Politics and Cultures of Islamic Education in Southeast Asia', in Robert W. Hefner (ed.), *Making Modern Muslims: The Politics of Islamic Education in Southeast Asia*. Honolulu: University of Halai'i Press, pp. 1–54.
Hermawan, Ary. 2009. 'David's Family to Present New Evidence to a Higher Court', *The Jakarta Post*, 1 August. https://www.thejakartapost.com/news/2009/08/01/david039s-family-present-new-evidence-a-higher-court.html.
Hirata, Andrea. 2009. *The Rainbow Troops. A Novel* (trans. A. Kilbane). New York: Sarah Crichton Books.
Indrawati, Sri Mulyani, and Ari Kuncoro. 2021. 'Improving Competitiveness through Vocational and Higher Education: Indonesia's Vision for Human Capital Development in 2019–2024', *Bulletin of Indonesian Economic Studies* 57(1): 29–59. https://doi.org/10.1080/00074918.2021.1909692.
Keats, Daphne M. 1969. *Back in Asia; a Follow-up Study of Australian-Trained Asian Students*. Canberra: Research School of Pacific Studies, ANU.
King, Kenneth (ed.). 2011. 'The Geopolitics of Overseas Scholarships and Awards: Old and New Providers, East and West, North and South', *NORRAG News* 45.
Kon, Yan. 1994. 'Amok', *British Journal of Psychiatry* 165(5): 685–89. https://doi.org/10.1192/bjp.165.5.685.
Laffan, Michael. 2004. 'An Indonesian Community in Cairo: Continuity and Change in a Cosmopolitan Islamic Milieu', *Indonesia* 77: 1–26. https://hdl.handle.net/1813/54309.
Lee, Christine. 2021. '"You Don't Look American": Race and Whiteness in the Ethnographic and Disciplinary Encounter', *American Ethnologist* 48(2): 206–17. https://doi.org/10.1111/amet.13014.

Lee, Raymond L.M. 1981. 'Structure and Anti-Structure in the Culture-Bound Syndromes: The Malay Case', *Culture, Medicine and Psychiatry* 5: 233–48. https://doi.org/10.1007/BF00050770.

Lewis, Tania. 2004. 'Meaghan Morris and the Formation of Australian Cultural Studies: A Narrative of Intellectual Exchange and Located Transnationalism', *Cultural Studies ↔ Critical Methodologies* 4(1): 45–70. https://doi.org/10.1177/1532708603259446.

Long, Nicholas J. 2016. 'Why Indonesians Turn against Democracy', in Joanna Cook, Nicholas J. Long and Henrietta L. Moore (eds), *The State We're In: Reflections on Democracy's Troubles*. Oxford: Berghahn Books, pp. 71–96.

———. Forthcoming. 'Afterlives and Alter-Lives: How Competitions Produce (Neoliberal?) Subjects in Indonesia', *Social Analysis* 66(4).

MacDougall, John James. 1976. 'The Technocratic Model of Modernization: The Case of Indonesia's New Order', *Asian Survey* 16(12): 1166–83.

Marsden, Magnus. 2016. '"We Are Both Diplomats and Traders": Afghan Transregional Traders across the Former Soviet Union', *The Cambridge Journal of Anthropology* 34(2): 59–75. https://doi.org/10.3167/ca.2016.340205.

Mayblin, Maya. 2012. 'The Madness of Mothers: Agape Love and the Maternal Myth in Northeast Brazil', *American Anthropologist* 114(2): 240–52. https://doi.org/10.1111/j.1548-1433.2012.01422.x.

Merkel, Ian. 2017. 'Fernand Braudel, Brazil, and the Empire of French Social Science: Newly Translated Sources from the 1930s', *French Historical Studies* 40(1): 129–60. https://doi.org/10.1215/00161071-3686080.

———. 2021. 'Primer: Intellectual Exchange', *World History Commons*. Retrieved 20 December 2021 from https://worldhistorycommons.org/primer-intellectual-exchange.

Mesakh, Eddy. 2009. 'Wiliam: Saya Yakin Adik Saya Dianiaya'. Retrieved 6 January 2022 from https://eddymesakh.wordpress.com/2009/03/05/wiliam-saya-yakin-adik-saya-dianiaya/.

Miller, Daniel. 2001. *The Dialectics of Shopping*. Chicago: University of Chicago Press.

Moore, Henrietta L. 2011. *Still Life: Hopes, Desires and Satisfactions*. Cambridge: Polity Press.

Newberry, Jan. 2017. '"Anything Can Be Used to Stimulate Child Development": Early Childhood Education and Development in Indonesia as a Durable Assemblage', *Journal of Asian Studies* 76(1): 25–45. https://doi.org/10.1017/S0021911816001650.

Nur, Yoslan. 2000. 'L'île de Batam à l'ombre de Singapour: Invetissement Singapourien et dèpendance de Batam', *Archipel* 59: 145–70.

Rani. 2009. 'Hujan Emas di Negeri Orang…'. Retrieved 28 December 2021 from https://staff.blog.ui.ac.id/rani/2009/03/06/hujan-emas-di-negeri-orang/.

Riza, Faisol. 2009. 'Iwan Piliang: Lindungi SDM Indonesia', *Perspektif Baru* (687). Retreived 29 December 2021 from http://www.perspektifbaru.com/wawancara/687.

Rudnyckyj, Daromir. 2010. *Spiritual Economies: Islam, Globalization, and the Afterlife of Development*. Ithaca, NY: Cornell University Press.

Sams, Iwan. 2009. 'Misteri Kematian David Hartono Wijaya'. Retrieved 31 December 2021 from https://isandri.blogspot.com/2009/03/misteri-kematian-david-hartono-wijaya.html.

Santosa, Riwaldo. 2020. 'Rahasia Mahasiswa Indonesia di Singapura Yang Belum Terpecahkan Hingga Sekarang: David Hartanto'. Retrieved 31 December 2021 from https://www.youtube.com/watch?v=Ik8ggi1Etac.

Schut, Thijs. 2019. 'The Promise of Education and Its Paradox in Rural Flores, East Indonesia', *Focaal*(83): 85–97. https://doi.org/10.3167/fcl.2019.830109.

Siagian, Partogi. 2009. 'Misteri Seputar Tewasnya David Hartanto Widjaya'. Retrieved 1 January 2022 from https://partogisiagianmpd.wordpress.com/2009/03/27/misteri-seputar-tewasnya-david-hartanto-widjaja/.

SidikRizal. 2009. 'Benarkah David Hartanto Widjaya Dibunuh?'. Retrieved 31 December 2021 from https://globalbekasi.blogspot.com/2009/04/benarkah-david-hartanto-widjaja-dibunuh.html.

Smith, Anto. 2009. 'Kebenaran Yang Tidak Diungkap Media Dalam Kasus David Hartanto!'. Retrieved 1 January 2022 from http://thedeathofdavidwidjaja.blogspot.com/2009/04/kebenaran-yang-tidak-diungkap-media.html.

Spykerman, Kimberly, and Sujin Thomas. 2009. 'Student's Death Ruled a Suicide', *The Straits Times*, 1 August. https://www.asiaone.com/News/Education/Story/A1Story20090730-158096.html.

Stewart, Kathleen. 1996. *A Space on the Side of the Road: Cultural Poetics in an 'Other' America*. Princeton, NJ: Princeton University Press.

Stutje, Klaas. 2013. 'Indonesian Identities Abroad: International Engagement of Colonial Students in the Netherlands, 1908–1931', *BMGN - Low Countries Historical Review* 128(1): 151–72. https://doi.org/10.18352/bmgn-lchr.8359.

Suwignyo, Andito. 2013. 'Honoris Causa Untuk SBY Dan Kematian David Hartanto '. Retrieved 29 December 2021 from https://anditoaja.wordpress.com/2013/04/24/honoris-causa-untuk-sby-dan-kematian-david-hartanto/.

Theo, Rika. 2018. 'Unravelling Indonesian Student Mobility to China: Politics, Identities, and Trajectories', Ph.D. dissertation. Utrecht: Universiteit Utrecht.

Throop, C. Jason. 2014. 'Moral Moods', *Ethos* 42(1): 65–83. https://doi.org/10.1111/etho.12039.

Tournès, Ludovic, and Giles Scott-Smith. 2018. 'A World of Exchanges: Conceptualizing the History of International Scholarships Programs (Nineteenth to Twenty-First Centuries)', in Ludovic Tournès and Giles Scott-Smith (eds), *Global Exchanges: Scholarships and Transnational Circulations in the Modern World*. Oxford: Berghahn Books, pp. 1–32.

Trawick, Margaret. 1990. *Notes on Love in a Tamil Family*. Berkeley: University of California Press.

van der Kroef, Justus M. 1957. 'Education in Indonesia', *Phi Delta Kappan* 39(3): 147–51.

Welch, A.R. 2007. 'Blurred Vision? Public and Private Higher Education in Indonesia', *Higher Education* 54(5): 665–87. https://doi.org/10.1007/s10734-006-9017-5.

Williamson, Thomas. 2007. 'Communicating Amok in Malaysia', *Identities: Global Studies in Culture and Power* 14(3): 341–65.

10

This Is the End?
The French Settler Community in Saigon and the Fall of Indochina in 1945

Christopher Goscha

> One thought alone preoccupies the submerged mind of Empire: how not to end, how not to die, how to prolong its era. By day it pursues its enemies. It is cunning and ruthless, it sends its bloodhounds everywhere. By night it feeds on images of disaster: the sack of cities, the rape of populations, pyramids of bones, acres of desolation.
>
> —J.M. Coetzee, *Waiting for the Barbarians*

Introduction

In his Nobel Prize-winning novel, *Waiting for the Barbarians*, J.M. Coetzee describes masterfully how the agents and members of empire struggle incessantly against the imperial state's demise by creating a constant state of fear against imminent barbarian attack. It is not enough to rule. The imperial state needs an enemy. It can then march the army into the borderlands to attack the nomads before they can descend upon the empire. The deployment of the army, the use of torture, and the suspension of rule of law are all necessary evils. The preservation of civilization depends on it. Empire simply cannot fathom its end. And yet, throughout his novel, Coetzee has his borderland administrator remind us that all empires must one day come to an end. Imperial time, the Magistrate whispers seditiously in our ear, is not universal: 'We have been here more than a hundred years, we have reclaimed land from the desert and built irrigation works and planted fields and built solid homes and put a wall around our town, but they still think of us as visitors, transients' (Coetzee 2004: 55). Driven almost mad by the failed military campaign against the approaching barbarians he has come to admire but still cannot see, the Magistrate finally admits that he 'wanted to live outside the history that Empire imposes on its subjects, even its lost subjects. I never wished it for the barbarians that they should have the history of Empire laid upon them. How can I believe that that is cause for shame?' (Coetzee 2004: 169). Our tortured colonial administrator had dared to imagine decolonization from the inside of empire.

Susan Bayly put her finger on this in a wonderful essay she penned in 2009 on one such rogue magistrate in French Indochina (Vietnam, Laos and Cambodia), Paul Mus. This colonial administrator had dared to imagine the decolonization of Vietnam from within the French empire in the wake of the Second World War. Like Coetzee's Magistrate, Mus lost his job at the head of the colonial academy (Bayly 2009). For the historian of French Indochina and its Vietnamese successor states, Coetzee's vision of the empire as an entity lashing out against its collapse finds something of a case study in Saigon and Hanoi in mid-1945 as Mus witnessed first-hand at the time. After building modern schools, hospitals and roads for eighty years, French settlers watched in fear from behind their shuttered windows in Hanoi and Saigon as the 'barbarians' took over as the Second World War came to a close in Asia. The Vietnamese were not only dancing jubilantly in the streets of both cities in August and September 1945; they also took control of the administration of the new nation-state they christened 'Vietnam'. 'The age of colonization is over', a newly appointed Vietnamese magistrate declared to Western reporters in Saigon on 17 September (Krull 1945: 12).[1] As he spoke, Vietnamese policemen did what they could to maintain order as their compatriots celebrated their liberation from eighty years of French colonial domination and five years of Japanese occupation.

The tables had been turned and yet everything still remained in flux. No one knew for sure in mid-1945 that the French would not return to retake Indochina having lost it briefly to the Japanese. Do all empires really die? Vietnamese nationalists were convinced that history was on their side; there was no going back. However, the overwhelming majority of the French settlers, colonial officers and administrators in Saigon disagreed vehemently that their time had come. Waves of Vietnamese nationalism surging around them did nothing to change their minds. To them, the Vietnamese revolution was an aberration. The Vietnamese were not, *could* not, be 'nationalists' or 'patriots'. They were 'pirates' and 'troublemakers'. At best, they were 'children', unready to assume independence (Hertrich [1956] 1999: 46–47).[2] Imperial time had briefly stopped because of the war. But it was now just a question of re-establishing order and resetting the clock. As one French planter told a journalist in September 1945: 'In 1942, I was in charge of re-establishing order at X. Well, we burned a few villages, jailed a few hundred natives, sentenced their leaders and that was all there was to that disturbance. Everything went back to order and the coolies went on working as before. They don't want anything else. They expect that of us' (Krull 1945: 9). Freed from Japanese internment, a ranking magistrate in Indochina repeated the same idea to Mus in a phrase the latter would carry with him: 'all the Annamese desire is our return' (*les Annamites n'attendent que notre retour*) (cited in Gentil 1972: 312).

Most scholars of modern Vietnam have understandably focused their attention on the birth of Vietnam in August–September 1945 in the form of the Democratic Republic of Vietnam (DRV). We owe much to this scholarship for putting the Vietnamese and their time before us. However, in this chapter, I would like to focus on the much less studied French community in Indochina whose members suddenly found themselves confronted with the end of empire in 1945. I would like to try to understand how the French in Saigon experienced the tumultuous events of August and September 1945, triggered by the end of the Second World War. How did they perceive Vietnamese independence? How did they understand the possible end of empire? How did they act to restore colonial rule, reset the imperial clock if you will? This chapter in no way responds definitively to all of these questions. Rather, it is a preliminary attempt to make better sense of how imperial time ended or didn't for the settler community in Indochina. This is something Susan engaged with in her work on colonialism. I would like to think that I'm following her lead, for her work has been of great inspiration to me over the years.

A Colonial World Turned Upside Down

The French Community in Colonial Indochina (1862–1940)

The French community in Indochina[3] numbered around thirty-five thousand people on the eve of the Second World War. Although the French had always been the smallest group of the thirty million people inhabiting Indochina by that time, they had always stood at the top of the colonial pyramid. Their violent conquest of Vietnam between 1858 and 1885 and their military superiority ensured this. The promulgation of the Indigenous Code in 1881 codified it by denying 'natives' equal rights with 'French citizens'. Besides a few hundred settlers and European missionaries, most of the *Français d'Indochine*, as they soon styled themselves, resided mainly in the urban areas of Vietnam. In 1940, seventeen thousand French lived in Saigon, six thousand in Hanoi, and over two thousand in Haiphong. A few thousand were scattered across the rest of the colony. Most pushed pencils in the civil service or served in the colonial army. A couple of thousand worked as planters, traders and entrepreneurs. Largely masculine immigration in the late nineteenth century led to mixed unions between French men and Vietnamese women. Several hundred children were born from these 'mixed' unions, referred to in French as *Eurasiens* or *métis*. Eurasians born to legal unions were often in a better situation than those born out of wedlock. William Bazé and Henri de Lachevrotière, for example, became powerful figures in the settler community, owned property and ran influential papers. Both were vociferous and indefatigable defenders of the colonial order and its French community well into the 1950s. Both had Vietnamese mothers (Meyer 2003).

Social interactions between the French and the Vietnamese occurred during the colonial period. Sports, for example, generated mixed teams and even saw the 'colonizer' and 'colonized' sit down together at the banquet table to celebrate a season, laugh together and reminisce (Larcher-Goscha 2009: 61–89, 1993). High school classrooms also brought some French and Vietnamese youth into contact with each other. French teachers often befriended their students. Jean-Michel Hertrich, who penned a gripping account of Vietnamese independence in 1945, had taught in Indochina in the 1930s and personally knew such future nationalist leaders as Pham Ngoc Thach and Pham Van Bach. Families often crossed paths and perhaps exchanged smiles in the Saigon markets or the beautiful Catholic cathedral in downtown Norodom Square (Hertrich [1956] 1999: 8).

However, this intermingling had real limits in colonial society. Other than learning a smattering of Vietnamese words to communicate with their domestic staff, few French spoke enough Vietnamese to interact proficiently with ordinary Vietnamese. Although the famous colonial country club in Saigon, the *Cercle Sportif*, was not officially segregated, in practice it only opened its membership to the well off, socially connected and almost exclusively French population (Franchini 1995: 77). The thousands of Vietnamese maids, 'boys', 'bep' (cooks) and drivers who worked in French households in Saigon had to carry permission slips in order to enter shops on the colonial city's chic *rue Catinat*. Many French and Vietnamese of comparable financial means lived in the same neighbourhoods and apartment complexes. And of course, not all *Français d'Indochine* were rich. But the French, Vietnamese and Chinese quarters remained distinct (see Babut 1931). Mixed marriages between Vietnamese men and French women were, on the whole, very rare. A notable exception was Dr Pham Ngoc Thach, future diplomat-at-large for Ho Chi Minh who married a French woman in Paris. The future novelist, Marguerite Duras, was another. But when her French classmates learned that she was dating a Vietnamese beau, a very wealthy one at that, they 'definitively distanced themselves from me. Those who frequented me until then dared no more to compromise themselves in my company' (Duras 2006: 41).

Contrary to the idyllic image many of the *Français d'Indochine* would later create about the peaceful, orderly and serene pre-Second World War period, the reality was different. Revolts against colonial rule had occurred repeatedly since the earliest days of the French conquest in the nineteenth century. Some were spontaneous peasant uprisings; others were nationalist and communist directed ones. The French community made no qualitative difference between any of them. They all threatened the colonial order. Massive peasant protests in central Vietnam in 1908 struck fear in colonial hearts and the European settler community used the image of the masses descending on the cities to pressure the government to roll back liberal reforms for the 'natives', suspend the rule of law for their 'subjects' and smash any insurrection. And that is what happened. Revolts occurred again during the First World War and then climaxed in massive ones in central and northern Vietnam in 1930–31 and a revolt in Cochinchina in 1940. The French relied on the colonial police, army and even the air force to smash and bomb these movements into submission. Torture became an all-too-common colonial practice in Indochina. The 'barbarians' had obviously not been invisible. The Vietnamese had always been there.

Japanese Occupation and the Collapse of Imperial Time (1940–45)

The Second World War weakened colonial power dramatically and discredited the French profoundly in the eyes of Vietnamese. Things first went badly when the French capitulated to the Germans in June 1940, dissolved the Third Republic, and allied the new State of France, better known as Vichy for the town from where it operated, with Hitler's Third Reich. Emboldened by French weakness, the Japanese moved their troops into northern Indochina from China in late 1940. However, rather than overthrowing the French colonial state under Vichy's control, the Japanese and the French ended up collaborating in an uneasy condominium based on the fact that Japan and France were now both partners with Germany. Rather than taking a stand against the Japanese, the French allowed the Japanese to occupy all of Indochina as the Germans had occupied all of France. As long as the French honoured their agreements with the occupiers and provided the required food, labour and natural resources, Japanese authorities were content to rule indirectly through the pre-existing French colonial administration. French Indochina became, if you will, a Japanese military protectorate.

It is not certain that the French grasped how an estimated fifteen thousand Indochinese elites and millions of increasingly hungry peasants may have interpreted their collaboration. While Vichy's Governor General Jean Decoux prided himself on keeping Indochina French (just as Pétain claimed to do in the metropole), it was clear to any thinking Vietnamese regardless of class that Decoux did so because the Japanese allowed him to do so. Second, that a 'yellow race' could so easily dominate a 'white one' debunked for good Social Darwinian arguments justifying French colonial rule since the nineteenth century. Vietnamese rickshaw drivers serving customers in Saigon understood perfectly well that Japanese soldiers strolling down the *rue Catinat* had upended the colonial order and the racism on which settler domination rested. Thanks to their military superiority, the Japanese occupied the top rung of the colonial ladder. Third, by collaborating with the Japanese, the French failed to honour duly signed international legal agreements binding them to defend their Asian colony. The French did not fight against the foreign occupiers in 1940–41. In the eyes of many Vietnamese nationalists, French prestige and invincibility had suffered a massive blow as a result of this, something which Vichy, its Republican successors and the French community in Indochina in particular failed entirely to grasp.

Vichy also applied its National Revolution in the colonies. Admiral Decoux faithfully applied anti-Semitic laws and clamped down on Republicans and their associations (Free Masons, the League of Human Rights, and the socialists). In their place, the admiral promoted the Fascist-minded *Légion française des Combatants et Volontaires de la Révolution nationale*. Thanks to volunteers from the French community, its ranks increased from 2,637 members in early 1942 to 6,576 by mid-1943, meaning about 25% of the total European population (Isoart 1982: 20). Decoux rolled back what little democracy the Third Republic had introduced to Indochina in the preceding decades. In November 1940, the admiral presided over the dissolution of all Indochinese local chambers and even the Colonial Council of Cochinchina. Like the Germans in France, the Japanese in French Indochina never required any of these antidemocratic measures (Jennings 2001; Raffin 2005; Namba 2012).

While Decoux did his best to build up Franco-Vietnamese collaboration, increasing the salaries of Vietnamese civil servants and stimulating local patriotism, little changed when it came to interactions between the Vietnamese and the French community. Each continued to live in separate worlds. Decoux's National Revolution may have mobilized tens of thousands of youths between late 1940 and early 1945, but I am unaware of any attempts to integrate French and Vietnamese youth groups. They remained segregated in practice. The Governor General had no real Vietnamese elites with whom he was willing to collaborate, other than the monarchy, and even then King Bao Dai was not really interested in collaborating with Decoux.[4]

The balance of power turned against the Axis powers, when the Allies debarked in Normandy in mid-1944 and brought down the Vichy government in France shortly thereafter. Worried by the prospect of an Allied landing in Indochina as the Germans retreated in Europe, on 9 March 1945 the Japanese occupiers easily overthrew the orphaned Vichy colonial state in Indochina, rapidly incarcerated its army, police force and ranking administrators, and declared the independence of Vietnam, Laos and Cambodia. France's Indochinese empire was no more. A few months later, the same was true for the Japanese one: on 15 August 1945, following the nuclear explosions at Hiroshima and Nagasaki, the Japanese emperor announced his country's capitulation to the Allies. It was in this context that Vietnamese nationalists, led by the Viet Minh, a nationalist front created by Ho Chi Minh's communist party in 1941, seized power in Hanoi on 19 August and then moved their way southwards, reaching Saigon a week or so later. On 2 September 1945, Ho stepped up to the microphone in Ba Dinh Square in downtown Hanoi, read the declaration of independence and announced the creation of the Democratic Republic of Vietnam (DRV) before tens of thousands of cheering Vietnamese citizens. National time was rapidly materializing.

From 9 March 1945, and especially after 15 August, French settlers found themselves in an unprecedented, extremely vulnerable and potentially dangerous position. With the colonial army behind bars, they were at the mercy of their Japanese rulers and then the Vietnamese nationalists. For the first time ever, the *Français d'Indochine* had no police or army to protect them between March and September 1945. Between 9 March and 15 August, the Japanese incarcerated an estimated 683 French civilians and high-ranking officers, including 150 in Saigon. They interned fifteen thousand members of the French colonial army, twelve thousand of them European. In Saigon, this included the *IIème Régiment d'infanterie coloniale* (11ème RIC). The Japanese confiscated weapons from the civilian population. In the same period, 400 French civilians and 1,800 French military personnel perished. Executions and torture of the French most certainly occurred. The Indochinese suffered in even greater numbers – six thousand 'Indochinese' civilians and seven hundred military personnel died in Japanese custody in equally horrible conditions. And under joint Franco-Japanese rule, at least one million Vietnamese died due to a massive famine in 1944–45. Strikingly absent from French accounts of their experiences in Indochina during this time is any mention of this massive Vietnamese loss of life and suffering (Goscha 2011: 388–89).

Many of the French living in the countryside fled to Saigon in search of safety; others did so on Japanese orders. As of 21 September, an estimated twenty-five thousand Europeans resided in Saigon (Goupy 1945). To accommodate this sudden influx in the population, longstanding French families in Saigon did their best to take in new arrivals. Twelve to eighteen people often lived in one house. Living conditions were often cramped – again, not all French lived in spacious villas (Goupy 1945). That said, the French community in Saigon never went hungry. To my knowledge, no French settler died from famine during this time. Western journalists arriving in early September reported that war-imposed autarchy, home gardening and animal husbandry had proven effective in Saigon: 'There was enough to eat and none of the necessities were lacking. On the whole, life had not changed much' (Krull 1945: 2).

Fear among the settlers, however, ran at unprecedented levels. Besides the Japanese assault on French civilians and combatants, including all sorts of humiliations, the colonizers suddenly found themselves at the mercy of the colonized, in particular the majority Vietnamese. By supporting the independence of Vietnam under Emperor Bao Dai following the 9 March coup, the Japanese had allowed nationalists, youth groups, scouts and workers to organize themselves and to take to the streets for the first time free of French control. The change in the balance of power immediately modified relationships between the French and the Vietnamese at all social levels. Vichy's scouting and youth groups morphed rapidly into the Youth Guard under Pham Ngoc Thach's leadership. Nationalist-minded presses and papers published scores of books and articles celebrating the heroes who had resisted the French since the 1860s. French settlers watched as Vietnamese nationalists ripped down colonial monuments and renamed streets celebrating French colonial heroes in favour of Vietnamese ones. The monument in Saigon dedicated to the French conqueror of Indochina, Francis Garnier, crumbled, as did another one in Norodom Square dedicated to the symbol of Franco-Vietnamese collaboration, the Bishop Pigneau de Béhaine (Barthouet 1947: 166). They had served as the all-important symbolic markers of imperial time. Their obliteration prepared the way for national ones, but their destruction convinced settlers that they had to be rebuilt and the Vietnamese put back in their place. It was essential to the re-establishment of imperial time and the reassurance that would come with it once the war was over. But there was no hiding the fact that the tables had been thoroughly turned on them. It was a humiliating, complex and powerful emotion for the settler community. 'Losing face' is how de Gaulle's new commissioner to Cochinchina described it upon arriving secretly in southern Vietnam (Cédile 1945: 1).

'Black Sunday': Vietnamese Independence and the Imperial Time Warp

French fear spiked when the Japanese capitulation of 15 August 1945 changed the balance of power firmly in favour of the Viet Minh, whose forces rapidly seized power in Hanoi on 19 August and in Saigon on the 25th. Until the Allies arrived, the Japanese remained in de facto control thanks to their 100,000 troops in Vietnam, including 70,000 in the south, not to mention their police forces. But as long as the Viet Minh didn't let things get out of hand, Japanese officers looked the other way as they waited for the Allied victors to take over. To the stupefaction of the French settlers, the Japanese refused to free incarcerated colonial troops, administrators and security forces in Hanoi or Saigon, for the simple reason that the Japanese did not recognize the French, 'new' or 'old', as an Allied power to whom they would surrender. Order no. 1 issued by Truman on 15 August 1945 had excluded the French and Dutch from joining the other Allied forces in occupying Japanese territories in the Asia-Pacific region. French settlers had to wait for the arrival of the British, who were to accept the Japanese surrender below the 16th parallel, repatriate Allied POWs and maintain order, while the Republic of China's troops under Chiang Kai-shek would do the same to the north of that line.

This was yet another blow to French prestige, for it confirmed for all to see the difficult situation in which France's wartime collaboration with the Axis had placed all of them. There was a general though unspoken realization among the settlers in Indochina that they had not quite been on the 'winning side'. In concrete terms, this meant that the French population could not free the imprisoned colonial troops to restore the colonial order and protect them. The French in Saigon thus continued to live in an expectative, troubled state of mind in August and September. The most powerful emotion was fear, alleviated somewhat by the belief that the Allies would soon arrive to protect them until the new French army sent by Charles de Gaulle could debark and put the Vietnamese back in their places, all of them.

Things became tense by early September 1945 as the Vietnamese moved fast to build a new nation-state on their terms. Nationalist leaders in charge of Saigon exhorted the population to refrain from aiding or collaborating with the French 'colonialists'. The Viet Minh issued orders to boycott French shops and urged colonial servants, maids, boys, cooks, suppliers and urban workers to abandon their masters and support the new Vietnamese nation by joining militias. Many did. Citing patriotic reasons or under pressure from Viet Minh authorities or friends, many rickshaw drivers stopped taking French passengers (Krull 1945: 6). Vietnamese hotheads taunted the French in the street. Fights often broke out and spitting on the former colonizer was not uncommon. *Métis* children, often fluent in Vietnamese, had to be very careful about how they spoke, what they said and with whom they consorted, for many militant nationalists now saw them as the visible traitors of their Vietnamese country because of the French 'blood' running through their veins. Caught between two identities, many had to choose their alliances at this very time. Some 'became' French in late August and early September; others chose 'Vietnam'. Names changed, as did language preferences. But pure fear often drove these choices as much as burning patriotism (Tran Van Giau undated : 273–84; Goupy 1945). Philippe Franchini, the *métis* son of the French owner of the Continental Hotel, recalled the terrible fright he experienced at this time as a child:

> 'Motherfucker, moron, son of a bitch, pig child, dirty Westerner, cocksucker'. The insults rained down on us, but worse than the words were the black faces filled with hate, the mouths contorted in fits of disgust, the rocks and trash being thrown at us, the obscene gesticulations and laughs, all of which welcomed us as we made our way before them. The Japanese soldiers who escorted us in order to 'protect' us only added to the horror. It seemed as unreal as a nightmare. We couldn't understand a thing about what was happening. (Franchini 1995: 128)

It was very real though and it was in this emotionally explosive atmosphere that southern Viet Minh authorities prepared a huge demonstration in downtown Saigon on 2 September 1945 to celebrate, as in the capital of Hanoi, the formal declaration of Vietnam's national independence and the official creation of the DRV under Ho Chi Minh's presidency. What happened in Vietnam on 2 September 1945 needs to be compared to what happened in the Algerian cities of Sétif and Guelma on 8 May of that same year. For just as 8 May 1945 marked the victory of the Allies over Nazi Germany in Europe, setting off independence demonstrations in Algeria, 2 September 1945 was the day on which the Allies celebrated victory over Japan and Ho Chi Minh declared Vietnam's independence. As de Gaulle's representative, General Philippe Leclerc, looked on approvingly as the American General Douglas MacArthur signed the instrument of Japanese unconditional surrender on the USS *Missouri* in Tokyo Bay, the French Expeditionary Corps was steaming towards Saigon to restore Indochina to the French empire under de Gaulle's rule. Two different times were about to clash.

In Algeria, where the French remained in control after the Allied landing in North Africa in 1942, Algerian calls for independence and spontaneous revolts resulted in a violent French crackdown on VE Day on 8 May. In Indochina, however, the French could do nothing to stop the Vietnamese from organizing massive independence demonstrations and celebrations, free of colonial interference. Unlike in Algeria, the French colonial state in Indochina no longer existed. The 2nd of September 1945 was a hot, muggy day in Saigon. Starting in the morning, the Viet Minh, led by Pham Ngoc Thach, Tran Van Giau and others, organized and presided over a massive demonstration of tens of thousands of Vietnamese to celebrate Vietnam's Independence Day. The participants consisted of youths, workers, students, women and men, young and old, rich and poor. Starting from different areas on the outskirts of the city, they all converged on Norodom Square, next to the cathedral in downtown Saigon. From there, Tran Van Giau, Pham Ngoc Thach and others would address the rally at 2pm. Thanks to big loudspeakers placed in the square, they would all listen together to Ho Chi Minh's address to the nation on this historic day in Vietnamese history.

The organizers had also learned that the first Allied teams had or would arrive possibly on that same day. The Viet Minh immediately plastered the city and the square with banners and posters reading in English, Chinese and Russian: 'Down with Fascism and Colonialism', 'Vietnam has Suffered and Bled under the Yoke of the French', 'Long Live the USSR and the USA', and 'Long Live Vietnamese Independence'. British, Chinese, American, Russian and the DRV's red flag with a yellow star in the middle hung from administrative buildings everywhere. If General Leclerc and the French flag were part of the Allied delegation celebrating the victory over Japan on the USS *Missouri* that day, in Saigon the Vietnamese intentionally excluded the French flag as the *Français d'Indochine* looked on with a mix of intense anger, fear and, no doubt, humiliation.

To complicate matters, earlier that day a group of five hundred Vietnamese youths carrying swords and light arms gathered in front of the military barracks where the Japanese had interned the French colonial army since March. In response to Vietnamese taunting and insults, the soldiers of the 11ème RIC reciprocated in kind and then burst out singing the *Marseillaise*. The Japanese stepped in to maintain order, but they also humiliated the colonial soldiers by keeping them confined while allowing some five thousand English, Australian, Dutch and American prisoners to walk free that day and move in and about Saigon and its sister-city, Cholon. As one of Decoux's closest collaborators wrote of his humiliation on 2 September: 'From our barred windows, we saw the English soldiers walking about in the streets, together with free Dutch soldiers. Only the French soldiers and seamen remained imprisoned!' (Franchini 1995: 131; Goupy 1945; Ducoroy 1949: 210–11 for the citation).

Significantly, many of these Allied POWs were very thankful to many in the French community for the assistance, food, care and compassion they had provided the POWs during the war. As a sign of their gratitude, many Allied POWs even loaned their passes and clothes to the local French so that they could circulate safely and shop 'undercover' as Allies (Marr 1995: 524–25). French families in Saigon welcomed liberated POWs from Japanese camps in Indochina, who helped with cooking and housework, and provided protection against possible Vietnamese molestation. Also riding into town that same day was one no-holds-barred, fluent French-speaking American war hero from Europe turned intelligence officer in Asia named Emile Counasse (his family had emigrated to the United States). He, his men and several American POWs immediately took the defence of the French community (personnel file for E. Counasse, NARA; Bartholomew-Feis 2006: 270–74).

Hotheads, shattered loyalties, powerful mixed emotions of fear and hate, feelings of nationalist invincibility and colonial insecurity were swirling all over Saigon as the Vietnamese marched in a very orderly fashion towards Norodom Square, where Viet Minh leaders awaited them that hot September day. It was a Sunday and noon mass had just let out. Standing on their balconies looking over the square, several French watched as Vietnamese gathered below them. Others looked on from the cathedral's steps. Jacques Le Bourgeois, the former director of *Radio Saigon* under Decoux, later recalled his thoughts that day as he walked through the burgeoning crowd of Vietnamese swirling around him:

> For the first time in Saigon, I felt terribly isolated. The 'Whiteman' whose face distinguishes him from everyone else and who understands nothing of what is being said around him or notices that everyone hushes up when he approaches ... There was a bit of everyone in the crowd around me. Curiosity more than politics must have drawn young secretaries in their silk vests (to the square), the coolies with their bare legs showing and towels wrapped around their foreheads, these women of the people wearing their black trousers, and the elegant Vietnamese women in their multicolored silk dresses falling to their feet (*ao dai*). I moved forward in a loud ocean of gossipy noise and laughter ... Further beyond, people were yelling, not out of meanness, but in support of the one who was holding up giant signs on which were written the words: 'We want the Viet Minh', 'Long Live the USSR and the USA', 'Down with Fascism and Colonialism!', 'Vietnam has long suffered and bled under French domination' ... The public applauded, except for the French whom could be seen from their presbytery balconies and posts. *Doc Lap!* Independence! So many Annamese who would never have thought of it now joined in the headiness of the moment to pronounce the word. But the desire for independence still remained theoretical. Regardless of what local newspapers advanced, few of these seemingly happy Cochinchinese were ready to 'fight to the death' against the French troops that had been announced to be on their way. Who after all really thought about death in such a jubilant crowd. (Le Bourgeois 1985: 310–11)

It is hard to know whether le Bourgeois actually understood what was happening before his very eyes that day. Did he understand Vietnamese? Did he seek out a translation of what the Vietnamese loudspeakers were blaring out? Did he ask why the people were clapping? After all, many of these 'elegant' Vietnamese women spoke beautiful French. Or had the troubled events occurring between that historic afternoon of September 1945 and the publication of his memoirs a few years later led him to leave many things out of his narrative in order to build his colonial case? What is striking in Le Bourgeois' account is the absence of any explanation as to what would attract so many people to converge in an 'orderly' fashion on Norodom Square. It couldn't be political, he says. These people were there out of 'curiosity'. He acknowledges their 'great joy', but fails to explain. Le Bourgeois acknowledged the use of the Vietnamese word *Doc Lap*; but, for him, 'independence' had no meaning for a Vietnamese.

Locked firmly in an imperial time warp, there is no place in his account of 2 September for the possibility of another historical time.[5] The Vietnamese were not mature enough for politics is all he can offer, echoing a colonial language common to so many colonizers save Coetzee's Magistrate and Bayly's Paul Mus. Other *Français d'Indochine* rejected the idea that the Vietnamese could even organize such an event themselves. It must have been the Japanese or the communists. As the Vietnamese marched calmly past the Hotel Continental on their way to Norodom Square, Frenchmen and women jeered: 'These country hicks (*niaques*) are taking advantage of the situation! It's the bastard Japs who are pushing them to do this'. The French promised to take their revenge: 'Go ahead, you opportunists! You'll see soon enough when you are singing *Doc Lap* behind bars' (Krull 1945: 3; Franchini 1995: 133).

Elation turned to frustration in Norodom Square in the afternoon, when the radio failed to work, denying the Vietnamese the chance to hear Ho Chi Minh's declaration of independence. Tran Van Giau quickly took to the stage, grabbed the microphone and rallied the crowd with a rousing, patriotic and anticolonialist harangue. He and others pleaded with the Vietnamese not to serve the French. Looking down from the balconies and across from the steps of the grand cathedral, Frenchmen and women watched but did not applaud. Silence. Some Vietnamese saw them and resented their failure to clap. Others said the radio's failure was due to a colonial plot (Marr 1995: 525; Ung Ngoc Ky 1995). Suddenly, each side eyed the other warily. And then, as the crowd began to disperse, shots rang out. French and Vietnamese alike ran for cover as pandemonium seized the square. We do not know who fired first and probably never will. The French said it was the Vietnamese, while some Vietnamese screamed 'French saboteurs...', 'Catch them ...' and 'Brothers, arrest the traitors', as well as '*trung tri chung no*' for 'wipe them out' (Ung Ngoc Ky 1995: 384–85). Hotheaded Vietnamese – and there were many of them present that day – attacked French houses and the church as the DRV security forces tried with little success to prevent things from spinning out of control. The French priests in the cathedral hustled nearby French civilians inside, but Father Tricoire lay dead on the steps, loved by as many Vietnamese as French. The Japanese did little to help. Dutch POWs came to the rescue of the French trapped in the cathedral. Tensions ran extremely high until the 3rd, as Vietnamese groups rounded up as many as five hundred French prisoners, including women and children. The mob riot that afternoon confirmed the worst suspicions of each side. As Germaine Krull wrote later from her interviews with those present that day: 'The French were watching from behind shuttered windows. At a given moment several shots rang out and the rioting started. An enraged mob rushed into the houses. Women and children were beaten up and men taken off to prison. A smoldering hatred was suddenly unleashed. The enemy was yesterday's houseboy and coolie seeking revenge on his former master' (Krull 1945: 3).

Hundreds of French fled towards the Continental Hotel, where the gunslinging Lt. Counasse had already taken charge of protecting the French holed up there. The latter had convinced the American OSS officer that the

Vietnamese 'had declared their intention to kill every white man in Saigon that night, their next objective being the hotel' (Bartholomew-Feis 2006: 271). Until now, the Japanese had refused to ensure the hotel's security. Again, it was French, not Allied property that they pointed out. In order to force the Japanese hand, Counasse convinced Mathieu Franchini, the owner of the Continental, to sign a contract by which the latter sold his famous hotel to the OSS for one (apparently American) dollar. The Japanese acquiesced and ensured the security of the hotel and the hundreds of French in it (personnel file, NARA; Bartholomew-Feis 2006: 270–74).[6]

The French population soon referred to what happened on 2 September 1945 as 'Black Sunday' or the *Vêpres sanglantes* in a well-known reference to the massacre of the French by the Sicilians in 1282. But there was no massacre on 2 September, unlike what happened in Algeria on 8 May 1945. In all, the Japanese and others reported, four Frenchmen died and about ten Vietnamese (Patti 1980: 256–57). But the events of 2 September marked a rupture between the two communities and struck even more fear and hate into French and Vietnamese hearts (Franchini 1995: 134). Fear is certainly what Le Bourgeois recalled after having hidden in the cathedral until the 3rd: 'Having become concerned about their security at night time at least, people stopped complaining about two or three families being crowded into one lodging. From the time the sun set, people returned home to barricade themselves in. Without weapons, we slept with wrenches and golf clubs within reach' (Le Bourgeois 1985: 314).

Settler Vengeance? The Coup of 23 September 1945

The *Français d'Indochine* now placed their immediate hopes in the arrival of the British and pressed de Gaulle's recently arrived commissioner for Cochinchina, Jean Cédile, to release the men of the 11ème RIC. But this he could not do, for the simple reason that the Japanese still did not recognize the French as an Allied power. There was another problem, too. The new French, Gaullist officers like Cédile were not only wary of the Vietnamese nationalists they met, but they were also distrustful of the *Français d'Indochine* welcoming them with open arms. *Franco-français* divisions dating from the Vichy period immediately made themselves felt in Saigon.

A Divided French House: The Problem of French 'Collaboration'

Like so many shattered empires and nations stretching across postwar Eurasia, people of all walks of life had to assert, deny, alter or simply forget earlier loyalties in view of the new balance of power and the delicate if not dangerous situations in which they suddenly found themselves following the Axis defeat. The French were no exception to this rule. Retribution, purges and even lynching occurred in France in 1944 as people turned on the *collabos*. Breaking with 'the old' was essential to inventing 'the new' (see Deak et al. 2000). The 'Free French' Gaullists arriving in Indochina in late August and early September, like Jean Cédile in Saigon and Jean Sainteny in Hanoi, had fought in the French resistance and Allied armies in Europe. These dedicated Gaullist nationalists were most certainly determined to reassert French sovereignty over Indochina and rebuild the French empire, but they had no sympathy, at least upon their arrival, for the French community, the colonial army and civilian administrators, who, in their eyes, had collaborated disgracefully with the Japanese. Cédile – and he was not alone in the Gaullist military and political class – despised Decoux, his officers and the 11ème RIC in particular for failing to put up a good fight on 9 March in Saigon. Cédile was more than happy to leave Decoux under house arrest in the southern Vietnamese countryside, where the Japanese had put him in March. Cédile recoiled before the settlers streaming into his office speaking of how much they had suffered and how well they had resisted, when, for this Gaullist, they had co-existed quite nicely with the Japanese until March 1945, with little resistance of which to speak in his view and that of other Gaullists. The Vietnamese nationalists were thus not alone in humiliating the *Français d'Indochine*.

The 'new French' nationalists arriving in Saigon held the settler community in contempt. In fact, Cédile and other Gaullist civil and military officers arrived with lists of names of French collaborators to arrest or investigate. They even carried orders to purge colonial administrators, military personnel and others for collaborating with the Japanese and Vichy. General Douglas Gracey, who was about to leave for Saigon, also carried a booklet with 'black' and 'grey' lists, containing the names of sixty-four well-known or highly suspected French and Vietnamese collaborators (Dunn 1985: 150). Cédile had already begun preparing épuration or purging committees for investigating, prosecuting and firing of colonial personnel.[7]

Of course, not all the *Français d'Indochine* collaborated. While I cannot treat the subject of French wartime collaboration in Indochina here, it is important to avoid black and white stereotypes turning everyone into 'collabos' or 'resisters'. Strategies of collaboration are always occupier driven and could change in time and space as the occupier's power waxed or waned, or as international events, like the Allied victory in Europe (8 May) and Asia (2 September 1945), radically changed the present and the prospects for the future (Gross 2000). There were Gaullists and resisters among the *Français d'Indochine*. Decoux arrested some but left others alone. The socialist and longtime resident of Indochina, Louis Caput, organized secret meetings in Hanoi with Gaullists and Vietnamese communists to find ways to resist the Japanese and help the Allies. During the Second World War, the *métis* and inveterate colonialist William Bazé refused to collaborate with the Japanese. He organized a resistance network in remote areas near his plantations in southern Vietnam. His choice cost him dearly when the Japanese captured, imprisoned and tortured him severely in mid-1945. On his liberation from prison, he had to be carried home on a stretcher. However, he was soon back on his feet, now a staunch Gaullist and defender of restoring the empire.

There is no denying that the newly arriving Gaullist officers and colonial administrators (Cédile was both) held the *Français d'Indochine* in suspicion. One such person was Le Bourgeois, the former director of *Radio Saigon* for the Vichy regime whom we met on 'Black Sunday'. Just as he couldn't believe that the Vietnamese were capable of understanding nationalism, so too was he caught off guard when he learned that he himself was not a good French nationalist. Arriving in Cédile's office in Saigon shortly before or after 2 September, Le Bourgeois describes his painful first encounter with this 'New France', in the person of a young, decorated French paratrooper who met him at Cédile's door. When Le Bourgeois asked whether he could see the new commissioner for Cochinchina, the young man disdainfully pointed the former high-ranking Vichy official towards Cédile's office without looking up. Writing in the third person, Le Bourgeouis described this humiliation in his memoirs as follows:

> The only impression the sight of the director of *Radio Saigon*, the official voice of the Governor General of Indochina until 9 March, could make on him was one of distrust. The gulf that had just opened between them and us would take me three more years to close ... No doubt this young man thought for good reason that I had 'collaborated' with the Japanese ... And yet I wanted to take him in my arms and embrace him as the first Frenchman from liberated France I had been able to meet ... But his mouth uttered not a word, his eyes never left his machine gun on which his hands rested. I was a suspect! (Le Bourgeois 1985: 307)

Le Bourgeois then either intentionally or disingenuously committed a terrible *faux pas* in Cédile's office. Sitting before the new magistrate, who had intentionally refrained from asking him to sit down, Le Bourgeois asked after the well-being of his former boss and friend, Admiral Jean Decoux. Visibly irritated by such impudence, Cédile brushed his question away with contempt, telling Le Bourgeois that his former boss would be sent off to France. And then he dropped the bombshell on his uninvited guest: 'His role here has been too antinational'. Devastated, Le Bourgeois had just had the nationalist tables turned on him yet again. Blindsided, he could not believe the word he had just heard, the dangers of which were aimed right at him – 'Antinational!' is all he could write in his memoir and it captures the emotion well (Le Bourgeois 1985: 309).[8] Cédile then casually informed him that his name was on the black list. When Le Bourgeois spoke of 'three years' above, he was clearly referring to his *épuration* and his legal battle to clear his name. Not only did many in the French community feel 'isolated' as they moved delicately among the exuberant Vietnamese national community, but they also feared being excluded or excommunicated from this new Free French definition of nationhood. 'Paris seems to have forgotten us as much as the (Free French) General headquarters in Calcutta. As for the (Free French) paratroopers in their villa (in Saigon), they had not yet announced a plan for re-establishing order' (Le Bourgeois 1985: 314).

This *Franco-français* divide is as important as the Franco-Vietnamese one in understanding the experience of the *Français d'Indochine* at this critical historical juncture in the history of France, French Indochina and Vietnam. As the Vietnamese nationalist government led by Ho Chi Minh rounded up those among the Vietnamese who had collaborated with the French, executing many, the French went after their own. No study exists as to how many French officials received sanctions or jail sentences, or were purged. But the French decree establishing the épuration commissions in Indochina in November 1945 required all those who had worked for the colonial army and administration between June 1940 and March 1945 to provide investigators with a full accounting of their activities during this period. The meeting of these 'two Frances' in Saigon in September 1945 resulted in the creation of a dividing line between the 'old' and the 'new' in Indochina, between 'liberal' Gaullist colonialists speaking of 'reforms' like Cédile and old 'colonial' Indochinese hands like Le Bourgeois and the 'settler community' seeking a return to the pre-1945 idyllic past. According to Le Bourgeois, 'this point of view' was the source of serious misunderstandings 'between new and old colonizers' (*entre nouveau et anciens coloniaux*). Jean-Michel Hertrich, a former settler in the 1930s returning to Saigon in September with the British as a war correspondent, agreed that many of the newly arriving paratroopers hated the 'Vichystes' adding that 'a gap had emerged that would be difficult to close' (Hertrich [1956] 1999: 58).

For the time being, the French had no real power on the ground in Indochina, either in Saigon or Hanoi. The Vietnamese and the Japanese were in control. But both the 'old' and the 'new' French were confident that the imminent arrival of the British would change the balance of power in their favour. Their common enemy were the nationalist Vietnamese who challenged the French claim to empire in Indochina. The British would disarm the Japanese, back the French led by the Gaullists, and overthrow the DRV. That shared goal at least, the *Français d'Indochine* were sure, would allow them to reposition themselves on the right side of history, the French colonial one.

The Coup of 23 September: Colonial Vengeance on Settler Terms

British troops under the command of General Douglas Gracey began to arrive in Saigon on 11 September. The Japanese solemnly received the British General and put their troops under his command. The Japanese High Command had seventy thousand troops at its disposal in the south, many of whom were battle-hardened, none of whom had suffered a single defeat in Indochina, and all of whom were still armed and disciplined. However, British military might was hardly impressive. Gracey's mainly Indian Gurkha troops only numbered around three thousand men in September. The British immediately flew out over nine thousand British POWs. As he set up his headquarters in the *Palais des gouverneurs* in Saigon, Gracey was uncomfortably aware that keeping order as tensions rose between the Vietnamese and the French settler community would not be easy (Dunn 1945: 153). The French community looked to the British for security, informing them of all the terrible things that had happened since 1940, on 9 March, and especially on 'Black Sunday'. They did everything they could to convince Gracey of the Vietnamese government's inability to maintain order. The settlers pleaded with the British to intervene directly or at least to release the 11ème RIC so that the French could restore order themselves. They 'knew' Indochina best. They could take care of this 'revolt'. They always had in the past (Ducoroy 1949: 211–12).

Over the next two weeks, the British did their best to maintain order as relations between the French and the Vietnamese deteriorated dramatically. A French administrator flown in from India to make an inspection tour of Saigon on 21–22 September reported that tensions between the two sides had taken a rapid turn for the worse since 2 September. He reported that the French community was obsessed with seeking vengeance against the 'Annamese' for the humiliations and suffering they had had to endure and made no effort to tone down the vitriol as the British seemed to introduce a more favourable balance of power. On the contrary (Goupy 1945). This official reported that the French tore down DRV flags and posters when they could, taunted DRV officials and insulted Vietnamese routinely. Looking on from the sidelines, they screamed with joy, he wrote, whenever Anglo-Indian troops removed DRV agents from their positions. Cédile ordered a stop to the rumour-mongering, convinced like Gracey that the French community's actions were only making things worse. On 12 September, a British officer reported phlegmatically that the 'outward welcome accorded to the Allied Force from both the French and the Annamese alike on our entry into French Indochina was decidedly embarrassing. Our forces obviously found themselves in a divided house' (Dunn 1945: 151).

The events leading up to the British-backed French coup dislodging the DRV from Saigon on 23 September 1945 are well known. At the core of the problem were two issues. First, the Vietnamese and French were sliding towards war, a war of national liberation for the Vietnamese, a war of colonial re-conquest for the French. There was no other way to put it. Second, the British did not have enough of their own troops on the ground to ensure security, and because they refused to use the Japanese to maintain order, Gracey reluctantly agreed that the 11ème RIC could be the solution he needed until General Leclerc's Expeditionary Corps arrived in three to four weeks' time. Gracey first tried to impose order by announcing a curfew and shutting down the Vietnamese press. Unwilling to give up its sovereignty, on 17 September the DRV organized a full-scale strike in a bid to force the British hand. It was counterproductive. Tensions escalated as the French settlers moved to expand their control over Saigon on every possible occasion. The British did their best to keep order while the French officers, including Cédile by this time, urged them to release the colonial army and let the French put their divided house in order. Gracey replaced the Japanese on 18 September, guarding the Continental Hotel with his Gurkhas. On the 21st, he began removing DRV authorities from their positions as the French cheered his men on from the sidelines. Anglo-Indian troops occupied civilian jails, police stations, the treasury, and the post and telegraph office. Gracey also agreed to start rearming the 11ème RIC in order to use them in a coup starting at 3am on 23 September 1945.

Gracey, and above all Jean Cédile, should have known better than to use the 11ème RIC. Using these long cooped up, very angry and humiliated colonial troops, many of whom had been a part of the very French community that was now working Saigon into a nervous breakdown, were as bent as the settlers on putting the Vietnamese back in their place and re-establishing the prewar colonial order. Cédile had visited the 11ème RIC personally before the 23rd, as did a special Free French investigator. Neither was impressed by what they saw. Hardly an 'anticolonialist', the French journalist Jean-Michel Hertrich was appalled by his visit to the 11ème RIC around 21 September. A longtime friend of Cédile and a member of the French resistance in Europe, Germaine Krull could not believe that the French would deploy such soldiers to retake Saigon. She, too, had inspected the 11ème RIC and was shocked by what she saw. They were a terribly undisciplined and motley crew, she wrote in her diary. 'I shuddered to think that these troops might be unleashed upon the city.' She concluded: 'It was like being on top of a volcano about to erupt' (Krull 1945: 16).

In the early hours of the 23rd, Gracey, pushed by the French, released the 11ème RIC and ordered them to replace the DRV and to help the British maintain order. The British-led operation easily dislodged the DRV from their headquarters in the Town Hall and rapidly occupied administrative buildings throughout the city without any Vietnamese casualties. Indeed, there was little Vietnamese resistance during the coup itself. It was rather the behaviour of the 11ème RIC and many in the French settler community that got out of hand. Around 8am, when it was clear that the Franco-British forces were in control, thousands in the French community, men and women, poured into the streets of Saigon without fear of reprisals from the Vietnamese or the Japanese. They then proceeded to go on a rampage through the city, breaking into Vietnamese homes, ransacking their stores and vandalizing their property. Soldiers and settlers walked together in the streets, grabbing any unfortunate Vietnamese they found in their path. French vigilantes seized around five hundred Vietnamese civilians in all and tied them up by their hands. They forced many at gunpoint to keep their hands in the air and kneel for hours. They then took them to British officers who could not believe their eyes. As one British officer reported: 'It hardly seemed necessary that women and striplings should be kept seated on the ground with their hands above their heads several hours after the shooting had stopped in the center of Saigon. This I saw' (Dunn 1945: 195). Settlers got hold of Pham Ngoc Thach's French wife and smashed in her teeth. She had been one of Gracey's most important contacts for talking to the DRV. She was lucky to get out of Saigon alive. Krull couldn't believe what she had witnessed that mad morning: 'I have never seen such unmilitary bearing or behavior. They beat up their wretched prisoners as soon as they got their hands on them.' 'I went all over town on foot and by car, in the company of Cédile, of various officers and journalists, and alone', Krull continued. 'I saw everything with my own eyes – Annamites tied up, some of them tortured, drunken officers and soldiers with smoking guns' (Krull 1945: 16).

> On the rue Catinat, I saw soldiers driving before them a group of Annamites bound, slave fashion, to a long rope. Women spat in their faces. They were on the verge of being lynched. In more distant sections, I saw French soldiers come out of Annamite houses with stolen shoes and shirts, saying 'at least, we will be able to wear clean linen this evening'. 'Aren't you ashamed of plundering like the Annamites?' I asked them? 'Certainly not', they replied, 'they have been stealing from us for months'. (Krull 1945: 19)

Blind revenge trumped maintaining order as French soldiers and settlers vented their pent-up feelings. A former *Français d'Indochine* himself, Jean-Michel Hertrich confirmed it: 'all of these people who only yesterday trembled in fear now only spoke of making the Annamese pay for the fear they had forced them to undergo. The (DRV's) mayoral office had not yet been seized before the threatening (settler) crowd surrounded it from a distance, prudent, before commenting on the operation of occupation in hateful terms. It was all so despicable and nauseating' (Hertrich [1956] 1999: 69). A few weeks later, Cédile reported to Leclerc that the 11ème RIC 'had arrested and tied up all the Annamese they found during their search for arms ... Women were arrested. The men were badly treated'. As the new French magistrate in Saigon told Leclerc, this deplorable action explained why so many Vietnamese civilians streamed out of the city fearing for their lives and for their future with the French (Cédile 1945: 4).

The British officer class in Saigon, General Gracey above all, was simply aghast at the French behaviour, both that of the colonial soldiers and the settler population. Hopping mad, Gracey ordered the 11ème RIC back to its barracks and decided that it was much wiser to rely on the Japanese than on the undisciplined French colonial troops. Gracey blamed these troops for worsening the security situation and his job as the DRV forces began counterattacking that night and initiated a war of terror on Saigon that would last for years. The French in Saigon, in perhaps one of the lowest points in their history in Indochina, showed the ugly side of what fear, hysteria and vengeance can do. And their actions that day only further widened the gulf between the French and the Vietnamese, convincing many that the only way to change imperial time was by the use of violence.

Had the troops been more disciplined, as Peter Dunn has argued, then the mob hysteria that rolled through Saigon that long September day would probably have been averted (Dunn 1945: 196–97). But the 11ème disappointed miserably. The French were convinced on the 23rd that they were on their way back to how it was 'before'. But of course there was no going back. In a perceptive reflection on what had 'just' happened, a British officer wrote that the French 'do not realize that in the eyes of the natives the French are no longer the superior beings that their domination and their force of arms made them appear in the past. The Annamites have seen the French dictated to, humiliated, and finally disarmed and kicked out of authority by an oriental race (the Japanese), and, perhaps equally important, they (the Vietnamese) have tasted power and known for a short time the pride of being a de facto government' (Nach n.d.: 42).

On 25 September, on her way out of town, Germaine Krull noted in her diary that 'Saigon was in flames'. And it was. She concluded her *Diary of Saigon* with a reflection on historical time that few in the French ruling class, including the 'new French', grasped: 'We may never regain face, but if we do, it won't be with the assistance of machine guns. The "good old days" are gone forever' (Krull 1945: 19). The 'barbarians' were now circling Saigon as the British and French turned to the Japanese to protect the city. But what the French forgot is that the Vietnamese had always been there. The question now was to what extent would the French ruling class go to ensure that imperial time, Empire, never ended?

Christopher Goscha is Professor of International Relations in the History Department at the Université du Québec à Montréal (UQÀM). He is a specialist of the Cold War in Asia as well as questions of colonization and decolonization in the Afro-Asian world. He teaches international relations, the Vietnam Wars and World History. He studied at the School of Foreign Service, Georgetown University (BA), the Australian National University (MA), the University Diderot Paris VII (MA) and l'École pratique des hautes études (PhD, La Sorbonne). He has published several books including *The Road to Dien Bien Phu: A History of the First War for Vietnam* (Princeton University Press, 2022), *The Penguin History of Vietnam* (Penguin/Random House, 2016), *Vietnam, A New History* (Basic Books, 2016, the American version of the preceding book and winner of the 2017 John K. Fairbank Prize – American Historical Association and finalist for the Cundhill History Prize).

Notes

1. My thanks to David Marr for kindly providing me with a copy of this diary.
2. See the long list of even more pejorative terms Jean-Michel Hertrich noted from his interviews in Saigon in September 1945.
3. For an overview of the French in Indochina to 1910, see Meyer (2003).
4. On colonial royalty, see Goscha (2020).
5. Franchini's *Continental Saigon* is the sole exception I have found to this rule.
6. The American government decorated Counasse for his actions that day, but I have never found mention of him in any French account of 2 September.
7. 'Epuration du personnel francais', *Journal de Saigon*, 21 November 1945, 1.
8. American OSS officers were well aware of this divide between the French. George Wickes wrote that Cédile 'would have liked to ship every colonial back to France and bring in an entirely new set of officials. Our views were also shared by the Free French soldiers who now began to arrive' (Wickes 1945: 8).

References

Babut, Ernest. 1931. 'Des petits faits qui nous font beaucoup de mal', *La Revue Franco-Annamite*, 16 February, 1–4.
Bartholomew-Feis, Dixee. 2006. *The OSS and Ho Chi Minh: Unexpected Allies in the War against Japan.* Lawrence: University Press of Kansas.
Barthouet, Arnaud. 1947. *Rancunes, autour de la tragédie franco-indochinoise.* Paris: Delmas.
Bayly, Susan. 2009. 'Conceptualizing Resistance and Revolution in Vietnam: Paul Mus' Understanding of Colonialism in Crisis', *Journal of Vietnamese Studies* 4(1): 192–205.
Cédile, J.M. 1945. 'J.M. Cédile to General Leclerc', Singapore, 28 September 1945, box 126, file grouping Etats-Associés de l'Indochine, Archives du Ministère des Affaires étrangères, France.
Coetzee, J.M. 2004. *Waiting for the Barbarians.* London: Vintage Books.
Deak, Istvan, Jan Gross and Tony Judt (eds). 2000. *The Politics of Retribution in Europe: World War II and its Aftermath.* Princeton, NJ: Princeton University Press.
Ducoroy, Maurice. 1949. *Ma Trahison en Indochine.* Paris: Les Editioins Inter-Nationales.
Dunn, Peter. 1985. *The First Vietnam War.* London: C. Hurst & Company.
Duras, Maguerite. 2006. *Cahiers de la guerre.* Paris: POL éditeur.
Franchini, Philippe. 1995. *Continental Saigon.* Paris: Editions Métailié.
Gentil, Pierre. 1972. *Derniers chefs d'un empire.* Paris: Académie des Sciences d'Outre-Mer.
Goscha, Christopher. 2011. *Historical Dictionary of the Indochina.* Honolulu/Copenhagen: University of Hawaii Press/NIAS.
______. 2020. 'Colonial Monarchy and Decolonisation in the French Empire: Bao Dai, Norodom Sihanouk and Mohammed V', in Robert Aldrich and Cindy McCreery (eds), *Monarchies and Decolonisation in Asia.* Manchester: Manchester University Press, pp. 152–74.
Goupy, M. 1945. 'Rapport sur la mission de liaison effectuée à Saigon les 20 et 21 septembre 1945 par M Goupy, Administrateur adjoint des Services civils d'Indochine', Calcutta, 25 September 1945, box 247, file grouping Conseiller politique, Centre des Archives d'Outre-mer (CAOM), France.
Gross, Jan. 2000. 'Themes for a Social History of War Experience and Collaboration', in Istvan Deak, Jan Gross and Tony Judt (eds), *The Politics of Retribution in Europe: World War II and Its Aftermath.* Princeton, NJ : Princeton University Press, pp. 15–36.
Hertrich, Jean-Michel. [1956] 1999. *Doc-Lap! (L'indépendance ou la mort !), choses vues en Indochine.* Paris: Editions Kergour.
Isoart, Paul. 1982. 'Aux origines d'une guerre: L'Indochine française (1940–1945)', in Paul Isoart (ed.), *L'Indochine française (1940–1945).* Paris: Presses Universitaires Françaises.
Jennings, Eric. 2001. *Vichy in the Tropics.* Stanford, CA: Stanford University Press.
Krull. 1945. *Diary of Saigon, Following the Allied Occupation in September 1945,* 12, held in the Department of State Special File RG59, lot file 54-D-190, box 9, National Archives and Records Administration (NARA), United States.
Larcher-Goscha, Agathe. 1993. 'Sports, colonialisme et identités nationales, premières approches du "corps à corps colonial" en Indochine, (1918–1945)', in Nicolas Bancel (ed.), *De l'Indochine* à *l'Algérie.* Paris: Editions La Découverte, pp. 15–31.

———. 2009. 'Du football au Vietnam 1905–1949, colonialisme, culture sportive et sociabilités en jeux', *Outre mer* 97: 61–89, 364–65.

Le Bourgeois, Jacques. 1985. *Ici Radio-Saigon, 1939–1945*. Paris: Éditions France-Empire.

Marr, David. 1995. *Vietnam 1945*. Berkeley: University of California Press.

Meyer, Charles. 2003. *Les Français en Indochine 1860–1910*. France: Le Grand Livre du Mois.

Nach, James. N.d. *History of the American Diplomatic Presence in Vietnam* (unpublished manuscript kindly made available by Mr Nach).

Namba, Chizuru. 2012. *Français et Japonais en Indochine (1940–1945)*. Paris: Karthala.

National Archives and Records Administration (NARA), Personnel File for Emile Counasse. United States: Department of State Files.

Patti, Archimedes. 1980. *Why Vietnam?* Berkeley: University of California Press.

Raffin, Anne. 2005. *Youth Mobilization in Vichy Indochina and Its Legacies, 1940–1970*. Lanham, MD: Lexington Books.

Tran Van Giau. N.d. *Hoi Ky, 1940–1945* (undated copy in the author's possession).

Ung Ngoc Ky. 1995. 'Ngay 2 – 9 – 1945: Khi The Phu Dong cua nguoi Sai Gon', in *Mua thu roi, ngay ham ba*. Hanoi: Nha Xuat Ban Cjhinh Tri Quoc Gai, pp. 381–87.

Verney, Sébastien. 2012. *L'Indochine sous Vichy*. Paris: Riveneuve Editions.

Wickes, George. N.d. *Saigon 1945* (personal memoir, 1945, electronic copy in the author's possession).

Afterword

James Laidlaw

This rich collection of papers is strikingly diverse thematically and in terms of intellectual style. This is partly because, as the contributors to the volume exemplify, the range of scholars on whom Susan Bayly has exerted a strong intellectual influence has been wide, and the threads they have chosen to follow from her work have led them in highly divergent directions. So, it was an insightful decision on the part of the editors to propose the concept of 'intellectual exchange', and it has exerted a rather productive gravitational pull on the contributions to the volume, resulting in a rich cross-cutting pattern of common themes running through the chapters. It has been able to do so, perhaps, because the editors have construed both 'intellectual' and 'exchange' in generously capacious terms. And the contributors have generally followed them in this. They have shown the richness of insight that may be gained from acknowledging that it is not only those assigned to do so in a specialized division of labour who engage reflectively with ideas, and nor is it the preserve of the affluent or leisured classes. And it is not only the conventionally 'cosmopolitan' who find themselves having to reckon with ideas (including concepts, values, narratives and so on) from different and conflicting frameworks and exercising reflection, judgement and sensibility as they do so. Susan Bayly's own ethnographic writing, exemplified in the two pieces here, consistently impresses for the patience and generosity with which it takes seriously the discriminations and differences, the distinctions and value judgements that matter to her interlocutors, and discerns a subtle life of the mind even in unlikely circumstances. In fact, the changing and often contradictory requirements of ideological conformity in an authoritarian regime turn out rather demandingly to *require* intellectual ingenuity, moral imagination, emotional discernment, and what Bayly calls the bridging of worlds. 'Intellectual exchange' turns out not to be a luxury, but a necessity.

In their Introduction, the editors have done an impressive job of highlighting the ways in which the contributors have severally addressed their theme, so there is little that I could add in that regard. It might be of interest, however, if I raise a couple of questions about what might happen to the notion of intellectual exchange at the edge of what might count as 'exchange'.

As editors and contributors have noted, exchange comes in many forms, not all implying bilateral interaction or balanced reciprocity between equals. Several contributors describe intellectual exchange in hierarchical relations, including but not limited to pedagogy, and relations that are in other respects asymmetrical. They have described various forms of gift giving, commerce, tribute and patronage, swapping and substituting, adopting and adapting. But (broadly speaking) intellectual converse is sometimes spoken of as a matter of sharing, which as many anthropologists have long emphasized is not best understood as a form of exchange at all, because that implies relations between separate parties, whereas sharing is a form of mutuality that occurs within and indeed works to constitute a 'we' as a singular subject. Perhaps because the rubric of the volume is exchange, only a few contributors (e.g. Sarbadhikary) mention sharing and the specific sorts of relations it engenders. I wonder: what might it add to our understanding of the (broadly defined) intellectual dimension of human sociality, if we observe that some of what happens to ideas (including concepts, values, narratives and so on) is that they are shared, and if we ask how is that different from when they are exchanged? This might be understood less as a call for a complement to the anthropology of intellectual exchange that is proposed and developed in this volume than as a suggestion that it be rounded out in a particular way. It would involve perhaps blurring the boundary of the 'exchange' in 'intellectual exchange', but might nevertheless enlarge our understanding of what one might think of as the intellectual dimension of human social life.

The distinction between exchange and sharing is relevant also to my second question, because it concerns a feature of exchange that is necessarily absent from sharing. It is easy to think of exchange as something that happens between parties whose existence and identity are postulated as being anterior to the transaction: you have two or more parties, and some object that is transferred from one to the other, giving rise to a relation between them. But it was an elementary observation of structural anthropology that this is not the only way in which to understand things. In the venerable domain of kinship and social structure, for example, whereas functionalist 'descent theory' took the existence of kin groups as given, and asked how they solved the problem of reproduction and managed relations with other such groups, 'alliance theory' took the practice of marriage, conceptualized as exchange, to be constitutive: it is through their relations that the parties come into existence as the things that they are. Both ways of seeing things have their merits, and some sorts of circumstances are illuminated more by one and some by the other. Anthropological accounts of intellectual life – this is conspicuously but not exclusively so in the anthropology of religion – tend towards the functionalist model: distinct 'religions', 'systems', 'cultures' or 'traditions' exist and are transmitted and reproduced through time, with contact, exchange, conflict, influence, borrowing and so on being processes that happen 'between' them. None of the contributors quite puts things this way, but repeatedly in reading the chapters in this book, it seemed to me that the analyses offered looked more like the structuralist 'alliance theory' account than the 'descent theory' picture. By foregrounding the processes of intellectual exchange themselves – rather than the different traditions and how they are transmitted, reproduced, bounded, mixed or hybridized – the social productivity of exchange itself comes into view. The entities between which exchange takes place are the emergent outcome of the relations. It is not just that worlds are bridged, but that some worlds are brought about by the activity of bridging. This is perhaps most explicit in Magnus Marsden's chapter, where he argues that at least some versions of 'the Islamic' consist not, as influential models in recent anthropology have assumed, in the transmission and boundary-policing of more or less bounded 'tradition', but in the very activity of exchange, which brings incommensurables into relation and creates and maintains 'a lived realm of thought, agency and relationality'.

Something like this picture emerges in a number of the other chapters in this volume, and one way in which the rubric of 'intellectual exchange', which is already amply vindicated by the rich array of analyses presented here, might prove to be of further theoretical importance in anthropology, is through a more relational and processual complement to the more usual way of imagining the 'entities' that frame intellectual life.

James Laidlaw is the William Wyse Professor of Social Anthropology and a Fellow of King's College at the University of Cambridge. His most recent book is *The Subject of Virtue: An Anthropology of Ethics and Freedom* (Cambridge, 2014).

Index

T

U

www.ingramcontent.com/pod-product-compliance
Ingram Content Group UK Ltd.
Pitfield, Milton Keynes, MK11 3LW, UK
UKHW021507250926
8884IPUK00009B/65

9 781807 581411